Painting as Model

OCTOBER Books

Joan Copjec, Rosalind Krauss, and Annette Michelson, editors

Painting as Model

YVE-ALAIN BOIS

An OCTOBER *Book*

The MIT Press
Cambridge, Massachusetts
London, England

First MIT Press paperback edition, 1993

© 1990 Massachusetts Institute of Technology

Figures 1–11 and 88 copyright 1990 Succession H. Matisse/ARS N.Y. Figures 12, 14, 17, 19–21, 23–24, and 26 copyright 1990 ARS N.Y./SPADEM. Figures 29–30, 34, and 63–64 copyright 1991 Estate of Piet Mondrian, c/o Estate of Harry Holtzman, New York, N.Y. Figures 66–81 copyright Annalee Newman.

This book was set in ITC Garamond by DEKR Corporation and printed and bound in the United States of America.

Library of Congress Cataloging-in-Publication Data

Bois, Yve Alain.
     Painting as model / Yve-Alain Bois.
          p.   cm.
     An October book.
     Includes bibliographical references.
     ISBN 0-262-02306-7 (HB), 0-262-52180-6 (PB)
     1. Painting—Philosophy.   I. Title.
ND1140.B59   1990
     750′.1—dc20

10 9 8 7 6

For Jean Clay, Dominique Jaffrennou, Rosalind Krauss,
my first readers

Contents

Acknowledgments

This book owes its existence to many benefactors. Numerous footnotes adorning these essays express my gratitude to a variety of friends and colleagues who provided me with pieces of information or useful comments, and the bibliographical note at the end of this volume acknowledges specifically the help I received from editors and translators. Help, however, can be provided in unspecific ways, and it is to the various circumstances that made my work possible that I would like to address myself here.

I have made explicit in the introduction the extent of my debt to Jean Clay, Dominique Jaffrennou, and Rosalind Krauss, the three persons to whom this book is dedicated; what I owe to Hubert Damisch is pointed out in the article that gives this volume its title. But many more people were important to the formation of my ideas and for the encouragement they gave me over the years to sustain my research. In France, where some of these texts were written prior to my arrival in the USA, I must make special mention of the group of friends who surrounded the now defunct journal *Macula* which I founded with Jean Clay in 1976 (I am thinking particularly of the painter Christian Bonnefoi, for our many heated discussions were to play a major role in my interpretation of abstract art).

But most of these essays were written in America, and the bulk of my debt rests on this side of the Atlantic. Since my sense of displacement remains acute, even after six years spent in this country, I will define the multidirectional field of my gratitude geographically.

Close to home, there is the intimate yet cosmopolitan milieu of The Johns Hopkins University: the daily conversations I have had with my colleagues in the History of Art department—Herbert Kessler, Charles Dempsey, Liz Cropper, Walter Melion, William Tronzo, and Michael Fried—have been extremely productive (I must insist on the richness of the dialogue with Michael Fried ever since my arrival here). Interdisciplinarity is more enacted than advocated at Hopkins, so I greatly benefited from the advice of colleagues from other departments, notably George Wilson (Philosophy), Neil Hertz (Humanities Center), and Werner Hamacher (German). Finally, I owe a great deal to the graduate students who suffered through my seminar: a number of essays included here were thought through during those sessions, and it is more often than not thanks to their questioning that a final (if far from perfect) form was found for them.

Farther away, but close at heart, another supportive community has been constituted by the makers of *October*—not only Rosalind Krauss, Annette Michelson, Douglas Crimp, and Joan Copjec, but the many authors publishing in this journal and sharing for this reason a sense of communal belonging. Among them, Benjamin Buchloh has become one of the few imaginary readers for whom I write, waiting to be criticized and challenged.

Finally, scattered around this country, without institutional links, there is a vast group of friends and scholars always ready to lend me their support and discuss my work in progress. To name them all is beyond my capacity, but I wish to thank especially Linda Francis, Richard Rand, Angelica Rudenstine, and Nancy Troy.

Exchanging ideas is not enough to shape a book; many small and sometimes unrewarding tasks have to be performed. Not only have my teaching assistants been most helpful over the years, but I would like to thank (superlatively) the staff of the interlibrary loan department at the Johns Hopkins University library, and particularly Jenny Newman, without whose dedication my work would have been almost impossible. For their help in assembling photographs I am most grateful, among many others, to Catherine Bock, Xavier Girard, Daryl Harnisch, Joop Joosten, Janina Ladnowska, Catherine Lawless, Annalee Newman, Hélène Seckel, and Nancy Troy.

To these names I must add those of Mark Rakatansky, who initiated the project, Roger Conover, his successor at the MIT Press, who kept up the pressure required for its completion, and Matthew Abbate, from the same publishing house, who bore the burden of the final anglicization of my often cumbersome English.

Finally I am grateful to Benjamin and Alexandre for having not too reluctantly allowed me to forsake their games in order to write these essays.

To introduce one's discourse is to attempt to situate it within a field, to measure what it shares with, and how it differs from, other discourses within the same field, to define its specificity. Yet such an analytical posture, which is the stuff of criticism and presupposes a certain distance, no matter how minimal, from the object of inquiry, remains fundamentally unavailable to anyone attending to his or her own discourse. One cannot be, at the same time, embedded in a field and surveying it from above, one cannot claim any secure ground from which one's own words could be read and judged as if written by someone else.

But this impossibility is far from being a loss, for it obliges the autoreferential discourse to admit that one always takes a stand. The strategic nature of the field, often repressed or simply taken for granted, cannot but be asserted: any field is a field of forces in which any discourse maintains a position. The coordinates of this position might be ill defined, its fragility or its strength unassessed, its motivations unconscious; still, the position stands, and stands *for* or *against*. Any critical discourse is programmatic in part, and it is this conscious part, floating above the surface of the water, that the autoreferential discourse can address, without any pretense at having the last word.

Anyone working in America today in the humanities, and most particularly in the field of art history, is confronted with certain intellectual pressures that require an immediate answer (even a refusal to answer, a refusal to confront the issues at stake, is a form of answer). Like anyone else, with whatever differences, I find some of these pressures oppressive, constituting a sort of intellectual blackmail. (This term, one with intense ethical connotations, represents to my mind any exclusionist imperative—either you do that or you are out—imposed upon the scholar.)[1] I aim to resist such pressures, obliquely at least, in the manner with which I handle the objects I am writing about. Yet they remain constantly at the horizon of my work; I constantly have to set them, successfully or not, as its negative. It is those pressures that I want to address here, not so much to make explicit what is implicit in the essays that follow, certainly not in the belief that I was never prey to the blackmails in question, but to provide, at my end of the spectrum (the other being you, dear reader, *amour de lecteur*, as the French poet Francis Ponge used to say), a map of the field of forces against which (or with which) these essays were written. For it is my contention that if one knows the ground (real or imaginary) on which something was constructed, one can have a better access to the construction itself.

Theory/Antitheory

I will first discuss *theoreticism*—the obligation to be "theoretical"—for, as a teacher, I sense it is one of the most powerful pressures at work today, one from which liberation is most wanted. "Theory" has become a catchword on American campuses (positions are advertised under this heading in the job market); more often than not, it functions as a superego, encapsulating, fueling, and, alas, discouraging the student's endeavor. It is not, of course, theory that I find oppressive, but the indiscriminate appeal to theory as a set of ready-made tools to handle a question, as the miracle-solution, no matter the problem. On the one hand, the "theory" in question today, far from being a homogeneous corpus or a fixed system, is constituted by a conglomerate of highly complex and often antagonistic works grouped under the fashionable label of "poststructuralism," and one of the most hasty results of theoreticism is the erasing of these differences. On the other hand, the relationship of theoreticism to theory is purely instrumental, and I would argue that such an instrumentalism cannot be productive. In fact, the first lesson to be learned from one of the theoreticians most likely to be invoked by theoreticists, Roland Barthes, is that one does not "apply" a theory; that concepts must be forged *from* the object of one's inquiry or imported *according to* that object's specific exigency; and that the main theoretical act is to define this object, not the other way around. To define an object, one has to know it intimately (on that level "poststructuralism" did not depart from structuralism; to overturn a critical tradition was in fact their common goal, but as a starting point this implied a scrupulous investigation of the object's materiality).

This brings me to a second type of blackmail, exactly symmetrical to the first, one that I would call *antitheory* (the obligation to be a- or antitheoretical). A symptom of this new kind of pressure is provided in America by the public dimension taken by the Paul de Man "affair" (just as in France, at the end of the '70s, after a formidable surge of theoreticism, the astounding media success of the so-called "Nouveaux Philosophes" set the tone for a huge tidal wave of antitheory that is still far from having run its course).[2] Theoreticism, or theoretical abuse, is based on the illusion that one could ingest swiftly, without previous homework, a mass of difficult and often contradictory texts. Without the background that would permit this material to be mastered usefully, the theoreticist first gives in to "theory" as if it were a new faith; then, more or less rapidly, grows disenchanted because "theory" did not perform immediately the expected miracles. Illusion leads to disillusionment, disillusion to resentment, and resentment to throwing out the baby with the bath water. As a consequence of this theoretical retreat, the old guard positivists, feeling vindicated— even though they had never lost an inch of their power—reemerge as more vociferous than ever.

Theory/antitheory: I find the ravages of this flux and reflux on one's thought devastating. In their modest way, it is as a mode of resistance against such pressures that the following essays were intended. But against other pressures as well.

Fashion

One of these, which can partake of either of the preceding types of blackmail, is *fashion* (the obligation to follow the latest trend in the market of ideas, be it theoretical, a-, or antitheoretical). A recent pamphlet provides a good example. In *Le mirage linguistique*, one of Thomas Pavel's main targets is structuralism, particularly the work of Claude Lévi-Strauss. This is not the first time, of course, that Lévi-Strauss's enterprise has undergone harsh criticism both from theoretical quarters (deconstruction) and antitheoretical ones (positivist ethnology). (Atheory as such has never concerned itself with his work.) But the argument is now of an altogether different order. Lévi-Strauss's endeavor, it is said, is a failure—as is structuralism as a whole— because it took something that was already passé for its main theoretical model: the structural linguistics of Saussure and the phonology of Trubetskoi. (Ironically enough, Pavel unwillingly undermines his own stance by giving Chomsky's generative grammar as the up-to-date model Lévi-Strauss "should have" adopted if, when he started his monumental study of myths, he definitely could not do without linguistics; for given the nativist basis of Chomsky's work, openly allying itself with Descartes, we are led to ask, if a seventeenth-century philospher is not altogether passé, why Saussure should be.)[3] This yielding to fashion has three implications. First, ideas are like commodities: they get used, abused, and worn out. Time to take on a new look. Second, the result of research is to be disconnected from its method (if, for one reason or another, the method is suddenly declared "old hat," either the result has to be discarded as pure fantasy, or the work has to be reframed entirely according to the "new" method). Third, there is only one method available at any one time in any given field.

In fact, what the blackmail by fashion refuses to consider is the heuristic function of the theoretical model; for it sees it as mere wrapping. To start with, Pavel's assumption is historically wrong: even if it could make some sense to say that the Saussurian model is "passé," it could not have been so when Lévi-Strauss "adopted" it. On the contrary, it was he, via his encounter with Jakobson in New York during World War II, who gave it the character of a model (Saussure's fame was utterly confined to the province of linguistics before Lévi-Strauss grabbed his work). Lévi-Strauss did not "adopt" this model because it was the latest trend, for it did not exist as a model yet. He founded it as a model because it was for him the best way to organize the immense amount of raw material that lay in front of him: as the scores of American Indian myths that he and others had collected were obviously evolving around binary oppositions, structural linguistics provided him with a system capable both of uncovering more pairs and of showing those oppositions to be constitutive of a vast semantic code shaping the cultures where the myths had originated. And it was with the help of this model that he was able to renew his field entirely—just as it was with the help of neo-Kantian formalism, as discussed in one of the following essays, that Kahnweiler was able to provide the first intelligent analysis of cubism.

Again, this is a question of the relationship between the object of one's inquiry and the theoretical model that is invented or imported for the occasion. The blackmail of fashion is a one-dimensional imperative: any theory makes a one-time appearance, during which it is not to share its power with any others, and then it is replaced without the possibility of ever making a return. Against this dogmatism of the chic, this opportunism of the marketplace, one has to oppose a certain openness—another kind of opportunism, if you will—whose vector is not the latest intellectual commodity but the specificity of the object of inquiry and the quality of the echo it sends back when investigated. This casuistic principle, which in my view is one of the most important legacies of Roland Barthes (I called it elsewhere the "principle of unbelief"),[4] has nothing to do with a lack of commitment to the realm of ideas. On the contrary it rebels against the overhasty consumption of "theory" that characterizes theoreticism, and it avoids the deflation of its antitheory aftermath. It asserts the right to store up, and the possibility of retaining parts of a system while not swallowing it whole. As Roland Barthes often told his students, critical ideas should not be let go of prematurely (hence, for example, his dedication of *Camera*

Lucida to Jean-Paul Sartre's *L'imaginaire*, Sartre whose existentialism had supposedly been entirely "undone" by structuralism): an "old" idea can always be called to the rescue when a "new" theoretical model fails to elicit insight into the object you are trying to interpret. The object's resistance is the leading clue; the object's demands are the foremost consideration. Thus in the essays that follow the reader will not find one particular model "applied" indiscriminately to Matisse, cubism, Newman, or Mondrian. It so happens that, experiencing the shortcomings of the classical formalist approach to Newman's paintings, I was helped by phenomenology to sketch what I wanted to write about it; in the same manner, Saussurian concepts proved extremely useful in sorting out what I read in Kahnweiler's interpretation of cubism. In those two cases, there was a contemporaneousness between the imported model and the object of my research that gave me a hint and helped me build my argument, but this is by no means necessary. Because I wanted to describe Matisse's dissolving of an opposition, a dialogue with deconstruction pervaded my discussion of his work; because I saw in Mondrian's late work a mutation at what I call the symbolic level (see the last essay of this collection), Walter Benjamin's symbolic grammatology became a powerful ally.

Antiformalism

All this is not to say, however, that a certain thread does not link the various essays presented here. To put it bluntly, I would stay that a certain notion of formalism is at stake—and that I would like to rescue what is called formalism from the bad press it has received in much art historical writing during the past twenty years. But two things must be signaled at the outset: (1) there is formalism and formalism (the formalist approach previously taken toward Newman's work did not satisfy me, but I would not recoil if my essay on that work were to be attacked as formalist); (2) my defense of formalism is part of the "right to store up" strategy (and a consequence of the necessity of starting with the specificity of the object).

I will start with the second point, which brings out a fourth type of blackmail, namely *antiformalism*. An anecdote will do for an introduction. More than ten years ago, when I was preparing for *Macula*, a journal I edited in France between 1976 and 1979, a Pollock/Greenberg dossier that was to contain all the critic's texts on the artist, my coeditor Jean Clay and I had a harsh discussion with the artist Hans Haacke, whom we both knew and whose work we admired. He could not understand why we wanted to devote any space to Greenberg, whose politics (in the sense both of his role in the art world and his public position on political matters—the Vietnam war for example) he found extremely discreditable. Greenberg was, for him, definitely passé. But for us on the contrary, rather ignorant of the art world politics in question and certainly unmoved by its local effects, Greenberg's discourse represented a serious blow to the extremely mediocre practice of French art criticism, dominated at best by the specific French phenomenon of the Writer's or Philosopher's essay on art, more often than not an efflorescence of condescending words uttered by a complacent man of letters. Not that we had anything against what Sartre could have to say on Giacometti, Artaud on Paolo Uccello, Leiris on Miró, Ponge on Braque, etc., etc., but we resented the fact that this type of discourse on art was the only one worthy of being read. We were indeed quite appalled by the fad of such a literary exercise among our "poststructuralist" mentors and even more by the slippery effect it had on their imitators' work. Since, if we ourselves wanted to import Saussurian or Lacanian concepts into our own studies of art, we first tried to get them right, we felt that if a philosopher or an intellectual wanted to take painting as a model, to import pictorial issues into his problematic, he too had to get acquainted with the specific and historical problems pertaining to it. Of course, there was something dogmatic in our demands, and a certain naiveté in our request for professionalism, but this was compelled by the context (no doubt our reaction would have been entirely different if we had been trained in the U.S.): we felt that art criticism needed less "inspired" prose, more serious discussion.[5]

Besides this literary genre, establishment art history, entirely governed by a positivist faction, had nothing to give us except raw material to be articulated; and art criticism as a whole represented what Jakobson had called mere *causerie*.[6] Like the Russian formalists we felt that sweeping measures had to be taken, and that the starting point was, once again, the specificity of the practices we wanted to analyze. It was at this juncture that we, belatedly, discovered Greenberg. We knew very little of the context in which his discourse had emerged, and although we did not agree with its essentialism or with its imperialism, compared to the vulgarity of what his French counterparts had to say about Pollock for example (if they mentioned his work at all), his formal analyses seemed a remarkable departure to us, a sort of ABC of criticism without which nothing serious could be written about that painter. On the one hand we had not suffered from Greenberg's "politics"; on the other, French art criticism, since Fénéon, had altogether dropped any interest in formal matters. A formal approach, considered passé and even reactionary on the other side of the Atlantic, would definitely prove discordant and stimulating in the moribund context of France at that time. In short, we could exercise our right to store up, while this possibility was ideologically closed to someone like Haacke. But then conservation did not mean absolution. We too disagreed with many aspects of Greenberg's enterprise, gradually becoming more and more conscious of the extent of this disagreement (most of the essays that follow bear some signs of this). Skimming through the pages of *Artforum* when it was still something to be read and not yet a glossy printout in the hands of dealers, we discovered at the same time that the vast corpus of American criticism of the late '60s and early '70s, so superior to the French, was largely dominated by a reaction against Greenberg. But the terms of this reaction were still entirely ruled by the tenor of his theory. What the critics writing at the time could not see, for the precise reason noted above (that one cannot be embedded in a field and survey it), was the dialectical relationship of their position to that which they were rejecting. What our outsideness to the context allowed us to perceive was the common ground of those adversaries, the closure of a whole universe of discourse whose divisions represented strategic positions on the same field rather than a radical rift.[7]

The Two Formalisms

I shall now turn to the other issue, the fact that the label "formalism" has at least two readings. Greenberg's dogmatic system of evaluation was declared both obsolete and reactionary by Haacke, and there were good reasons for it. It had been gradually closing its doors on most of the artistic production following abstract expressionism, to admit into its pantheon only a handful of artists whose works neither we nor Haacke found particularly compelling. But in the heat of the discussion, the terms of the polemical opposition were given thus: either one is a formalist, hence necessarily oblivious to "meaning," or one is an antiformalist, hence entirely uninterested in formal matters. The either/or structure, that is, the generic structure of blackmail, seemed to be inescapable. Jean Clay and I nonetheless tried to convince our interlocutor that such an opposition was a false one, and that he himself could not avoid taking the issue of form extremely seriously in his work, on two different levels at least, that of morphology and that of structure. If the magnesium plates of his Mobil piece, *On Social Grease*, had not look exactly "as if they would be at home in the lobby of corporate headquarters or in the boardroom," as he wrote himself, their significance would have been entirely lost. As to this significance, a critique of that recent invention of the culture industry called corporate sponsorship, it rested on a very specific semantic strategy, a highly demanding structure of discourse, a type of rhetoric of which Haacke has become the master, and which I call elsewhere the tit-for-tat strategy.[8] Both formal levels were of paramount importance for the functioning of Haacke's work, as they are for any work, and furthermore the success of this work rested on the fact that those two levels were constantly interacting.

This distinction between the morphological and the structural or rhetorical, although it did not prove very useful in our debate at the time, became essential to my attitude toward "formalism." If Greenberg's discourse was flawed, I realized, it was because it deliberately disjoined the two levels and chose moreover to speak only about the first one, leading to such insipid statements as "the quality is the content," and to the transformation of structural oppositions ("opticality versus tactility") into purely morphological criteria of judgment. But this was by no means a necessary bias of formalism as such. Although I do not agree with Medvedev/Bakhtin's assessment of the Russian formalist school of criticism, which was far less monolithic than portrayed in "their" book, and far from being wholly uninterested in meaning, the way "they" oppose the methods of that school to those of the formalist trend in European *Kunstwissenschaft* is of particular significance here. Speaking of Riegl, Hildebrand, Fiedler, and others whose names eventually recur in the essays that follow, Medvedev/Bakhtin first remark on the context in which their work originated. It was in opposition to idealist philosophy and to positivist scholarship that the "main line of European formalism" emerged; it was against both the projective aesthetics of idealism, which conceives form as the embodiment of a transcendental a priori meaning, and the stubborn worship of facts that European formalism declared the "primacy of the constructive function," which these authors saw as the most important agent of signification in the work of art:

> European formalism not only did not deny content, did not make content a conditional and detachable element of the work, but, on the contrary, strove to attribute deep ideological meaning to form itself. It contrasted this conception of form to the simplistic realist view of it as some sort of embellishment of the content, a decorative accessory lacking any ideological meaning of its own.
>
> The formalists therefore reduced form and content to one common denominator, although one with two aspects: (1) form and content were both constructive elements in the closed unity of the work, and (2) form and content were ideological elements. The principle of contrast between form and content was thus eliminated.[9]

Bakhtin/Medvedev go on to say that Russian formalism sharply differs from the European variety on this point: "The Russian formalists began from the false assumption that an element acquires constructive significance at the cost of losing its ideological meaning."[10] This charge is ungrounded, in my view, if one sets aside a few slogans awkwardly launched by Shklovsky in the heat of the polemics of the time, but one certainly could bring it against Greenberg. In "Strzemiński and Kobro: In Search of Motivation," I allude to his astounding assertion that "if the past did appreciate masters like [Leonardo, Raphael, Titian, Rubens, Rembrandt, or Watteau] justly, it often gave wrong or irrelevant reasons for doing so," and that a modernist gaze at the works of these masters, supposedly unconcerned by their "literary" content, could be the only one able to unravel their "true" content.[11] Such a baffling statement would not have been possible had not Greenberg gradually lost, as Wölfflin also did at the end of his career, the sense that the formal structure of any given work is both a part and a determinant of its signification.

Thus Haacke's hostility is indeed understandable. Form, for Greenberg, had become an autonomous ingredient, and meaning a virus that could be dispensed with. The content/form and form/matter oppositions that have governed the idealist and dualistic aesthetic of the West beginning with Plato and Aristotle—and that modern art as a whole had sought to annihilate—were reconsolidated by his special brand of formalism. Idealism, which had been one of the main targets of European formalism, proved entirely victorious once again (and one might add that the other target, positivism, had reentered by the back door, as Greenberg himself, characterizing his own distrust for "interpretation," has been ready to acknowledge).[12] If I insist on this issue it is precisely to invoke the possibility of a *materialist* formalism, for which the specificity of the object involves not just the general condition of its medium, but also its means of production in its slightest detail. I speak of this materialism as a "technical model" in the article that gave its title to this volume, but it is also discussed in most of the essays that follow, and moreover, I would hope, it is the link between them.

Greenberg's strategies provide a good counterexample. Although he speaks about the medium of any art as its principal horizon, he seldom discusses the actual stuff of any work of art (or when he occasionally does, it is with gross errors: Barnett Newman, for example, was absolutely enraged when reading Greenberg's assessment of his color-field canvases as bearing a "dyer's effect").[13] Form became an a priori for Greenberg, an idea preexisting its actual "projection," its actual descent into the realm of matter, just like the "image" had been for Sartre. All the following articles strive to combat such a rampant idealism. In that sense, I cling steadfastly to the conception of what Medvedev/Bakhtin call European formalism:

Such a conception of the means of representation allows no suggestion of a contrast between the technique of representation taken as something inferior, as an auxiliary, and creative intention as something higher, as a superior goal. Artistic intention itself, being artistic, is from the very beginning given in technical terms, so to speak. And the object of this intention, its content, is not thought of outside the system of the means of its representation. From this point of view there is no need to draw a line between technique and creativity. Everything here has a constructive meaning. Anything incapable of such meaning has nothing to do with art.[14]

Formalism/Politics

A brief return to our early dialogue with Haacke will introduce yet another type of blackmail, the *sociopolitical* (the obligation to offer a sociopolitical interpretation of a work of art, recently supplemented by the obligation, for an artist, to make explicit the sociopolitical implications of his work). In our 1977 debate about Greenberg, politics had been the stumbling block, the dividing line: if you were a formalist, you were a reactionary. Both Jean Clay and I, ex-*soixantehuitards*, found the violence of the resentment rather puzzling: we had never expected to find ourselves labeled as conservatives. I face today the same astonishment when confronted with the political demands that are made of art in America more than anywhere else. (Here is a country for which politics seems to have very little significance—witness the vapidity of the last presidential campaign, the general lack of political awareness of graduate students—and yet it is perhaps here that these demands are the strongest. Comparing Japan to the USA, Roland Barthes once wrote: "In Japan . . . sexuality is in sex, not elsewhere; in the United States, it is the contrary; sex is everywhere, except in sexuality."[15] I would say that in the USA politics pervades everything but politics per se.)

But the terms of the opposition are not new: as is well known, the extraordinary adventure called today the "Soviet avant-garde" of the '20s was abruptly put to an end according to the lines of a similar sociopolitical blackmail. Not only the Russian formalist critics, but also scores of artists, film directors, writers, architects, etc., were silenced on the grounds of their "formalism," and in the name of "Marxism." Although Medvedev/Bakhtin are right when they affirm that, in general, the formalist-Marxist debate in Russia has been "essentially fruitless" (p. 67), the intervention of one of its participants rings truer to my ears than ever.

In 1932, as Stalin's lid was tightened on the cultural affairs of Russia, and in conjunction with the festivities commemorating the fifteenth anniversary of the October

Revolution, the journal *Kino* unfurled the slogan: "Our cinema must head for ideological plenitude!" Very courageously, Eisenstein set out to rebuff this dictate in the following issue of the magazine. Starting by looking at a dictionary ("I have a bad case of fondness for dictionaries, it's a kind of illness"), he finds that the word "ideology" derives from the Greek *idea*, and then immediately plunges into his Greek/Russian dictionary:

> "*idea*, Ionian. (1) aspect, external appearance; (2) image, genre, manner, attribute, quality . . . ; in particular: manner of expression, form and genre of the discourse; (3) idea, archetype, ideal."
>
> Thus: necessity to call to mind once again the genetic inseparability of the *idea* (point 3), of the *manner of expression* (point 2), and of . . . the *aspect*, the *appearance* (point 1).
>
> Is that new? As new as Popov's name, used to write Sacha Tchierny of such "discoveries." Yet, if it is not new, it is one of those truths that one has to repeat continually to oneself, before lunch and before dinner. And for those who don't dine, before going to bed. But most of all while awake, for one has to realize it in one's own practice.[16]

Eisenstein's argument, matching what Medvedev/Bakhtin see as the main claim of "European formalism," is that "form is *always ideological*,"[17] and that *Kino*'s slogan, in presupposing that any form could be ideologically "empty," deprived of content, is either entirely naive or entirely dishonest—depending on the level at which "form" is taken into consideration. His first stance, after the definitional introduction, is to rebuke the label "formalism": "as soon as a film director starts thinking about the problem of the expressive means of the materialization of an idea, the suspicion or accusation of formalism falls on him with a revenge. . . . To baptize such a director 'formalist' partakes of the same hasty lack of foresight as that of calling scientists studying the manifestation of syphilis 'syphilitic.'"[18] But Eisenstein's wit does not stop there, and in order to reaffirm his commitment to formal issues (the article is entitled "In the Interest of Form"), he adopts a very astute strategy, that of disarming the weapons of his adversaries. If "form" is described as a nuisance in the name of Marxism, it is in the name of Marxism that he will rescue it from the grip of what he calls an ideological "Ku Klux Klan":

> It is precisely of the misappreciation of form, the form that one forgets, that Engels spoke in his letter to Mehring dated July 14, 1893:
>
> > "I must simply draw your attention to the fact that a point is lacking, something that neither Marx nor I have examined thoroughly enough in

our works. On this issue, we are all equally guilty. To put it bluntly: we have all put the center of gravity, and we had to do it at the time, on the deduction of political, juridical, and ideological representations in general, as well as the actions determined by them, from the economical facts that lay at the basis of these representations. In doing so, because of the content, we did not pay to the formal side the attention that is due to it: in what way those representations are formed, etc. . . . This is an old story: at first, because of contrent, one never pays any attention to form. . . . I wanted to point that out to you for the future."[19]

It is "an old story indeed," and although Engels's formulation still presupposes a possible separation of the attention devoted to form and that devoted to content, this passage proved a formidable piece of ammunition for Eisenstein in his demonstration that such a separation is impossible. To cast this inseparability in another light, I would like to resort once again to Roland Barthes. For the thousandth time answering a question regarding the ahistoricity of his formalism, Barthes replied:

> It's remarkable how often one hears it stubbornly repeated that formalism is congenitally antipathetic to history. I myself have always tried to state the historical responsibility of forms. Thanks to linguistics and translinguistics, we will perhaps finally avoid the impasse to which sociology and history always lead us: the improper reduction of history to the history of referents. There is a history of forms, structures, writings, which has its own particular time—or rather, *times*: it's precisely this plurality which seems threatening to some people.[20]

What Barthes is alluding to here had been an essential issue for Russian formalism in its later years, although in their treatment of it Medvedev/Bakhtin rather dishonestly omit the idea in order to reformulate it themselves in the same manner.[21] Undoubtedly written in reaction against the "Marxist" antiformalist campaign, Jurij Tynjanov's brilliant article "The Problem of Literary Evolution" (1927), and the subsequent "Problems in the Study of Literature and Language" (1928) by Tynjanov and Jakobson, are both critiques of Shklovky's early defense of the absolute autonomy of the work of art, and, in the same vein as Barthes's words just mentioned, an affirmation of the compatibility—more: mutual support—of historical and structural studies.[22] Rejecting the vulgar "Marxist" theory of the work of art as a "reflection" of the economic basis of society, the authors stress that the relationships between this basis ("infrastructure") and "superstructure" (the ideological productions of mankind) should not be analyzed too swiftly and cannot be observed directly. For them, such precipitousness always leads to a conception of art as a mere illustration of a sociopolitical construct, as a mere projection of reality; and art's specificity is sacrificed on the altar of a transcendental signified. In order to avoid the trap of the reflection theory, which in Russia eventually led to so-called "socialist" realism as well as to the organized murder of every artist or writer who did not share this view, they proposed that one must first trace a picture, an overall diagram of the interrelationships between every sector of the superstructure at any moment of history. Only after these relationships were clearly charted, for example between religion, philosophy, science, and art, could one begin to try analyzing how both the overall chart (series of series, system of systems) and the particular fields it maps relate to the society contemporary to it. But because these different cultural series (art, religion, philosophy, etc.) are always evolving at different rhythms, and this is a decisive point in their argument, each historical cross section or map would bear a specific characteristic that would be the epistemological picture of the epoch under consideration—what Michel Foucault would later call the *tableau* or the *épistémé* of a given time. This insistence on the historical specificity of structural relations between the various "ideological" series is what Barthes had in mind when he spoke of the "historical responsibility of forms"; and it is what guided his overall rejection of militant discourse as typically ahistorical.

On this matter I hope to have remained faithful both to Barthes's lesson and to the Russian formalists' caution. In the following pages, the reader will not find any direct sociopolitical analysis of any work, for if indeed art can fulfill a political demand it is at its own level, that is, an ideological level, itself stratified. Which does not mean in the least that in the end the sociopolitical does not permeate the analysis. Concepts such as "Western metaphysics" or "a priori projection" appear often in the following essays, each time to note that the works discussed are in various ways struggling against what they embody. A blunter way to put it would be that most of these works represent extremely powerful attacks against idealism. No one would deny that the materialism-idealism antagonism, which is ideological, both informs and is informed by the sociopolitical, yet cannot be reduced to it. It is my contention that if one does not want to limit the relation between art and the sociopolitical to a mere question of thematic (one would then be left with a useless dichotomy between "political" and "nonpolitical" art), it is to refine the ideological analysis that one must work (and indeed the best examples of what is called "political art" have always consisted in a deciphering of the codes and strategies of the dominant ideology—today more than ever). This implies a most special attention paid to the "history of structures, of forms," for "form is always ideological."

To end this discussion of formalism, I quote from Barthes:

We should not be too quick to jettison the word *formalism*, because its enemies are our own: scientists, causationists, spiritualists, functionalists, "spontaneists"; attacks against formalism are always made in the name of content, the subject, the Cause (an ironically ambiguous word, referring as it does to a faith and a determinism, as if they were the same thing); i.e., in the name of the signified, in the name of the Name. We don't need to keep our distance from formalism, merely to take our ease (ease, on the order of desire, is more subversive than distance, on the order of censure). The formalism I have in mind does not consist in "forgetting," "neglecting," "reducing" content ("man"), but only in *not stopping* at the threshold of content (let's keep the word, provisionally); content is *precisely* what interests formalism, because its endless task is each time to push content back (until the notion of origin ceases to be pertinent), to displace it according to a play of successive forms.[23]

Asymbolia

This last quotation hits the center of a last type of blackmail, one that encapsulates all the preceding except the theoreticist one, entirely dominating the field of art history, with a particular force in the subfield of twentieth-century studies. Borrowing one last time a concept from Barthes, I would call it *asymbolia*. A kind of pathological disease that affects the human capacity to perceive and accept coexisting meanings, asymbolia is an atrophy of the function of symbolization.[24] But the disease is extremely hard to diagnose, for no one is more vocal about content than its victim, no one speaks more about the need for a "return to content." To pursue the medical metaphor at another level: just as the antiformalist critic refuses to see form as anything but a dispensable virus, the asymbolic critic conceives meaning as an ingredient that could at some point be absent. He is never as pleased as when he has proven that something "has" a meaning. But who ever thought that Mondrian's or Malevich's or Rothko's art, for example, was meaningless? A lot of people, to be sure, with whom the victims of asymbolia share a fundamental tenet based on their confusion between the meaning and the referent of a work of art, or, in the words that Barnett Newman borrowed from Meyer Schapiro, "subject-matter" and "object-matter." In the same way as the antiformalist enemies of abstract art held the latter meaningless because it had no apparent referent in the phenomenal world ("but what does it represent?"), the asymbolic critic finally admits it to his aesthetic pantheon because he is able to pinpoint such a referent. He can only rest in peace when he has unveiled this referent and heralded it as the only possible signification of the work in question. Now that he has found the "woman underneath," to speak like Balzac's dumbfounded beholders of Frenhofer's "unknown masterpiece," he feels that his task is at an end.

It would not be difficult to set forth scores of examples of such an asymbolia. If its attraction is stronger in the subfield of twentieth-century art studies (hence my insistence on the necessity to resist such a pressure), perhaps this is because the referentiality of the sign was precisely the main ethos of mimetic representation that modern art as a whole wanted to question. But it is only more apparent there: as a whole, art history as a discipline, especially in America, is heavily under its spell. One of the causes of this phenomenon, I think, is the strength of the iconological model in this country, which brings me to Panofsky.

Iconological Blindness

The famous essay in which Panofsky coined the term *iconology* appeared in at least two different versions: in 1939 in *Studies in Iconology*, and in 1955 in *Meaning in the Visual Arts*. (The 1939 version was itself a revision of a 1932 article based on arguments first presented in a 1930 book.)[25] Despite Panofsky's remarks to the contrary in the preface to *Meaning in the Visual Arts*, his corrections in the 1955 version are extremely significant (qualitatively if not quantitatively). As Michael Holly observed, what Panofsky referred to in 1939 as "iconography in the deeper [as opposed to narrower] sense" became "iconology" as opposed to iconography in 1955.[26] I interpret this slide from "iconography" to "iconology" as a strategy of disavowal, a mask intended to dissemble the fact that, in practice, iconology had too often become a sophisticated, extremely intelligent and cultivated version of traditional iconography. Panofsky was aware of this fact (hence the mask), and he must have interpreted it as his own betrayal of the ideas of his youth. Holly cites a letter to Booth Tarkington about *Studies in Iconology* that is significant in this regard:

> What I have tried to make clear is really not entirely original. It is perhaps only in contrast with so many purely formalistic interpretations of works of art that iconographic efforts appear as something unusual. In reality, my methods are reactionary rather than revolutionary, and I should not be surprised if some critics would tell me what the old doctor in "Doctor's Dilemma" tells his young friend: "You can be proud that your discovery has been made forty years ago," or something to that effect.[27]

By 1966, the mask itself was not felt as necessary anymore. Prefacing the French edition of *Studies in Iconology*, Panofsky wrote: "Today, perhaps I would have replaced the key word of the title, *iconology*, by *iconography*, more familiar and less controversial; but—and to admit this fills me with melancholic pride—the very fact that this substitution is henceforth possible is precisely a consequence, in a certain way, of the existence of these *Studies in Iconology*."[28] We could, of course, take Panofsky at his word and dismiss the iconological method he developed as old wine in new bottles, but it would be both unfair and unwise. What interests me more is the sense of disappointment conveyed in the letter, and the "melancholic pride" of the 1966 preface. Indeed, in his early texts, most of which are still inaccessible in English, Panofsky had sought to write the kind of history that would link various formal systems embedded in works of art with a social, psychological, and ideological explanation of stylistic change. If he was able in the '20s to pursue such brilliant lines of inquiry as those leading to his famous articles on theories of human proportion or perspective, it is because he was then entertaining the idea that artistic form, at the structural level, plays a major role in shaping a *Kunstwollen*, to use the concept of Riegl's that he tried to clarify in a remarkable essay. That is, because he did not regard form as a supplement. Gradually, though, Panofsky abandoned this elaborate concept and began developing a much more direct and less stratified way of connecting the history of art, the history of ideas, and the history of society. What emerged was a much simpler emphasis on theme, understood in relationship to texts. The entire complex structure of meanings that he had earlier wished to articulate in works of art—his investigation of a dialectical link between (1) a "structural scheme" (perspective, for example), (2) a theme, (3) a "vision of the world," and (4) the history of society— was finally reduced to the act of identifying a theme, which was considered as the sole agent of signification: every work of art became a one-dimensional rebus, the carrier of a veiled allegory that had to be properly deciphered. It is thus not by chance, as iconology became the governing method of art history in this country, that scholars grew less and less committed to the study of the *possibility* of meaning, of the structure of signification as such (which encompasses thematics indeed, but only as one of its components): I set as one of the purposes of my work to disturb this state of affairs. Once again, I have nothing against the iconological inquiry into twentieth-century art, provided that its rather limited concept of meaning does not prevent the analysis from reaching other levels of interpretation, other strata of signification. To give an example, I am perfectly happy to learn that Picasso had always endowed the figure of the guitar with anthropomorphic (more than that: feminine) connotations; but I would resent anyone's insisting on the fact that the "meaning" of his *Guitar* is "woman." On the one hand "woman" is not a meaning as such, but a referent to which a vast array of meanings can be attached; on the other hand, I am more interested in studying the structural possibility of such a semiological fluctuation of the signs in Picasso's cubism.

Last but not least, and strange as it may seem, Panofsky warned against the iconological mania when directed toward modern art, and specifically toward abstract art, an art with which a good portion of the subsequent essays is concerned as is indeed the bulk of my studies. Let us return to my earlier philological comparison of the two versions of "Iconography and Iconology." In the passage that contains the terminological substitution discussed above, Panofsky is in the process of concluding the exposition of his famous trilevel theory, with its hierarchical nesting of three strata of interpretation (the identification of the motif as preliminary to interpretation of the image's historical or allegorical significance, which is itself preliminary to interpretation of its "intrinsic content"). However, this expositional passage concludes with a restriction that does not seem to have caught the attention of Panofsky's devotees: the hierarchy of interpretive strata is necessary, he writes in the 1939 version of the essay,

> unless we deal with such works of art in which the whole sphere of secondary or conventional subject matter is eliminated, and a direct transition from *motifs* to *content* is striven for, as is the case with European landscape painting, still-life and genre; that is, on the whole, with exceptional phenomena, which mark the later, over-sophisticated phases of a long development.[29]

As Bernard Teyssèdre observes in the French edition of this text, Panofsky's sentence underwent three revisions in the 1955 version: (1) the final clause (beginning with "that is, on the whole, with exceptional phenomena") was deleted; (2) the pejorative "is striven for" was replaced with "is effected"; and (3) to the list "landscape painting, still life, and genre," Panofsky appended "not to mention 'non-objective' art."[30] The third transformation is obviously the one that concerns me here, although I should point out that the deletion of the implicit negative value judgment of landscape, still life, and genre does not at all mean that Panofsky had finally withdrawn his claim for the universality of his method and was restricting it to works of the Renaissance humanist tradition, that is to works of art based on texts.[31] But the mention of abstract art here is a warning: he is discouraging an iconological approach to it. This caution was no doubt engendered by his own bafflement with the phenomenon (as Barnett Newman somewhat exaggeratedly puts it, we should not expect too much from "one who has consistently shown himself to be unfeeling towards any work of art since Dürer"),[32] but at least Panofsky did not dare to put in writing that if his method did not work, it was the object's fault. The important point is that iconology was declared by its founder to be not the best tool with which to approach abstract art. On that point, he was absolutely right.

    Maybe Panofsky's growing asymbolia was a consequence of his transmigration to the United States. Although he was not a refugee (as were most German art historians emigrating to the USA, or for that matter to London), Panofsky did share with his less fortunate colleagues a compulsion to perfect his integration into the cultural tissue of his new country. In "Three Decades of Art History in the United States," a rather inaccurate title for this "immigrant" essay, he provides a clue. After noting the liberating effect of being plunged into a new scholarly atmosphere that knew nothing of the provinciality and national *parti pris* characterizing European research at the time, he marvels at the linguistic and epistemological mutation he was forced to endure. Even if he mentions in passing the possibility of a conflict with the tradition he is discovering, Panofsky sees as a "blessing" the fact that the European scholar arriving in America came into contact with "an Anglo-Saxon positivism which is, in principle, distrustful of abstract speculation."[33] The rapid mastery of the English language was, for Panofsky, the vehicle of a much-needed transformation. "Forced to express ourselves both understandably and precisely and realizing, not without surprise, that it could be done," the German emigré willfully underwent a drastic ablation:

> The German language unfortunately permits a fairly trivial thought to declaim from behind a woolen curtain of apparent profundity and, conversely, a multitude of meanings to lurk behind one term. The word *taktisch*, for example, normally denoting "tactical" as opposed to "strategic," is used in art-historical German as an equivalent of "tactile" or even "textural" as well as "tangible" or "palpable." And the ubiquitous adjective *malerisch* must be rendered, according to context, in seven or eight different ways: "picturesque" as in "picturesque disorder"; "pictorial" (or, rather horribly, "painterly") as opposed to "plastic"; "dissolved," "sfumato," or "non-linear" as opposed to "linear" or "clearly defined"; "loose" as opposed to "tight"; "impasto" as opposed to "smooth." In short, when speaking or writing English, even an art historian must more or less know what he means and mean what he says, and this compulsion was exceedingly wholesome for all of us."[34]

Making fun of his debuts, Panofsky-the-great-philologist immediately wins the reader over to his side. (Who did not struggle, as he had himself, with the various signifi-cations of Riegl's *Kunstwollen*?) But the self-inflicted irony masks in fact a terrible sense of mourning: much as his American texts can be read as a refutation of the anti-positivist stance of his youth (a refutation prompted by the "failure" to achieve the "transcendental-scientific" history he had been striving for), his embrace of an eco-nomic view of language—one meaning per word—his final refusal to admit that lan-guage has a life of its own and that its signs bear connotations that are infinitely open to interpretation, will shape the shrunken conception of meaning that his iconology will espouse. For if, in the name of clarity, only one of the seven or eight possible meanings of *malerisch* is retained, it is not a gain, but a loss—just as the allegorical reading of Picasso's *Guitar* as referring to a woman, and as only that, is a terrible reduction that, I feel, must be fought at all costs. Between claiming that only one meaning could be assigned to any word, to any work of art, and that a pure lack of meaning could ever be possible, there is only a difference in degree, not in nature, and in fact one claim often proceeds from the other (if not *this* signification, then it must be nothing at all). Both fantasies presuppose a frozen world of signs (as if mean-ings did not change in history, as if new meanings did not emerge from old signs); both symptoms of asymbolia, they cut short the interpretative chain, close Pandora's box when the task of the critic is to open it.

Theoreticism, antitheory, fashion, antiformalism, sociopolitical demand, asym-bolia: those are the forces at work within the field in which I move, the various vec-tors that map the territory to which I belong. At least, those are the forces I am able to recognize and that I regard as the most lethal, the forces against which I target my labor, albeit always implicitly, in the essays that follow. This does not mean that I am always successful at keeping these forces at bay. Nor does it mean that many other forces, undetected or whose might I do not perceive with enough accuracy to find their repudiation most urgent, are not casting their shadow on the field in question nor shaping my discourse without my being aware of it. For those last I obviously cannot provide an antidote; they are my blind spot, the unseen part of my horizon. I do hope, however, that enough has surfaced in my perception of the field for my work to prove consistent and for the essays that follow to constitute in some way a lesson in resistance.

A final note regarding these essays and the context in which they were written, a note that will have to look a bit like a list of acknowledgments. I shall start with one of the first pages of this book, the dedication: three names are given, that of my first three readers, in alphabetical order—Jean Clay, Dominique Jaffrennou, Rosalind

Krauss. But Dominique Jaffrennou, my wife, should be singled out as the very first reader of all those texts: I rarely dare send off any article prior to her approval, and she has continually been my most generous (but also harshest) editor. I could not be more grateful for her constant support.

I have mentioned several times Jean Clay, with whom I had founded *Macula*, and whom I have known since my teens: most of the ideas expressed here were first elaborated as part of our uninterrupted dialogue, to the point that it is sometimes hard for me to pay due tribute to him, having cannibalized his contribution to my thinking in a most unconscious way. The collective experience that the editing of our journal represented has played a major role in the formation of these essays, even if all of them are posterior to the end of its publication.

As for Rosalind Krauss, whose voice has been essential in my decision to come work in America, the reader of these essays will quickly acknowledge the extent of my debt to her work. Some of these articles appeared in *October*, the journal she has been editing with Annette Michelson for more than a decade, and it is with some sense of pride that I see this collection appear among the *October* book series. But I want to emphasize that, even more than a friend, Rosalind Krauss has been for me, ever since I set foot in this country, a most powerful ally. Not so much because she has ceaselessly supported my work with all her institutional weight, not so much because there are probably very few issues on which our views diverge, but because, in my resistance to the various forms of blackmail I have tried to sketch above, her combative stance has constantly represented for me a rock to which I could return at moments when my strength was threatening to fail.

Finally, the essay from which this volume takes its title departs from the others. Although I have written many reviews over the years, considering it almost a moral duty on the part of the intellectual, this, on a book by Hubert Damisch, is the only one I include. I have not mentioned his name in this preface, although I could well have at every turn. He was, with Roland Barthes, the advisor for my graduate studies at the Ecoles des Hautes Etudes en Sciences Sociales, that haven of the French system of higher education where the positivism and humanism (idealism) of the old university are shunned as trite disgraces. As my indebtedness to his work is sketched in the essay I just mentioned, I shall not insist on it here. I simply want to point to the fact that if his name does not figure in the dedication, it is because I almost never dared to send him anything before publication. The urge to take painting seriously, or any kind of art for that matter, and to understand it not as the illustration of a theory but as a model, a theoretical model in itself, I owe directly to him. My wish is that in the pages that follow, part of that legacy has been successfully put to work.

I Totems of Modernity

Matisse and "Arche-drawing"

It is solely a question of playing up differences.

—Matisse to Gaston Diehl, 1947

An incongruity in the text published under the title "Modernism and Tradition," of which the original French manuscript is missing, unexpectedly attests to the difficulty of the most radical aspects of Matisse's enterprise. As late as 1935, the year in which the article appeared in the venerable London review *The Studio,* Matisse's intentions still remained partially obscure, even to those most favorably disposed to him. The passage in question reads: "A great modern attainment is to have found the secret of expression by color, to which has been added, with what is called fauvism and the movements which have followed it, expression by design; contour, lines and their direction."[1] The problem lies in the phrase "expression by design": not only is there no word in French corresponding to the concept of "design," but more importantly (since the term could have been used to translate a periphrasis), nothing could be more alien to Matisse's thought.[2] Indeed, the concept of design presupposes a kind of plastic grammar transcending all genres, all media, a kind of esperanto allowing for a flattening out of all differences, and an escape from the dictates of materiality: for a "designer," scale does not count; he sketches a cigarette lighter as if he were dealing with a scale model of a skyscraper, or plans a skyscraper on the basis of a mock-up the size of a lighter. Design is an entirely projective practice (the designer, imitated all too frequently by architects, projects on paper in a priori fashion what others will go on to realize); for the designer, the formal idea is prior to the actual substance: all of Matisse's art is violently opposed to such tawdry Aristotelianism.[3] "Expression by design" is impossible, a judgment confirmed at the end of the same sentence, where Matisse speaks of "contours, lines and their directions," in other words, drawing (*dessin*). But if the translator could not bring himself to translate what must have been "expression par le dessin" as "expression by drawing," it is clearly because he had no more idea of what Matisse meant by it than anyone else at the time. The translator's infelicity is certainly understandable: wasn't fauvism always referred to elsewhere, as Matisse himself puts it, as "the exaltation of color" (a statement made to Tériade in 1952, Flam, p. 134)? What are we to make of the almost playful way in which, along with the "movements that followed," fauvism is singled out for its "drawing" and presented as what *followed* the "great modern attainment" of color? In my view, the stakes bound up in this sentence are high, and the present essay is simply an attempt to show that, far from being a slip or mere approximation, the statement turns out to be confirmed by the great majority of Matisse's writings and remarks, as well as by his most important works, encapsulating as it does what is essential in the break he produced in the history of painting. Before dealing with what Matisse understands by the at first sight enigmatic phrase "expression by [drawing]," we must first examine the "secret of expression by color" that is said to have been discovered before fauvism. To do so, a close reading of "Modernism and Tradition" proves to be absolutely essential.

Let us begin by noting the exceptional place of this text in Matisse's theoretical output: he was then at the midpoint of his career as a painter and, after the Nice odalisques, had just begun to reexamine the exemplary work of 1906–17: if we exclude one very brief "autobiographical note" that appeared in 1930 (*EPA,* pp. 77–78), it was the first written text published by Matisse since the famous "Notes of a Painter" from 1908. Certainly, in the intervening years the artist confided in numerous visitors, and his various remarks, notably those addressed to Tériade, are far from being insignificant. But, from "Notes" to *Jazz,* Matisse frequently expressed his repugnance for writing, too frequently for his deigning to take up the pen after a quarter of a century not to have exceptional significance:[4] we can be sure that every word in "Modernism and Tradition" must have been carefully weighed.

And yet the article is full of surprises: "expression by [drawing]" is not the only one it has in store. In fact, it would be true to say that a whole series of strange, skillfully arranged moments prepares the way for it. To begin with, contrary to what is suggested by the title, Matisse opens with an homage to "the enterprise and the courage" said to have been demonstrated by the artists working in Paris for the preceding fifty years (in other words, since 1885): "elsewhere, artists are content to follow where others have led." Then follows a slightly ironic passage on the very earliest years of his apprenticeship, during which Matisse supposedly did not stand out from the crowd (this is implied, at least, by his use of "we": "When I first began to paint, we did not disagree with our superiors and advanced our opinions slowly and cautiously"). Then comes a kind of litany reeling off everything he had to reject in order to be able to "create something out of [his] own experience":"I felt that the methods of the impressionists were not for me"; "what I saw at the Louvre did not affect me directly." Even his old professor Gustave Moreau ends up being snubbed, Moreau who was so often praised by Matisse precisely because, contrary to academic norms, he had urged him both to visit the Louvre and to go out into the street to paint.[5] The first couplet in the litany ends with a sentence that highlights the movement from "we" to "I": "so I began to work alone." Immediately after, however, and as if to refute this remark in the very same breath, we find: "It was then that I met . . . Derain." The return to "we" is quite unusual, for although, as he says, Matisse was undoubtedly stimulated by the young Derain's arrival in Collioure in 1905, he always tended to downplay the effect it had on him.[6] At the end of the article, Matisse cannot resist running down the label "fauvism," one of his bêtes noires, because all labels "limit the life of a movement and militate against individual recognition"; but, at this point in the text, immediately after noting a certain tendency to work alone, he comes to insist on the collective nature of the revolt against the elders, in other words, he picks up the litany at another level, that of the atmosphere of the day: "We lived together for some time at Collioure, where we worked unremittingly, urged by the same incentive. The methods of painting employed by our elders were not adequate to the true representation of our sensations, so we had to seek new methods. And, after all, this urge is felt by every generation."

So far, the word "tradition" has appeared only in the title and the reader is entitled to wonder whether Matisse doesn't conceive the relations between modernism and tradition solely in antagonistic terms. Now, the word figures in two passages, the first just after this historicist appeal to the category of "generation" ("At that time, it is true, there was more scope than there is today, and tradition was rather out of favor by reason of having been so long respected"), the second immediately following the enigmatic sentence concerning fauvism and "expression by [drawing]" ("In the main, tradition was carried forward by new mediums of expression and augmented as far as was possible in this direction," a sentence followed by another on the "continuity of artistic progress from the early to the present-day painters," then by a fairly hollow dogmatic assertion that could easily pass for an academic profession of faith, were it not for everything that precedes it: "In abandoning tradition the artist would have but a fleeting success, and his name would soon be forgotten"). Indeed, framed by these two sections in which the word "tradition" appears, we find a third moment in the litany. This passage, which makes for all the richness of this text, begins with a flashback consisting of a long development on Matisse's brief divisionist experiment, then discusses its rejection, which, with the advent of fauvism, in turn led to "discarding verisimilitude."

Let us first pause for a moment to examine his use of the word "tradition." Matisse bestows two contradictory meanings on it: there is a good and a bad tradition, and we seem to move surreptitiously from the second to the first. Indeed, what does Matisse mean when he notes that in the fauvist period "tradition was rather out of favor by reason of having been so long respected"? He is certainly not talking about museums, in spite of what is suggested by the beginning of the text (for almost all the fauves came out of Moreau's studio, Moreau who "took [them] *back*" to the Louvre—and not simply "took" them, as Flam's translation has it; Flam, p. 65; cf. *EPA,* p. 90, and note 5 above), but about what he later calls, in the preface to *Portraits,* a book published posthumously, "the dead part of tradition," namely "the rules of the School, remnants of the teachings of the masters who came before us" (Flam, p. 151). It was fauvism's task to throw off this dead weight, but with the aid of the good tradition, the one that "confirms your efforts" and "helps you jump the ditch" (a remark made to Diehl in 1947, concerning the East and some icons he had seen in Moscow, Flam, p. 116)—aided by Courbet who "reoriented" Matisse in the Louvre,[7] by Cézanne who spent who spent "his afternoons [there] drawing . . . at the time he was painting the portrait of Vollard and who would say to Vollard: 'I think that tomorrow's sitting will be a good one, for I'm pleased with what I did this afternoon in the Louvre'" ("Observations on Painting," 1945, Flam, p. 101), and by many others. All of which is very canonically modernist; the good tradition is not the Louvre as such, but a certain way of using it: those who merely imitate the old masters are the gravediggers; keeping a tradition alive means being aware of one's own historical situation with respect to it and thus transforming it; the good tradition belongs to the present which reinterprets the old; abandoning a tradition means abandoning it to its entropic fate by refusing to unsettle it.[8] See Baudelaire, Eliot, Adorno, Greenberg, etc. There would be no end to the list of theoreticians of the tradition of the new. What is truly striking in the economy of Matisse's text is on the one hand its dynamic symmetrical arrangement (with the bad tradition on one side, the good on the other, and between the two an arrow indicating the history of his own liberation), on the other hand what is designated as the trigger that, in engendering the reaction that gave rise to fauvism, allowed Matisse to relocate himself on the axis of the good tradition that goes "from the early to the present-day painters"—namely, his passage through divisionism.

Certainly, "Modernism and Tradition" makes it clear that it was his abandonment of divisionism that led Matisse to fauvist painting, "which is not the whole
story," but which is "the basis of everything," as he later says.[9] But the very structure
of the text indicates that the conversion from the bad to the good would not have
been possible without what was much more than a simple excursion through divisionism. The negation of divisionism carried out by fauvism, and even more so by
"the movements which . . . followed it," was heuristic only because the failure of his
divisionist efforts (which were actually much more conscientious than is generally
conceded) had revealed to Matisse his own singularity: his road to Damascus was
thoroughly dialectical. Now, nothing in Matisse's previous and subsequent remarks
accords with such a hypostasis of the divisionist phase. Certainly, as he remarks to
Apollinaire in 1907, Matisse "never avoided the influence of others" (Flam, p. 32),
never sought to conceal the effect that his elders, including the divisionists, had on
him. But in all his statements on the question (to Tériade, 1929 and 1952, Flam,
pp. 58–59 and 132; to Diehl at the end of his life[10]), the divisionist episode is always
viewed as an aberration in his own itinerary, a false, obsessive trail on which he
claims to have gone astray before the big fauve clean-out: "Fauvism overthrew the
tyranny of divisionism. One can't live in a house too well-kept, a house of country
aunts. One has to go off into the jungle to find simpler ways which won't stifle the
mind" (1929, Flam, p. 58).[11] Now, even if "Modernism and Tradition" repeats the
same refrain ("actually I knew very well that achievement by these means was limited
by too great an adherence to strictly logical rules"), Matisse, in retrospect, does not
hesitate to admit his enthusiasm: "This new technique made a great impression on
me. Painting had at last been reduced to a scientific formula; it was the secession from
the empiricism of the preceding eras. I was so much intrigued by this extraordinary
method that I studied post-impressionism." Not only does Matisse here admit something whose very possibility he had ruled out in the "Notes," namely the at least provisional fascination held for him by a theory making it possible to break with
impressionist empiricism (marking himself off explicitly from Signac, he had said at
that time "my choice of colors does not rest on any scientific theory," Flam, p. 38,
without implying that it ever had), but throughout this text littered with negations,
divisionism is the *only* previous pictorial practice to which he refers in positive
terms: it was "the great innovation of that day." It was the point of departure, what
Matisse had to rub up against in order to become Matisse. None of the great totemic
figures is mentioned here: neither Cézanne, "the master of us all,"[12] this "sort of god
of painting" (to Guenne, 1925, Flam, p. 55), to whom "[he] indubitably owe[s] most"
in modern art (to Russell Howe, 1949, Flam, p. 123), nor the Orientals ("my reve-

lation came from the Orient," to Diehl, 1947, Flam, p. 116). Of the four traditions from which, as the autobiographical note tells us, he drew his inspiration in order to move from the "somber gamut" of the Louvre to the "brightened palette" of fauvism and the works, "mainly decorative in character," that followed—the "impressionists, the neoimpressionists, Cézanne, and the Orientals" (*EPA*, p. 77)—the last two are ignored here and the first immediately declared irrelevant ("not for me"): the chain reaction that will end with "fauvism and the movements which have followed it" is attributed solely to divisionism, or neoimpressionism. What does this mean? Quite simply that Matisse attributes to divisionism the discovery of "the secret of expression by color." Certainly, "the impressionists cleared the way" in this domain (to Diehl, 1945, Flam, p. 99), and the Orientals contributed a great deal, but "it was later . . . that this art touched me" (to Diehl, 1947, Flam, p. 116).[13] As for Cézanne, even if Matisse on one occasion attributes to him "the definitive impulse" in the rehabilitation of color (to Diehl, 1945, Flam, p. 99),[14] the fauves' use of pure colors owes nothing directly to him.[15] André Marchand even reports the following remark, which forces us to reconsider Matisse's claimed indebtedness to the Aix master: "Cézanne constructed his paintings, but the magic of color still remained to be found after him" (1947, Flam, p. 114). Matisse's discourse is inflexible on this point: even if we are dealing with "a purely physical systematization . . . of the means of impressionism," with a "mechanical means," even if he "didn't stay on this course" (to Tériade, 1929, Flam, p. 58), divisionism, before fauvism, was what allowed him to glimpse "possibilities of expression beyond the literal copy" ("The Chapel of the Rosary," 1951, Flam, p. 128),[16] by means of the atom of color freed from any mimetic function. It was this potential autonomy of color that constituted the secret unveiled by neoimpressionism.[17]

I do not intend here to reopen the file on the enormous impact that neoimpressionism had on Matisse: this question has been analyzed with great verve by Catherine Bock, who has forced Matisse criticism as a whole to surrender the ill-gotten gains of its permanent contempt for the procedure of color division.[18] A brief summary of the matter will suffice. I would rather reexamine the reasons that led Matisse to abandon divisionism and to agree with Henri-Edmond Cross when Cross said to him, "You won't stay with us long," a remark Matisse reported in "Modernism and Tradition" and in numerous other places.

First, the summary. And to begin, a correction to what I have said so far: contrary to what is suggested by "Modernism and Tradition" and Matisse's other statements on the same question, we find not one but *two* divisionist phases in his career.

The first was even shorter than the second, and its failure less productive—at least if one concedes that the years immediately following it, marked by a great stylistic diversity, have nothing of the triumphant assurance that apparently characterizes his oeuvre during the decade following the advent of fauvism. Summarily put, Matisse "repressed" this first phase in his remarks: it comprised an important stage in his apprenticeship, but the reaction it engendered, the celebrated "return to Cézanne" of the years that Barr calls "dark" (1900–04), was much less determinative for the constitution of his pictorial system than that which emerged from the second divisionist phase. Or rather, this first reaction was determinative above all in a negative way: during these "dark years," Matisse confronts and solves problems raised by his dissatisfaction or disappointment with divisionism, which makes it possible for him to move on to something completely different during phase two. This first incursion thus also warrants a brief outline.

In 1898, shortly after following Pissarro's advice to go to London to see the Turners, Matisse is confronted for the first time with the light of the south during a stay in Corsica. His apprenticeship years with Moreau had not prepared him for this exposure to the sun, and he is far from having adequately mastered the impressionist palette, which he had only just discovered, too far to know how to "organize [his] sensations," to use the Cézanne expression he himself often used (including in "Modernism and Tradition").[19] As Pierre Schneider puts it, the canvases of this period have a "panicky character"[20] (see fig. 1), and Matisse himself is somehow stricken by them. Soliciting the opinion of Henri Evenepoël, a cohort from Moreau's studio, he sends him some of the hurried sketches done in Corsica, not without forewarning him that "it was epileptic." His friend reacts even more wildly, replying that "yes, it is furious painting, done by someone gnashing his teeth."[21] Less than a week after receiving this letter, Matisse is in Paris for a few days, discussing the new development with Evenepoël, failing to convince him: it is doubtless at this time that he purchases two issues of *La Revue blanche,* in which the first six chapters of Paul Signac's *De Delacroix au néo-impressionnisme* had just appeared.[22]

The reading does not have an immediate effect: Matisse clings momentarily to the style of his "sketches," a style that, with the exaggerated thickness of the paint, could be dubbed "couillard," after the period of the same name in Cézanne's oeuvre. Apart from a bare handful of fauve canvases like *The Gypsy* [*La Gitane*], this is the only time in Matisse's entire career when he succumbs to the "prestige of matter" (Schneider), to the effects of impasto: one of the most immediate effects of Signac's pamphlet is to liberate him from this failing. In any case, at the end of his stay in the south (in the meantime Matisse and his family have moved to Toulouse), he is completely

1. Henri Matisse, The Tree [L'Arbre], *Corsica, 1898. Oil on cardboard, 18 × 22 cm (7¹/₁₆ × 8⁵/₈ in.). Musée des Beaux Arts, Bordeaux. Photo Alain Danvers.*

engrossed in trying to put Signac's principles into practice. Signac's treatise (perhaps the first text by a painter that Matisse had read since Goupil's technical manual, which in autodidactic fashion he had pored over when he was just starting out) presents an impressive historical overview of the chromatic evolution of painting since Delacroix, and provides a particularly effective reference grid for the young painter once again working in complete solitude (note that Gustave Moreau, whose studio he left at the beginning of 1898, died in April, during Matisse's stay in the south).[23] If we exclude Delacroix, whose art had at that point barely touched Matisse, Signac assigns almost all the artists whose contradictory influences had up to that point affected Matisse a definite place in the historical sequence that according to him necessarily ends with divisionism: Fantin-Latour, Turner, Monet, Pissarro.[24] Even Cézanne figures as a precursor here, and it was perhaps the very fact of his reading of Signac's

2. Henri Matisse, Sideboard and Table [Buffet et table], *Toulouse, early 1899. Oil on canvas, 67.5 × 82.5 cm (26½ × 32½ in.). Private collection, Switzerland.*

treatise, where the color stroke is defined as a perfectly nonmimetic element, that led Matisse to be more attentive to the work of this "god of painting."[25]

I shall not attempt to retrace Matisse's various trial and error efforts to apply Signac's theory in the absence of any concrete model for him to refer to. Let us simply note that at the end of his few months of apprenticeship, Matisse is, as Bock observes (to whom I owe this summary), in a position to produce an orthodox divisionist piece, a painting that could be seen as even more faithful to the theory than those done by divisionist painters of the same period.[26] Indeed, whereas from 1894 on Signac had simplified his color contrasts by enlarging his brushstrokes and abandoning color-value modeling in favor of reinforcing the flatness of the picture, Matisse works from the very infrequent specifically technical passages in *De Delacroix au néo-impressionnisme* in order to paint *Sideboard and Table* [*Buffet et table*] (fig. 2), without paying any attention to the corner cutting found here and there in the course of the treatise. Not only does he try to follow the compositional rules elaborated on the basis of Seurat's and Charles Henry's theories on the psychology of the line (dyna-mogeny versus inhibition) and the necessary harmony between the deployment of this latter and the picture's color system (ascending line + warm hues + light tones = joy, etc.), but he also diligently endeavors to "spread" his complementary contrasts over the entire surface of the canvas, as recommended by Signac in the brief tech-nical remarks on the divisionist method at the beginning of his treatise. Result: the surface of his canvas is "jumpy," as Matisse will later say of his works from 1904–05, and, as in Seurat's *Poseuses,* the colors self-destruct.[27] Faced with such a disappoint-ing result after such a consuming effort, Matisse's reaction is instantaneous: *Still Life with Oranges* [*Nature morte aux oranges;* The Washington University Gallery of Art, St. Louis], done in Toulouse, is constructed in large, flat planes of saturated colors, following a method very close to what will be that of fauvism; but above all, in *Still Life against the Light* [*Nature morte orange (ou nature morte orangé à contre-jour*)] (fig. 3), painted in Paris toward the end of 1899, he increases the intensity of his col-ors to a level previously unattained in his oeuvre. As Bock writes, "The whole room is inundated with light that is almost heat; the effect is that of a furnace. The colored areas are large; the brushstroke is broad, gestural, ample. In contrast to the red/green, yellow/purple scheme of the pointillist still life, the binary colors are stressed here: orange, blue, purple, and some green. The colors are intensified, but they are not juxtaposed complementaries. It is as though Matisse relaxed from the effort of the pointillist still life by painting another version which flouts the conventions of the first. As opposed to the rather cold luster of the neoimpressionist work and the marked three-dimensionality of its forms, the orange still life is ablaze with a color that dissolves the outlines of glasses and bowls and produces a relatively flat effect."[28] This last point is particularly well taken, although I would modify it slightly: the tra-ditional structure of perspective + light and dark is especially marked in *Sideboard and Table,* but, as Schneider notes, it is largely contradicted, if not totally annihilated, by the chromatic texture.[29] In other words, the flatness of these first "reactive" works, far from being a solution to the color/volume contradiction evident in the pointillist still life, is merely a restatement of it in a different mode. The true reaction comes with the general abandoning of this fiery range of colors in the years that follow, with a few important exceptions which Catherine Bock is right to emphasize. Even if (as she says) it is wrong to place this "somber" period exclusively under the sign of Cézanne, the fact is that Matisse seems at first glance to be interested in what seems to be cruelly lacking in his 1899 canvases, namely the rendering of volume, and that

3. *Henri Matisse,* Still Life against the Light [Nature morte orange (ou nature morte orangé à contre-jour)], *Paris, 1899. Oil on canvas, 74 × 93.5 cm (29¾ × 36½ in.). Private collection, France.*

he then returns to modeling. Hence his new-found passion for sculpture, hence his return to school and his choice of Eugène Carrière as master, a painter whose grisaille canvases deliberately ignore color, hence, yes, his recourse to Cézanne, from whom he tries to learn how to unite value and color. As he later wrote to his son concerning the 1903 *Studio under the Eaves* [*Atelier sous les toits*], it was a time "of transition between values and color."[30] Up until his rediscovery of divisionism in 1904, Matisse's constant concern is with modeling and the representation of space. Breaking volume down into planes, which he picks up from Cézanne, is now the procedure he most frequently, although not exclusively, turns to.

We now approach phase two. And to begin, let us note that in 1904, when he accepts Signac's invitation to spend the summer with him in Saint-Tropez, Matisse has incomparably more strings to his bow than he had five years earlier. He has just had a personal exhibition at Vollard's, a retrospective of his work since 1896. He is much better acquainted with Cézanne's oeuvre (the first three works done in Saint-Tropez are the only ones in his entire output in which he openly imitates the Aix master),[31] he has discovered Redon's pastels, has confronted Rodin, been inspired by Nabi art, familiarized himself with Van Gogh and above all Gauguin whose work had been presented at the Salon d'Automne in 1903 (a mini-retrospective) and at Vollard's in a monster exhibition in November of the same year. And finally, he has had numerous opportunities to see divisionist pictures, first at the Salon des Indépendants, which the neoimpressionists resurrected in 1901, then at the Galerie Druet, which opened in 1903 with the stated intention of promoting this tendency.[32]

It is generally agreed nowadays that Matisse's second conversion to divisionism dates from August 1904, as if somehow he had to await the arrival in Saint-Tropez of a neoimpressionist less fervent than Signac, namely Henri-Edmond Cross, in order to allow himself to be persuaded to try the experiment once more. Impelled by his two mentors, whom he watches at work, he undertakes a large symbolist composition featuring nudes in a landscape that, like them, he begins with studies on the motif. *Luxe, calme et volupté* (fig. 4), one of the rare pictures by Matisse bearing an explicitly literary title (an allusion to Baudelaire's *L'Invitation au voyage*), was painted in Paris, after he had seen the Cézanne, Redon, and Puvis de Chavannes retrospectives at the Salon d'Automne, but the scene's landscape decor was conceived in Saint-Tropez: Matisse still believes he can separate conception and realization. We shall see that the rupture with divisionism stems in part from discovering that for him such a separation is just not possible.

When it was exhibited at the Salon des Indépendants in 1905, an exhibition including Seurat and Van Gogh retrospectives, the critics most favorably disposed to Matisse found the picture offensive; it provoked this judgment from Denis: "*Luxe, calme et volupté* is a theoretical diagram,"[33] a judgment reinforced a few months later by the following outbursts: "it's dialectics!," "it's artificiality," "it's pictorial noumena [*des noumènes de tableaux*]."[34] Signac, though, was delighted to have produced a disciple of this caliber, and he bought the painting—which in any case shows that he felt it conformed closely enough to the rules of divisionism as he had outlined them (which flies in the face of a veritable cliché of Matisse criticism). Nevertheless, *Luxe, calme et volupté* didn't satisfy Matisse for long, and what he considered to be relatively speaking a failure made him resolve to seek an alternative to the neoimpressionist technique.

4. *Henri Matisse,* Luxe, calme et volupté, *1904. Oil on canvas, 98.3 × 118.5 cm (37 × 46 in.). Musée National d'Art Moderne, Centre Georges Pompidou, Paris. Photo of the museum.*

In order to better understand Matisse's rapid disaffection for what remains an important phase in his career as a painter, let us return to "Modernism and Tradition." Immediately after reporting Cross's prophecy, he writes: "In the post-impressionist picture, the subject is thrown into relief by a contrasting series of planes which always remain secondary. For me, the subject of a picture and its background have the same value, or, to put it more clearly, there is no principal feature, only the pattern is important. The picture is formed by the combination of surfaces, differently colored, which results in the creation of an 'expression'" (Flam, p. 72). Then follows a comparison—at the time quite banal—between music and color, and then what constitutes one of the recurrent themes in Matisse's statements, namely the possibility, if not the necessity, of color transposition (the example provided is that of translating a red-green-blue-black harmony into a white-blue-red-green harmony), a possibility associated, as is often the case with Matisse, with the metaphor of the chess game.[35]

At first sight, Matisse's formulation seems to be quite ill-chosen: is not divisionism, especially in its "pointillist" version, in itself a demonstration that "there is no principal feature" and that "the subject of a picture and its background have the same value"? As Meyer Schapiro long ago observed, isn't this what constitutes the very novelty of Seurat's system?[36] A remark Matisse makes to Gaston Diehl, embroidering on the idea found at the beginning of the passage just cited (the "contrasting planes . . . always secondary"), sheds some light on the problem Matisse had at the time with divisionism: he was striving, he says, to paint by "marking out zones of influence which elicit reactions, proceeding by successive gradations of tones." But: "I just couldn't get into the swing of it. Once I had laid my dominant, I couldn't help putting on its reaction, equally intense: I would be working on a small landscape built up in dots of color [taches], and I just couldn't achieve a luminous harmony by following the prescribed rules. I was continually forced to start all over again."[37] What are we to make of these "reactions" that Matisse cannot help making as strong as his "dominants"?

According to Bock, we are dealing with the proselyte's zeal here: "The neo-impressionists also worked with 'dominants' that challenged one another with nearly equal intensity, but they did this in much larger areas, thus avoiding the 'breaking up' (morcellement) of which Matisse speaks"[38] (cf. further on for Matisse's complete sentence). In wanting to graft the divided color stroke onto academic modeling Matisse is said to have become entangled in the color and light contrasts analyzed by this procedure (local tone, reaction to this local tone; the effect of light on the local tone, reaction to this effect; shadow effect, reaction, etc.). In seeking to deploy the whole panoply of such contrasts on a very small surface, for example the one defined by the leg of one of the nudes in *Luxe, calme et volupté,* Matisse is said to have gone astray and become discouraged. Hence these remarks to Tériade: "The breaking up of color led to the breaking up of form, of contour. Result: a jumpy surface. There is only a retinal sensation, but it destroys the calm of the surface and of the contour. Objects are differentiated only by the luminosity given them. Everything is treated in the same way. Ultimately, there is only a tactile vitality comparable to the 'vibrato' of the violin or voice" (1929, Flam, p. 58).

Bock's diagnosis is very convincing, in that it is based on a very tight decoding of the picture in terms of the reading grid offered by Signac's theories. Indeed, some of the first fauve works, still largely tributary to the divisionist system, although the regular division of brush strokes is abandoned—notably the famous *Women with the Hat* [*Dame au chapeau*] of 1905, but also *Girl Reading* [*Intérieur à la fillette,* also entitled *La Lecture*], of 1905–06—seem to directly rectify the flaws of *Luxe, calme et volupté* by bestowing much vaster "zones of influence" on the color contrasts. Nevertheless, as was the case with Matisse's first conversion to divisionism, this first "reaction" is not a reaction: the surface of these canvases is just as "jumpy" and the forms are just as optically overwhelmed by the color. But Bock's argument, perhaps overhasty in its denial of any discontinuity between divisionism and fauvism, an understandable swing of the critical pendulum, in my opinion does not go far enough. Matisse's inability to pursue a career as a divisionist painter is not just the result of his overscholarly application of the theory, an application said to be the essential cause of the "breaking up." On the contrary, there is something much more fundamental going on here—something that in my view comes through very clearly in the way in which Matisse relates his defection. Once again recalling Cross's prediction, he tells Diehl: "Indeed, a few months later, working in an exhilarating landscape, I no longer thought of anything but making my colors sing, without worrying about all the rules and regulations. From then on, I composed with my drawing so as to enter directly into the arabesque with the color."[39] An observation that, after a long detour, brings us back to the enigmatic locution "expression by [drawing]," whose scope I shall now go on to examine.

Contrary to what one might think, it was only after the fauvist Salon d'Automne in 1905 that Matisse permanently abandoned the divisionist technique (he doesn't manage to finish *The Port of Abaill, Collioure* [*Port d'Abaill, Collioure*] for the Salon, but nonetheless does not abandon the picture itself, painted later on in accordance with the technique).[40] A few months later, however, exactly one year after having exhibited *Luxe, calme et volupté* there, Matisse shows *Le Bonheur de vivre* (fig. 5) at the Salon des Indépendants. Signac is furious. Shortly before the opening of the Salon, which was to some extent his fiefdom, Signac writes to Charles Angrand: "Matisse, whose attempts I have liked up to now, seems to me to have gone to the dogs. Upon a canvas of two-and-a-half meters, he has surrounded some strange characters with a line as thick as your thumb. Then he has covered the whole thing with flat, well-defined tints, which—however pure—seem disgusting . . . ah! those rosy flesh tones! It evokes the worst Ranson (of the "Nabi" period), the most detestable of late [Anquetin]'s *'cloisonnismes'*—and the multicolored shopfronts of the merchants of paints, varnishes and household goods!"[41]

In order to try to unravel what happened during the year separating the two pastorals, *Luxe, calme et volupté* and *Le Bonheur de vivre,* let us begin with the letter Matisse wrote to Signac during the "fauve" summer he spends with Derain in Collioure. He is discussing *Luxe, calme et volupté:* "Did you find a perfect harmony in my *Bathers* picture between the character of the drawing and the character of the painting? To me they seem totally different from each other and even absolutely contradictory. One, the drawing, depends on linear or sculptural form [*plastique linéaire ou sculpturale*], and the other, painting, depends on colored form [*plastique colorée*]." And he adds: "Remember the cartoon for the picture and the canvas, and you will notice, if you have not already done so, the discordance of their artistic approaches [*leur discordance de plastique*]. To color the cartoon, all that was needed was to fill its compartments with flat tones, à la Puvis, for example."[42] Here we learn something that at first sight seems very surprising, namely that in order to paint *Luxe, calme et volupté,* Matisse resorted to the academic practice of the cartoon. As Bock observes, Matisse is therefore following the same procedure he saw Signac and Cross using in Saint-Tropez: just as Signac in his treatise insists on making the divided brush strokes proportional to the size of the painting, so in his journal he records the necessity of drawing his composition on the same scale as the final picture: "to seek only the idea in the sketch, and to seek the arrangement only on a cardboard with the [size and] format of the definitive painting. For our researches into lines and angles, the squaring up of a little sketch seems impossible to me. An angle which works well in small dimensions can look very bad when enlarged."[43] This accords perfectly with the "Notes of a Painter": "An artist who wants to transpose a composition from one canvas to another larger one must conceive it anew in order to preserve its expression; he must alter its character and not just square it up onto the larger canvas" (Flam, p. 36). But although Signac's example may have been a determining factor in this realization of the importance of scale, in my opinion one of the

5. *Henri Matisse,* Le Bonheur de vivre, *1905–06. Oil on canvas, 174 × 238.1 cm (68½ × 93¾ in.). The Barnes Foundation, Merion, Pennsylvania. Photo The Barnes Foundation.*

most important stakes in Matisse's art (see below), I am far from assuming the existence of any direct filiation here: it is rather in learning to dispense with the cartoon that he will discover his true measure. Indeed, what has been the purpose of the cartoon since the procedure appeared in the Italian Renaissance? It was either used for fresco work, especially when it was impossible for the painter to visually control the immense surface to be covered (it was absolutely indispensable when dealing with a ceiling), or, used as a stencil, it served to transfer the composition in drawing form onto a bigger canvas. In both cases, the cartoon more often than not presupposes squaring (a practice that, as we just saw, Matisse later condemns), and above all a clear separation, not to say hierarchization, between conception and realization on the one hand, and between drawing and color on the other (color comes after the fact, "à la Puvis," for example; it is coloring-in). Or again: resorting to a cartoon is surely a sign of a (practical) concern with scale, but *from inside* a projective system whose principal component is the compositional or figurative *idea* that is prior to any material constraints. As we shall see, Matisse will oppose this classical view of conception with all his might, but not before his break with divisionism; there again both his divisionist apprenticeship and his subsequent rejection of the movement prove to be determinative. Indeed, the use of the cartoon seems to characterize Matisse's divisionist period, almost exclusively so. *Woman with a Parasol, Collioure* [*Jeune femme à l'ombrelle, Collioure*] (fig. 6) for example, painted during the "fauve" summer in accordance with divisionist procedure even as the artist is writing to Signac to express his doubts, bears the traces of squaring off,[44] and the cartoon of *The Port of Abaill, Collioure* has been preserved, a canvas he finished in Paris when exhibiting his fauve works at the Salon d'Automne. Everything thus seems to suggest that, at the very time he is again learning to use nothing but pure colors, at the very time he is discovering "the secret of expression by color," Matisse had found practically nothing in divisionism to enable him to break away from the old academic prejudice that, since Aristotle, had seen color merely as a supplement to drawing. There seems little doubt that *Le Bonheur de vivre* was done with the aid of a cartoon,[45] but here we are dealing with the moment when Matisse's oeuvre is tilting into a universe that belongs to him and him alone. The cartoon subsequently disappears from his technical arsenal, with the notable exception of the one he did for *Le Luxe I* and *II* (in other words, shortly before writing the "Notes"), which is quite visibly squared off (there is room for wondering whether this cartoon wasn't drawn *after* the painting of *Le Luxe I,* so as to reproduce the composition as exactly as possible in *Le Luxe II,* in such a way that the "theoretical experiment" Matisse carries out here on the difference in effect between a work done entirely in "passages" à la Cézanne

6. *Henri Matisse,* Woman with a Parasol [Jeune femme
à l'ombrelle], *1905. Oil on canvas, 46 × 38 cm (18⅛*
× 15 in.). Musée Matisse, Cimiez. Photo of the museum.

and another painted, by contrast, entirely flat, could only have had even clearer
implications).[46] Whatever the case, this resurgence of the traditional practice of the
cartoon in the course of Matisse's second divisionist phase explains one of his statements that at first sight contradicts the thesis I am patiently elaborating concerning
"expression by [drawing]," which is said to have stemmed from the reaction against
"confettism," as it was then called. Indeed, when Matisse, again discussing his brief
divisionist phase, declares to Diehl, "Above all, I was no longer able to restrain my
drawing and I was tempted to put in too much of it [*d'en mettre trop*],"[47] all he is
doing is stating the widening gap between his drawing and his use of color. This has
nothing to do with what I should like to distinguish here, which on the contrary has
to do with the fundamental inseparability Matisse discovers between drawing and
color shortly after his fauve summer.

We are dealing with two concepts of drawing: drawing in the restricted sense, as a practice—and Matisse is one of this century's great masters in drawing, regardless of the medium he used (pen, charcoal, lithographic pencil, etc.); and drawing in the larger sense, as a generative category, which in my opinion led to the best of his painted oeuvre from 1906 to 1917, and from 1931 to his death—two periods that I shall henceforth arbitrarily group together under the name of "the Matisse system." Drawing in this larger sense could be called *arche-drawing* by analogy with the "concept" of "arche-writing" developed by Jacques Derrida (and we shall see later on that it is not by chance that I choose to propose this admittedly not terribly rigorous analogy: in order to give a brief glimpse of what I have in mind, I would say that, on the point we are concerned with, Matisse provides a lesson in "deconstruction," if not to the author of *Of Grammatology,* at least to those who draw their inspiration directly from his work in order to deal with the question of the relations between color and drawing.)[48] Just as "arche-writing" is "prior" to the hierarchization of speech and writing, and, being productive of difference itself, forms their common "root" (which goes for all the hierarchical oppositions out of which western metaphysics is woven, notably the opposition between sign and meaning), so "arche-drawing" would be "prior" to the drawing/color opposition, that is, without in any way denying the specificity of drawing and color in the history of painting, it would constitute the "originary" source from which both emerge. In my opinion, it is this "arche-drawing" (which governs Matisse's drawing practice *as well as* his most important discovery in the domain of color) that is the fundamental category at issue in "Modernism and Tradition," to the considerable bafflement, as we have seen, of the English translator. The "Matisse system" was designed to "directly" reveal this "arche-drawing" at work—and it is therefore clear that my analogy can only be superficial, since Derridean "arche-writing" is not open to being made present and can in no way surrender itself to the present.

Without further ado, I shall outline what I consider to be Matisse's fundamental discovery concerning color. It can be very simply stated: "1cm^2 of any blue is not as blue as a square meter of the same blue,"[49] or again "the quantity of color was its quality" (to Tériade, 1929, Flam, p. 59), and finally, when discussing the two versions of *The Dance* [*La Danse*] (1933): "the colors, which are the same, are nonetheless changed; as the quantities differ, their quality also changes: the colors applied freely show that it is their quantitative relation [*leur rapport de quantité*] that produces their quality" (letter to Alexandre Romm, 1934, Flam, p. 68). This theme of quantity as quality returns time and again in Matisse's writings and remarks,[50] but it is when he discusses the luminous pen and ink drawings that punctuate his oeuvre and that become increasingly important in his work from 1928–29 on that he is at his most eloquent: "In spite of the absence of shadows or half-tones expressed by hatching, I do not renounce the play of values or modulations. I modulate with variations in the weight of line, and above all with the areas it delimits on the white paper. I modify the different parts of the white paper without touching them, but by neighborings" ("Notes of a Painter on His Drawing," 1939, Flam, p. 82.[51] Or again, pointing out to Aragon that none of his drawings "has lost the touching whiteness of the paper," Matisse adds: "even if a stroke divides them into compartments of varying quality."[52] And finally, in "The Roles and Modalities of Color" (remarks reported by Diehl in 1945), Matisse declares: "What counts most with colors are relationships. Thanks to them and them alone a drawing can be intensely colored without there being any need for actual color" (Flam, p. 99). A little further on, immediately before reminding us that "it is not possible to separate drawings and color," he makes his meaning quite explicit: "With a drawing, even if it is done with only one line, an infinite number of nuances can be given to each part that the line encloses. Proportion plays a fundamental role" (ibid.). What Matisse discovers in his drawing practice is not just that "in art, what is most important is the relationship between things" (to Tériade, 1930, Flam, p.60), but that color relations are above all quantity relations. Invention always takes place after the elimination of certain parameters, albeit those on which such invention will have the most effect: color "proper" *had* to be absent for Matisse to discover not only that black and white are colors, but that what makes them act as colors (modulation through quantity) plays an essential role in the behavior of all color. Transferred to the domain of painting, this discovery translates in the following way: it is the area (and thus form) of a surface, or rather, what differentiates the latter from the area (and form) of the other colored surfaces of a painting, that, above all else, governs the quality of the hue and the tone (in other words, the saturation of a color and its luminous intensity, its value).[53]

At least four of the founding principles of Matisse's art proceed from the fact that color relations, which determine expression, are above all relations between surface quantities. These are consequences of the imposition of "arche-drawing": distributing surface quantities, that is, dividing up a surface, "compartmentalizing" it, as Matisse says, putting what Derrida calls *spacing* to work in it, all this is a matter of drawing in the large as well as the restricted sense (just as writing is more directly affected by the grammata of "arche-writing" than is the *phoné,* so the effect of "arche-drawing" is perhaps better grasped at the outset in the domain of drawing itself, but only at the outset, as we shall see).

1. The first of these consequences concerns the *all-over* nature of Matisse's best works. Since the expression of the picture or of the drawing results from the differences in quantity between the colored surfaces, it is impossible to work without immediately considering the totality of the surface to be covered (the problem is identical in the case of a painting and a drawing—only somewhat more complex in the case of the painting—since two surfaces of the same color but different sizes do not have the same quality: in this respect, two white surfaces behave no differently than two surfaces of an altogether different color). I shall come back to this question of the *all-over.*

2. The second effect of the quantity-quality equation, the corollary of the first, concerns the form, the very format of the picture, and thus the fundamental role of its limits as an element of the drawing: "The four sides of the frame are amongst the most important parts of a painting," Matisse later says (to Diehl, 1943, *EPA,* p. 196); or again: "Think of the hard lines of the chassis or the frame, they have an influence on your motif's lines";[54] or finally: "The arabesque is effective only when contained by the four sides of the picture. With this support, it has strength" (to Verdet, 1952, Flam, p. 143). The limit itself has such a determining influence that it is internalized. In the famous passage of *Jazz* entitled "My curves are not mad," we find the following remark: "The vertical is in my mind. It helps me give my lines a precise direction and in my quick drawings I never indicate a curve—for example, that of a branch in a landscape—without an awareness of its relationship to the vertical" (Flam, p. 112; trans. modified). The slightest displacement in relation to this parameter transforms all the relationships: Matisse is furious when, in the books and articles published about him, the reproductions are out of balance (to Rouveyre, 1947, "What a pity that being out of balance in a reproduction completely destroys a drawing," *EPA,* p. 146, note 8). "The balance [*l'aplomb*] and the proportion in relation to the page [are] two essential elements" (to Romm, 1934, Flam, p. 68). Both are a function of the quantity-quality equation (the quantity of white surrounding the reproduction of an image will be irregular if the latter is out of alignment and this inopportune intrusion from the outside will modify the perception of the image's internal relationships).[55]

3. The third point, concerning scale, is of paramount importance (a point already evoked above in relation to squaring). All too often, scale is confused with size, which is always absolute (any given painting measures so many square centimeters, a figure that can be calculated with precision); scale, on the other hand, is relative and is only concerned with proportions, whether it is a question of internal relationships (quantity relations between a painting's different colored surfaces or a drawing's various areas of white) or of external relationships (between a canvas

and the wall on which it is hung, between the size of a sculpture and that of the person looking at it, etc.). Size determines the scale on which the artist has to work (it is impossible to approach a small etching in the same way that one approaches, as Matisse did for the Merion *Dance,* "seventy-two square meters of white canvas" (*EPA,* p. 138).[56] But paradoxically, it is in being attentive to the size of the support, thus in working on the scale imposed by the latter, that one "transcend[s] . . . size for the sake of scale," as Barnett Newman says.[57] When Matisse declares to Verdet, in 1952, that "the size of a canvas is of little importance," he is not suddenly overturning everything he otherwise said and wrote concerning quantity. He means that absolute quantity (size) is entirely modifiable by relative quantity (scale). In fact, he goes on to say that "what I always want is to give the feeling of space, as much in the smallest canvas as in the Chapel at Vence" (Flam, p. 145). Matisse is perfectly clear on this point: "the work can be large in spite of its restricted format," and it is perfectly logical that the latter remark should immediately follow his suggestion that "we are now returning to surface painting" (to Florent Fels, *EPA,* p. 154, note 14; the year is 1929, a time when Matisse is going through a pictorial crisis, which he tries to escape with a trip to Tahiti, and which is resolved by working on the illustrations for the *Mallarmé* and on the Merion *Dance,* in other words, by a return to "surface painting," to the "Matisse system" equating quantity and quality).

Being relative, scale is determined by internal and external relations of quantity. One very important problem arises from the fact that, apart from when his work is destined for a specific architectural location (or when he is illustrating a book—and Matisse's predilection for this genre is well known), the painter has practically no way of controlling or anticipating these external relations (which will vary with the spaces in which the painting is hung). We know that Matisse, like certain abstract expressionist painters during the 1940s, at one time envisaged the eventual disappearance of easel painting in favor of mural painting.[58] The energy and enthusiasm he displays in elaborating the Merion *Dance* (from which stem, in large part, his reencounters with the "Matisse system"), and his numerous statements concerning this gigantic work (no doubt amongst some of the most enlightening he left us with) show that he did not take this possibility lightly—and the same could be said of the Vence chapel, which he considered (this is the only time that he ever voices the idea of an ending) "the end-point of [his] researches" (to Lejard, 1951, *EPA,* p. 242).[59] Matisse, however (was it due to a lack of demand for murals?),[60] only resolved to abandon easel painting at a very advanced age when, bedridden, he was obliged to draw using a cane two and a half meters long, or, using pieces of colored paper that his assistant would glue in place for him, he was able to "cut directly into color"

(*Jazz,* 1947, Flam, p. 112). In fact, Matisse seems actually to have taken pleasure in meeting the challenge presented by the unavoidable autonomy of easel painting (his pictorial ethic is based on emulation and struggle: "I have always believed that a large part of the beauty of a picture arises from the struggle which an artist wages with his limited medium," he writes in "Modernism and Tradition" [Flam, p.73], and numerous statements echo this theme). Having no control over external relations in his easel painting, he compensated for this loss by clarifying the internal (quantity) relations, which had by force of circumstance become the sole factors determining scale, having them play a paroxystic role absolutely unprecedented in the history of painting.[61]

4. The discovery of "expression by [drawing]" had a fourth repercussion: not only are saturation and value entirely relative (since they depend on quantity relations), but they are henceforth inseparable, meaning that, as we have seen, Matisse can "modulate" (to use the Cézanne expression Matisse himself employs) without in any way being restricted to the traditional modeling that led to the failure of his divisionist efforts. In what I am calling the "Matisse system," "it is the proportion of things which is the chief expression" (to Verdet, 1952, Flam, p. 143).

Dominique Fourcade offers us a remarkable summary of Matisse's way of proceeding in his best drawings (see fig. 7): "Take a penstroke on a sheet of paper: if there is another stroke parallel to it five centimeters away, the blank space formed by these two strokes will not have the same color as another space enclosed by two penstrokes twenty centimeters apart. Or again, a black line drawn with a pen in more or less close proximity to another black line will produce a space whose color will vary according to its dimension. With a third line, the relationship between the resulting two spaces differing in shape and dimension will produce a color relation in which "what is most important" is to be found. In this way, on the blank parts of the paper he will have *drawn* all the space, even the space that isn't actually space, even the empty spaces between the leaves on different branches of a tree, for example, even the space where the pen does not venture, even the space where the line encloses nothing."[62] The reader will notice the absence of the word "value" in this description: if Fourcade doesn't mention it when talking exclusively about works in black and white, it is because the very concept of value has changed: we have henceforth entered the pictorial field of *color-value*. From 1906 up until what is today called his "first Nice period," which between 1917 and 1930 constitutes a reaction in relation to the "Matisse system" and in a way a returns to the problematic of the years 1900–04, Matisse turns his back on traditional modeling. He even totally inverts its fundamental principles, making black, for instance, "a color of light and not a color

7. Henri Matisse, The Rumanian Blouse [La Blouse roumaine]*, 1937. Pen and black ink on white paper, 63 × 50 cm (24¹³/₁₆ × 9¹¹/₁₆ in.). The Baltimore Museum of Art. The Cone Collection. Photo of the museum.*

of darkness,"[63] an inversion that returns in force in his late work, culminating in the glittering *Egyptian Curtain* [*Intérieur au rideau égyptien*] of 1948. Let us note in passing a further inversion produced in the usual value system by the quantity-quality equation, the inversion of the old law of contrasts governing the practice of highlighting, a law that states that the less extensive a white line or surface is in relation to the darker zones from which it stands out, the more luminous it will appear.[64]

Finally, since from now on saturation and value overlap (the luminous whiteness of certain "compartments" in Matisse's drawings is the magistral index of this essential solidarity: Matisse here invents what is a radical incongruity for the classical system—various degrees of saturation in the white), and since "we have abandoned relief, perspective,"[65] the whole spatial construction of the picture will be taken on by the organization of color.

Such were the broad repercussions of Matisse's discovery of the quantity-quality equation. Its four aspects are as intricate as Le Corbusier's "five points of modern architecture." Together, they highlight the already mentioned fact that, for Matisse, pictorial (or graphic) practice is not projective: in his work, there is no image—in the classical sense of *disegno*—that is not coextensive with the field. Compositional a prioris are impossible, there is no preformulated "idea" informing an inert matter. There is one apparent contradiction, however, that has to be dealt with: in his "Notes," as well as in several of his statements, Matisse says that "all is in the conception" (Flam, p. 37), seemingly indicating that he is far from having abandoned the idealist aesthetic of the Renaissance, as impressively presented by Panofsky in *Idea*.[66] What does Matisse mean? Immediately after stating this axiom, he goes on to say that "I must therefore have a clear vision of the whole from the beginning" (Flam, p. 37), which is followed by a critique of Rodin's practice of composing in fragments, to which Matisse opposes that of Cézanne. Matisse's "conception" is the other name for working "all-over." I am not suggesting that he stands before his blank canvas without having the slightest idea of what he is going to do with it (although he often talks of being frightened of a virgin canvas, or of the mental blank he experiences when beginning what he calls a "variation" type drawing), but that his "idea" is concomitant with the quantity of the surface he has to cover: this is why, writing to Camoin to tell him he hasn't begun his "big Tangiers picture" (*The Moroccans*), he says, "the dimensions of the canvas I've nailed up don't match my conception of the subject" (1913, *EPA*, p. 117, note 72). "I have my conception in my head," says Matisse (to Dégand, 1945, Flam, p. 103), but this means he also has the surface in his head, as he says of *The Dance*. And, since modulation is a function of scale, everything is in play at the same time: it is impossible, for instance, to go back and add veins to the leaves on a tree drawn *alla prima* ("See, if I add veins afterward, I destroy the light in the leaves, so I have to mark them out straightaway—that is, before drawing them, I have to see them as forming an integral part of my drawing. And so, there you have it—the whole of drawing": to Courthion, 1942, *EPA,* p. 168, note 18). The "conception" Matisse refers to does not exist prior to the surface destined to receive the inscription: the veins have to be involved from the very beginning as parameters of his compartmentalization of the paper, and compartmentalization cannot exist ideally, it is inseparable from its actualization: all of Matisse's art hangs on the impossibility of a gap between conception and realization.

Let us now try to date the invention of the quantity-quality equation, find the rupture in his oeuvre, not so much in the name of chronological fastidiousness, but because here Matisse clarified his relationship to the four great artists who at the time loomed over young painters as unsurpassable models, namely Cézanne, Gauguin, Van Gogh, and Seurat (filtered through Signac), and, in doing so, changed century so to speak, and began to "be able to sing freely," to use one of his favorite expressions.[67] The breakthrough, the veritable *eureka,* took place in my opinion with the three woodcuts (cf. figs. 8, 9) that Matisse exhibited at the Galerie Druet in March and April of 1906, was consolidated in a series of extraordinarily cursive lithographs presented at the same exhibition, and was first elaborated in painted form in *Le Bonheur de vivre,* which was simultaneously reigning at the Indépendants. Alfred Barr suggests, and the bulk of Matisse criticism since is in agreement with him, that the woodcuts come immediately after the great 1906 painting: by contrast—and this is one of the enigmatic senses of "expression by [drawing]"—I take these prints (which were initially sketched in ink using a brush, in accordance with the quasi-Chinese technique that Matisse returned to very late in life)[68] to be the inauguration of his complete break with divisionism (with which his fauve canvases were still impregnated), the work that crystallized for Matisse the developments of an entire summer and produced, indeed invented, an entirely new system.

There are several reasons for this hypothesis. First of all, there is the intensively worked character of these woodcuts, in spite of their apparent wildness (they constitute one of the obligatory openings for any study devoted to Matisse's "primitivism"). The largest of them, *Seated Nude* [*Nu de profil sur une chaise longue (grand bois)*] (fig. 9), is almost like a stylistic exercise detailing the different possibilities of modulation through quantity: around the brilliant whiteness of the nude, Matisse

8. Henri Matisse, Seated Woman [Femme
assise, petit bois clair], *1906. Woodcut,
34.2 × 26.6 cm (13⁷/₁₆ × 10⁷/₁₆ in.). The
Baltimore Museum of Art. The Cone Collection. Photo of the museum.*

seems to have wanted to explore the entire spectrum of luminous intensities, looking for what I shall call the "degree-zero" of expression by drawing. He was looking
for the simplest way of expressing both the largest and smallest of differences. To do
so, he virtually eliminates one of the parameters of graphic art—varying the thickness of the strokes—and concentrates on line direction (or line form, since some of
the lines are reduced to large dots) and above all on the density and extension of
the various "patterns" produced by the lines, all of them very different. Apart from
the internal "contours" that just faintly impinge on the whiteness of the torso, there
is not a single zone that does not demonstrate the infinite variety of effects Matisse
achieves with the most rudimentary means: the white of the floor is "whiter" than
that of the wooden leg of the chaise longue (since the spaces between the two strokes
are larger at this point, as is the overall zone defined by this set of strokes and spaces),
but it even varies from the right-hand corner of the print to the bottom left-hand

9. Henri Matisse, Seated Nude [Nu de profil sur une chaise longue (grand bois)]*, 1906. Woodcut, 47.5 × 38 cm (18¹¹/₁₆ × 14¹⁵/₁₆ in.). The Baltimore Museum of Art. The Cone Collection. Photo of the museum.*

edge. Why? Because in this latter section, the network of lines figuring the slats is tighter; because the direction of the lines is less dynamic (they have gone from being oblique to being vertical); and finally because the space between the bottom edge of the print and the leg of the chaise longue is less extensive in area; reducing the amount of white reduces the amount of light. To be more precise, in each case the white both *is* and *is not* the same: physically, as light of a specific wavelength, as what Josef Albers calls a "factual fact," it is the same; but in terms of the way it acts, its effect, which is not fixed but subordinate both to the context in which it appears and to a subject's perception—thus, as an "actual fact"—it is not the same.[69] The demonstration could be repeated for all the peripheral zones of the print, whether for the swirling striations in the top left-hand corner (a progressive loosening of a network of lines, harmonizing or contrasting plastically with the contours of the nude, a centrifugal movement from light to dark), for the upper portion of the figure's hair, for the narrow space to the right of her neck, or else for the herringbone motif at bottom left, which seems to metonymically figure the (otherwise ignored) marquetry on the floor: each one of these surfaces is streaked with parallel lines, but their direction and, once again, the density of their respective networks (in other words, the quantity of white separating the individual lines) are different in each case. In order to test even further his ability to modulate, Matisse introduces a second kind of lattice, this one properly decorative—in the positive sense that Matisse gives to this word— a lattice that perhaps constitutes an ironic adieu to divisionism. Made up of black dots (and once again producing a different luminous effect depending on their shape and distribution: some are circular and thinly scattered, others elongated like abortive lines and more tightly grouped), the surface defining the cloth stretching between the legs of the chaise longue not only adds an extra possibility to the arsenal that Matisse seems to want to display here in exhaustive fashion, it also provides us with a direct link between the woodcuts of 1906 and the painter's final graphic works, the pen and brush drawings dating from 1948 to 1951. Indeed, we find this same speckling effect in the 1948 drawing entitled *Still Life with Pineapple* [*Nature morte à l'ananas*] (fig. 10) about which the very least one can say is that the painting that repeats the same composition (but dispensing with the speckling) comes nowhere near attaining the same luminous fulgurance.[70] This late echo of the experimental work of 1906, at the moment when the "Matisse system" perhaps reached its fullness in painting, just prior to the final adventure of the cutouts, is a further mark of the inaugural character these woodcuts had for him, especially the largest of them. *Seated Nude* is like a catalogue of effects, an exploratory board on which Matisse wanted to try for the greatest number of differences in modulation through quantity:

10. Henri Matisse, Still Life with Pineapple [Nature morte à l'ananas]*, 1948. Brush and ink on white paper, 104.1 × 74 cm (39¹/₆ × 29¹/₈ in.). Private collection. Photo Pierre Matisse Gallery.*

in the almost hyperbolic demonstration he indulges in here, there is something of the intoxicated glee of the scientist whose hypothesis is in the process of being experimentally confirmed. By contrast, after the exuberance of the fauve canvases, *Le Bonheur de vivre* will, without quite managing it, tend to reduce this multiplication and extreme diversification of color-value zones: a "synthetic" reordering after the scattered variegation engendered by the graphic analysis carried out in the *Seated Nude*.

The second motif in the chronology I am proposing is the obvious link between these woodcuts and the work of Van Gogh and Gauguin, both frequently mentioned in the discussions between Matisse and Derain during the summer they spent in Collioure.[71] Certainly, Matisse knew Van Gogh's work well (he had owned several of his drawings since 1897), but in his struggle to escape the "tyranny of divisionism," the need for a much closer examination of the Dutch painter's oeuvre must have made itself quite vehemently felt. In the first place, Derain was at the time very close to Vlaminck, who swore by Van Gogh (Matisse elsewhere mentions having met Vlaminck, in the company of Derain, at the Van Gogh exhibition at Bernheim-Jeune);[72] secondly, he had himself just helped to hang the Van Gogh retrospective presented at the Salon des Indépendants in 1905, to which he lent one of the works he owned.[73] Finally, as Ellen Oppler observes, certain extracts from Van Gogh's correspondence, republished on the occasion of his retrospective, sound like a call to free oneself from all constraints having to do with the textural organization of a picture:

> I don't follow any brushstroke system, I daub the paint onto the canvas in uneven strokes, which I leave as they are; patches of thickly laid on color, places here and there where the canvas is left bare, portions that are left completely unfinished, parts I've gone back over, rough qualities, the final result is (I'm inclined to believe) disturbing and irritating enough not to please people with preconceived ideas on technique.[74]

Although Matisse's statements on Van Gogh are, to say the least, ambiguous (and his painting actually seems to owe him little, at least directly),[75] most commentators have noted the remarkable similarity between the Dutchman's drawings and Matisse's graphic work of 1905: a work like *Madame Matisse in the Olive Grove* [*Madame Matisse dans les oliviers*], with its lattice of multidirectional cross hatching, almost seems like a pastiche of Van Gogh (there again, it is notable that the resulting painting, neoimpressionist in treatment, seems dull and labored by comparison).[76]

Matisse's indebtedness to Van Gogh should not be exaggerated, however: he borrows his sense of decorative "pattern," his way of creating very diverse surfaces with differently oriented, rhythmically varied linear networks—a kind of disproportionate magnification of old techniques borrowed from engraving, an accelerated zoom effect of which the 1906 woodcuts would be the outcome—but Matisse seems to use the procedure against the grain. Whereas in Van Gogh it is the very organization of the diverse lattices that articulates the planes in establishing them as so many zones, consequently producing differences in quantity, in Matisse the reverse happens, notably in *Seated Nude*. Later on, around 1908, Matisse becomes the great master of the "decorative"; but the various "patterns" that he deploys in this work are nowhere near having the function they will have in *Harmony in Red* or *Interior with Eggplants* [*Intérieur aux aubergines*], for example. They in no way accentuate the flatness of the image and do not create any sense of lateral extensibility: they are there only in order to "verify" or reinforce the modulation produced by the interrelationships of proportion between surfaces, not to engender it. Van Gogh's drawing more or less collapses once it is stripped of its "snarls"—by contrast, Matisse's drawing lights up: the Dutch painter overdoes it in order to make his expression assertive, Matisse "prunes," or rather uses a minimum of inscription in order to let the "touching whiteness of the paper" resonate more and more. It is only after learning to modulate by relying solely on the quantitative play of the surfaces, without resorting to the expedient of the lattice, that Matisse will be able to reincorporate "decorative feeling" into his art and make it play a determining role.

His relationship to Gauguin is much more complex, and perhaps more essential. Ellen Oppler quite rightly criticizes the "myth of the Sudden Revelation," which traditionally saw the big Gauguin retrospective at the Salon d'Automne in 1906 as the radical point of departure in the latter's emergence as an essential figure in French painting.[77] Certainly, Matisse had long appreciated Gauguin's work: just after acquiring Cézanne's *The Bathers* he had bought a Van Gogh drawing from Vollard, as well as a Gauguin canvas, *Head of a Boy* [*Jeune homme à la fleur*] from 1891, which unmistakably evokes his own works, without it being possible to say exactly why— is it the touching strangeness of the flower on the young man's ear, slightly reminiscent of what Matisse found striking about Morocco, and which he sought to render in *The Arab Café* [*Le Café arabe*] (1913), "These huge fellows who stand for hours contemplating a flower and a goldfish"?[78] But all historians mention as being particularly important Matisse and Derain's summer 1905 visit, organized by Maillol, to Georges-Daniel de Mondfreid, whose country house was a "veritable shrine" to the glory of the wild painter (Oppler). Depository of a great number of Gauguin canvases, most of them predating the contract the artist had signed with Vollard late in 1899, of numerous letters, unpublished writings, and above all, the woodcuts, which did not interest the dealer, de Mondfreid was wholly devoted to the cult of his recently deceased friend (Gauguin had died two years earlier). Everything suggests that his visitors didn't exactly need to plead with him to respond to their voracious questioning concerning various aspects of the dead painter's theory. Although in the simplicity of their black and white contrast and the absence of any trace of the medium involved they are more reminiscent of Valloton's work (in the wake of an error by Madame Matisse, and with Barr's sanction, they were long thought to be linocuts), the woodcuts Matisse did some months later were no doubt stimulated by the abundance of prints he had seen at de Mondfreid's. But the question of Matisse's relationship to Gauguin cannot be reduced to a simple matter of technique and his momentary fascination with a graphic medium little in keeping with his own cursive gestures and with his desire—however naive this word he constantly uses might be—for "spontaneity."

In *Matisse, ce vivant,* citing the statements reported by Tériade in *Minotaure* in 1936 (Flam, p. 74), Raymond Escholier inserts some of Matisse's unpublished annotations, which the artist had no doubt made directly on Escholier's manuscript (Escholier tell us that "apart from the final pages," which concern his death, the painter reviewed the whole work). The annotated passage is perfectly characteristic of Matisse's theory. Since it contains a certain number of elements that will be relevant later on, I shall cite it at some length, underlining the additions in Escholier's version:

> At each stage, I reach a balance, a conclusion. At the next sitting [*séance*], if I find a weakness in the whole, I find my way back into the picture by means of this weakness—I re-enter through the breach—and reconceive the whole. Thus everything becomes fluid again and as each element is only one of the component forces (as in orchestration), the whole can be changed in appearance but the feeling remains the same. A black could very well replace a blue, since basically the expression derives from the relationships. One is not bound to a blue, to a green or a red *whose timbres can be interverted or replaced if the feeling so dictates.* You can change the relationships by modifying the quantity of the components without changing their nature. That is, the painting will still be composed of blue, yellow and green, in altered quantities. *A kilogram of green is greener than half a kilo. Gauguin attributes this saying to Cézanne in a*

visitor's book at the Marie Gloanec boarding house in Pont-Aven. Or you can retain the relationships which form the expression of a picture, replacing a blue with a black, as in an orchestra a trumpet may be replaced by an oboe. (Flam, p. 74, trans. slightly modified)[79]

Here we recognize the great theme of color transposition, already discussed, most often associated in Matisse with the question of quantity relations. The second annotation merely confirms this solidarity and immediately calls to mind the sentence mentioned above on "one square centimeter of any blue" that is "not as blue as a square meter of the same blue." But what is surprising here is both the substitution of weight for the notion of surface area, and Gauguin's attribution of such a maxim to Cézanne. What is even more surprising is that Matisse should have had the maxim stored in his memory since his first trip to Brittany in 1895, and that he should mention it only at the end of his life: perhaps he was troubled by a certain ambiguity in the statement, an ambiguity he would now have considered entirely eliminated— and rightly so—by the context in which he makes the annotations: when he says quantity relations, it is understood that he means the relative proportions of the surfaces, not the heaping up of matter, nor the profusion of colors.[80] Now, not only is the sentence deflected here from its initial meaning, as we shall see, but it does not figure anywhere in Cézanne's statements, although Gauguin did peddle it on numerous occasions as genuine. It first appears in a short story by Duranty, "Le Peintre Marsabiel," published in 1867 and later incorporated, with slight alterations, into another story. From the outset, the caricature is clearly identifiable as the Cézanne of the "couillarde" period (an "ultra-Marseilles" accent, slight paranoia, bald with a beard, the "philosophical" themes of his paintings, "the painting is done more with temperament (pronounced *dammbéramminnte*) than with brushes," etc.) Marsabiel briefly contemplates a sketch by one of his friends and admirers, Cabladours, and exclaims: "You must be going crazy, there's no paint on that at all." Later versions of the text are more comical: "That's not painting, that's just a *wash*. You want to see the way *we* do it? [Ce n'est pas de la peinture, ça, c'est de la *frotasse*. Voulez-vous voir comme nous faisons, nous ottres!]." "Frotasse," that is, heavily diluted paint, an almost insubstantial wash letting the whiteness of the canvas show through; in other words, a certain liquidity in the pigment that Matisse takes a particular liking to around 1911–12. Duranty's story continues:

He dipped the spoon into one of the paint pots and pulled out a real trowelful of green, which he then applied to a canvas where a few lines indicated a landscape; he twisted the spoon, and if you looked very closely, you could make out a meadow in what he'd just daubed on. In fact, it was then I noticed that the color on his canvases was about a centimeter thick, forming hills and valleys, like a relief map. Marsabiel felt that a kilogram of green was greener than a gram of the same color, by the inverse of the reasoning that makes certain people think that a pound of feathers is lighter than a pound of lead.[81]

Whether Gauguin simply felt that the accusation wasn't overly malicious, or, on the contrary, he heard Cézanne actually voice the phrase, he does in fact attribute it to him in the Gloanec boarding house visitors' book,[82] but more importantly, he attributes it to him in "Diverses choses," a text as yet unpublished in its entirety that forms a sequel to the manuscript of *Noa Noa* held at the Louvre. Far from interpreting it as Duranty does, Gauguin turns the theorem into a plea for the maximum saturation of colors. After ridiculing those who see the phrase as further proof of Cézanne's madness ("the craziest one isn't the one they have in mind"), Gauguin launches into a long argument against photographic exactitude and local tone.[83] A few pages later, as if to outdo Cézanne when he supposedly said "I was pleased with myself when I discovered that the sun, for example, could not be reproduced, but had to be represented by something else, by color" (a statement reported later by Maurice Denis),[84] Gauguin states that the only possible equivalent of light is "pure color!" and that "everything has to be sacrificed for it." It is at this point that the statement attributed to Cézanne reappears:

> A tree trunk of local color blue-gray becomes pure blue, and the same goes for all the hues. The intensity of the color will indicate the nature of each color: for example, the blue of the sea will be of a more intense blue than the grey tree trunk, which has also become pure blue, but is less intense. Then, since a kilo of green is greener than half a kilo, in order to achieve the equivalent (your canvas being smaller than life-size), you have to use a green greener than nature. There you have the truth behind the lie. That way, deriving its light from a subterfuge, a lie, your picture will be true to life since it will give you the impression of something real (light, strength, and size), as varied in its harmonies as you could wish for.[85]

Gauguin never interprets the notion of weight in terms of *impasto* effects. But, even though he mentions the size of the painting, he doesn't interpret it in terms of surface quantity either: for him, it is simply a matter of color intensity, of saturation, and even though he paints in flat planes and in compartments as Matisse will later

on, in *Le Bonheur de vivre* for example (see the "detestable" return to "cloisonnisme" that Signac detects in it), Gauguin at no stage considers the extension of a
colored surface to be what essentially determines its degree of saturation.[86] If he
mentions "the laws of relative size" and writes that "in decorative art it is necessary
to properly establish the size of the surfaces to be painted," it is only in connection
with the importance of what I am calling external quantity relations, and only in so-
called applied art (the size of the painted figures in a fresco or of sculptures in relation to the dimensions of the architecture framing it).[87] In short, as far as the quantity-
quality equation is concerned, Matisse has nothing to learn from Gauguin, which is
no doubt what he means when he says "the basis of Gauguin's work and mine is not
the same" (to Howe, 1949, Flam, p. 123) and "what prevents Gauguin from being situated among the fauves is that he does not construct space by color."[88]

   Does this mean that Matisse owes nothing to the older painter? We know about
the animosity that separated Gauguin from Seurat and Signac, animosity that followed a period of camaraderie:[89] wouldn't it have been logical for Matisse, when he
was trying to escape the hold that the divisionist system had on his work, to have
glanced in his direction? He himself provides us with a few quite succinct observations on the matter:

> I never saw Gauguin. I instinctively avoided his already set theory, since
> I was a student of the galleries in the Louvre, which made me aware of
> the complexity of the problem that I had to solve in relation to myself,
> and I was afraid of doctrines which tend to operate like passwords. At the
> time, I wasn't all that far from agreeing with Rodin who used to say "Gau-
> guin is a curiosity!" I subsequently changed my mind once my studies had
> enabled me to see where Gauguin's theory was coming from. I was even
> able to add to Gauguin's Seurat's theory of contrasts, simultaneous reac-
> tions of colors and the relation of their luminosity.[90]

or again: "I wanted an art of expression and equivalence, and basically Gauguin
seemed more likely than the neoimpressionists to give me a push in the direction
I wanted to go" (*EPA,* p. 95, name of interlocutor omitted).

   The first fragment is a response to a question from Escholier concerning
Matisse's second stay in Brittany, in 1896: "at the time" refers to the years he spent
in apprenticeship with Moreau. In both of these passages, Gauguin is immediately
associated with divisionism, but whereas in the first of them Matisse implies that he
came to understand Gauguin's theory before he did Seurat's, in the second Gauguin
appears as a model that Matisse, after the fact, when reexamining his divisionist

phase, regrets not having turned to earlier. I interpret this hiatus, this split temporality as a symptom of the perhaps unconscious importance of Gauguin in Matisse's struggle, in 1906, to break away from the "tyranny of divisionism."[91]

As numerous historians have remarked, Seurat's and Gauguin's doctrines were not all that remote from each other when it came to the actual goal of painting: both men were symbolists. But in spite of the "abstraction" of the divisionist brushstroke, neoimpressionism, as its name suggests, still avows its indebtedness to impressionism conceived as a "realism" of light—the optical mix being theoretically charged, at the right distance from the picture, with recomposing a synthetic image that would render imperceptible everything that is jarring in the atomization of color. Even though Signac no longer shows any sign of believing in this possibility, in *De Delacroix au néo-impressionnisme* he constantly proposes two contradictory arguments: on the one hand, the divided brushstroke is seen as being akin to a musical note, an arbitrary convention, an artifice in the same way that "Ribot's black, Whistler's grey, Carrière's brown, Delacroix's hatchings, Monet's commas" are artifices; on the other hand, "better than any other procedure," it conforms to the technique of nature itself, since "[nature] paints exclusively with the colors of the solar spectrum, with an infinite number of gradations, and does not allow itself so much as a square millimeter of flat hue."[92] The first argument will seduce the Delaunays, the Kupkas, and the Mondrians of the world, and will play an important role in the development of abstraction proper (they won't follow Signac's advice, who invoked Rembrandt—"painting is not made to be sniffed"—in recommending that divisionist canvases should not be looked at from too close up);[93] the second argument places the whole divisionism problematic back into a traditional mimetic framework and negates everything that is radically new about the autonomization of pure colors that it deployed—hence the comparison Gauguin makes on several occasions between neoimpressionism and color photography.[94] Starting from the same symbolist premises as Seurat (including the psychology or "dynamogeny" of lines and colors, and the necessity of color division), Gauguin develops a theory of equivalences that is more elaborate and much less doctrinaire, in many respects very close to that of Matisse's transposition, the theory that prompted him to abandon local tone.[95] Although he claims to have been aware of it from the "Moreau years" on, Matisse can only have had indirect access to it (through the articles of Gabriel-Albert Aurier, Maurice Denis, Charles Morice, etc.—the latter two, moreover, come down quite hard on this own work). But the paintings were much more important than the theory behind them. All historians have pointed out that in *Le Bonheur de vivre,* for the first time in his painted work, at least in such a consequential way, Matisse resorts to the broad, flat applications of color that Gauguin used so extensively in his canvases, applications denounced on every page of Signac's treatise (with no mention of Gauguin's name). But why this "borrowing" at this stage in his career? Quite simply because Gauguin makes Matisse realize that *color can be divided* (you can refuse to mix colors and use only pure tones), *without having to divide brushstrokes.* Certainly, Gauguin himself is a long way from renouncing traditional modeling and ruling out all mixing of color in his canvases, but his numerous flat compartments of saturated color pointed the way toward the possibility of shaking off the "tyranny of divisionism" without sacrificing its major advantage.[96] "I have a great love for bright, clear, pure color, and I am always surprised to see such lovely colors unnecessarily muddied and dimmed," writes Matisse in "Modernism and Tradition" (Flam, p. 73): Gauguin shows him that the divided brushstroke is not the only possibility available to those who want to accentuate pure color, that a larger atom of color, the "compartment," can be substituted for the small dots. In appropriating this substitution (and in according it much more weight than Gauguin had been able to do, for whom extension was clearly not a matter of importance), Matisse outstrips the "arbitrariness" of color promoted here and there by Signac and permanently renounces all impressionism, arriving at an aesthetic of transposition based on "the relationship between color relations in the object and color relations in the painting," as Lebensztejn puts it so well.[97]

This long detour through Van Gogh and Gauguin was motivated, to begin with, by a chronological question. Before examining one last time the nature of the relations between the "Matisse system" and the "Signac system," which will, paradoxically, lead us to Cézanne, I want to return briefly to the question of chronology. There is a third reason that makes me inclined to place the woodcuts before *Le Bonheur de vivre.* In "Modernism and Tradition," Matisse talks of "contour," "lines" and "their direction," and I noted above, with respect to *Seated Nude,* the numerous changes in direction to which the thick black lines are subjected, lines that form its various "patterns." Line and contour direction will become one of the most important elements in Matisse's drawing (his glorification of the arabesque is entirely dependent on it): just as in a Rembrandt engraving it is not a matter of indifference whether the hatchings move upward or downward, that they are oriented, so in Matisse every line has its relevant starting point and endpoint ("one must always search for the desire of the line, where it wishes to enter or where to die away"; note by Sarah Stein, Flam, p. 43). This bears no relation to symbolist dynamogeny: line direction is what allows for the refinement of modulation-through-quantity-relations and makes it possible to indicate the concavity or convexity of volumes. In this respect, if the 1906 woodcuts are compared with *Le Bonheur de vivre,* one can only be struck by their crude character where the drawing of the figures is concerned. On the one hand, there is a minimum of internal contours, as if Matisse had been afraid they might make him lose the major benefit of the equation he is verifying; on the other hand, all the contours are clumsy, jarring, almost willfully so: the lines always seem to be hesitating as to where they want to end up. There is nothing of the extraordinary fluidity that, even though they have the thickness of a thumb (much to Signac's disgust), characterizes the contours of almost all the figures in the painting. The poses assigned to the figures are no less elaborately ornate in the woodcuts than in *Le Bonheur de vivre,* but whereas in the former Matisse relies entirely on the overlapping of the limbs to indicate the relative position of the volumes in space, in the painting he only needs to slightly inflect the curves used to draw the nudes in order to transform their flat color applications into solid bodies, and this in spite of the ethereal atmosphere in which the scene is bathed. The rare internal contours that encroach onto the white expanse of the torso in the *Seated Nude* (at the shoulder blade, the thigh, and the armpit) succeed in differentiating the depth planes only at the price of highly redundant redoublings: with the figures in the painting, however, the slightest deviation in line trajectory is sufficient to accomplish this task.

I mentioned earlier the series of lithographs that Matisse exhibited at the same time as his woodcuts at the Galerie Druet: in my view, it was in working on these lithographs, through an extremely subtle analysis of the modulating power of linear direction, that he learned to perfect what he discovered with such jubilation in the woodcuts. There we are still dealing with what are almost stylistic exercises, still a little scholarly at times, as in *Reclining Nude, Hiding Her Eyes* [*Nu mi-allongé, les bras dissimulant les yeux*], where the contour, which remains jerky, alternates almost regularly between indicating concavity and convexity (but even here notice to what extent the tiny arc marking the navel, from the simple fact of its being open at the top, indicates the bulge of the lower belly). In *Standing Nude with Downcast Eyes* [*L'Idole*] or *Nude, Back View* [*Figure de dos au collier noir*] (fig. 11), perhaps the two most successful pieces in the series, the line is refined, the cursive gesture is only interrupted when the line has run its course, which is always calculated minimally; all redundance is outlawed.[98] Whereas the woodcuts were pushed to extremes in order to underscore the novelty of the invention, Matisse now understands that his "system" implies a radical economy of means. Chardin used to say "I add until it looks right," and citing him, Matisse adds: "or I take away, because I scrape out a lot" ("Notes of a Painter on His Drawing," Flam, p. 82). The remark has to do with color, but it was in the 1906 lithographs that the principle of radical economy was first

11. Henri Matisse, Nude, Back View [Figure de dos au collier noir]*, 1906. Lithograph, 45 × 27.9 cm (16¹/₈ × 10¹³/₁₆ in.). The Baltimore Museum of Art. The Blanche Adler Fund. Photo of the museum.*

explored in and for itself, at least in such an extreme manner: there again, "expression by [drawing]" was determinant.[99] After which, even if some of these plates were done after *Le Bonheur de vivre* (I'm inclined to see them as concomitant, since Matisse often stated that a change in medium helped him to "order his thoughts"),[100] in totally abandoning divisionism he was able to compose "with [his] drawing so as to enter directly into the arabesque with the color" (quoted above).

Let us now come back to the Seurat-Signac system. It harbors two radical incompatibilities with the "Matisse system," two negations of the quantity-quality equation. As we saw, Signac is not insensitive to the question of scale: for example, he recommends modifying the size of the brushstrokes in accordance with the size of the picture. But he does not recommend modifying their size inside the painting itself: each atom of color has to cover the same quantity of surface. It is impossible to modulate using quantity: all the quantities resulting from the division of the brushstrokes are equal.[101] Certainly, in any given zone of the painting there is always a dominant color. But whatever the number of strokes of red he applies to the canvas, the divisionist painter will never manage to bestow the same intensity on his red, the same pigmentary force as the artist working with flat applications. Matisse one day jokingly recalls this naive definition of fauvism: "it's when you have red."[102] Now, in spite of everything I said earlier about the autonomization of pure color in the divisionist system, using red as such, insisting on red or on any other color in particular for the purposes of expression is precisely what this system rules out. Jean-Claude Lebensztejn quite rightly notes that Matisse is not opposed a priori to local tone, since the choice of individual colors matters less than their interrelationships.[103] It can even be the starting point of a harmony, its dominant, if its presence in the painting is able to translate something of what it was that moved the painter in the scene that he wants to evoke (by contrast, in order to emphasize the color strength of a particular locale, the other colors in the painting will have to be transposed). I mentioned earlier that what struck Matisse about the Moroccans crouching and sipping their coffee was their silent contemplation of a pink flower and a bowl of gold fish. "Well, if I make them [the fish] red, the vermilion is going to make my flower violet! So? I want it pink, otherwise it no longer exists. The fish, on the other hand, could be yellow, it doesn't bother me; they'll be yellow!" (to Marcel Sembat, 1913, *EPA*, p. 47, note 10).[104] "I want my flower pink!" Signac's response would be: "Impossible. It will be pink, but it will also be the opposite of pink," etc. No color or figure in the painting can be singled out: the impersonality of divisionist technique concerns not only the brushstroke but the motif itself. It is an absolute pictorial democracy.

The second incompatibility in the Seurat-Signac system for Matisse, which again directly concerns the quantity-quality equation, emerges very clearly in this passage from *De Delacroix au néo-impressionnisme:* "It mustn't be thought that the painter who *divides* indulges in an insipid riddling of his canvas from top to bottom, and from right to left, with small, multicolored brushstrokes. Beginning with a contrast between two hues, without worrying about the surface to be covered, he will oppose, gradate, and proportion the various elements on each side of the line of demarcation, until he comes to another contrast, the motif of a further gradation. And, moving from contrast to contrast, the canvas will be covered."[105] "Without worrying about the surface to be covered"! Reading this, one is almost led to wonder how it could have taken Matisse so long to abandon the divisionist option (this would be misguided, however, since it was in becoming aware of his inability to work within its confines that he discovered the quantity-quality equation). Matisse's space is tabular; any linear or narrative unfolding is unthinkable—which applies just as much to the production process as it does to the perception of the picture. On the level of reception, Matisse is opposed to Klee, who feels that "the eye must 'graze' over the surface, sharply grasping portion after portion, to convey them to the brain which collects and stores the impressions" (Klee, who used pointillism a great deal, albeit in parodying it, and whom Matisse nevertheless considered a painter of "rare sensibility").[106] For Matisse, "expression comes from the colored surface which the spectator perceives as a whole" (to Tériade in 1929, when discussing *Music* [*La Musique*], Flam, p. 58; not at all unexpectedly, this sentence follows one of the variations on the quality-quantity equation: "the color was proportioned to the form"). As for production, only once in the entire corpus of his writings and statements does Matisse seem to evoke the kind of temporality Klee refers to:

> When I make my drawings—"Variations"—the path traced by my pencil on the sheet of paper is, to some extent, analogous to the gesture of a man groping his way in the darkness. I mean that there is nothing foreseen about my path: I am led. I do not lead. I go from one point in the thing which is my model to another point which I always see in isolation, independent of the other points towards which my pen will subsequently move. . . . Just as the spider throws out (or fastens?) its thread to some convenient protuberance and thence to another that it perceives, and from one point to another weaves its web.[107]

But here it is a question of pointing out the "unconscious" nature of this kind of pen drawing ("I rely on my subconscious self [*je m'en remets à mon inconscient*]," to

Carco, Flam, p. 84), a type of drawing prepared over a long period of time through more "conscious" [*volontaires*] charcoal studies, as he himself says; in other words, through a previous working of the surface to be covered and of the characteristics of the model. Matisse often spoke of the difference between these two genres. When he works on a theme drawing (as he calls the "conscious" studies), where the palimpsest and erasing are permissible, he can chat with his model; but if the latter should ask him the time while he's at work on a variation drawing (necessarily done *alla prima*), the contact with the work is broken, as Pollock would say. "I am done for, the drawing is done for [*je suis fichu, le dessin est fichu*]," as Matisse puts it.[108] This tension comes from the fact that, contrary to what he himself seems to believe, he constantly has to have if not "in mind" then "in hand" the totality of the surface to be covered, since this is the basis of the quantity relations, and therefore of the modulation of the whiteness of the paper. Even if he draws with his eyes closed (he tried the experiment several times), before he can begin Matisse first has to have incorporated the measurements of the surface area. He hardly ever works spider-fashion (for that matter, can we be sure that spiders rely so little on planning); each one of his strokes and lines is like the end of a dance in which his hand has surveyed the space, skimming the surface of the canvas without quite touching it. In a film made in 1945–46 by François Campeaux and Jean Cassou (*Henri Matisse*), we see him painting a face in large black strokes, that of a figure in a canvas entitled *Young Woman in White, Red Background* [*Jeune femme en blanc, fond rouge*] from 1946.[109] The sequence is filmed at normal speed, then a second sequence shows him painting this same face in slow motion (not the same sequence but another stage of the painting, no doubt filmed the next day; in the meantime, as was his custom, Matisse has erased the "first" face with turpentine). While watching this slow motion sequence of the film, Matisse "suddenly felt naked" (and both Merleau-Ponty and Lacan were greatly struck by his reaction):[110]

> There was a passage showing me drawing in slow motion. . . . Before my pencil ever touched the paper, my hand made a strange journey of its own. I never realized before that I did this. I suddenly felt as if I were shown naked—that everyone could see this—it made me feel deeply embarrassed. You must understand, this was not hesitation. I was unconsciously establishing the relationship between the subject I was about to draw and the size of my paper. *Je n'avais pas encore commencé à chanter* [I hadn't yet started to sing].[111]

This lack of awareness has nothing to do with the gropings of a man feeling his way in the dark (in his commentary accompanying this sequence, Cassou compares the movement of the hand to that of a bee just before settling on a flower), and the fact that Matisse mistakenly substitutes drawing for painting in his memory here sounds like a denial of the spider's step by step approach. We don't have "spider-like" drawing on one side and "bee-like" painting on the other: both of them are constructed in the same way, both follow the same choreography of extension.

Certainly, short of running over the entire surface with a roller, like a house painter, and producing a monochromatic canvas, there is no way of avoiding a consecutive placement of the strokes of color on the canvas, no way of eliminating a certain residue of division.[112] But this minimal consecution is resolved in Matisse's work in the flat application that unites the separate brushstrokes in one plane, and allows for a change in level: the passage from the brushstroke to the compartment (which becomes the atom, the undivided element) transforms division, which in Seurat-Signac had an optical and textural function, into a major composition question—namely the articulation of the picture's planes in an indissoluble unity. Yet it was at the level of the brushstroke itself that Matisse became aware of the compositional role of division—and this realization sealed his incompatibility with divisionism. Let us return once again to "Modernism and Tradition." In order to explain his break with this system, after noting that "the picture is formed by the combination of surfaces, differently colored, which results in the creation of an 'expression,'" and before discussing transposition, Matisse says: "In the same way that in a musical harmony each note is part of the whole, so I wished each color to have a contributory value" (Flam, p. 72). In a sense, it seems that this is precisely what the divisionist theory maintained: once the whole is "synthesized" through optical mixing, each divided color stroke contributes to the general harmony of the picture. Why, then, does the painter feel uneasy? In fact, in the beginning, Matisse doesn't understand why "once [he] had laid [his] dominant," he couldn't help "putting on its reaction, equally intense," finding himself "continually forced to start all over again" (cited above). It was during the fauve summer that he realized just how hard it was for him to adapt his work to the do's and don'ts outlined by Signac: "During the time at Collioure I began with an idea that I had heard expressed by Vuillard, who used the word the 'definitive touch.' . . . This helped me a lot because I had a sensation of an object's coloring; I applied the color, and this was the first color on my canvas. I added to this a second color, and then, if this second color did not appear to agree with the first, instead of taking it off, I added a third, which reconciled them. I then had to continue in this way until I felt that I had established a completely harmonious canvas, and that

I was emptied [*je me trouvais déchargé*] of the emotion that had made me begin it."[113] At first sight, we seem close to *De Delacroix au néo-impressionnisme* here, whereas we are in fact dealing with its opposite: "harmony through a third color" is impossible in a divisionist picture, with its myriad brushstrokes of pure color. Short of having a computer in place of a brain, it is impossible to control all the interactions between the atoms of color, and it is from just such control that the possibility of this kind of harmony emerges (a harmony that is unthinkable unless the number of atoms is reduced, hence the broad, flat planes). Matisse was constantly forced to start from scratch because each color stroke implied a further dissonance, ricochet-like, and necessitated an unsettling of the picture's global color harmony.

Although Matisse invokes Vuillard (which should encourage those who deny the importance of Nabi art in his formation to be more prudent),[114] and although the idea of a harmony between two colors as the result of an extra color formed a part of the overall problematic of what is unhappily called "postimpressionism" (we find this idea in Gauguin, for example[115]), everything suggests that Cézanne was the exemplary figure here. We remember, for example, what Cézanne said to Vollard concerning the two small spots on the hands in his portrait that weren't yet covered with pigment: "maybe tomorrow I will be able to find the exact tone to cover up those spots. Don't you see, Monsieur Vollard, that if I put something there by guesswork, I might have to paint the whole canvas over starting from that point?"[116] Matisse was well aware that the apparently "unfinished" quality of Cézanne's canvases had an essential function in their construction. But it wasn't just because the sections left blank enhanced the overall tonality (the luminous effect of the white, which became so important in his own paintings, to the point of determining his preference for a very light coating leaving the canvas visible, something he learnt from Signac): as we shall see, the "unfinished" in Cézanne's canvases is always at least a provisional finish. And despite being repeatedly given the run-around by Vollard, an experience that was to fuel his mistrust of dealers and make him intractable in his business dealings, Matisse always payed homage to him for finding a way of saving Cézanne from a calamity "in having his canvases photographed": "this had considerable importance because without it others surely would have "finished" all the Cézannes, like they used to add trees to all the Corots" (to Guenne, 1925, Flam, p. 56).

Renoir used to say of Cézanne: "How does he do it? He can't put two strokes of color on a canvas without it already being very good."[117] How does he do it? He does it by constantly thinking of his picture, in its totality, as a play of forces to be "balanced." The two brushstrokes Renoir mentions are forces opposed to each other, but also to the white of the canvas: the intensity and luminosity of the colors are the result of this internal struggle.[118] At the end of each sitting, in its very "unfinished-ness" the painting has attained a form of static equilibrium, but, being based on a radical dynamism, the equilibrium is totally precarious, functioning somewhat like the force of deterrence in the arms race (the metaphor comes from Mondrian).[119] The painter cannot leave his easel before placing the brushstroke that, whatever stage the canvas is at, will achieve this state of equilibrium. At each new sitting the painter has to begin working as if he were starting from scratch, since each new mark he makes, adding to the forces already present in the painting, implies a rupturing of the equilibrium.[120] Emile Bernard mentions a canvas on which Cézanne worked for the entire month he spent with him in Aix: "This painting changed form and color almost every day, and yet when I first arrived at his studio, you could have taken it off the easel as an adequate work."[121] Adequate, but not necessarily satisfactory, since the canvas "did not yet join hands."[122]

The same is true of Matisse. Let me quote once again these remarks to Tériade, which Escholier repeats: "At each stage, I reach a balance, a conclusion. At the next sitting [*à la séance suivante*], if I find a weakness in the whole, I find my way back into the picture by means of the weakness—I re-enter through the breach—and reconceive the whole. Thus everything becomes fluid again and as each element is only one of the component forces (as in an orchestration), the whole can be changed in appearance but the feeling still remains the same" (Flam, p. 74). Matisse unques-tionably owes this strategic and energetic conception of the picture to Cézanne, who "constructed by means of relations of forces,"[123] and who wanted "the tones to be forces in a painting" (to Guenne, 1925, Flam, p. 55). If, from a purely morphological standpoint, his oeuvre apparently has so little to do with that of the old Aix master, it is because he retained its fundamental principle, the notion of dynamism, and not the effects: indeed, it was impossible for Matisse to imitate Cézanne's "constructive brushwork," at least after the discovery of the quantity-quality equation. By contrast, the idea of a constant opposition of forces, which necessarily implies an all-over treatment of the surface, could only have reinforced his determination to abandon divisionism. The only difference between the "Matisse system" and the "Cézanne sys-tem" is the serious consideration Matisse affords to extension as a parameter of the way color behaves, which requires a usage of flat color planes that Cézanne would have virulently condemned.[124] But his discovery itself would not have been possible without Cézanne's support: "In moments of doubt, when I was still searching for myself, frightened sometimes by my discoveries, I thought: 'If Cézanne is right, I am right'; because I knew that Cézanne had made no mistake" (to Guenne, 1925, Flam, p. 55).[125]

The energetic conception governs the possibility of transposition in Matisse's work—and the same conception was already implicit in Cézanne: see what Bernard says about the painting that constantly changes color. Commenting on a visitor who thinks he's seeing a different painting when confronted with *Harmony* [repainted] *in Red,* Matisse says: "He has no idea. It's not another painting: I'm looking for forces and an equilibrium of forces" (*EPA,* p. 129, note 96). This conception also implies that everything counts, absolutely everything, in the relations between these forces; not just the quantities but the materials, for example. Discussing the Merion *Dance,* he says: "I had placed the darkest tones, which were my blacks, against the arcades themselves, but when I replaced the paper with my color [i.e., paint], I again had to undertake a certain number of modifications because of the inherent brilliance of the pictorial material, which upset the previously established equilibrium."[126] Matisse's statements abound with this preoccupation with the slightest detail.

"There is no principal feature." Once again, it is the relationship with Cézanne that helps in understanding this at first sight strange remark from "Modernism and Tradition," which was his way, as will be remembered, of expressing his disaffection with divisionism. Referring to *The Bathers,* which he bought from Vollard, Matisse says that "everything in it was so well hierarchized," that "the trees, the hands counted as much as the sky." [127] The crucial notion here is "hierarchy,": we are dealing with a relation of dynamic forces, not with a democratic equalization settled in advance. In a Cézanne painting, no point is more important than another for the final effect because each point plays a different role in the "orchestration." By contrast, the a priori democracy of divisionism outlaws this diversification of roles. The result: a stroke of dark color will automatically have a secondary role, "always secondary," in relation to a stroke of light color.

Finally, the energetic conception that Matisse inherits from Cézanne engenders what could be called the economy of the sitting, each of which has to end in a "discharge" (*décharge;* Matisse makes frequent use of the word, especially when referring to his drawings: cf., for example, the statement to Bonnard, *EPA,* p. 183). He often mentions the number of sittings that have been necessary to bring a painting to its conclusion, and is greatly worried by the fact that young painters risk being taken in by the "apparent facility" of his drawing (Flam, p. 120; his letter to Henry Clifford published in the catalogue of his 1948 Philadelphia exhibition is entirely taken up with the question). Lydia Delectorskaya, who started out as his favorite model (from 1935 to 1939) and went on to become his lifetime assistant, reports that "most of the canvases were usually concluded in a few sittings, but it was almost a rule that, during "the working season" (from September to June, July), at least one picture would drag on." Particularly for these more "resistant" paintings (but the idea came to him while working on the 1933 *Dance*). "Matisse had decided to bring in a photographer . . . to photograph the panel each time that, at the end of a sitting, he either felt the work was finished or that it had reached a significant stage. He knew that the next morning he would find an imperfection in it, and, hurrying to eliminate it, he would disrupt the whole equilibrium, the general harmony attained the day before, even if it meant many extra days of struggle before finding a new solution that would satisfy him."[128] Thanks to this desire to preserve a trace of the preceding "discharge," before the breach he detects in the work has even begun to be filled in (Matisse always erased at least "the compartments of the undesirable color,"[129] if not the entire canvas, before starting work again),[130] we have at our disposition an almost complete file, put together by Lydia Delectorskaya, not just on the elaboration of *The Pink Nude* [*Nu rose*], for which Barr had already provided photographs of the different stages, but on the elaboration of all the important canvases from 1935–39. This is not the place even to begin to sketch what there is to learn from all these traces of a long process—each painting would need to be examined separately, in detail. I simply want to underscore how agonistic painting was for Matisse: each painting is the trace of a struggle in which the painter takes all the risks, the photographs of the different stages merely helping to ensure the conservation of a previous attainment before, as he himself often says, "getting a better jump" [*mieux sauter*]. In a letter to his son in 1940, he writes: "in short, virtually every one of my paintings is an adventure, this is what gives it its interest—since I only exhibit it once the adventure is successfully ended, I'm the only one taking the risks" (*EPA*, p. 184; he is discussing a painting he has just finished after working on it for a year).

The foregoing has been, to begin with, simply an attempt at explaining the special place that Matisse, in his exceptionally important text "Modernism and Tradition," assigns to divisionism in the evolution of his oeuvre. My hypothesis, namely that the quantity-quality equation, the essential key to his work, was discovered in reacting against the "tyranny of divisionism," led me to examine the relations between Matisse and Van Gogh, Gauguin, Signac, and Cézanne in the course of a long "chronological" detour. It now remains for me to verify the permanence of the equation in Matisse's oeuvre, and to show how it entirely revolutionizes the pictorial tradition. Just before doing so, I want to outline what changes my hypothesis produces in the common appreciation of Matisse's art.

I have stated throughout that it was divisionism and not fauvism that enabled Matisse to find "the secret of expression by color." I should add that it is not fauvism so much as "the movements which . . . followed it" that represented for him the discovery of what he calls "expression by [drawing]." At first sight, such a claim seems inoffensive enough, yet it implies that for Matisse fauvism was a moment of transition before the blossoming of what I have tried to bring out as his most fundamental contribution. In "Modernism and Tradition" he himself insists on what is false about the label "fauvism" when it artificially groups together painters—"individuals"—who, even though they work "along the same lines," as he says to Tériade, have each been led to "find their own path" (1952, Flam, p. 132). Moreover, in this same interview with Tériade, he refers to fauvism as a "lively but somewhat limiting theory" (Flam, p. 133). Now, if you look at Matisse's output during the fauve summer and even during the first months of 1906, what is most striking about it is its eclecticism—a sign, at the very least, of the absence of any fixed theory. Matisse, it seems, is still of two minds, without of course being aware of it. First of all, he is a long way from having abandoned divisionism proper (as evidenced by *The Port of Abaill* or *Woman with a Parasol,* mentioned above);[131] secondly, in a certain number of works that renounce the divided brushstroke, he seems to be trying to rectify the freedom of impressionist brushwork through the rigors of simultaneous contrast (or vice versa), with a partial return to traditional modeling (*Girl Reading, Woman with a Hat*); in still others, like *The Idol* [*L'Idole*] or *The Gypsy,* in order to free himself from the Signac system he again resorts to impasto, which he had abandoned since his Corsican period. The most important canvases, however, are those in which the quantity-quality equation was being sought, before it was isolated as such in the woodcuts: the extraordinary *The Open Window, Collioure* [*Fenêtre à Collioure*], *The Green Line* [*Femme à la raie verte*], and *The Siesta* [*La Sieste*]. Matisse refers to this last painting, moreover, in the following terms: "the same red is used for the child's dress and elsewhere in the picture, well, *you cannot see* that it's the same red shown in light and in shadow, and that the difference between them is a matter of relationships."[132] But as a general rule we are only dealing with partial analyses here, bearing on various parts of various paintings: in itself, the overall construction of these canvases is not yet elaborated in accordance with the axiomatic of quantity-quality as described above (all-over, frame, scale, color value). It was not until the woodcuts, their refinement in the lithographs, then the application of the results to painting in *Le Bonheur de vivre,* that Matisse understood what was causing the gap between color and drawing that he so deplored in his divisionist works. In Collioure, he still didn't realize that the gap is inevitable once you start thinking in terms of color versus drawing where each is assigned a distinct role. We find, for example, the following observation in the notes he took at the time: "To use drawing to indicate the expression of objects in relation to one another . . . To use color for its luminous intensity, in its various combinations and harmonies, and not for defining objects."[133] The construction of space through color, which depends on "expression by [drawing]," in other words on quantity relations, was yet to be discovered.

In my hypothesis, *Le Bonheur de vivre* becomes at once the end of fauvism and the birth of the "Matisse system," the moment of break (even if certain works that come after it seem to entirely deny the break its untimely character—most notably, the brief return to modeling in 1907–08 with, for example, the three *Nudes* that illustrate the "Notes"). As everyone has noticed, flashbacks are frequent in Matisse's work, the sign of a strategy that could be called the strategy of consolidating gains. He makes a gigantic leap forward that keeps him in a state of extreme tension for several months, then, in order to "discharge" this tension, he goes back to what he was doing before the breakthrough; the flashback subsequently allows him to plunge back, refreshed and less anxious, into the new problematic that had both excited and disconcerted him. Whatever the case, Matisse was certainly aware that with *Le Bonheur de vivre* he was onto something entirely new, hence the imposing format he gave to the canvas, his largest painting up to that point. Certainly, the work is not without its faults (Jack Flam goes so far as to say that in looking at it, you alternate between "a sense of the sublime and the feeling that it is almost a bit silly").[134] Matisse himself was quite hard on it, his own criticisms echoing some of those he had heard: "This picture was painted through the juxtaposition of things conceived independently, but arranged together. Whereas afterwards, I tried to get more unity in my compositions."[135] It will be recalled that the picture was probably done with the aid of a cartoon, which is probably what lies behind Matisse's later harsh judgment of it . For it was in working on this painting that Matisse learned how to dispense with the cartoon (see above for the remarks on the exceptional status of the two *Luxe* canvases): perhaps he still needed this "compass" because he did not yet know whether the equation he had just discovered in drawing was going to be verified in his painting, but immediately after *Le Bonheur de vivre,* he relegates the old procedure to the scrap heap. From now on, through "expression by [drawing]," he will work directly in the color. This painting was like a talisman for Matisse, the mark of a radical conversion, which, paradoxically, is maybe why he never explicitly referred to it again, until right at the end of his life. Indeed, I cannot agree with Pierre Schneider when he says that *Le Bonheur de vivre* "simply vanished from his life after Leo Stein bought it."[136] In my opinion, Matisse's silence indicates instead too great a proximity to the work and the necessity to withdraw from the commotion so as to be able to measure its effect with the necessary objectivity. At any rate, Matisse was clearly aware of the inaugural character of his great composition. In 1952, summing up a lifetime's work, he declares to Maria Luz that: "From *Le Bonheur de vivre*—I was thirty-five then—to this cut out—I am eighty-two—I have not changed; not in the way my friends mean who want to compliment me, no matter what, on my good health, but because all this time I have looked for the same things, which I have perhaps realized by different means" (Flam, p. 136). There follows a description of the expansive space of the chapel ("a spiritual space; that is, a space whose dimensions are not limited even by the existence of the objects represented"), which is another way of stating what he says in the various remarks on scale I reported earlier. Then, as if to confirm everything I've tried to disentangle here, comes an explicit evocation of "expression by [drawing]," in other words expression through relations of quantity: "On a painted surface I render space to the sense of sight: I make of it a color limited by a drawing. When I use paint, I have a feeling of quantity—surface of color—which is necessary to me, and I modify its contour in order to determine my feelings clearly in a definitive way. (Let's call the first action 'to paint' and the second 'to draw.') In my case, to paint or to draw are one. I choose my quantity of colored surface and I make it conform to my feeling of the drawing, like the sculptor moulds clay by modifying the ball which he first made and afterwards elicits his feeling from it" (Flam, pp. 136–137). Fauvism is perhaps "the basis of everything," but this is because the initially confused negative reaction to divisionism leads to *Le Bonheur de vivre,* the real point of departure. Matisse often insisted on the indebtedness of the Moscow (1910) and the Merion (1933) *Dance* to the central ring in his great 1906 painting, and all historians have remarked that this ring does in fact prefigure the farandole on the panel commissioned by Shchukin. To my knowledge, however, no one has pointed out that the equation I have discussed at length here is at least equally involved in this filiation (and Matisse is particularly eloquent on this matter, concerning both the painting of 1910 and the "decoration" of 1933). Which once again goes to show that in limiting oneself solely to the iconographic level, one is bound to overlook what constitutes one of the most important stakes in every problematic, if not the most important.[137]

In order to delineate one last time the silent omnipresence of the work of "arche-drawing" and the quantity-quality equation in Matisse's entire oeuvre, I want to return to this best-known text, "Notes of a Painter," to which I suggested that "Modernism and Tradition" may have constituted a corrective by putting us on the trail of divisionism and the reaction that followed. The text is introduced by his friend Georges Desvallières, all in all a rather traditional but obviously very open-minded colleague from the Moreau studio. Is it far-fetched to believe that Matisse had a hand in this introduction? Now, even though the article is only illustrated with six of Matisse's canvases—almost all of them chosen, moreover, as Roger Benjamin notes, from amongst those that return to traditional modeling (apart from *Joueurs de boules,* the biggest of them, paradoxically in a tiny reproduction here), as if the painter didn't want to frighten his reader off—Desvallières focuses above all on his drawing.[138]

He beings by noting that, like the romanesque workers who "deform" (as was said at the time) in taking architecture into account, "Matisse takes the rectangle formed by his paper into account when he draws upon it," then, still seeking to explain the "deformation" of one of the reproduced figures, he writes that the "various parts of the body are themselves studied so that the whites left between the paper's edge [while we are dealing here with a painting on canvas] and the black lines form an expressive ornamentation." He concludes his discussion with these words: "he enlarged our understanding of drawing" (*EPA,* pp. 39–40).[139] In the space of a few words, he mentions the importance that drawing had for Matisse, the role of the paper's format (and therefore the role of scale) and that of spacing (modulation by quantity). Color is barely mentioned, and then only as if by chance, on order to signal Matisse's indebtedness to the carpets and the "findings of modern science" (Chevreul was working at the Gobelins when he carried out his research on simultaneous contrast, which would so fascinate Delacroix, then Seurat).

Let us now move on to Matisse's text proper.[140] After putting on a performance about having dared to put pen to paper, and after making it plain that he is not concerned with theory, he immediately launches into a definition of "expression," which is "what [he is] after, above all." The definition starts out negative, antiexpressionist, so to speak: "expression, for me, does not reside in passions glowing in a human face or manifested by violent movement." Then comes the affirmative part of the definition: expression "rests in the entire arrangement of my picture: the place occupied by the figures, the empty space around them, the proportions, everything has its share." The principle of the all-over is thus posited from the outset. Then comes its practical result, the precept of radical economy: "In a picture every part will be visible and will play its appointed role, whether it be principal or secondary. Everything that is not useful in the picture is, it follows, harmful." What does this compositional rule immediately lead to, or rather, of what is it the essential condition? The question of quantity:

> Composition, the aim of which should be expression, is modified according to the surface to be covered. If I take a sheet of paper of a given size, my drawing will have a necessary relationship to its format. I would

not repeat this drawing on another sheet of different proportions, for example, rectangular instead of square. Nor should I be satisfied with a mere enlargement, had I to transfer the drawing to a sheet the same shape, but ten times larger. A drawing must have an expansive force which gives life to the things around it [*force d'expansion qui vivifie les choses qui l'entourent*]. An artist who wants to transpose a composition from one canvas to another larger one must conceive it anew in order to preserve its expression; he must alter its character and not just square it up onto the larger canvas. (Flam, p. 36)

Before the question of color is even raised, then, the importance of the "surface to be covered" is foregrounded, and with it everything that flows from a focus on scale, including the role of expansion in Matisse's art. The text then broaches the question of "condensation" (what others used to call "synthesis" a few years before) and the difference between Matisse's output and impressionism. After recapitulating his aesthetic of evocation, in terms very close to those of Mallarmé, Matisse is back to quantity again (it should again be pointed out that there is still no mention of color). This time, the question of quantity relations is dealt with head on, with a noteworthy differentiation between absolute quantity (that of the isolated mark) and relative quantity:

I must precisely define the character of the object or of the body that I wish to paint. To do so, I study my method very closely: If I put a black dot on a sheet of white paper, the dot will be visible no matter how far away I hold it: it is a clear notation [*une écriture claire*]. But beside this dot I place another one, and then a third, and already there is confusion. In order for the first dot to maintain its value I must enlarge it as I put other marks on the paper." (Flam, p. 37)

Here we have an explanation, referring exclusively to the domain of drawing, of the appearance of the flat color planes and the abandonment of divisionism. Indeed, the painter moves straight on to this question, finally raising the issue of color:

If upon a white canvas I scatter some sensations of blue, of green, of red, each new stroke diminishes the importance of the preceding ones. Suppose I have to paint an interior: I have before me a cupboard; it gives me a sensation of vivid red, and I put down a red which satisfies me. A relation is established between this red and the white of the canvas. Let me put a green near the red, and make the floor yellow; and again there will

> be relationships between the green or yellow and the white of the canvas which will satisfy me. But these different tones mutually weaken one another. It is necessary that the various marks I use be balanced so that they do not destroy each other. To do this I must organize my ideas; the relationship between the tones must be such that it will sustain and not knock them down. A new combination of colors will succeed the first and render the totality of my representation. I am forced to transpose. (Flam, p. 37)

There are several points to be noted here. First of all, the Cézannian idea of a permanent equilibrium of the totality of the forces at work on the canvas. Secondly, the fact that in moving from drawing to painting, we run into color transposition. Whereas in drawing the first dot had to be enlarged as other marks appeared on the paper, the painter has to change color combinations so that the relationship between the tones maintains them rather than destroys them. One might be tempted to think that Matisse is abandoning the problematic of quantity-quality here, but this is far from being the case: saturation and value, as I said earlier, are essentially determined by quantity, but these differences in quantity operate in and through colors, which have their own character, a character modified in accordance with the needs of "expression." Certainly, Matisse is always thinking in terms of color interaction— never, for example, as Lebensztejn points out, in terms of any kind of "psychology of colors," in the manner of a Kandinsky. Hence the possibility of transposition ("a black could very well replace a blue, since basically the expression derives from the relationships," he says to Tériade in the passage picked up by Escholier).[141] But we have seen that he was sensitive to the behavior of individual colors, and that most of the time he began with a specific color that he wanted to feature in his canvas (the *pink* flower, in *The Arab Café*). Now the expression of this behavior, the particular affect of a particular color, which gives rise to, amongst other things, the necessity of transposition, is once again made possible by quantity relations. In *Jazz,* for instance, consider two cutouts representing a torso, one white, the other blue. At first sight, they appear to be in a positive-negative relation: the white-on-blue torso seems to be what remains after the blue-on-white silhouette on the opposite page has been cut out of it. But this is not the case: "In order to give the same visual weight to the white torso and the blue torso, originally identical, the upper part of the blue torso has had to be made heavier (assertion of the fact: '1 cm^2 of one color is not equal in weight to 1 cm^2 of another color,' this is a basic principle of the science of colors)."[142]

Let us return one last time to the 1908 "Notes." After outlining his aesthetic of transposition (it is here that he refers indirectly to *Harmony in Red*), and reaffirming the necessity of composing everything together (a dig at Rodin, who works in fragments, and whom Matisse has not forgiven for snubbing him), Matisse notes that his color is expressive because it is polarized. This pole—an individual color that, in the manner of a tuning fork, regulates the painting's overall harmony (the pink flower, for example)—is at times chosen unconsciously: "If at first, and perhaps without my having been conscious of it, one tone has particularly seduced or caught me, more often than not once the picture is finished I will notice that I have respected this tone while I progressively altered and transformed all the others" (Flam, p. 38). As we have seen, this expressive system (using red as red) goes completely against the grain of divisionism, and it is thus perfectly logical that Matisse should then move into a discussion of what separates him from Signac. How does he encapsulate the break? Once again, through the quantity-quality equation: "I simply try to put down colors which render my sensation. There is an impelling proportion of tones that may lead me to change the shape of a figure or to transform my composition" (ibid.). Quality and quantity have become so inseparable that here it is the tone one has decided on (the one that seduces or catches the eye) that dictates the quantity necessary for it to vibrate at maximum intensity in relation to the other planes in the painting: however you interpret Matisse's remarks in "Notes" on his color and drawing, you always find yourself returning to his system's foundational equation.

Perhaps the reader will complain that I'm guilty of overkill, that the point has long since been made and taken. Perhaps, but if I choose to drive the point home with reference to a text that has been the object of innumerable commentaries, even of an entire book, it is because to my knowledge no one has ever detected this principle in it, in part because no attention has ever been given to the way in which the text is articulated, to the sequencing of the ideas.[143] Now, all or almost all of Matisse's texts, and the bulk of his statements, follow a trajectory very close to the one found here: whether you reread his declarations on the Merion *Dance*, the extraordinary "Notes of a Painter on His Drawing" from 1939, his "Témoignage" [Testimonial] from 1943 (*EPA*, pp. 195–196), the "Notes on Color," published in 1962 (*EPA*, pp. 205–207), "How I Made My Books" from 1946, his declarations on the cutouts, on Vence, you will always find the quantity-quality equation, more often than not forcefully introduced like some theoretical deus ex machina charged not with "resolving" but with dissolving "the eternal conflict between drawing and color," to use the slightly deceptive expression Matisse employs in a letter to Rouveyre (1944, *EPA*, p. 188). You will also encounter over and over one of Matisse's constant anxieties: what if he doesn't manage to find the equivalent in painting of what he had discovered in drawing—his drawing that in the late twenties brings him back to "surface painting"? "I believe that in drawing I have been able to say something, I have worked a lot on that problem," says Matisse to Marchand in 1947 (Flam, p. 114), "but a colorist drawing is not a painting. You would have to find an equivalent in color—this is what I can't quite manage" (to Bonnard, 1940, *EPA,* p. 183). He alternates between moments of doubt and moments of jubilation ("I'm convinced there are signs of the emergence of the great things I expect of color, analogous to what I did in drawing last year," to Rouveyre, 1943, *EPA,* p. 192).[144] There are times when, wholly absorbed with color, drawing no longer interests him ("I've purged my mind on that score," to Rouveyre, 1947, *EPA,* p. 193), but in 1944 he also tells Tériade, who asks him to write something on color, that "to tell the truth, I loathe color at the moment, and I dare not write on it" (*EPA,* p. 197). From the late twenties on (in other words, from the time that his pen drawings predominate, the ones that best correspond to Fourcade's description cited above), the majority of Matisse's statements concerning the relations between his painting and his drawing show that he is convinced of having "found something" in drawing, and testify to the difficulty of finding an equivalent in painting (I quote one passage among many others: "Wanting to produce painting in keeping with my drawings, those that come straight from the heart and set down with the greatest simplicity, I started down a terribly arduous path that seems overwhelming because of the little time remaining to me," to Rouveyre, 1947, *EPA,* pp. 193–194). We even find Matisse giving himself a pat on the back in a remarkable handwritten admission in the album of photographs of the different stages put together by Lydia Delectorskaya: "I must also say that I achieved a very rare voluptuousness and elegance of line [in the pen drawings]. I poured my entire sensibility into them, and if it weren't for the social obligation to provide my contemporaries with works somewhat richer in terms of means, the humble pen drawing, well prepared by an analytic study, would be entirely adequate to purge me [*me décharger*] of my passionate emotions."[145]

To conclude, I want to return to the notion of the "eternal conflict between drawing and color," which as I said seems somewhat equivocal. In fact, when things don't go as Matisse would like them to, it is more a question of a gap than a conflict. In these moments of blockage, he says "my drawing and my painting go their separate ways" (to Bonnard, 1940, *EPA,* p. 182). Now, the entire "Matisse system" is based on an originary structure, what I am calling "arche-drawing," designed to make this gap impossible, to suppress any eventuality of it in advance. In this system, not only is it "not possible to separate drawing and colour" (Flam, p. 99), but "drawing represents a kind of painting executed with limited means" (to Fels, 1929, *EPA*, p. 200, note 62). It is "a painting made with reduced means" (to Charbonnier, 1952, Flam, p. 141). Precisely because of the quantity-quality equation, "arche-drawing" is just as much at work in the practice of drawing proper as it is in pictorial practice (hence the sentence that follows this declaration to Charbonnier again raises the question of modulation through quantity: "On a white surface, a sheet of paper, with pen and ink, by creating certain contrasts, you can create volumes; by changing the quality of the paper you can give supple surfaces, bright surfaces, hard surfaces, without, however, using either shading or highlights"). The difference between a painting and a drawing is determined not by the axis presence/absence of color (since "a drawing can be intensely colored without there being any need for actual color," as we have seen; Flam, p. 99), but by the number of color parameters implicated in the relations of the whole. "Painting is obviously a thing which has more to it [*une chose plus nourrie*], which acts more strongly on the mind" (Flam, p. 141),[146] says Matisse, again to Charbonnier (where we have a somewhat idealized echo of the famous statement to Tériade where he discusses "beautiful blues, beautiful reds, beautiful yellows— matter to stir the sensual depths in men," 1936, Flam, p. 74; translation slightly modified). But this is no reason to think that Matisse remains immersed in the hierarchization consecrated by the tradition and the market (where drawing is said to be preparatory to paintings, whose value is incommensurable). Not only is it in drawing, through the restriction of means (the suppression of a certain number of parameters), that he discovers the quantity-quality equation crucial for his work on color, but this restriction, this simplification of means, makes the draftsman's task even more of a gamble, and thus, in accordance with the agonistic ethic mentioned earlier, all the more respectable if it actually pays off.

Thus it will come as no surprise that Matisse, whom everyone agrees deserves the title of the century's greatest colorist, often considered his drawing more successful than his painting: as I remarked when first invoking the "concept," "arche-drawing" is more directly at work in drawing, the deployment of spacing is layed bare. But we still need to isolate what the invention or rather the locating of this "originary" level displaces in the Western pictorial tradition. And since the concept of "arche-drawing" is modeled on the concept of "arche-writing" proposed by Jacques Derrida, we should no doubt spend a moment or two examining what the theory of deconstruction has to teach us about it.

Curiously enough, nothing. Indeed, the long passage devoted to color in *Of Grammatology* consists in pointing out the supplementary nature of color in Western aesthetics, and in tracing the effects of this supplementarity in the economy of our metaphysics (Derrida starts with Rousseau, but he could have gone back to Aristotle or continued the analysis with Kant).[147] Pursuing Derrida's analysis, Jean-Claude Lebensztejn has compiled a list of all the expressions of contempt heaped on color— seen as a mere cosmetic—since Plato.[148] He approaches Matisse using the same schema of repression used by deconstruction:[149] his remarkable essay, already mentioned several times here, begins with a history of the subordination of color from the Renaissance to impressionism. He opens with one of Matisse's statements: "To say that color has once again become expressive is to write its history" (to Diehl, 1945, Flam, p. 99), explaining his art from fauvism on as one of overturning, as an inversion of the hierarchy via the revelation of the Orient ("In order to give color back its powers of expression, Matisse had to step outside the classic Western tradition"),[150] reminding us that Matisse thought little of Ingres's definition of drawing ("the probity of art"). Strictly speaking, there is nothing *wrong* with the demonstration, and the statements made to Diehl to which Lebensztejn refers fully support the idea that Matisse is bent on undoing all supplementarity ("To say that color has once again become expressive is to write its history. For a long time color was only the complement of drawing. Raphael, Mantegna or Dürer, like all the Renaissance painters, constructed with drawing first and then added the local color," Flam, p. 99; translation slightly modified). But by enclosing Matisse's use of color in this purely reactive logic (whereas in the same series of remarks, as was to be expected, the discussion opens onto the question of quantity and modulation in drawing [coloring without color]), one runs the risk of overlooking what constitutes the specificity of his work and his intervention in the history of art. To be fair, Lebensztejn does insist on the quantity-quality equation (alone among all of Matisse's commentators, as I pointed out), and his text is patiently constructed so as to end with the "solution" of the cutouts, which enabled Matisse to "draw directly in the color" (to Lejard, 1951, *EPA,* p. 243). But the very use of the word "solution" suggests that Matisse's long quest is still being thought of as the resolution of a conflict, and not as the suppression of the very possibility of the conflict, as a general displacement of the problematic.

Let us examine the way that deconstruction functions: Derrida tells us that its strategy is one of a "double science": "On the one hand we must traverse a phase of *overturning.* To do justice to this necessity is to recognize that in a classical philosophical opposition [as here with drawing and color] we are not dealing with the peaceful coexistence of a *vis-à-vis,* but rather with a violent hierarchy. One of the two terms governs the other (axiologically, logically, etc.) or has the upper hand. To deconstruct the opposition, first of all, is to overturn the hierarchy at a given moment. To overlook this phase of overturning is to forget the conflictual and subordinating structure of the opposition." But "to remain in this phase," continues Derrida, "is still to operate on the terrain of and from within the deconstructed system." Thus: "By means of this double, and precisely stratified, dislodged and dislodging writing, we must also mark the interval between inversion, which brings low what was high, and the irruptive emergence of a new 'concept,' a concept that can no longer be, and never could be, included in the previous regime." Thus, the new concept of "arche-writing" forged by Derrida is a concept "that *simultaneously* provokes the over-turning of the hierarchy speech/writing, and the entire system attached to it, *and* releases the dissonance of a writing within speech, thereby disorganizing the entire inherited order and invading the entire field."[151]

The reader will have recognized there, I hope, part of the argument developed here on Matisse's invention of "arche-drawing": Matisse, we might say, is a deconstructor. But his strategy is not that of canonical deconstruction, and we can even ask ourselves whether deconstruction might not be able to learn a lesson or two from the painter: grammatology begins by reversing the hierarchical opposition subordinating writing to the plenitude of speech, to the voice, to the *phoné;* then, once the reversal has been carried out, it forges the concept of "arche-writing," which "precedes" the speech/writing opposition, a concept that henceforth "invades the entire field" and governs speech just as much as it does writing proper (although its solidarity with the latter is more apparent). Had Matisse followed the same movement, after the reversal described by Lebensztejn (and aiming to lower the status of drawing and raise that of color), he would have invented a concept of "arche-color" that would have shaped his painting as well as his drawing. But it didn't happen, and it is in part because what used to be an instrument of "oppression" became in his art an instrument of "liberation," to put it crudely, that the effect of his approach was as radical and determining for the pictorial production of this century as it was. Not only does Matisse not believe in the existence of the conflict between drawing and color (the old clan struggles that have troubled criticism of French art since the eighteenth century, the fierce battles between "Rubinistes" and "Poussinnistes," between "draftsmen" and "colorists," leave him completely cold—his painting does not mark the *n*th swing of the pendulum in the history of this famous antinomy),[152] but he is only able to fully exalt his color after discovering, through his drawing, the quantity-quality equation that relegates this supposed conflict to the status of a chimera.

His letter to Signac discussing *Luxe, calme et volupté* now becomes perfectly understandable: the intolerable paradox of this canvas (and of divisionist painting in general) was that it claimed to be the liberation of color, to be expression through pure color, but drawing had not been taken into account in this liberation. The result? Drawing is still seen as inhibiting color, as being too loud ("I was no longer able to restrain my drawing, and I was tempted to put too much of it," cited above). But a further confirmation of the indissociability of drawing and color is that drawing is also "inhibited" here, reduced to just one of its functions, that of contour. The letter to Signac includes this sentence, omitted above, immediately after the self-critique concerning the gap between "linear or sculptural plasticity [*plastique linéaire ou sculpturale*]" and "color plasticity [*plastique colorée*]": "Result: the painting, especially because it is divisionist, destroys the drawing, which derives all of its eloquence from the outline."[153] Hence the overcompensation ("tempted to put too much of it"). Just as Cézanne, the other great deconstructor of this hierarchical opposition (but employing altogether different means), deplored the black outlines of neoimpressionist canvases, "a flaw that has to be forcefully resisted,"[154] so Matisse was particularly frustrated at not being able to dispense with the contours governing the color in *Luxe, calme et volupté* and his other divisionist pictures.[155] It was when the black line ceased to be the border of a compartment that is filled up with color, "à la Puvis, for example," when it became impossible to distinguish between the border and the partitioning it forms on the surface, impossible to oppose a contour to what it contains, when drawing "dominated" to the extent that spacing itself became the essential determinant of color relations, it was then that Matisse could begin to exalt color. In one (but only one) sense, "Modernism and Tradition" actually falsifies things: the discovery of the "secret of expression by color," which precedes fauvism, had only a deferred effect on Matisse's elaboration of color, an effect that can only have appeared after the fact, after the invention of "expression by [drawing]."

Kahnweiler's Lesson

If we find fault with hypotheses, just let us try to undertake history without them. We cannot say that something exists, though, without saying what it is. No matter how we may consider facts, we have already related them to concepts whose selection is far from indifferent. If we realize this, we can decide and choose among possible concepts those which are necessary to connect the facts. If we do not wish to recognize this, we abandon choice to instinct, accident, or the arbitrary; we flatter ourselves that we possess a pure empiricism that is completely a posteriori, while we have, in fact, an a priori vision that is perfectly partial, dogmatic, and transcendent.

—Fragment 226 of the *Athenaeum,* vol. 1, no. 2 (1798)

When Daniel-Henry Kahnweiler declared to Francis Crémieux, "I think my case is quite unusual and won't repeat itself very often,"[1] he was well aware of his unique experience in the history of modern culture. Not only was he a great art dealer; not only was he a courageous and pioneering publisher (the first of Apollinaire, Artaud, Leiris, Max Jacob, and many others); not only did he have a fantastic "eye" during the heroic years of cubism; but beyond that he was from early on a champion of the painting that he both loved and sold, a passionate critic whose breadth we have only begun to appreciate.

Although Kahnweiler did not write his defense of cubism until the outbreak of World War I, he had always understood his role of art dealer as a partisan and propaedeutic one. A 1912 interview shows him to be accessible, generous with explanations, and responsive to his visitor's questions.[2] We know, furthermore, that his role as interpreter of cubism went much farther, and that he assigned the titles, based on descriptions provided by the painters, to the majority of Braque's and Picasso's cubist paintings. He provided these titles to help the public "read" the pictures—"to facilitate assimilation" and "to impress its urgency upon the spectator"—that is, to prevent their erroneous interpretation as pure abstraction.[3] I will return to this metaphor of reading, which induced in Kahnweiler a real and increasingly dogmatic blindness toward abstract art;[4] what is important here is his absolute certainty from the very start of his career as a dealer: "I did not have the slightest doubt as to either the aesthetic value of these [cubist] pictures or their importance in the history of painting."[5] Kahnweiler mistakenly likened his confidence to that of the artists he defended, as for instance when he explained their decision not to exhibit in public ("They knew what they were doing, and they only wanted to do their work").[6] We have, of course, Picasso's famous "I don't seek, I find," but this is more a habitual boast than an exact description of his work process. Kahnweiler's conviction was steadfast (which the artists who sought comfort from him knew well), and his theory of art scarcely evolved from his first to his last texts. As an adolescent, he had wanted to be an orchestra conductor—an intermediary, but an organizer; the same desire, he said, drove him to become an art dealer.[7]

In a letter dated June 13, 1924, Kahnweiler wrote to his friend Carl Einstein, "I no longer wish to publish because I am an art dealer again; it no longer seems appropriate. As for my own conscience, I could publish because I buy only things that I love, but the public would see commercialism in it. Therefore, I am silent."[8] This remarkable scrupulousness explains why Kahnweiler did not devote himself to writing before the outbreak of the First World War. It accounts, as well, for the division of his theoretical work into three sections: the texts of 1915–20; the monograph on Gris written during World War II; and the abundance of articles published after the war, when he was no longer officially the dealer of the artists he was defending. This compunction further explains the minimal evolution of his theory, and its consequent blindness to new developments; one cannot abstain from writing for more than twenty years without suffering from rigidity of thought. Kahnweiler's scrupulousness, however, proved to be his good fortune, as well as ours. Because he waited until his 1915–20 exile to write, he was able to give cubism its first theoretical account of some interest, one that remains in many respects unequaled today. Kahnweiler's analysis is often so apt precisely because it was not hurried.

Kahnweiler's exile, for him a tragedy, gave him the opportunity to develop as a critic, aesthetician, and art historian.[9] At Berne, he became acquainted with various currents of neo-Kantian philosophy (Georg Simmel's sociology, for example, from which Kahnweiler quoted the extraordinary article on the problem of historical time).[10] His simultaneous discovery of the entire German aesthetic tradition after Kant, and of new developments in art history and criticism infused by this tradition, was of crucial importance. He encountered the writings of the formalist critic Konrad Fiedler, so close to Kahnweiler in many respects, as well as those of Fiedler's friend Adolf von Hildebrand, whom Kahnweiler attacked.[11] Through Wilhelm Worringer he became familiar with the work of Aloïs Riegl and Heinrich Wölfflin, who offered him concepts that enabled him to theorize the historicity of all artistic production. With Carl Einstein's work as mediation, he could analyze his interest in "Negro" art and thus elaborate a general theory of sculpture. In brief, he familiarized himself with critical tools unknown in France, and these helped him to crystallize what he had not precisely formulated during the long hours spent in his gallery at rue de Vignon.

Overall, this temporary displacement allowed Kahnweiler to become the only critic to give an intelligent account of cubism, after he had been a privileged witness to its beginnings. If we compare him to the contemporary French critics, we must ask whether any of them possessed the means to go beyond the brawling, congenial journalism of an Apollinaire (a journalism that Kahnweiler did not esteem very highly).[12] Art history was moribund in Paris (or rather, it was vitally concerned only with the Middle Ages, and not at all with the theoretical-historiographical and perceptual problems that preoccupied Kahnweiler in Switzerland). The aesthetic was the province of specialists who repeated their investigations of the beautiful or of "the harmony of the arts." None of the events in art for half a century seemed to have affected the theorists in France, whereas Wölfflin and Fiedler, for example, were influenced in their theoretical work by the emergence of impressionism, even if they did not refer to it explicitly. Even so, there was Bergson, and on the basis of several of Jean Metzinger's remarks on duration, Alexandre Mercereau and André Salmon attempted briefly to make this national glory a comrade on cubism's path (although his vitalism was a much more direct influence on Italian futurism).[13] Certainly, just like Kahnweiler, critics such as Maurice Raynal or Olivier Hourcade referred to Kant, but in such a way that Raynal, for example, found it possible to invoke him simultaneously with Berkeley, while Kant's refutation of Berkeley's "dogmatic idealism" stands as one of the most famous passages of the *Critique of Pure Reason*.[14]

Clearly, the question is not whether it is more appropriate to refer to Kant than to Berkeley in regard to cubism; either one can be cited, although not simultaneously.[15] It is more useful to locate the effects of their influences on conception, to identify what they "liberate" in the course of argument. It is therefore unnecessary to expand on Kahnweiler's Kantianism here; I wish simply to note that, unlike his peers, he was not satisfied with just mentioning the German philosopher's name (he resorts to this only once in *The Rise of Cubism*).[16] Kahnweiler read Kant by way of his followers' works—on perception, on history, on art and art history—texts that supplied him with concepts. He set these concepts in play without having to brandish their ultimate source each time like a trophy. Kahnweiler's Kantianism would have little consequence had it not been the springboard that enabled him to conceptualize cubism, just as it led him to an occasional error of appreciation. Some examples of his misjudgment were: his interpretation of the *Demoiselles d'Avignon* as an unfinished painting, due to his conception of the work of art as a coherent whole— a position that led him, in regard to Gris, to a veritable neoclassicism as early as 1929;[17] his rationalist and spatial understanding of Picasso's strange remark, "In a Raphael painting it is not possible to establish the distance from the tip of the nose to the mouth. I should like to paint pictures in which that would be possible";[18] his conception of a work of art as fulfilled in the minds of its spectators once they decode its signs and receive what he called its "message"—a position that caused him a profound uneasiness, as described in his book on Gris, before the ambiguities of "hermetic" cubism in 1911;[19] his dogmatic opposition between the beautiful and the agreeable, which led him, from his first texts, to categorically reject not only Matisse but abstract art as hedonistic decoration; and so on. There are many aspects of Kahnweiler's aesthetics that are now out of date, and not a few of them derive from a normative application of Kant (that is, a Kant reread by the neo-Kantians).

All this means that Kant is not necessarily the indispensable sesame of cubism, although he may have been for Kahnweiler. It is more important that Kahnweiler had a theory, unlike his French colleagues, and that he paid his tribute to the clichés of cubist criticism on "multiple points of view" or the "object's geometrical essence" through a body of doctrine that enabled him to arrive at other ideas. As the epistemologist Alexandre Koyré has written, "The possession of a theory, even a false one, constitutes enormous progress in comparison with the pretheoretical state."[20] For Kahnweiler, German aesthetic Kantianism authorized the emergence of a formalist criticism in the best sense of the term (attention to processes, to the means by which a work of art produces itself). The Kantianism of German art history provided him with a distinct consciousness of the historical implications of all artistic production. If we reread the astonishing text Kahnweiler wrote in 1920, "The Limits of Art History," we see that, in opposition to psychological interpretation based on analysis of the artist's hypothetical intentions, and against all positivist perception, which would abstain from evaluating facts by fixing them on the grid of a homogeneous and empty time frame, Kahnweiler proposed an almost structuralist conception of the historian's work. Historians determine their object, the historical series, "or they suffer the degeneration of history into sterile professional ratiocination." Only the constitution of this theoretical object permits critical appreciation of the work of art: "No work is too insignificant if the series's integrity is jeopardized without it; none is important enough to figure there if the series exists as complete in its absence."[21] It is of little consequence if certain assertions of this shattering text partake of the naiveté of the supposed "science of art" (*Kunstwissenschaft*) in fashion at the time; nor is it important if the historicism of these assertions appears debatable today. In combining the formalism of a Fiedler or an Einstein and the historical concepts of a Simmel or a Riegl, Kahnweiler was the only critic, until the appearance of Clement Greenberg's text dedicated to the *papiers collés* in 1958, to understand what was crucial in the evolution of cubism. He was the only critic to perceive that *Pitcher and Violin* [*Broc et violon*] (1909–10) and *The Portuguese* [*Le Portugais*] (1911), both by Braque, were essential moments in cubism's history;[22] and he was the first to comprehend that a rupture had occurred for Picasso at the time of his stay at Cadaqués during the summer of 1910. Above all, he alone recognized, although in works after *The Rise of Cubism,* that the construction titled *Guitar* [*Guitare*] (fig. 12), completed by Picasso in 1912, is at once the origin of "synthetic" cubism and of a new era in the history of Western sculpture.

I wish to pause here and examine a question that only Kahnweiler, it seems to me, truly understood: the relation between cubism and African art. We might be surprised, on rereading *The Rise of Cubism,* to find no mention of African art in relation to the *Demoiselles d'Avignon,* and scarcely one vague allusion to this art in connection with the 'Negro' period that followed for Picasso—even though Kahnweiler had discussed thoroughly at the end of the text the Ivory Coast mask (fig. 13), to which I shall return momentarily.[23] For Kahnweiler, to use Pierre Daix's expression, "there is no 'Negro' art in the *Demoiselles d'Avignon,*" or rather, if there is any borrowing it is only superficial; it concerns only African art's appearance and not its substance.[24] Kahnweiler is completely explicit on this point in his book on Gris, in his 1948 article

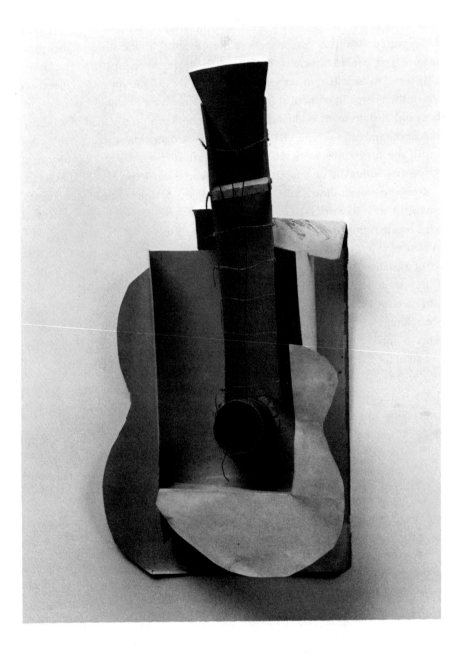

12. Pablo Picasso, Guitar [Guitare], *fall 1912. Cardboard and string (restored), 66.3 × 33.7 × 19.3 cm (26⅛ × 13⅜ × 7⅝ in.). The Museum of Modern Art, New York. Gift of the artist. Photo of the museum.*

13. Grebo Mask, Ivory Coast or Liberia. Painted wood and fiber, 64 cm high (25¹/8 in.).
Musée Picasso, Paris (formerly collection Pablo Picasso). Gift of Marina Luiz-Picasso.
Photo Réunion des Musées Nationaux.

"Negro Art and Cubism," and especially in his preface that same year for Brassaï's book of photographs, *Les Sculptures de Picasso*. As if criticizing in advance the recent Museum of Modern Art exhibition titled "'Primitivism' in Twentieth-Century Art: Affinity of the Tribal and the Modern," Kahnweiler maintains that, in spite of appearances, the formal affinities between African art and Picasso's painting in 1907–08 are illusory.[25] To summarize, so that I might in turn offer a different formulation, Kahnweiler proposes two types of formal influence: one is morphological, the other structural. We see the morphological influence of "Negro" art in the "barbaric aspect" of Vlaminck's paintings (his art "certainly shows the influence of the *appearance* of African sculptures, but not the slightest understanding of their spirit").[26] We observe, on the other hand, a structural influence in the importance of the Grebo mask, purchased in the course of Picasso's many "chasses aux nègres," for the elaboration of the 1912 *Guitar*.

In spite of Kahnweiler's and Daix's assertions, there are indeed traces of African art in Picasso's "Negro" period (figs. 14, 15), but in a certain way, Kahnweiler was right to affirm that "the 'savage' quality of those pictures can be fully explained by the influence of Gauguin's paintings and—above all—of his sculpture."[27] Kahnweiler describes a specific kind of formal borrowing, for which Gauguin's work provided the archetype. Regardless of its quality or novelty, the cubist work of Picasso's "Negro" period does not relate to African art in a fundamentally different manner from that of the formal relation posed by his 1906 *Portrait of Gertrude Stein* to the Iberian sculptures that had interested him at the time.[28]

As Jean Laude has remarked, Picasso first noticed African *masks* for two reasons: as reliefs, mixtures of painting and sculpture, they worked in the limited space that Gauguin had admired in Khmer and Egyptian art;[29] and they served as marks of psychological absence, an aspect whose interest for Picasso is part of an expressionist quest that originated in the symbolist tradition and the *fin de siècle* aesthetic[30]— Ensor, for example, inverted the absence of psychological traits on a mask's face into a sign of morbidity. When Picasso became interested in African statuary, and completely abandoned all reference to Iberian sculpture, his curiosity derived from a purely morphological-expressionistic point of view. What he sought from African objects seen at the Trocadero or bought at the flea markets were *models* for deforming anatomical proportions, for deviating from a norm. We could say, exaggerating for the sake of argument, that his method of borrowing was not fundamentally different from the way in which a mediocre proto-art-deco sculptor like Jacob Epstein employed certain formal characteristics taken from his African objects, or again, from the way in which the German expressionists worked.[31] (As Picasso, unlike others,

14. Pablo Picasso, Head of a Woman [Tête de femme], *1907–08. Oil on canvas, 73.3 × 60.3 cm (28⅞ × 23¾ in.). Private collection, New York.*

15. Fang Mask, Gabon. Painted wood, 50 cm high (18⅝ in.). Collection Vérité, Paris.

never literally copied any African object, this comparison is an obvious oversimplification. Certainly at the start, however, Picasso was more interested in the formal vocabulary than in the syntactic arrangement of this art.)

With the *Demoiselles d'Avignon,* and throughout the following two years, Picasso worked within the kind of morphological relation initiated by Gauguin. If these works are in themselves radically new, it is the sources of the "deforming canon," and their connotations, that are new, but not essentially the manner of using a model. This is what Kahnweiler meant when he affirmed that the *true* influence of African art in Picasso's work did not occur during the "Negro" period but began in 1912, after Picasso's discovery of the previously mentioned Grebo mask. Kahnweiler's insight, in saying that "the discovery of [Grebo] art coincided with the end of analytic cubism,"[32] was his understanding that henceforth the imitation of an object's specific formal traits was no longer at issue, even if in certain respects the *Guitar* resembled the Grebo mask. Rather, what was significant was the understanding of its principle, what Picasso called the "*raisonnable*" character of African sculpture.[33]

"It was the [Grebo] masks which opened these painters' eyes," wrote Kahnweiler in reference to Braque and Picasso.

> For example, the hollow of the guitar in some of Picasso's reliefs is marked by a projecting lead cylinder, in others by a plastilene cone. How can we fail to recognize in these the means (identical in the first case) by which the Ivory Coast artists create a volume whose limits they only indicate by the height of the cylinders representing the eyes?[34]

From Grebo art, Picasso received simultaneously the principle of semiological arbitrariness and, in consequence, the nonsubstantial character of the sign.

> These painters turned away from imitation because they had discovered that the true character of painting and sculpture is that of a *script*. The products of these arts are signs, emblems, for the external world, not mirrors reflecting the external world in a more or less distorting manner. Once this was recognised, the plastic arts were freed from the slavery inherent in illusionistic styles. The [Grebo] masks bore testimony to the conception, in all its purity, that art aims at the creation of signs. The human face "seen," or rather "read," does not coincide at all with the details of the sign, which details, moreover, would have no significance if isolated. The volume of the face that is "seen," especially, is not to be found in the "true" mask, which presents only the contour of that face. This volume is seen somewhere before the real mask. The epidermis of the face that is seen exists only in the consciousness of the spectator, who "imagines," who creates the volume of this face *in front of* the plane surface of the mask, at the ends of the eye-cylinders, which thus become eyes seen as hollows.[35]

Kahnweiler called this capacity to represent virtual volume in space "transparency." The term is particularly ill chosen and confusing. No surface transparency provides access to a central core of the Grebo masks or of the *Guitar* (nor to the famous *Glass of Absinth* [*Verre d'absinthe*] that Kahnweiler summoned to support his terminology). "Transparency," as well, seems to promise an immediate communicability; an idealistic dream of an art without codes, without semantic opacity; a state of apprehension where art would speak directly to the mind of the spectator. This dream is not at all what Kahnweiler proposed.[36]

"The overwhelming novelty for European sculpture of these reliefs," Kahnweiler wrote about Picasso's constructions, "consisted in that they burst open 'opaque'—so to speak—volumes. The forms of these tumblers, of these musical instruments, is in no degree *described* in its continuity; continuity arises only in the creative imagination of the spectator."[37] In order to read this sentence correctly, and to understand what Kahnweiler meant by "transparency," I believe we must refer to Carl Einstein's famous text *Negerplastik,* published in 1915, which Kahnweiler read during his stay in Berne and cited in "Negro Art and Cubism." We must also return to the remarkable article Kahnweiler wrote during those years of war, "The Essence of Sculpture" (Das Wesen der Bildhauerei), to which he referred as well.[38] For both Einstein and Kahnweiler, "Christian European sculpture" was not sculpture but rather "painting" that dared not speak its name. Adolph von Hildebrand served as a target for both, with his elevation of the compromise represented by bas-relief to the dignity of an unsurpassable ideal. For Einstein, as for Kahnweiler, Western sculpture was frontal, pictorial. What Hildebrand's theory enabled them to see was that frontality and pictorialism were aberrations resulting from *fear* of space, fear of seeing the sculptural *object* lose itself in the world of objects, fear of seeing the limits of art blur as real space invaded the imaginary space of art. Hildebrand never articulated this fear better than when he condemned the panorama, that nineteenth-century art that effectively plays with confused boundaries, or condemned the figures in wax museums, or denounced Canova's tombs (fig. 16), to which he opposed those of Michelangelo:

> Canova entirely separated his architecture from his figures, with the result that the architectural part has in itself the effect of a monument, while the figures appear to be set up in front without regard to any total spatial impression. The figures, indeed, belong more to the public than they do to the tomb; it seems as though they had just climbed up into their positions. The single bond of unity between the architecture and the figures lies in the suggested act of their entering the tomb. What is here constructed is not a picture seen, but a drama acted out: —the figures are real men and women turned to stone. . . . There is no definite line drawn between the monument and the public; —as well bring a few stone spectators on the scene![39]

I have quoted this passage at length because it explains perfectly the terror of real space that was, for Carl Einstein and Kahnweiler, Western sculpture's indelible defect (hence their severe judgments on Bernini and Menardo Rosso, on sculptural

16. Antonio Canova, Tomb of Maria Christina, *1798–1805.*
Marble, 574 cm high (225⁷/8 in.). Augustinerkirche, Vienna.
Photo Eric Garberson. The sculpted figures are life-size, as
the presence of a spectator makes clear. The fence was prob-
ably not original (Canova's various bozzetti *for this and*
other similar monuments do not bear any trace of it). The
fact that it has been felt necessary to put up such a fence is
just another sign of Canova's unorthodox confusion of the
public space and the space of art.

pictorialism at its apogee).[40] In many respects, this position is still held, and it has led the majority of critics to a fundamental misunderstanding of Picasso's cubist constructions.[41] This thesis, articulated most convincingly by Greenberg and long since adopted, is that the 1912 *Guitar* originated from "collages," meaning *papiers collés:*

> It was as though, in that instant, he [Picasso] had felt the flatness of collage as too constricting and had suddenly tried to escape all the way back— or forward—to literal three-dimensionality. This he did by using utterly literal means to carry the forward push of the collage (and of Cubism in general) *literally* into the literal space in front of the picture plane.[42]

Such a thesis—which makes the *Guitar* a painting in space, a painting become sculpture—allowed Greenberg, in another context, to argue in favor of an optical, flat, pictorial sculpture, a sculpture that remains painting and that demonstrates the identical fear of space as Hildebrand's bas-relief.[43] Above all, it denies the inaugural character of the 1912 *Guitar,* its role as the point of departure for synthetic cubism.

This classical interpretation of cubism was challenged by William Rubin in 1972, when he dated the *Guitar* as spring 1912 on the basis of conversations with Picasso. However, the painter's memories only further complicated matters. Picasso stated, in fact, that the *Guitar* preceded his first collage (*Still Life with Chair Caning* [*Nature morte au cannage de chaise*]; fig. 17) by "several months." It would therefore date from the end of 1911 or the beginning of 1912, because this last work belongs to the cycle of oval sill lifes from spring 1912.[44] This possibility seems absurd in every respect, as Picasso was, at that time, completely absorbed by the dialectic between literal surface and flat depth, so well analyzed by Greenberg, that led to the introduction of printed characters in his painting. We could counterpropose here the protean character of Picasso's career, the fact that he often worked in many directions simultaneously. However, his work from the end of 1910 up to the summer of 1912 remained more homogeneous than ever, exclusively involving "purely" pictorial problems with which the dialogue with sculpture, so important in his preceding phase, had little to do. My hypothesis is simple: Picasso confused "first collage" with "first *papier collé*" in his memory, a common confusion and quite explicable almost fifty years after the fact.[45] While the collage of spring 1912 originated from the dialectic described by Greenberg in relation to "analytic" cubism—the introduction of an *actual* element on a flat surface serving as contrast, like the printed letters of 1911–12 or the nail in Braque's "trompe l'oeil" in 1909–10—the first *papier collé* of late autumn 1912 derived from the *Guitar,* which should have been finished, as Edward Fry convincingly suggests, during the early fall.[46]

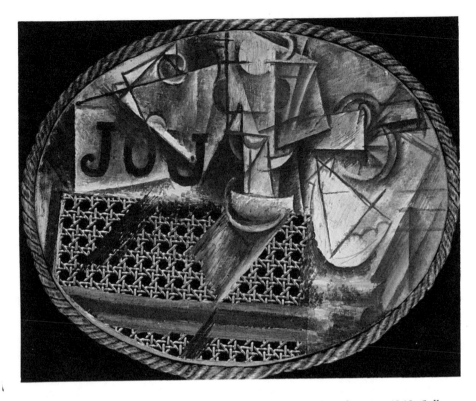

17. Still Life with Chair Caning [Nature morte au cannage de chaise], *spring 1912. Collage of oil, oilcloth, and paper on canvas, surrounded with rope, 27 × 35 cm (10⅝ × 13¾ in.). Musée Picasso, Paris. Photo Réunion des Musées Nationaux.*

Is all this chronological quibbling? On the contrary, it is a question of articulating the development of a certain formal logic (that of the "Picasso system"), and not of retracing the biography of the individual Picasso. I would like to mark indelibly the birth of a new paradigm or an epistemological break (the terminology is of little importance), to indicate the radical transformation of the ensemble of conventions that constituted the domain of plastic art until this·period—to provide by means of a formal analysis an instrument of historical inquiry. If we graft peremptorily the *Guitar* onto the problematic of the first collage, if we refuse to reconstruct the specificity of that invention, then we will not comprehend its full force and effect. We will not see that if the principal rupture in this century's art was indeed that of cubism, this break was probably not made by the *Demoiselles d'Avignon* nor by analytic cubism but in the collusion between the Grebo mask and the *Guitar*.[47] We will not perceive that from this event arose synthetic cubism, almost all this century's sculpture, and, to a great extent, the semiological investigation called abstraction. This thesis may seem excessive because it requires, at least, a rewriting of cubism's history (as well as a good part of the subsequent history of this century's art). Nor can it be understood without accepting my proposed chronology and realizing what is at stake in it. It is insufficient simply to reject Greenberg's "opticality" in order to render justice to the "objecthood" of the *papiers collés;* it is still necessary to reveal the mechanism of "Greenbergian" repression and respond to it. This repression is founded on a continuous narrative presentation of a formal problem's gradual resolution. Chronology is its backbone. To contest its chronology is to undermine the discourse's foundation. We cannot respond to Greenberg except by using his own particularly efficacious weapons.[48]

Returning to Kahnweiler, Carl Einstein, and African art: if African sculpture proposes a new solution to the problem of its inscription in space, according to Einstein, it is in the dissociation of volume from mass. This sculpture gives an instantaneous impression of volume, not due to a pictorial illusion that the unseen mass lies just behind what we see, but through abrupt visual discontinuities (see fig. 18). Einstein's essential point is that there is little or no modeling in African art (and though he does not use the term *montage,* his description of African art relies on this concept, explored by Picasso's *papiers collés* and constructions).[49] If we agree with Einstein's proposed formal reading, as Kahnweiler did, we are in a position to understand why Picasso's art could support only a morphological relation with African art during his "Negro" period. As Kahnweiler and many critics after him have remarked, the art inaugurated by *Les Demoiselles d'Avignon* strove to transcribe the volumetric properties of sculpture onto a two-dimensional surface. The question remains, what were

18. Figure, Bambara or Dogon, Mali. Wood and metal, 69 cm high (27⅛ in.). Private collection.

19. *Pablo Picasso,* Seated Male Nude
[Homme nu assis], *winter 1908–09. Oil on
canvas, 92 × 73 cm (36¼ × 28¾ in.).
Musée d'Art Moderne du Nord, Villeneuve
d'Ascq. Donation Masurel. Photo Routhier.*

the means of that transcription? If we bracket the representation as seen from its different sides, a procedure whose tradition goes back to the polemics of the Renaissance *paragone,*[50] we perceive an intensification of light-dark contrast on the surface
of solids (see fig. 19), a dramatic chiaroscuro that owes nothing to Rembrandt's "aesthetic of Bengal lights" (to quote Henri Focillon), but on the contrary exaggerates
the physical opacity of represented bodies. The illusionism of this process irritated
Picasso, who limited his "realistic" intention as much as possible by the use of multiple, contradictory light sources. He did not, however, find a means to free himself
from this process. Kahnweiler reports that in a lost painting of 1909, *Le Piano,* Picasso
tried to replace chiaroscuro by true relief, but this timid use of real shadow remained
a makeshift gesture that only brought the problem of painting back to Hildebrand's
solution.[51] Only after dissociating the contrast of shadow and light from its function
as modeling in translating sculptural qualities into painting, only after understanding
this function as one pictorial code among others, was Picasso in a position to value
African art other than as a reservoir of forms—and then to become interested in what

precisely in African sculpture owes nothing to modeling.[52] After this moment of dissociation, Picasso was able to glimpse possibilities for sculpture other than the direct carving that informed his primitivist attempts of 1907. He could then definitively thrust aside the pictorialism that he had brought to its height in the sculptures preceding his stay at Cadaqués by several months, such as the famous *Head of a Woman* [*Tête*] at the end of 1909, where "the contrast of shadow and light is systematically employed; it follows a rigorous rhythm: bright zone, dark zone, light, shadow."[53]

It is not by chance that I mention here Picasso's frustrating sojourn at Cadaqués, for Kahnweiler locates the rupture in question at that point. Picasso brought back to Paris from his summer of work several "pictures that did not satisfy him but in which rigid constructions were no longer imitations of solids in the round, but a kind of scaffolding" (fig. 20).[54] According to Kahnweiler, "Picasso had pierced the closed form";[55] chiaroscuro, if it must have a role in painting, could no longer serve to define solids. If we must wait two more years for the "true" discovery of African art, it is because the dissociation previously mentioned led Braque and Picasso first to a new analysis of Cézannean "passages" whose ambiguity drew them away from considerations of tactile space. Beginning by reflecting on the minimal conditions for the readability of pictorial signs, Braque and Picasso came to question all the qualities of these signs. Only after this comprehensive inquiry, which lasted through the period of "hermetic" cubism (of which Kahnweiler's portrait [fig. 21] constitutes one of the peaks), could Picasso experience a new interest in "Negro" art.

In order to give a more specific account of the lesson Picasso drew from the Grebo mask, and to follow Kahnweiler's thought, another text on African art, strictly contemporary with Carl Einstein's work, is particularly fecund here.[56] This work is *Iskusstvo negrov* [The Art of the Negroes], written in 1913–14 by Vladimir Markov, a painter and critic linked to the milieu of the Russian avant-garde. In spite of a certain number of clichés (due to its overreliance on Leo Frobenius), this book, posthumously published in 1919 thanks to Mayakovsky, offers a particularly striking analysis of African art. According to Markov, its three essential characteristics are: (1) its statuary's powerful sense of volume, brought about by the inorganic *arbitrariness* of its articulations (this idea resembles Einstein's, but is formulated differently); (2) the diversity and *arbitrariness* of its morphological elements (called "plastic symbolism" by Markov, and corresponding to the semiological character that struck Kahnweiler in the Grebo masks); and (3) the diversity and *arbitrariness* of its materials, whose articulation seemed to be governed by the principal of montage.[57]

This text, so similar to Einstein's in many respects, is significant in that it refers explicitly to Picasso, while Einstein was satisfied with an allusion to modern French art in general,[58] and for its triple insistence on the arbitrary character of African art's plastic system. Markov gives numerous examples of the three types of arbitrariness, which he makes explicit by a series of photographic montages that "strip" certain pieces (fig. 22). The syntax is "arbitrary" in that it no longer relies on anatomical knowledge, and therefore on the pictorial illusionism that always springs from this knowledge (the face and hair can be separated in two equal volumes, disposed on one side and the other of a cylindrical neck—an example to which we can add the protuberant quality of the Grebo mask's eyes). The vocabulary is arbitrary and, in consequence, extends to infinity because the sculptural elements no longer have need of any direct resemblance to their referent. A cowry can represent an eye, but a nail can fill the same function. From this second type of arbitrariness unfolds the third (that of materials), as well as a complete range of poetic methods that we might now call metaphoric displacements. A cowry can represent an eye but also a navel

20. Pablo Picasso, The Guitar Player [Le guitariste], *summer 1910. Oil on canvas, 100 × 73 cm (39⅜ × 28¾ in.). Musée National d'Art Moderne, Centre Georges Pompidou, Paris. Gift of Mr. and Mrs. André Lefèvre. Photo of the museum.*

21. Pablo Picasso, Portrait of Daniel-Henry Kahnweiler, *autumn 1910. Oil on canvas, 100.6 × 72.8 cm (39½ × 28⅝ in.). The Art Institute of Chicago. Gift of Mrs. Gilbert Chapman in memory of Charles B. Goodspeed. Photo of the museum.*

22. *Reliquary figure (six views), Fang, Gabon or Equatorial Guinea. Photographed by Vladimir Markov at the Musée d'ethnographie du Trocadero, Paris. From* Iskusstvo negrov [The Art of the Negroes], *1919.*

23. *Pablo Picasso,* Mask and Heads [Masque
et têtes], *1907. Pencil, 22 × 16.3 cm
(8⅝ × 6⅜ in.). Formerly collection Jacque-
line Picasso, Mougins.*

or a mouth; therefore, an eye is also a mouth or a navel. Picasso, in fact, had perceived
African art's potential for metaphoric extension as early as 1907, as we can see by a
drawing of that year where an African-Oceanian head engenders, through a simple
formal declension, a head in tears, a head-as-leaf, and a head-as-flowerpot (fig. 23).
Just before Picasso's discovery of the Grebo mask, he insisted on the possibility of
plastic metaphorization at the heart of cubism by his use of the decorator-painter's
"comb" (normally used to imitate the grain of wood) to portray the hair of the 1912
The Poet [Le Poète]. Werner Spies correctly writes that we "should like, in analogy
with Freud's 'dream work,' to speak of 'cubist work.'"[59]

It is well known that the concept of the arbitrariness of the sign, drawn from
the conventionalist linguistics of William Dwight Whitney, an American specialist in
Sanskrit, was formulated by Ferdinand de Saussure in his *Course in General Linguistics,* delivered in three years between 1907 and 1911 and published posthumously in 1916. There is indeed no chance that a young painter such as Markov
would have been acquainted with Saussure's *Course* (the book, moreover, did not
appear in Russia, at the earliest, until two years after its publication, when Markov

was already dead),[60] but this does not affect the argument I wish to pursue. Indeed, Roman Jakobson has frequently maintained that the members of the Moscow Linguistic Circle understood that an interrogation of the arbitrary character of the linguistic sign was at the heart of all modern poetry because of their knowledge of cubist works before the Revolution (and not just any cubist work, but the exceptional selections in the Shchukin and Morozov collections).[61] Jakobson expressly associates Saussure's work, after he was finally directly acquainted with it, with that of the cubist': "Arriving in Prague in 1920, I procured myself the *Course in General Linguistics,* and it is precisely the insistence, in Saussure's *Course,* on the question of relations which especially impressed me. It corresponds in a striking manner with the particular accent given by cubist painters such as Braque and Picasso, not on the objects themselves, but on their relations."[62] Markov, with his responsibilities at the center of the Union of the Youth of Petrograd, was not only necessarily abreast of the great debate that then agitated Jakobson's friends Kasimir Malevich, Mikhail Matyushin, Alexei Kruchenykh, and Velimir Khlebnikov on the possibilities of an abstract poetry, but he was also in direct contract with the future theorists of Opoyaz, Viktor Shklovsky and Osip Brik, and perhaps even with the linguist Baudouin de Courtenay, who occasionally participated in the meetings of the Union and whose studies anticipated those of Saussure.[63] What is important here is not the hypothetical meeting between Markov and a particular linguist, Saussurian or otherwise; it is that the notion of the arbitrary, even if not formulated as such, was at the heart of the debates of Russian modernity. It is equally crucial that Markov formulated this concept as such in relation to African art, and at the same time as Saussure's theoretical elaboration.

There is no space here, of course to enter into a technical exposition of Saussure's concept of the arbitrariness of the sign, as it fluctuates through the *Course* and as it has given rise to innumerable discussions among linguists, discussions that are moreover not closed.[64] A digression is, nonetheless, necessary, because it will enable us to understand what Kahnweiler had intuited. I wish to emphasize that Saussure went far beyond the conventionalist notion of the arbitrary as an absence of a "natural" link between the sign and its referent, despite the fact that his first example of arbitrariness is typically conventionalist (the simple existence of multiple languages). For Saussure, the arbitrary involves not the link between the sign and its referent but that between the signifier and the signified in the interior of the sign. His principal target was the Adamic conception of language (from Adam's performance in Genesis: language as an ensemble of names for things). This notion represents for him "what is crudest in semiology," and he qualifies it as "chimeric" because it presupposes the existence (as Whitney still does) of invariable, a priori signifieds that receive in each particular language a different formal vestment.[65] This angle of attack led Saussure to separate entirely the problem of referentiality (which he did not treat) from the problem of signification, understood as the enactment in what he called *parole* of an arbitrary but necessary link between an acoustic signifier and a "conceptual" signified.

This diagram, for example:

$$\text{objects} \left\{ \begin{array}{l} x \text{ ------ } a \\ x \text{ ------ } b \\ x \text{ ------ } c \end{array} \right\} \text{ names}$$

was false for Saussure, who added: "The true signification is a-b-c, beyond all knowledge of an effective rapport like x-a founded on an object. If any object could be the term on which the sign was fixed, linguistics would immediately cease to be what it is, from the summit to the base, and so would the human mind,"[66] that is, the very possibility of language. For Saussure, language is a form whose units are differential (whether acoustic units [signifiers], "conceptual" units [signifieds], or signs, that is, conjunctions of signifiers and signifieds)—or, in the celebrated passage from the *Course:*

> In language there are only differences. Even more important: a difference generally implies positive terms between which the difference is set up; but in language there are only differences *without positive terms.* . . . The idea or phonic substance that a sign contains is of less importance than the other signs that surround it.[67]

In the numerous references made to these lines, however, the inflection cast by the following paragraph is often omitted: "But the statement that everything in language is negative is true only if the signified and the signifier are considered separately; when we consider the sign in its totality, we have something that is positive in its own class."[66] The acoustic signifier and the "conceptual" signified are negatively differential (they define themselves by what they are not), but a positive fact results from their combination, "the sole type of facts that language has," namely, the sign. Why is this positive, when everywhere else Saussure insisted on the *oppositional* nature of the sign? Wasn't he reintroducing a substantive quality here, when all his linguistics rests on the discovery that "language is form and not substance"?[69]

Everything revolves around the concept of *value,* one of the most complex and controversial concepts in Saussure. The sign is positive because it has a value "determined (1) by a dissimilar element that can be exchanged, which we can also represent as ↑, and (2) by similar elements that are comparable:

$$\leftarrow \leftarrow \uparrow \rightarrow \rightarrow \rightarrow$$

Both elements are necessary for value."[70] In other words, according to René Amacker's formula, "(a) all value is defined in relation to the system from which it is taken, but (b) all value is necessarily determined, as well, by the use we make of it, by what we can exchange for it, that is to say, by the class of things, exterior to it, that have that value."[71] A word's value derives from its position on the two axes of language: the axis of succession, of syntagm, which is governed by grammar (for example, in a sentence), and the axis of simultaneity, or paradigm, which defines the lexicon (a group of words that could occupy the same place in the sentence). This value is absolutely differential, like the value of a hundred-franc bill in relation to a thousand-franc bill, but it confers on the sign "something positive."

To explain his concept of value (and to differentiate it from signification, or the relation between a signifier and a signified, which fluctuates as it is realized in *parole*), Saussure invoked the metaphor of a chess game, a metaphor used by Matisse at the same time for rather similar reasons.[72] If, during a game, a piece is lost—for example, if the knight is carried off to some obscure corner by a child—it does not matter what other piece replaces it provisionally; we can choose arbitrarily (any object will do, and even, depending on the players' capacity to remember, the absence of an object). For it is the piece's function within a system that confers its value (and I am tempted to say that it is the piece's position at each moment of the game that gives it its signification). "If you augment language by one sign," Saussure said, "you diminish in the same proportion the [value] of the others. Reciprocally, if only two signs had been chosen . . . all the [concrete] significations would have had to be divided between these two signs. One would have designated one half of the objects, the other, the other half."[73] Value is an economic concept for Saussure; it permits the exchange of signs (in social communication or in translation), but it prevents, as well, a complete exchangeability. (Saussure's famous example is the different values of English *sheep* and French *mouton,* for *sheep* opposes *mutton* in English. "In speaking of a piece of meat ready to be served on the table, English uses *mutton* and not *sheep*. The difference in value between *sheep* and *mouton* is due to the fact that *sheep* has beside it a second term, while the French word does not.")[74]

This concept of value, finally, is paradoxically linked to the notion Saussure called the "linguistic sign's relative motivation," which has often been misunderstood. "Everything that relates to language as a system must, I am convinced, be approached from this viewpoint, which has scarcely received the attention of linguists: the limiting of arbitrariness."[75] While in the first place, value concerns the opposition of signs to each other, "relative motivation" pertains to their "solidarity" in the system. And this solidarity, contradictory as it may seem, enters into the production of value. "*Dix-neuf* is supported associatively by *dix-huit, soixante-dix,* etc., and syntagmatically by its elements *dix* and *neuf.* This dual relation gives it a part of its value."[76] Relative motivation, however, should not be considered as a negation of the semiological principle of the arbitrariness of the sign (which we must distinguish, as Saussure did, from the linguistic sign's relatively *unmotivated* character). "In every system," as Rudolph Engler notes, "even not entirely arbitrary signs and modes of expression draw their value from rules of usage much more than from their natural expressiveness. Signs of politeness, onomatopoeias, and exclamations offer examples of this [in the *Course*]."[77] "Not only are the elements of a motivated sign themselves unmotivated (cf. *dix* and *neuf* in *dix-neuf*), but the value of the whole term is never equal to the sum of the value of the parts. *Teach* × *er* is not equal to *teach* + *er*."[78] In other words, "relative motivation" demonstrates that *not everything is possible in a given system of values,* that of each particular language. This guarantees the system's force much more than it compromises it, associating its combinatory infinitude with the rigor of its laws. In no case does it indicate unconsciously in Saussure, as it has seemed to after the awkward interventions of the *Course*'s editors, the linguistic sign's dependence on the referent.[79]

I hope to be excused for this linguistic excursion, for I believe it closely encompasses Kahnweiler's discussion of African art's *scriptural* character, discovered by Picasso in his Grebo mask and explored in his 1912 *Guitar* and the *papier collés* of the following months. It seems necessary inasmuch as the vulgar notion of the arbitrariness of the sign, which often remains simply the conventionalist view, obliterates the operative analogy here, first intuitively traced by Kahnweiler, between cubism and language.

What, in fact, did Picasso see in the Grebo mask's protuberant eyes? It is erroneous to think that he arrived only at the conventionalist conception of the arbitrariness of the sign (that there is no resemblance between these protuberant eyes and what we habitually call, after Leonardo, "the windows of the soul"). As Kahnweiler understood, Picasso became aware, more specifically, of the differential nature of the sign, of its value: the value of the plastic sign/eye as a mark on an unmarked ground, within a system that regulates its use (to recall Kahnweiler's text, "The [Grebo] masks bore testimony to the conception, in all its purity, that art aims at the creation of signs. The human face 'seen,' or rather 'read,' does not coincide at all with the details of the sign, whose details, moreover, would have no significance if isolated").[80] The traditional anatomical syntax can be set aside entirely because the sign's positive value as a semantic mark, "which depends on [the] presence or absence of a neighboring term"[81] and which allows its exchange, can be produced by any operation. Hence, Picasso's continuous exploration of the immense mutability of signs at the heart of the same system of values: the mouth can undergo a rotation of 90° and surge forward from the face, producing a disquietingly vaginal, predatory kiss, or it can be multiplied according to a metaphoric play founded on the exchange of signs (the same sort of play that Markov observed in African art).[82] This can be seen in Picasso's play on the minimum sign, prepared by all of "hermetic" cubism prior to the Grebo mask/*Guitar* conjunction and taken to an extreme in the series of *papiers collés* from spring 1913.[83] Picasso's reduction of his plastic system to a handful of signs, none referring univocally to a referent, causes their value to meet with numerous significations. A form can sometimes be seen as "nose" and sometimes as "mouth," a group of forms can sometimes be seen as "head" and sometimes as "guitar." Again, Kahnweiler writes:

> The discovery of [Grebo] art coincided with the end of analytical Cubism. The period of investigation of the external world was over. The Cubist painters now meant to represent things by invented signs which would make them appear as a whole in the consciousness of the spectator, without his being able to identify the details of the sign with details of the objects "read."[84]

We can see in this last citation, however, that the "system of values" governing Picasso's art, if not anatomical (illusionist, mimetic), remained figurative. This creates the "relative motivation" of his signs, the syntax of which the discovery of "Negro" art had liberated. The celebrated remark reported by Leo Stein ("A head . . . was a matter of eyes, nose, mouth, which could be distributed in any way you like—the head remained a head")[85] corresponds exactly to the work accomplished in the notebooks of drawings from summer and autumn 1912, at the presumed moment of Picasso's discovery of the Grebo mask and his elaboration of the *Guitar*.

Finally, and I believe this is the essential reason for the Grebo mask/*Guitar*'s inauguration of the series denoted as "synthetic cubism," Picasso realized for the first time that a sign, because it has a value, can be entirely virtual, or nonsubstantial. Here we have returned to what Kahnweiler called "transparency," which is rather an acceptance of absence, of emptiness, as a positive term.

The volume of the face that is "seen," especially, is not to be found in the "true" mask, which presents only the contour of that face. This volume is seen somewhere before the real mask. . . . The overwhelming novelty for European sculpture of these reliefs consisted in that they burst open "opaque"—so to speak—volumes. The forms of these tumblers, of these musical instruments, is in no degree *described* in its continuity; continuity arises only in the creative imagination of the spectator.[86]

As Kahnweiler clearly saw, this understanding of the sign's nonsubstantial character led Picasso to his "open" constructions. The sculpture no longer had to fear being swallowed up by the real space of objects; it could formally employ space, transform emptiness into a mark, and combine this mark with all kinds of signs. In a sense, Picasso's *Guitar* is his response to Hildebrand.[87] This is confirmed in Picasso's subsequent experiment, in which he fabricated a *papier collé* figure that emerged from its vertical support, held a real guitar in space, and extended its paper legs under an actual table, on which was arranged a still life of a real bottle, pipe, and, most important, newspaper (an actual newspaper, i.e., the object that furnished the pasted figure's raw material; fig. 24). This mixing of real space and the space of art, similar to what Hildebrand abhorred in the panorama, the wax walls, and Canova's tomb, is at the heart of cubism, of the *objecthood* that it wishes to confer on the work of art and that Greenberg's reading tends to minimize if not efface. Rather than resort to a trivial conception of the "return to reality" that the collages should have achieved (and whose vacuity Greenberg has shown so adroitly), we should consider, from the perspective of cubist semiology, how "reality" in these works (the addition of real objects, the sculpting of real space) could have been incorporated—once it had been caught in a network of differences, in a system of values, once it had been transformed into a sign. Another equally significant experiment is that of Braque's only paper sculpture of which a trace has been conserved (fig. 25). Fixed in a room's corner, the construction annexes architectural space, its real context, by what we can call an indexical contiguity. The image's field is not separated from the supporting field; the real architectural corner is simultaneously support and part of the image. This directly anticipates Vladimir Tatlin's corner *counter-reliefs*.[88]

The infinite combination of arbitrary and nonsubstantial signs at the heart of a finite system of values—this is the *raisonnable* model disclosed by African art, for which, in a certain manner, the iconographic reduction of Picasso's work (emphasized, moreover, between 1912 and 1914) was preparatory.[89] When, in a moment of irritation, Picasso declared to a journalist that the African objects scattered through-

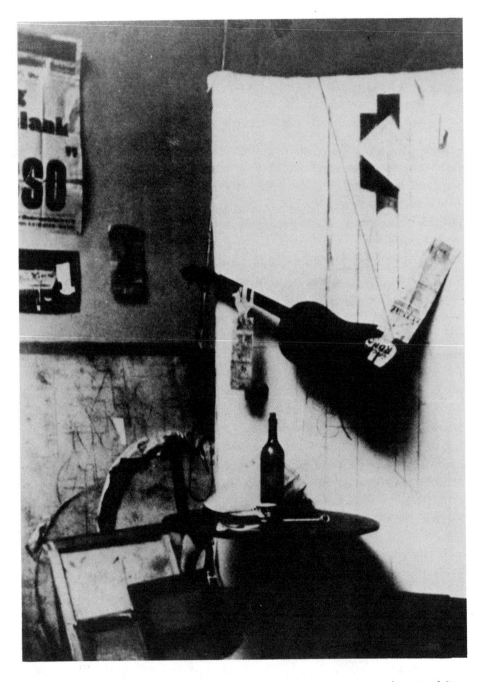

24. *Pablo Picasso,* Construction with Guitar Player [Construction au joueur de guitare] *(in Picasso's studio), 1913. Paper, guitar, and various objects; destroyed.*

25. Georges Braque, Construction (in Braque's studio), *1913. Paper and cardboard; destroyed. This is the only existing document of Braque's paper sculptures, which were all destroyed.*

out his studio were "more *witnesses* [*témoins*] than *examples*," he meant not only "witnesses" in the judicial sense but "landmark" [*borne*] and "evidence" [*preuve*] as well. The Grebo mask proved to him that it was not a sign's morphology that was important but its function, its value within a system. And Kahnweiler, I believe, was the first (other than Picasso, of course) to understand this,[90] just as he was the first to see how the 1912 *Guitar* opened up new perspectives. In a conversation reported by Kahnweiler, dated March 9, 1955, the artist described his repugnance before an exposition titled "The Creators of Cubism":

> *Picasso:* There is no cubism in all that. Everything disgusts me, my own things first of all. There is nothing good but Braque's *papiers collés* and Raynal's picture. All the rest is painting. The painted tables are even basically in perspective. What has led people astray is simply the multiple representation of objects. Whereas the *papiers collés* and the *Guitar* . . .
> *Kahnweiler:* Yet superimposed planes were no longer perspective.
> *Picasso:* No, but they were still a means of replacing it.[91]

And André Salmon, one of Picasso's closest friends during the years of cubism, relates the emblematic function that the enigmatic *Guitar,* confusing all categories, played in Picasso's studio.[92]

I have mentioned Kahnweiler's idea, expressed unflaggingly in his texts, that cubism is a writing (implying, thus, a reading). Unfortunately, he extended this metaphor to all of painting (defined as "formative writing"), and in terms of an obsolete linguistic conception. Not only did he commit a substantial error in his estimation of nonalphabetic writing and of the possibility of a pure pictogram, a concept now abandoned by the historians of writing, but again, as corollary, he stopped at an Adamic conception of language, in spite of his vivid understanding of the sign's differential nature.[93] We can only lament that he did not have access to Saussure, for the Genevan linguist's theory would have allowed him to emerge from this imprisoning contradiction. We can see this contradiction in germ in Kahnweiler's first texts, indicating that perhaps he was not so much of a Kantian after all. In fact, in spite of his use of the Kantian notion of "dependent beauty" in speaking of the viewer's recognition of the object represented in cubist work—and in spite of his refusal to see in this act of recognition (which he called "assimilation") the scene of aesthetic pleasure[94]—Kahnweiler founded his argument on an associationist theory of perception that obliged him to define "assimilation" as the final moment toward which all empirical commerce with the work of art is directed. Kahnweiler conceived cubism's "illegibility" early on as a provisional ill, its difficulty founded on a difference of degree and not of kind:

> We also understand now why a new manner of expression, a new "style" in the fine arts often appears illegible—as impressionism at its time and now cubism: the unaccustomed optical impulses do not evoke memory-images in some viewers because there is no formation of associations until finally the "writing," which initially appeared strange, becomes a habit and, after frequently seeing such pictures, the associations are finally made.[95]

The incompatibility between Kahnweiler's Kantianism and his associationism produced a rift in his discourse. This all-too-apparent rift led him to stigmatize the "naive" spectator, who "identifies the sign with the signified" when rejecting the "askew nose" of Picasso's women, while allowing him to conceive what he called the reading of the painting as this same act of identification.[96] Once the painting is "read" according to a code, it "exists" in the spectator's "consciousness" because henceforth "he will have identified the sign with the object signified."[97] In fact, Kahnweiler lacked the concept that would have made his scriptural analogy other than an analogy: that of the referent. The naive spectator does not confound the "sign" and the signified, but, like Kahnweiler and the majority of art historians and critics, confuses the signified and the referent. As a result of this logical error, Kahnweiler's text fluctuates from siding with the "naive" spectator when speaking against the "stunted aesthetes" on the "subject in Picasso"[98] or when repudiating abstract painting (which had no signified for Kahnweiler because it had no referent in the world), to becoming formalist again when insisting on the kinship between Mallarmé's project and that of synthetic cubism.

I wish to conclude at this point, for when Kahnweiler speaks of cubism and Mallarmé, he is not satisfied with simply an anecdotal connection between this or that work of Picasso and *Un Coup de dés* (the most striking of which, participating in what we can call, after Freud, the logic of cubist "wit," occurs in the *papier collé* where the title of the newspaper article, "un coup de théâtre," becomes "un coup de thé").[99] Kahnweiler links the virtuality, the nonsubstantiality of cubist signs with Mallarméan art, an art of folds, of spacing, of differentiation—of an exacerbation of the characteristics of writing, in Jacques Derrida's broad sense. He insists on the object's "vibratory suspension," on the poem's incantatory character that makes the reader a creator. He even notes the war against chance that Mallarméan poetry endeavors

26. Pablo Picasso, Guitar, Sheet Music, and Glass [Guitare, partition et verre], *late autumn 1912. Charcoal, gouache, and pasted paper, 48 × 36.5 cm (24⁵/₈ × 18¹/₂ in.). The Marion Koogler McNay Art Museum, San Antonio, Texas. Photo of the museum.*

to wage (the work's totalizing structure, the determination of elements by "rela-tions"), and links the "cubism" of Apollinaire's *calligrammes* to the importance of blank spaces in Mallarmé's work and their check on the signifier's linearity.[100] Kahn-weiler's linking of cubist painting and Mallarmé is itself a theoretical act that makes us pardon his dogmatic anathemas against abstract painting (for which even Picasso reproached him).[101] Although he certainly was not the first to make this connection (as early as 1911, Ardengo Soffici wrote in *La Voce* that Braque's and Picasso's paint-ings "have the quality of a hieroglyph that serves to write a lyric reality . . . identical to a certain extent with Stéphane Mallarmé's elliptic syntax and grammatical trans-positions"),[102] he was the first to understand its significance.

Rather than enter upon this issue in detail, which would be the subject of another article, I would like to quote these lines of Mallarmé's *Magie,* which served as a basis for Kahnweiler's connection. I cite them in relation to *Guitar, Sheet Music, and Glass* [*Guitare, partition, verre*] (fig. 26), one of Picasso's first *papiers collés,* which was completed some months after the *Guitar,* once the shock of the Grebo mask had been absorbed:

> To evoke, in deliberate obscurity, the silenced object by allusive, indirect words, that amount to a uniform stillness, admits an attempt close to creating: verisimilar at the edge of the idea solely set into play by the enchanter of letters until, indeed, some illusion equal to the gaze shim-mers. Verse, incantatory trace! and we will not deny to the circle that rhyme perpetually closes and opens, a resemblance with the fairy's or the magician's rounds amid the grass.[103]

II   Abstraction I

There are three ways of defining De Stijl, and all three are used simultaneously by Theo van Doesburg in his 1927 retrospective article on the movement:[1] De Stijl as a *journal,* De Stijl as a *group* of artists assembled around this publication, and De Stijl as an *idea* shared by the members of this group.

The first definition is the most convenient, for it is derived from a definite corpus: the first issue of the journal appeared in Leiden in October 1917, the last in 1932, as a posthumous homage to van Doesburg shortly after his death in a Swiss sanatorium. Yet the very eclecticism of the journal, its openness to all aspects of the European avant-garde, could lead one to doubt that De Stijl had any specific identity as a movement. According to this definition, everything that appeared in *De Stijl* is "De Stijl." But to rank the dadaists Hugo Ball, Hans Arp, and Hans Richter, the Italian futurist Gino Severini, the Russian constructivist El Lissitzky, and the sculptor Constantin Brancusi among the "main collaborators" of De Stijl, as van Doesburg does in his recapitulatory chart of 1927 (not to mention the inclusion of Aldo Camini and I. K. Bonset, that is, van Doesburg himself under a futurist and a dadaist guise), is to miss entirely what made the strength and the unity of the Dutch avant-garde *group.*[2]

Indeed, it is the second definition, that of De Stijl as a restricted group, that is the most commonly accepted. It establishes a simple hierarchy, based on historical precedence, between a handful of Dutch founding fathers and a heteroclite detachment of new cosmopolitan recruits who joined at various times to fill the gaps left by defecting members. Generally speaking, the founding fathers are those who signed the *First Manifesto* of De Stijl, published in November 1918: the painters Piet Mondrian and the Hungarian-born Vilmos Huszar, the architects Jan Wils and Robert van't Hoff, the Belgian sculptor Georges Vantongerloo, the poet Antony Kok (who published little), and of course van Doesburg, the *homme-orchestre,* the only real link between the members of the group and mainspring of the movement. To those names one must add that of the painter Bart van der Leck (who had already left De Stijl before the publication of this manifesto), and that of the architects Gerrit Rietveld and J. J. P. Oud (the former had not yet joined the group at this point, although he had already produced an unpainted version of the *Red and Blue Chair,* which—in its painted form—was to become the landmark of the movement; the latter never signed any collective text). The new recruits, with the exception of the architect Cornelis van Eesteren, all pursued careers independently from De Stijl and were only briefly associated with the movement when it was already approaching the end of its course. For example, the American musician George Antheil, who got his degree in avant-gardism with his score for Fernand Léger's film *Ballet mécanique;* the creators of reliefs, César Domela and Friedrich Vordemberge-Gildewart; the architect and sculptor Frederick Kiesler; and the industrial designer Werner Gräff. But despite its usefulness, this second definition turns out to be only slightly more precise than the first, based as it is on what seems to be a purely circumstantial criterion of inclusion. It cannot explain, for example, van der Leck's defection from the movement during its first year, or Wils's and van't Hoff's during the second, Oud's during the fourth, Huszar's and Vantongerloo's during the fifth, and finally that of Mondrian in 1925.

There remains therefore the third definition, De Stijl as an *idea:* "it is from the De Stijl idea that the De Stijl movement gradually developed," writes van Doesburg in his retrospective article. Although this definition seems the most vague of the three, it turns out, by its conceptual nature (as opposed to the purely empirical character of the two others), to be the most restrictive. Moreover, it is the only one that can take into account that "De Stijl" means not only "the *Style*" but even more ambitiously "*The* style." What follows is an attempt at a brief presentation of this "idea."

De Stijl was a typically modernist movement, whose theory was grounded on those two ideological pillars of modernism, historicism and essentialism. On historicism, because on the one hand De Stijl conceived of its production as the logical culmination of the art of the past, and on the other because it prophesied in quasi-Hegelian terms the inevitable dissolution of art into an all-encompassing sphere ("life" or "the environment"). On essentialism, because the motor of this slow historical process was an ontological quest: each art was to "realize" its own "nature" by purging itself of everything that was not specific to it, by revealing its materials and codes, and in doing so by working toward the institution of a "universal plastic language." None of this was particularly original, although De Stijl's formulation of this modernist theory developed quite early on. The specificity of De Stijl lies elsewhere: in the idea that a single generative principle might apply to all the arts without compromising their integrity, and moreover, that it is only on the basis of such a principle that the autonomy of each art can be secured.

Although this principle was never explicitly formulated as such by any of the movement's members, I would say that it involves two operations that I would like to call *elementarization* and *integration. Elementarization,* that is, the analysis of each practice into discrete components and the reduction of these components to a few irreducible elements. *Integration,* that is, the exhaustive articulation of these elements into a syntactically indivisible, nonhierarchical whole. The second operation rests upon a structural principle (like the phonemes of verbal language, the visual elements in question are meaningful only through their differences). This principle is a totalizing one: no element is more important than any other, and none must escape integration. The mode of articulation stemming from this principle is not additive (as in minimalism, for example) but exponential (hence De Stijl's blanket rejection of repetition).[3]

This general principle rapidly displaced the ontological question—the "What is the essence of painting or architecture"—by leading artists to consider the question of delimitation, of what distinguishes a work of art from its context. As a result, all of the De Stijl painters were interested in playing with the frame and the polyptych format: see for example *Mine Triptych (Composition 1916, no. 4)* by van der Leck (fig. 27), or *Composition XVIII* in three parts, by Theo van Doesburg (1920, Dienst Verspreide Rijkskollecties, The Hague).[4] The logic of this shift goes something like this: as a constitutive element of every form of artistic practice, the limit (frame, boundary, edge, base) must itself be both elementarized and integrated; but its integration will remain incomplete as long as the inside and the outside (which the limit articulates) lack a common denominator, that is, as long as the outside itself has not also been subject to the same treatment. Thus, De Stijl's environmental utopia, however naive it may seem to us today, was no mere ideological dream, but a corollary of the movement's general principle. However, this utopia, which is an essential motif of Mondrian's writings, did not prevent him from treating his paintings as isolated objects, as independent entities (and the same can be said for Rietveld's furniture). For the general principle had first to be realized within each individual art form, before they could be joined together and then integrated into the larger world.

De Stijl was initially a congregation of painters, to which the architects later joined (according to legend, it is this addition that compelled van der Leck to flee), and it was the painters who laid the foundation for De Stijl's "general principle."

27. Bart van der Leck, Composition 1916, no. 4 (Mine Triptych) [Mijntriptiek], *1916. Oil on canvas, 113 × 222.3 (44½ × 87½ in.). Dienst Verspreide Rijkscollekties, on loan to the Gemeentemuseum, The Hague. Photo Stedelijk Museum.*

Although only Mondrian managed to fully translate this principle into practice, with the elaboration of his neoplastic oeuvre from 1920 on, both van der Leck and Huszar contributed to its formulation.

It is known that van der Leck was the first to elementarize color (Mondrian credited his own use of the primary colors to him),[5] but he was never able to achieve the integration of all the elements of his canvases. As "abstract" as some of his paintings may seem (and through the direct influence of Mondrian on his work he almost reached total abstraction in 1916–18), he never relinquished an illusionistic conception of space. The white ground of his paintings behaves like a neutral zone, an empty container that exists prior to the inscription of forms. Thus it is not surprising that van der Leck left the movement in 1918 to "return" to figuration (the ostensible reason he gave for his desertion, that is, the invasion of the journal by architects, was only a pretext): once the other painters had solved the problem of the ground, van der Leck found that he no longer spoke the same language.

As for Huszar, a handful of compositions—among them, the 1917 cover design for *De Stijl* and a 1919 canvas entitled *Hammer and Saw* (the only painting ever to be reproduced in color in *De Stijl*)—reveal his one pictorial contribution to the movement, namely the elementarization of the ground, or rather of the figure/ground relationship, which he reduced to a binary opposition. In one of his most successful works, a black and white linocut published in *De Stijl* (fig. 28), it is impossible to discern the figure from the ground. Unfortunately Huszar stopped there and even regressed, for, like van der Leck, he was incapable of integrating other pictorial elements into his work. Having begun with the latter's illusionistic conception of space (see Huszar's 1917 painting *Composition II, Skaters,* in the Gemeentemuseum of The Hague), he returned to it in his mediocre figurative works of the 1920s. These are too often antedated by dealers, though having nothing whatsoever to do with the principle of De Stijl.

Having perfectly assimilated the lessons of cubism while he was in Paris in 1912–14, Mondrian was much faster than the other members of De Stijl to resolve the question of abstraction; thus he was able to devote all his attention to the issue of integration. His first concern, after the choice of primary colors, was to unite figure and ground into an inseparable entity, but without restricting himself to a binary solution, as Huszar had done, for this would jeopardize the possibility of a full play of color. The evolution that led him from his cubist work to his three first breakthrough canvases of 1917 (the "triptych" mentioned in note 4: *Composition in Color A, Composition in Color B, and Composition with Black Lines*), and from there to neoplasticism is too complex to be analyzed here in detail.[6] Let us simply note that Mondrian managed to rid his pictorial vocabulary of the "neutral ground" *à la* van der Leck only after he had used a modular grid in nine of his canvases (1918–19; see fig. 29). The problem Mondrian faced was the elementarization of the division of his

28. Vilmos Huszar, Composition 6, *1918.*
Linocut, printed in De Stijl *1, no. 6 (April 1918), 11.4 × 14.4 cm (4½ × 5⅝ in.).*

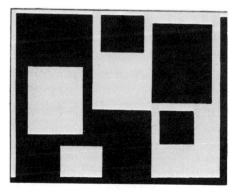

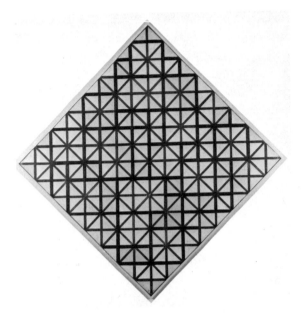

29. Piet Mondrian, Lozenge with Gray Lines [Losangique met grijze lijnen]*, 1918. Oil on canvas, diagonal 121 cm (47⅝ in.). Gemeentemuseum, The Hague. Photo of the museum.*

paintings, that is, finding an irreducible system for the repartition of his colored planes, a system grounded on one single element (hence the use of the modular grid, the module being of the same proportions as the surface of the very painting it is dividing).[7] Mondrian very quickly abandoned this device, which he found regressive because it is based on repetition and privileges only one type of relationship between the various parts of the painting (univocal engendering). But in passing the modular grid allowed him to solve an essential opposition, not considered by the other members of De Stijl, that of color/noncolor. Back in Paris by mid-1919, he spent the next year and a half ridding the canvas of the regular grid: the first truly neoplastic painting is *Composition in Red, Yellow, and Blue* (fig. 30), which dates from the end of 1920.

Van Doesburg, on the contrary, needed the grid throughout his life; for him it constituted a guarantee against the arbitrariness of the sign. Despite appearances and despite his formulations that sometimes bear "mathematical" pretensions, van Doesburg remained paralyzed by the question of abstraction: if a composition must be "abstract," it had to be "justified" by "mathematical" computations, its geometrical

30. Piet Mondrian, Composition in Red, Yellow, and Blue [Com-
position met rood, geel and blauw], *1920. Oil on canvas, 51.5 ×
61 cm (20½ × 23⅝ in.). Stedelijk Museum, Amsterdam. Photo of
the museum.*

configuration had to be *motivated*. Before he arrived at the grid formula (through
his work in decorative art, especially stained-glass windows), this obsession made
him hesitate for a long time between the pictorial system of Huszar (see van Doesburg's *Composition IX—Cardplayers* of 1917, Gemeentemuseum, The Hague) and
that of van der Leck (*Composition XI*, 1918, Guggenheim Museum). Then it led him
to a concern with the stylization of natural motifs (a cow, a portrait, a still life, or a
dancer as, for example, in *Rhythm of a Russian Dance* [1918], for which all the
sketches remain in the Museum of Modern Art in New York). He even tried for a short
period to apply this type of "explanation" to his modular works (as in the absurd
presentation he made, in 1919, of his *Composition in Dissonances* as an *abstraction
from* "a young woman in the artist's studio" [fig. 31]).[8] But this was a false trail, for
if van Doesburg was seduced by the system of the grid, it was for its repetitive and
further for its *projective* nature (since it is decided beforehand and applied *onto* the
picture plane whose material characteristics are of no importance). That is, for the
very reason that led Mondrian to consider this system foreign to the De Stijl idea, thus
to abandon it.[9] Hence the famous quarrel about "Elementarism" (the extremely inap-

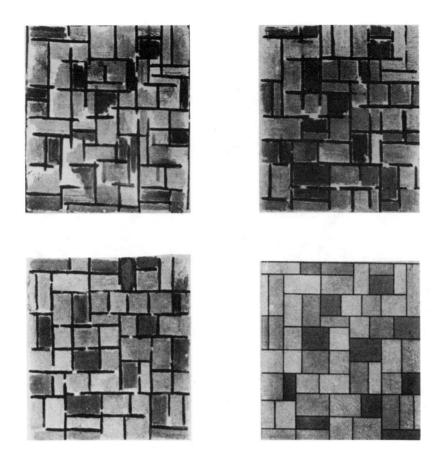

31. *Theo van Doesburg,* Studies, *1919. This sequence was first published by van Doesburg in* De Hollandsche revue *24, no. 8 (1919) as illustration for one of his articles, entitled "Van 'natuur' tot 'kompositie'" [From Nature to Composition]. It was again chosen by him as an illustration for the first sympathetic and lengthy study ever devoted to De Stijl (Friedrich Markus Huebner, "Die Holländische 'Styl-Gruppe,'"* Das Feuer *2, no. 5 (Oct.–Nov. 1921), pp. 267–278; each of the eight images bears the caption "Mädchen im atelier" [Young Woman in the Studio]). The last image of the sequence is* Composition in Dissonances [Compositie in dissonanten]*, 1918. Oil on canvas, 63.5 × 58.5 cm (25 × 23 in.). Oeffentliche Kunstsammlung, Basel. The dimensions and whereabouts of the six studies are unknown.*

Many works by Van Doesburg dated from 1917 to 1920 are acknowledgedly based on studies from nature, gradually "abstracted." But even after he had abandoned this process under the influence of Mondrian, he retained in the publications of his earlier works the "pedagogical" device of the linear sequence starting from a photograph and ending with a geometrical painting. He used it as late as in his Bauhaus book (Grundbegriffe der Neuen Gesteltenden Kunst *(Munich: Albert Langen, 1925; English tr. Janet Seligman,* Principles of Neo-Plastic Art *[London: Lund Humphries, 1968]), where he "explained" in such a manner the elaboration of* Composition VIII (The Cow)*, 1917 (Museum of Modern Art, New York).*

32. *Theo van Doesburg,* Counter-composition XVI in Dissonance, *1925. Oil on canvas, 100 × 180 cm (39⅜ × 70⅞ in.). Gemeentemuseum, The Hague. Photo of the museum.*

propriate word chosen by van Doesburg to label his introduction of the oblique into the formal vocabulary of neoplasticism in 1925, as for example in his *Counter-composition XVI in Dissonance* of the same year [fig. 32]). As is well known, it is this quarrel that led Mondrian to leave De Stijl in 1925. But if Mondrian violently rejected van Doesburg's "improvement," as the latter referred to it, it is not so much because it disregarded the formal rule of orthogonality (which he himself had broken in his own "lozangique" canvases, as he called them) as because in a single stroke it destroyed all the movement's efforts to achieve a total integration of all the elements of the painting. For as they glide over the surface of the canvas, van Doesburg's diagonals reestablish a distance between the imaginary moving surface they inhabit and the picture plane, and we find ourselves once again before van der Leck's illusionist space. For an evolutionist like Mondrian, it was as if the clock had been turned back eight years. In short, although van Doesburg's achievement in painting is very interesting, it does not partake of the general principle of elementarization and integration that characterizes De Stijl. However, there are two areas in which he did work much more efficiently toward the elaboration of this principle, that of the interior as art, and that of architecture.

The importance given to the *interior* by the De Stijl artists stems both from their questioning of the limits of painting and from their distrust of any kind of applied art. The common view of De Stijl as a movement that applied a formal solution to what is now referred to as "design" is erroneous: decorative art in general did not interest the De Stijl artists, with the temporary exception, in the case of van Doesburg and Huszar, of stained glass (which Rietveld judged moreover as "ignominious").[10] If the arts were to remain faithful to the principle of De Stijl, then they could not simply be applied to each other, but would eventually have to join together to create an indivisible whole. The stakes were quite considerable, and almost all the movement's internal quarrels resulted from a power struggle between painters and architects over precisely this issue. The invention of the interior as a hybrid art form was not easy; it developed in two moments, in two theoretical movements.

The first movement: only when an art has defined the limits of its own field, only when it has achieved the greatest possible degree of autonomy and discovered the artistic means specific to itself, that is, only through a process of self-definition and of differentiation from the other arts, will it discover what it has in common with another art. This common denominator is what allows for the combination of the arts, for their integration. Thus the members of De Stijl thought that architecture and painting could go hand-in-hand today because they share one basic element, that of planarity (of the wall and of the picture plane). As van der Leck wrote in March 1918 (and one could cite many similar declarations from the same period by van Doesburg and Mondrian, as well as the text Oud published in the first number of *De Stijl*):

> Modern painting has now arrived at the point at which it may enter into a collaboration with architecture. It has arrived at this point because its means of expression have been purified. The description of time and space by means of perspective has been abandoned: now it is the flat surface itself that transmits spatial continuity. . . . Painting today is architectural because in itself and by its own means it serves the same concept as architecture—space and the plane—and thus expresses "the same thing" but in a different way.[11]

From this first movement stems the totality of van der Leck's mostly unrealized interior coloristic projects, the first interiors of Huszar and van Doesburg (see fig. 33), Mondrian's Paris studio and his *Projet de Salon pour Madame B . . . , à Dresde* of 1926 (fig. 34). These works share a conception of architecture as static: each room is treated in isolation, as a sum of walls, a six-sided box, which is explicable by the fact that in each case the artist was working within the confines of an already existing architecture.

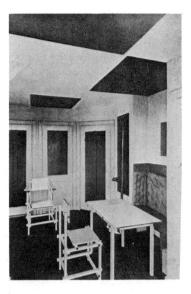

33. Theo van Doesburg, Example of Coloristic Composition in an Interior [Proeve van kleurcompositie in intérieur], *1919. Published (in black and white) in* De Stijl *3, no. 12 (November 1920). The colors of this interior composition (realized for the anarchist philosopher Bart de Ligt, with furniture by Rietveld) were orange, green, and blue. However, when van Doesburg published this photograph in color (in* L'Architecture vivante *3, no. 9 [1925], special issue on De Stijl) he corrected the color scheme so as to match the red, blue, and yellow neoplastic orthodoxy.*

34. Piet Mondrian, Salon de Madame B . . . , à Dresden, *1926. Ink and gouache on paper, 37.5 × 57 cm (14⁹/16 × 22⁷/16 in.). Staatliche Kunstsammlungen, Dresden.*

35. J.J.P. Oud, De Vonk, Noordwijkerhout, *1917–18. Illustrated in* Klei, *no. 12 (1920). The color scheme of the window frames, doors, and shutters and the tile triptych above the entrance are by van Doesburg.*

The second movement is the consequence of a collaborative enterprise turned sour, the first genuine collaboration between a painter and an architect of the De Stijl group, that is, van Doesburg and Oud's teamwork for the *De Vonk* vacation house of 1917 (at Noordwijkerhout), and later for the *Spangen* housing complex at Rotterdam (1918–21). If this collaboration resulted in divorce (Oud refusing the last coloristic projects of van Doesburg for *Spangen*), it is because, despite van Doesburg's heroic attempt to integrate color into architecture (throughout each building, both inside and out, doors and windows are conceived according to a contrapuntal color sequence), the mediocrity of the architecture itself (fig. 35) led the painter to plan his color scheme independently from the constructive structure of the building. This color scheme was conceived in relation to the entire building, the wall no longer being the basic unit, and in opposition therefore to individual architectural elements.[12] There is a paradox here: it was precisely because Oud's symmetrical, repetitive architecture was absolutely antithetical to the principle of De Stijl that van Doesburg was drawn to invent a type of *negative* integration based on the visual abolition of architecture by painting. (With the exception of his *Project for the Purmerend Factory* of 1919 [fig. 36], strongly influenced by Frank Lloyd Wright, Oud's early work is characterized by repetition and symmetry; his contribution to De Stijl is thus limited to a few theoretical pieces in the journal).[13]

"Architecture joins together, binds—painting loosens, unbinds," van Doesburg wrote in 1918.[14] Thus, the "elementarist" oblique, which appears for the first time in a 1923 van Doesburg color study for a project for a "university hall" by van Eesteren

36. *J.J.P. Oud,* Project of a Factory in Purmerend, *1919. Pencil and watercolor on paper, 37.1 × 64.2 cm (14⅝ × 25¼ in.). Nederlands Documentatiecentrum voor de Bouwkunst, Amsterdam. Photo of the museum.*

37. Cornelis van Eesteren, with color by van Doesburg, Interior Perspective of a University Hall, *1921–23. Ink, tempera, and collage on tracing paper, 63.4 × 146 cm (25 × 57¼ in.). Van Eesteren-Fluck & van Lohuizenstichting, Amsterdam.*

(fig. 37), a year later in van Doesburg's design for a "flower room" in the villa Mallet-Stevens built in Hyères, and finally, on a grand scale, in the 1928 *Café Aubette* in Strasbourg, is each time launched as an attack against a preexisting architectural situation. While the oblique contradicted De Stijl's integration principle within the realm of painting, it fulfilled that principle in the new domain of the abstract interior. There, it is not "applied"; rather, it is an element with a function (ironically, an antifunctionalist one), that of the camouflage of the building's horizontal-vertical skeleton (its "natural," anatomical aspect). Such camouflage was, for van Doesburg, absolutely necessary if the interior was to work as an abstract, nonhierarchical whole.

But the oblique was not the only solution to his new integrative task, as Huszar and Rietveld demonstrated in their extraordinary Berlin Pavilion (1923; fig. 38): the articulation of architectural surfaces (walls, floor, ceiling) could itself be elementarized by using the corner as a visual agent of spatial continuity. In this interior, colored planes painted on the walls do not stop where the wall surfaces meet, but overlap, continue around the corner, creating a kind of spatial displacement and obliging the spectator to spin his body or gaze around. Stretching to the utmost its own possibilities, painting solves a purely architectural problem—circulation in space. Conversely, as the architectural space was not preexisting, this project of a pavilion marked the birth of an architectural problematic that would become proper to De Stijl (it is hardly coincidental that this is a piece of exhibition architecture,

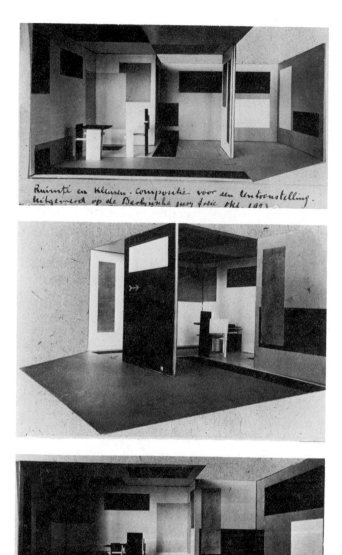

38. *Gerrit Rietveld and Vilmos Huszar,* Spatial Color Composition for an Exhibition [Ruimte en Kleuren-compositie voor een
tentoonstelling], *Berlin, 1923. Three views of the model for the
Berlin Pavilion (it is not certain that this abstract interior was
ever realized). Photo Stedelijk Museum, Amsterdam.*

engaged explicitly in demonstrating its own modernity). No better proof could have
been provided of the proposition that the union of the arts can be achieved only
when each has arrived at the greatest degree of autonomy.

De Stijl's contribution to architecture is quantitatively far less important than
is generally believed: the two little houses Robert van't Hoff built in 1916 (before the
foundation of the movement) are amiable and talented pastiches of Wright; Jan Wils's
constructions flirt somewhat with art deco (it is not by chance that he leaves the
movement almost immediately); as for Oud, his most interesting architectural work,
executed after he had broken with van Doesburg, partakes much more of the Neue
Sachlichkeit so-called International than of De Stijl (one could even say that its functionalism annuls whatever superficial features it might have of De Stijl's idiom). De
Stijl's architectural contribution consists in fact of the projects exhibited by van Doesburg and van Eesteren in *Galerie de l'Effort Moderne,* (see fig. 39) directed by Leonce
Rosenberg (Paris, 1923), and in the work of Gerrit Rietveld as a whole.[15]

As for the Rosenberg projects, a somber argument over attribution initiated by
van Eesteren has confused the issue for too long. Attribution here is a wrong question, or a question badly asked: what is essential is that there is a striking formal difference between the first project (an elegant *Hôtel particulier* that anticipates the
International Style by several years) and the last two (a *Maison particulière* and *Maison d'artiste*). For the difference is the direct consequence of the intervention not
of the painter (who worked on all three), but of painting: the model of the first project is white, the last two are polychrome. The starting point of those last projects was
indeed the possibility of conceiving simultaneously their coloristic and spatial articulation. And van Doesburg's inflated yet enigmatic claim that, in these projects, color
becomes "construction material" is not simply rhetorical: it is color indeed that
allowed the wall surface as such to be elementarized, culminating in the invention
of a new architectural element—the indivisible unit of the *screen*. The entire architecture of the last two Rosenberg projects, as the groundbreaking axonometric drawings van Doesburg executed for the show demonstrate (fig. 40), stem from the
limitation of the constructive vocabulary to this new element, the screen. For the
screen combines two contradictory visual functions (in profile it appears like a van-
ishing line, frontally it is a plane that blocks spatial recession), and this contradiction
promotes the visual interpenetration of volumes and the fluidity of their articulation.
Thus, the desire to integrate painting and architecture, to establish a perfect coincidence between the basic elements of painting (the color planes) and architecture
(the wall), led to a major architectural discovery—walls, floor, ceiling as surfaces

39. View of the Exhibition Les architects du Groupe "de Styl," *Paris, Galerie de L'Effort Moderne (Leonce Rosenberg, director), 1923. Photo Nederlands Documentatiecentrum voor de Bouwkunst. In the foreground, one can see the first Rosenberg model by van Does-burg and van Eesteren* (Private Villa [Hotel particulier]), *with its ground plans displayed on the wall. Behind it is the third model,* House of an Artist [Maison d'artiste]. *On the other wall one can recognize Oud's* Project of a Factory, *and in front of it a model for a "tramway shelter with a florist kiosk" by Willem van Leusden, who was very briefly associated with De Stijl. In the second room, there are works by Huszar and Rietveld.*

40. A: *Cornelis van Eesteren and Theo van Doesburg*, Axonometric Projection of a Private House [Architecture vue d'en haut], *1923. Ink, gouache, and collage (sand paper), 57 × 57 cm (22⁷/₁₆ × 22⁷/₁₆ in.). Van Eesteren-Fluck & van Lohuizenstichting, Amsterdam. Photo Nederlands Documentatiecentrum voor de Bouwkunst.* B: *Theo van Doesburg,* Counter-construction [Analyse de l'architecture], *1923. Pencil and ink on tracing paper, 50.2 × 35.5 cm (19³/₄ × 14 in.). Nederlands Documentatiecentrum voor de Bouwkunst, Amsterdam. Photo of the museum.*

While the first illustration shows how van Doesburg applied his color scheme on an axonometric drawing made by van Eesteren (after they had designed the house together), the second explains the process of the formation of the many "counter-constructions" related to this project: van Doesburg "edited" van Eesteren's drawing while tracing it, choosing to keep or delete certain elements so as to enhance his "analysis of the architecture."

without thickness that can be duplicated, or unfolded like screens and made to slide past one another in space (see fig. 41). Once invented, the screen had no further need of its chromatic origins: thus, the only genuinely De Stijl element in the white studio-house van Doesburg built for himself at Meudon just before his death is a rectangle that completely masks the stairway leading to the first-floor entrance, and that becomes a second skin for the façade it almost entirely repeats.

Van Doesburg was not mistaken when he claimed that Rietveld's Schröder House (1924; fig. 42) was the only building to have realized the principles theoretically laid down in the last two Rosenberg projects,[16] with the provision that the screen is used there in a much more extensive way, for Rietveld managed to elementarize what had remained a bête noire for van Doesburg, that is, the building's frame itself. The Rosenberg projects treat the frame from a constructive perspective (for which van Eesteren claims responsibility). That is, the frame is still treated as "natural," anatomical, motivated, and above all functional. While the elementarization of the wall surface had led van Doesburg and van Eesteren to make intensive use of overhanging horizontal planes (the cantilever is one of the most distinctive formal features of the Rosenberg projects), Rietveld's invention was to displace the cantilever to the level of the frame itself. In doing so, he ironically subverted, most of the time by a minimal transformation, the opposition supporting/supported upon which every constructive frame is based. The Schröder House is full of those inversions that continually pervert the functionalist ethic of modernist architecture—the dictum that would have one meaning per sign (the most famous is the corner window that, once opened, violently disrupts the structural axis constituted by the intersection of two walls [fig. 43]). Rietveld's furniture is based on the same model: in the famous *Red and Blue Chair* of 1918 (fig. 44), for example, one of the vertical elements is both supporting (it bears the armrest) and supported (it hangs off the ground).[17] Whether architecture or furniture, Rietveld understands his works as pieces of sculpture (and these are often very similar to the best sculptures of Vantongerloo), that is, as independent objects in charge of "separating, limiting and bringing into a human scale a part of unlimited space," as he wrote in an autobiographical text of 1957.[18] This is in direct opposition to Mondrian, for whom the three-dimensional nature of architecture was its inherent flaw, but also to the entire body of texts on the interior in the early numbers of *De Stijl,* which focused on architecture as closure.

41. *Theo van Doesburg and Cornelis van Eesteren,* Model, House of an Artist, *1923. This photomontage, by van Doesburg, was first published in* De Stijl 6, no. 6/7 (1924). *Photo Dienst Verspreide Rijkscollecties, The Hague.*

42. Gerrit Rietveld, Schröder House, 1924, Utrecht.

If Rietveld is the only De Stijl architect properly speaking, it is because he was able to substitute for the functionalist ethic another one, which Baudelaire in his time had called the "Ethic of Toys."[19] Everything is deployed in such a way as to flatter our intellectual desire to dismantle his pieces of furniture or architecture into their component parts (and there is in fact a photograph showing all the elements that are necessary to build the *Red and Blue Chair*);[20] but like Baudelaire's infant, who takes the toy apart in order to locate its "soul," we would learn nothing from this operation (probably not even how to reassemble the parts), for the "soul" in question resides elsewhere—in the articulation of these elements, in their integration.

43. *Gerrit Rietveld, Schröder House, 1924.*
Detail of the corner window. Once open,
the window destroys the axis joining two
façades. This break is doubled by the roof
that hovers over it in a decentered manner.

44. *Gerrit Rietveld,* Red and Blue Chair,
1918. Painted wood, 86 × 63.8 × 67.9 cm
(33⁷⁄₈ × 25¹⁄₈ × 26³⁄₄ in.). Stedelijk
Museum, Amsterdam. The first model of this
chair, designed prior to Rietveld's acquain-
tance with De Stijl, was uncolored. The
color was applied after 1920. Photo of the
museum.

Strzemiński and Kobro: In Search of Motivation

Some works appear too early and make a comeback too late, their very pre-cocity interfering—and continuing to interfere—with their reception. The belated discovery of such works plunges us into a state of confusion: we confront them the same way we would confront an improbable species that does not fit comfortably into the categories of our evolutionist reading of natural history. Władysław Strzem-iński's and Katarzyna Kobro's texts and works from the '20s and '30s belong to this category. We would wish to call them "seminal," so much do they seem to have directly influenced the art and aesthetics of the '60s. But this is impossible, since they have been condemned to a double oblivion. First, as part of the Eastern European avant-garde, they were tightly covered up with the lugubrious lid of stalinization (this is common enough and I do not need to say more on this point, but in their case this oblivion was abetted by the Nazi destruction—only about 15 of Kobro's sculptures have survived, 6 of which are reconstructions). Second, their work was ignored by artists and critics in the West who would later ask the same questions and often adopt the same solutions, despite the fact that, with Gomulka's return to power in 1956, nothing prevented the rediscovery of this work. "*Re*discovery" is slightly inaccurate, in fact, for in comparison to those of the Russian avant-garde of the '20s the ideas and works of the Polish avant-garde had not circulated very widely in Europe prior to World War II.

Given the historicist bias of our aesthetic judgment, our first impulse is to "rehabilitate" Strzemiński's and Kobro's work, and to contest the novelty of what was produced later—to argue, for example, that Yves Klein invented nothing with his monochromes, or that Frank Stella was truly presumptuous in claiming that Euro-pean art had never been anything more than a balancing act ("You do something in one corner and balance it with something in the other corner").[1] However well-intended such rehabilitation may be, it has the perfect uselessness of an academic

45. Władysław Strzemiński, Architectonic Composition 9c, *1929. Oil on canvas, 96 × 60 cm (37³/₄ × 23⁵/₈ in.). Museum Sztuki, Łodz. Photo of the museum.*

debate. For we "discover" Strzemiński and Kobro at a time when the system of values we call modernist has floundered—a system that they themselves formulated very precisely, some 30 years before the theories that are more familiar to us. So that rehabilitation is no longer the order of the day; what *is* in order is an attempt to understand the causes, mechanisms, and effects of the mortal crisis, or declared death, of modernism (which means, by the same token, the necessity to reexamine its history).

It is precisely this task that a close reading of Strzemiński and Kobro's work and theory, which they baptized *unism,* can help us to achieve. Why? Because the historicism that makes us evaluate works of art as a function of their date, that is, of their position within an unbroken chain of events, this very historicism was an essential condition of modernism. Because our disarray in front of their works and their texts, itself the product of a theory of history they had coined better than others, should help us understand that this theory is wrong (that history is not linear and that temporalities are not synchronous), and that it is partly because modernism was explicitly grounded on such a theory that it is nowadays in crisis and might have reached the end of its course.

The fact that the oblivion to which they have been consigned continues is itself instructive and can no longer be explained by circumstances alone. Their works have been exhibited widely during the past 15 years in the major museums of modern art in the West. Both were represented in the 1976 exhibition "Constructivism in Poland," which appeared in four U.S. museums, including the Museum of Modern Art in New York; Kobro's work was markedly featured in the exhibition "The Planar Dimension," organized by Margit Rowell at the Guggenheim Museum in 1979; a good selection of their writings has been available in English since 1973 and a larger one in French since 1977. Still, there has been no serious study of their work in the West, no critical evaluation.[2] This lasting oblivion, it seems to me, stems from the specific historical situation of these texts and works, a situation of "in between" that obliges us to periodize history differently and to rid ourselves of such traditional conceptual tools as genealogy, influence, and style.

Strzemiński's and Kobro's texts are dense. They are also singularly consistent: there was no radical theoretical modification between 1922 and 1936, that is, during the whole period one could call "the unist adventure" (the anthology of their texts published in French by Antoine Baudin and Pierre-Maxim Jedryka covers exactly this time span, framed by the first and last texts Strzemiński wrote before the war).[3] Of course, one can observe mild inflections over the years—and in his introduction Baudin shows how those inflections are tied, directly or indirectly, to the social and political history of Poland. But the fundamental question raised in these texts remains the same. This question is the main vector of the theory of art we call the modernist theory, a theory whose initiator was Baudelaire but that only got its label with the appearance of "abstraction" in painting. And if those texts help us to better frame the question, and thus to understand the relative "failure" of the answers that were proposed in time, a "failure" whose measure is given today by the difficulty we find in mourning modernism, it is because of the strange "in-between" situation I just mentioned.

In a few words: the modernist theory had two major moments during this century (they are not the only moments, but all others proceeded from them, either by derivation or by confrontation). The first moment, itself derived from cubism, reached its apogee at the beginning of the '20s, just before the academic "return to order" of those very same years; the second moment climaxed in the '60s. It is the texts of the first nonexpressionist abstract *painters* that constituted the first theoretical corpus (Malevich's and Mondrian's writings are here the paragons); the writings of the so-called "formalist" American *critics,* that is, of Clement Greenberg and those who proceeded from his work, constituted the second corpus.[4] No doubt because it was the product of critics and not of artists, the second wave of modernist theory wished to be rationalist, positivist: one gained in clarity (the mystical tone that emanated from Mondrian's or Malevich's texts disappeared), but one lost the scope of vision. (The work of art is no longer for Greenberg an epistemological model, the metaphoric announcement of a future classless society, but a specific answer to a given formal problem.) Now, the rarity of Strzemiński's and Kobro's texts stems from the fact that they partake simultaneously of those two theoretical sets (not chronologically, of course, for they are just about contemporaneous with the first wave, but logically). This hybrid situation leads these texts to displace constantly the position of either theoretical series and, moreover, to emphasize via these displacements what was their common question. What those texts teach us remarkably is that modernism in the broad sense of the term was not merely an operation of ontological reduction—Greenberg's canonical interpretation—but rather a vast enterprise of motivation, of *motivation of the arbitrary.*

That essentialism and historicism are two strategies of motivation, and are the two fundamental strategies of the modernist discourse, we can certainly read between the lines of Greenberg's essays, as well as of those who followed him. But if this axis of motivation is more manifest in Strzemiński's and Kobro's writings, it is because in becoming rationalist their theory did not abandon a third strategy of motivation, which was specific to the first moment of the modernist theory, that is, utopia. Moreover, this third strategy caps the other two, motivates them in turn. Strzemiński's and Kobro's essentialism was never simply an aesthetic program (pursuit of degree zero, of the specificity of each art); it was, rather, articulated onto a social program and found its "justification" in the history of the social division of labor.[5] Charged with a historical function, their essentialism was formulated with the utmost seriousness: they did not share Mondrian's horror of three-dimensionality (which the Dutch painter condemned as the fatal flaw of architecture and sculpture); nor did they treat as a liability the fact that sculpture belongs to the same space as ordinary objects—the space of everyday life—as Greenberg would in the '60s. On the contrary, this was for them the essential condition of sculpture itself, what must be magnified and worked through. For a Mondrian or a Greenberg, the plea for medium-specificity remained vastly rhetorical (they judged architecture or sculpture according to pictorial criteria); for Strzemiński and Kobro it was the key point of their theory and practice. But if their "laocoönism" is among the most incisive, it is because it was a primary aspect of their utopian teleology: "the aim of modern painting and sculpture is . . . a creative experiment, an invention of form, which stimulates the growth of opportunity provided by daily life";[6] but, like all experiment, artistic experiment is elaborated upon, and is the function of, conditions that are each time specific. Not to consider the specific properties of each art was, in their view, to repeat the past rather than extend it, to adopt ready-made solutions, to ignore the properties of materials and to project onto them instead an a priori vision, to impose upon art a "universal system," a transcendental content. Hence their criticism of the baroque's indifference to materials, of the use of proportional grids in Renaissance painting, or of what they called Malevich's "universalism."[7] Because the essentialism of the theoreticians of unism is an integral part of their utopianism, it is exacerbated. From those essentialist premises, Strzemiński and Kobro were perhaps the only modernist artists to isolate and define four different arts (painting, sculpture, architecture, typography), *without making any one of them dependent upon any other*.[8] Even more importantly, their utopianism led them to question this exacerbated essentialism, forced them to refine it (one strategy of motivation working "against" another, dialecticizing it). Although he defined pictorial investigation as a quest for the "natural essence" of painting (absolute flatness), Strzemiński was aware that the object he sought was a myth:

> Two-dimensional, atemporal space is a fiction, as is the one-dimensional space used to measure all dimensions (meter, cubit, etc.). The fact that the meter, the ideal one-dimensional space, does not exist—that we never find ourselves in this space—does not mean that this fiction (if indeed it is one?) is unproductive.[9]

A *fiction:* must I insist on the intelligence of this critical distancing? Again I hold this as a symptom of the "in-between" situation mentioned above. Neither a Mondrian nor a Greenberg would have accepted a relativization of their credo in this manner, that is, its historicization.

It is at this juncture that the displacement produced by this "in-between" situation of Strzemiński's and Kobro's texts in the realm of modernist historicism must be examined. First, let us look at the similarities: much the same way neoplasticism was for Mondrian the necessary culmination of the whole art of the past, unism for its theoreticians is the result of what they call the "visual acquisitions," and is situated at the end of a chain that comprises impressionism, cubism, and suprematism. For Strzemiński and Kobro as for Greenberg, a work of art derives its meaning only from the way it measures up to its recent past, to its present (the measurement of the topicality of a work of art is that of a perfection that is accessible only today"),[10] and to its future ("only the ulterior artistic evolution will provide the justification of current abstract art").[11] But even if Strzemiński considers abstract art as the resultant of an evolutionist line, as "the synthesis, the crystallization of the visual acquisitions" of the precedent artistic movements,[12] he never thought, as Mondrian or Greenberg did, that he was telling the *truth* of the art of the past. For a Mondrian, painting had always already sought abstraction—only it had not been conscious of it because this desire was "veiled" by the charm of "appearances." For Greenberg, modernist art shows us that if our ancestors were right to appreciate the art of "Leonardo, Raphael, Titian, Rubens, Rembrandt and Watteau," they "often gave wrong or irrelevant reasons to do so."[13] Nothing as naive appears in the texts of Strzemiński and Kobro. Their evolutionism is not blind to the scansions of history. If Strzemiński is perfectly aware of the difficulty of breaking totally with one's tradition (which is why one must not merely repudiate it),[14] he is far from conceiving a kind of atemporal universality that would negate the specificity of this tradition. His extraordinary formal analyses led him to regard Cézanne's art and cubism, as strange as that might seem at first, as offspring of the baroque tradition that, for him, it was essential to eradicate. But such a reading never drove him toward an undifferentiation of the criteria of judgment in history. On the contrary, unlike what will be the case for unism, "A picture that contained little contrasts, that was in agreement with its innate qualities and with itself—was a dull picture from the baroque point of view."[15] The elaboration of a typology of formal systems that were adopted in the course of human history was a task of paramount importance for Strzemiński; his structural attention made him a historian of the long duration, an analyst of what remains the same behind the apparent changes, a sharp critic who does not get easily fooled by any avant-gardist triumphalism.

Taking scientific experimentation with its "epistemological breaks" as a model for artistic work, Strzemiński and Kobro never lost sight of the collective dimension, precisely because they had a utopian aim. This collective dimension is clearly more affirmed in the texts of the '30s, that is, at the time when the accusations of "bourgeois" and "asocial" formalism were more the rule than the exception. ("The artist's goal is not to express his individuality, but to work collectively toward the creation of objective values whose measure is form.")[16] But it was already asserted in one of the earliest texts by Strzemiński, dating from 1924, a text that contradicts beforehand any denunciation of modern art as an iconoclast *tabula rasa*:

> He is the winner in art who steadily attempts to develop a system, who aims at objective perfection: he tests and improves the system again and again. Such an effort is beyond an individual's capacity; it requires collective endeavors. And thus: to undertake the work of one's predecessors; to investigate the assumptions; to mend the system and to continue—this is the way of creating true cultural values. Contemporary creation has to arise on the basis of previous efforts, but its beginning must be where everything already done ends. Tradition is the raw material that must be used for construction, which means that it must be transformed into what it has never been. The further we go, the more faithful we are to tradition.[17]

We are reaching here a point where essentialism, historicism, and utopia meet—the great dream of an "objective" language, the fantasy of the degree zero, common to all avant-garde movements of the '20s. But Strzemiński did not entirely subscribe to this myth, and his reservations stem from the rigor of his historicism. Here, for example, is the way he criticizes Malevich:

> *Shapes as natural as nature*—said Malevich about the deepest assumption of suprematism. Universal cosmic shapes as the sign and shape of universal cosmic dynamism. The fault of suprematism was that, attempting to discover the laws of cosmic organicity, it overlooked the fact that it was creating its own shape in dependence on the environment that it wanted to overcome. . . . It is impossible and vain to speak at all about shapes.[18]

And again, more generally: "it is not a question of assimilating some supposedly perfect, extratemporal form. Such a form does not exist and never will, because the artistic criteria are in fact a sublimation of the criteria of life, which are different at every epoch."[19] Strzemiński and Kobro believed in an "objective logic of the evolution of art"[20] that would be "as absolute as the evolution of nature";[21] but this absoluteness concerns not the formal configurations of such or such a system, but the law of historical determination ("nothing valuable can arise all by itself, without being reliant upon something preceding," wrote Kobro;[22] "a new form does not spring from itself, but appears thanks to a modification of the objective conditions," added Strzemiński[23]). "Hence the necessity for the artist to recapitulate the entire trajectory of the evolution of art, so that he will be able to elaborate in full consciousness the form appropriate to our own time."[24] This formulation, repeated more than once, will undoubtedly be regarded with skepticism today; but the fact that information gradually took precedence over experience in artistic formation in the era of so-called "late capitalism" is not foreign to the crisis of modernism. This theme of ontogeny recapitulating phylogeny was not a mere accessory to the historicist theory of Strzemiński and Kobro: it constituted one of its central tenets, that which made it a strategy of motivation. For what this evolutionist conception of history legislates is the *quality* of the work of art. As early as 1922, in his "Notes on Russian Art," perhaps one of the most illuminating essays ever written on the art of the Soviet avant-garde (together with the lecture Lissitzky delivered in Berlin at the same time),[25] Strzemiński remarked: "it is the quality that is crucial, not the quantity. Numerous artists now famous (Rodchenko, Stepanova, etc.) cannot even conceive of the efforts that were deployed to attain the solutions of cubism and suprematism. Unconscious of the values contained in the realizations of the new art, they make a "new art" all the same, without developing it, without raising new questions, but by compiling in their works fragments of those of their predecessors."[26] This is a text one might find prophetic, as it seems to describe in advance the climate of cultural amnesia that surrounds today's artistic production (the same text gives a definition of expressionism that matches even more exactly the international neoexpressionist "postmodernism" that invaded the galleries in the '80s).[27] Absolutist in his historicism, Strzemiński condemned redundancy without reservation: in the same manner that there are for him useless artists (Kandinsky is one of those), there are useless works of art. Like the scientist, the artist is an experimenter, hence he must never repeat himself: "An abstract painting has no other raison d'être than the discovery of new data, new in comparison to those offered by preceding works. This is why one should paint only when one has something to say."[28]

The context in which these lines occur—Strzemiński is discussing one of his late "still lifes" and "landscapes" heavily influenced by Arp's biomorphism—tends to obscure their tragic dimension. For this text was written in 1934—that is, at the precise moment at which his unist work came to an end. The paragraph continues: "This justifies, I believe, the possibility of painting not only abstract pictures, but also paintings born from contact with nature, whether as an experiment or for pleasure." This could be interpreted, wrongly, as a verbal pirouette. In fact, Strzemiński himself was forced to abandon unism once he reached the point at which his system left him nothing more to say (and we should probably explain the abrupt halt of Kobro's career in the same way, and not, or not only, as the result of circumstances).[29] A sense of having reached an impasse is, in my view, the inevitable consequence of unist theory—in fact, of every modernist theory, bound as it is by a desire to eliminate all arbitrariness (the same sense of doom occurred many times during the course of modernism—we could even say it is one of the conditions of possibility of modernism).[30] But this impasse is more than formal; it is also political, in the broadest sense of the term, and concerns the utopian daydream that was one of unism's driving forces as it was of all the movements of the first modernist wave. One year after he wrote the lines cited above, Strzemiński reiterated the same excuses in a text that stands as the last apology for unism (it is not indifferent that it is a polemical text):

> Those marine landscapes that I exhibited in Lwow [see fig. 46] are not signs of my abandonment of abstraction nor of my getting closer to "reality." I painted them as a hobby, for they are less demanding. I do not think that the reproduction of reality is closer to life than the transformation of that reality, than its organization. Which is closer to life: relating its events or investigating the laws and principles that regulate it? Today it is not submission to reality and its reproduction that are needed, but its transformation. I therefore consider anti-unism to be a betrayal of the fundamental direction of the aspirations of our age.[31]

However, Strzemiński's work from the moment he wrote these lines to his death must be described as anti-unist. Every characteristic—centered compositions, figure/ground opposition, dynamism, illusionistic depth, nondeductive structure, etc.—contradicts unism's basic principles. How can one account for this contradiction? By the time he wrote these lines, Strzemiński no longer believed in art's value as a model, in its role as the herald of a new social reality, because he no longer believed in the possibility of a future Golden Age. His duplicity was not hypocritical, but desperate: he defended to the death a faith of which he had been the prophet,

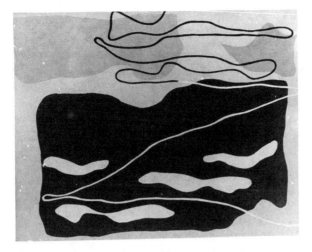

46. Władysław Strzemiński, Sea Landscape, *1934. Distemper on cardboard, 21 × 27 cm (8¼ × 10⅝ in.). Museum Sztuki, Łódz. Photo of the museum.*

but in which he himself could no longer believe, because it had been disproved by the facts of history. The last article he published before the war, "Aspects of Reality," deals with surrealism, whose principles are exposed with clarity and sympathy, so much sympathy that one might think for a moment that Strzemiński has adopted them (all the more since the only description contained in the text, concerning works by the unnamed Arp, could be applied word for word to the drawings he is doing at the time [see fig. 47]). The text concludes as follows:

> We know today that the tangling of the biological line of the surrealists, desperately wriggling while searching for a way out, that the explanation of man by recourse to the movements of his unconscious and of biology, are the reflection of the blood pulse and irrational play of blind forces that are forming the events of present history. . . . Let us oppose to the contemplation and to the passive apprehension of surrealism the productive utilitarianism of a functional art in the service of a society organized in a positive and homogeneous system, freed from the blind play of incoherent forces.[32]

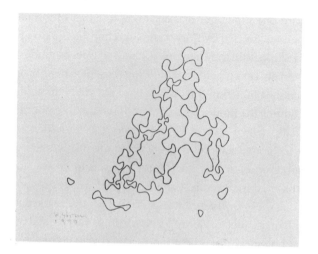

47. *Władysław Strzemiński,* Cast Forth 3, 1940. *Pencil on paper, 30 × 38 cm (11¾ × 15 in.). Museum Sztuki, Łodz. Photo of the museum.*

The rhetoric is lurid but these lines must be read in context. Confronting the Nazi threat (it refers explicitly to *Mein Kampf*), what this text tells us is that there is only one solution: to continue to believe that there is a way out, other than barbarism.

Strzemiński's and Kobro's disillusion, around 1936, matched in density the intelligence of their utopia. Unlike the Russian productivists, whose position Strzemiński had criticized harshly as early as 1922,[33] they insisted at length on the necessity of a mediation between formal experimentation and its use in daily life: "An experimentation from which new plastic values emanate does not yet imply the possibility of an immediate realization."[34] And elsewhere: "Abstract art constitutes a laboratory of research in the formal domain. The results of these researches enter daily life as definitive components. This does not imply, however, that an immediate use of a work of abstract art is necessary."[35] And finally: "Thus, the social influence of art is indirect."[36] It is true that, during a brief moment when they felt outflanked from the left, Strzemiński and Kobro seemed to adopt the very same instrumental conception of art that they combated all their lives. But a closer look is instructive. The topic at stake was architecture and, in architecture, functionalism. At first condemned for its massive use of standardized forms (that is, "projected," determined a priori), then for its technical fantasy that more often than not masks a complete lack of formal invention,[37] functionalism is then envisioned by Kobro and Strzemiński as a possibility of direct action. But the functionalism they imagine is a radical one, grounded on a phenomenology of space and not on a typology of buildings based on their program: "the ground plan and sections of the building do not have any value in themselves, but only as structures orienting the movements of man, as the spatiotemporal rhythm of the life of man in his daily activity."[38] So in 1934–36, when the theoreticians of unism expressed the desire to "go beyond the conception of the picture as the unique field proper to the realization of artistic intentions,"[39] it was in no way to adopt the positions of productivism. If their interest shifted toward architecture, it was not, despite appearances, that they considered it as an outlet for their "formal experimentation." It was rather that architecture bore for them, in its very stuff, that is, space, a wealth of effects (psychological, kinesthetic, and social) that painting and sculpture could only take into account in a metaphorical way. Two texts, one by Strzemiński (1931), the other by Kobro (1934) help to define the terms of this debate:

1. The elements of architecture are:
a) places where a man stops during any activity;
b) motion when he passes from one activity to another.
2. The aim of architecture is an organization of the rhythm of consecutive motions and stops, and thereby the forming of the whole of life.
3. The final goal of architecture is not the building of convenient houses; it is also not the blowing up of abstract sculptures and calling them exhibition pavilions. Its aim is: to be a regulator of the rhythm of social and individual life.[40]

As long as we remain within the limits of a picture as the only kind of a work of art that is deserving of an artist, we shall never grasp the essence of functionalism. A work of art cannot be more or less "functional." It can be simply a field of a plastic experiment, offering more or less useful solutions of forms for a utilitarian realization of functionalism.[41]

Chronologically sandwiched between these two texts is a project by Kobro that wholly contradicts the theory that there is a radical distinction between a work of art, which is not functional, and a building. This is a project for a *Functional Nursery School*, which is nothing less than the clumsy enlargement of one of her sculptures (fig. 48). How could we account for such a discrepancy between words and deeds?

48. *Katarzyna Kobro,* Project for a Functional Nursery School, *after 1932. Illustrated in* Forma, *no. 5 (1936), p. 11. The sculpture that is at the base of this architectural model is* Space Composition 8, *ca. 1932. Museum Sztuki, Łodz. Photo of the museum.*

Simply, Strzemiński and Kobro, not being architects, did not have at their disposal the means to put their anthropological theory of architecture into practice (one would have had to be Rietveld for that).[42] All the same, their radical functionalism is one of the very rare theories of modern architecture (with Le Corbusier's idea of the "picturesque promenade") to have taken into consideration the movement of man in the building.[43] In this radical functionalism, "what is at stake is not a rhythm incorporated into the determined scheme of a superimposed form, but a rhythm derived from life in all its complexity."[44] In short, this radical functionalism denounces as fraudulent the functionalist claim of modern architecture in general.

Conceiving artistic work as a kind of quasi-scientific research, Strzemiński and Kobro rejected art for art's sake without stepping onto this fatal stumbling-block of the Russian avant-garde, the instrumentalization of art: "works of pure art that propose neither a formal solution nor a perfecting of form . . . have no raison d'être."[45] They rejected the notions of "beauty,"[46] of "formal richness,"[47] and of taste.[48] A metaphor (motivation) was at the base of their utopia (the unist work whose every part is equivalent and interdependent is *like* the socialist society). Such a metaphor might sound naive; in a certain way, however, I hold it as accurate, and I believe that Strzemiński and Kobro were right to think that they were achieving, or trying to achieve, in their art a fundamental mutation, much greater than a merely aesthetic one, that is, the deconstruction of a whole series of oppositions upon which Western metaphysics and hence social order are grounded.

But what was unism, then, from a "purely" formal point of view? Among other things, it was a response to one of modernism's fundamental questions: what is the mode of existence of the work of art once its expressive function has been discarded? "A work of plastic art," Strzemiński wrote, "does not express anything. A work of plastic art is not a sign of anything. It is (exists) in itself."[49] This seems simple, tautological, but it warrants closer scrutiny. The general principle of unism runs as follows (from 1924 on):

> A real = autonomous existence in the plastic arts: when a work of art is plastically self-sufficient; when it constitutes an end in itself and does not seek justification in values that subsist beyond the picture. An item of pure art, built in accordance with its own principles, stands up beside other worldly organisms as a parallel entity, as a real being, *for every thing has its own laws of construction of its organism.* When we build one thing, we cannot do it according to the laws and principles belonging to another thing.[50]

In each art, and in necessarily different manner in each, the artist must strive to produce a "real" work, one that has a "real" existence—that is, one that refers to nothing outside itself, that relies upon no transcendence. A work of art is "baroque" (that is, "arbitrary") when its formal configuration is not completely justified by its material conditions (dimensions, materials, etc.) but originates instead in an a priori system, in a preexisting vision. In what Strzemiński and Kobro call the "pictorial baroque," "the idea, alien to painting, stands in the way and bars the understanding that a picture is not an illusion of a phenomenon seen elsewhere or even calculated right away and transported to a picture, but that it is itself, in itself, and for itself."[51] From such a passage, however, one should not conclude that illusionism is the essential target of unism: illusionism is only the ineluctable consequence of the projective nature of the "baroque," of its dependence upon literature, not so much for what concerns its themes (that would just be a cliché) as for the major role devoted in painting, after the relinquishment of medieval symmetry, of that mode of ordering called *composition*. According to Strzemiński, composition rests on a rhetorical model (more recently, Michael Baxandall has advanced a similar argument).[52] Any composition stages a drama (thesis/antithesis) whose resolution (synthesis) must be convincing. ("The basic assumption underlying the baroque is that a picture should be a sign of the dramatic pathos. The pathos is that which finds its expression in the dynamism of directional tensions and in the drama of the blows inflicted by lines upon other lines.")[53] But this resolution, Strzemiński declared, is not "real," because the plastic problem it resolves is based on metaphysical oppositions "artificially" imposed on the pictorial and sculptural matter. This resolution, in fact, is itself metaphysical ("A form that is strung to infinity, a form that is being fed but is never saturated, a hampered rush—this is the essential content of a Baroque painting").[54] Unism's war machine against what Strzemiński and Kobro called the baroque—that is, all past art, including cubism and suprematism—was a war machine against the rhetoric of composition, against Western metaphysics. Dualism was to be abolished:

> Against this dualistic conception, attempting to connect things that cannot be connected, and finding its reason not in the attainment of its intended objective, but in the power of the struggling forces and in the too strenuous effort wasted to subdue them, against this conception producing forces in order to fight them continuously, but never to conquer them—we have to oppose a conception of a picture as a reconciled and organic unity. The dualistic conception must be replaced by the unistic one. Rather than the sublime dramatic outbursts and the power of forces—a picture, as organic as nature.[55]

What do Strzemiński and Kobro mean by this notion of "organicity" (a notion that, as we will see, reincapsulates their enterprise within the confines of Western metaphysics at the very moment it was thought to struggle against it)? The "law of organicity" stipulates that the work of art must be engendered from its "primary given," according to its "first principles," which means that this law functions differently for different media. As far as painting is concerned, these "first principles" belong to three different orders, all of which are indissolubly linked to the fact that "a picture is, or rather ought to be, a thing designed for *looking at* only:[56] flatness, deduction of forms from the shape of the frame, abolition of the figure/ground opposition. As soon as a form is not "motivated" by the "natural" limits of the painting—that is, not derived from the shape of the frame—it floats (thereby introducing a nonpictorial, rhetorical element—namely, time). It detaches itself from the ground, it hollows out the "natural" planarity of the picture and creates an illusionistic depth. Everything Strzemiński said about the necessity of abolishing time in painting, about the "absolute simultaneity of phenomena," about "pure opticality," is part and parcel of the modernist tradition that goes back to Lessing and (in Greenberg's account) to

Kant.[57] Indeed, one can find the same kind of preoccupations in the texts of the most radical artists of modernism, for example Mondrian during the '20s. But the specificity of Strzemiński's discourse, by which he anticipated American artists of the '60s, was his association of the abolition of temporality in painting with that of all contrasts, of all "unmotivated" division, that is, of compositional equilibrium. Thanks to the radicality of his theory, he was an outstanding analyst, not easily intimidated by stylistic effects and able to propose a transversal reading of many works preceding unism. Here are some examples: the surfaces of Mondrian's neoplastic canvases are flat, to be sure, but his pictures are not yet flat because he did not rid himself of the compositional ideology ("The painter still looks for contrasts; painting flat, he still fails to understand what consequences it should imply");[58] the centered composition of cubist paintings results in a "greater intensity of forms,"[59] the contrast between the linear network of the central figure (horizontal/vertical lines) and that of the peripheral areas (curves, shadings off) is explained by the necessity, for the cubist artists, to "camouflage their propensity toward volume";[60] Malevich's obligation to renounce color, that is, to limit the possibilities of his art, results from the contradiction between the dynamism of his shapes and his desire to break with the linearity of contours;[61] Tatlin's incapacity to abandon the centered composition, essential to baroque dynamism, comes from the contradiction between the materiological determinism of his shapes (a cylinder for sheet iron, a T or L profile for steel, etc.) and the absence of determination in their articulation.[62] One could multiply the examples: Strzemiński's formal analyses are brilliant demonstrations from which art historians could benefit enormously. I shall mention only one more case: among all the artists of the constructivist tradition, Strzemiński was perhaps the only one not to overestimate the power of geometry. While his own style is almost entirely geometrical, in 1927–28 he wrote: "It is time to clear up the misunderstanding by which geometrical construction is almost a strict work, almost a piece of engineering. Actually, geometrical composition is as arbitrary and subjective as any other."[63]

Strzemiński's painting, however, had never really lived up to his theory. Or rather, theory and practice were not in sync.[64] We can distinguish three periods in his work: pre-unist (cubist apprenticeship, early abstract works inspired by Tatlin and Malevich and thus vulnerable to the same charges Strzemiński leveled later against these artists), unist (1924–32), and post-unist (inspired by Arp's idiosyncratic surrealism). The unist period is itself divisible into four sections, and this division is not exactly chronological. The earliest canvases that Strzemiński dubbed unist (1924–28) resemble puzzles: a single plane, bordered by a rectilinear "margin," has

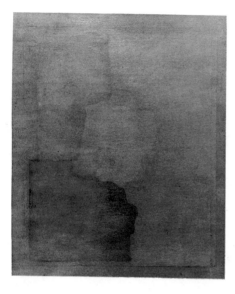

49. Władysław Strzemiński, Unist Composition 7, 1929. *Oil on canvas, 77 × 63 cm (30⁵/₁₆ × 24³/₄ in.). Museum Sztuki, Łódz. Photo Zdzisław Sowinski.*

been divided over and over into color areas of equal saturation with zigzagging contours (see fig. 49). The shape of the plane itself has been derived from the form of the frame, but not the internal divisions of that plane. What is more, bordered as it is by a margin, it distinguishes itself from a "preexisting" ground. The three other sections are constituted by (1) the extraordinary series of *Architectonic Paintings* (1926–30; see figs. 45, 50); (2) a few exceptional canvases like *Unist Composition 9* (1931; fig. 51) in which the geometric division of the architectonic painting is counteracted by a homogenization of facture and color saturation, which makes those works almost indecipherable in black and white reproductions (the surfaces of these paintings are constituted of textured lines of paint reminiscent of television scan lines that carry the division of color and upset the figure/ground opposition); and (3) monochromes (figs. 52, 53). Although the will to abolish every contrast (of color, form, facture), expressed by Strzemiński as early as 1924, implies an all-over monochromatic painting, he did not adopt this solution until the end of his unist period, ca. 1932, and then only in a handful of works (a great number of them, it is true, might have been destroyed).

"Unism begins with the principle that a divided composition is never homogeneous," Strzemiński will say in 1934.[65] But until he finally produced even-textured monochromes (they are not all that way), Strzemiński sought a way to motivate the

50. *Władysław Strzemiński*, Architectonic
Compositon 1, *1926. Oil on canvas, 90 ×
64 cm (35⁷/₁₆ × 25³/₁₆ in.). Museum Sztuki,
Łodz. Photo Jolanta Sadowska.*

51. *Władysław Strzemiński*, Unist Composition 9, *1931. Oil on canvas, 48 × 32 cm
(18⁷/₈ × 12⁹/₁₆ in). Museum Sztuki, Łodz.
Photo of the museum. The configuration of
this painting is similar to that of the* Architectonic Compositions, *although less strictly
geometric. If it cannot be seen in a black
and white reproduction, it is because there
Strzemiński's art matches perfectly his theory: not only is the rippled texture even
throughout the whole canvas (each ripple is
composed of two lines, a high relief line
and a low relief line), but the colors are of
exactly identical value and saturation. Furthermore, the unity of the surface is reinforced because one of every two "ripples" is
plain pink; the other ripples, each compris-
ing a yellow and a green segment, carry
out the vertical color division of the painting (there are two areas, a pink-yellow area
and a pink-green area). For a detailed
analysis of this canvas, cf. Pierre-Maxime
Jedryka, "Ellipses," in* L'Espace uniste,
p. 195.

52. *Władysław Strzemiński,* Unist Composition 10, *1931. Oil on canvas, 74 × 50 cm (29⅛ × 19⅝ in.). Museum Sztuki, Łodz. Photo of the museum.*

division of the canvas. Hence the deductivist injunction, already in place in his earliest texts but not applied until he had found a plastic solution to the problem of division with his "architectonic" canvases. This solution is enunciated in his great text of 1927–28, entitled "Unism in Painting":

> Starting the construction of a picture, we should take its length and breadth as the basic dimensions and as the starting point, while the breadth and length as well as the place of each shape should be dependent on them. In this way the dimensions of a picture become the main thing in it, rather than a secondary one, existing as if beyond our awareness, as it used to be in the baroque; they become something basic and determine the construction and its character.[66]

The paintings Strzemiński called "architectonic" demonstrate this principle: the canvas has been divided geometrically into two or three surfaces (supposed to be of equal color intensity, which was hardly the case), in such a way that we cannot decide which is "form" and which is "ground." The division of the surface is indeed derived from the painting's proportions (all internal divisions are based on the ratio of its length to its width). However, the sheer variety of these works, most of which were

53. *Władysław Strzemiński,* Unist Composition 8, *1931–32. Oil on canvas, 60 × 36 cm (23⅝ × 14³/₁₆ in.). Museum Sztuki, Łodz. Photo of the museum.*

executed in the same format and size, as well as the quite common introduction of a curvilinear form (which violates the deductivist law, at least in a rectangular painting), suggest that Strzemiński was constrained to bend his theories to fit his practice (see fig. 54). He explained himself only in an extraordinary text on sculpture, dating from 1929 and coauthored with Kobro: "The offered method of conduct concerns only the size of the shapes and their arrangement, it says nothing about the shapes themselves. This is up to the artist, who knows himself what shapes he needs."[67]

This kind of reintroduction in extremis of the "arbitrary," of the artist's subjectivity, must have been problematic for Strzemiński (to repeat: it is the impossibility of eradicating entirely the "arbitrariness," except if one chooses the solution of the monochromes—and maybe not even then—that is at the base of our current mourning of modernism). Even before he opted for the monochrome, Strzemiński tried to push the limits of this arbitrariness further back, and in one stroke he made his entire system crumble into pieces. His question was: if the divisions of the painting

54. Władysław Strzemiński, Architectonic Composition 14d, *1929–30. Oil on canvas, 96 × 60 cm (37¾ × 23⅝ in.). Museum Sztuki, Łodz. Photo of the museum.*

are determined by its dimensions, then what motivates these dimensions? The answer marks a logical impasse that destroys the essentialist specialization of the different arts and radically violates the "law of organicity" on which unism was based. Using architecture as a reference—in architecture, Strzemiński wrote, "the homogeneous rhythm of movements must be a function of the dimensions of man"—he arrived at a kind of ideal proportion ($n = 8:5$) applicable to both painting and sculpture (see fig. 55).[68] Most of his "architectonic" paintings employ this proportional system derived from the Fibonacci series.[69]

It is impossible to eliminate the arbitrary: wishing to reduce it to a minimum, Strzemiński in the end returned to precisely what he had condemned in 1924, humanism and the use of a projective system—the confusion "between art and the hieromathematics of Pythagoras."[70]

Strzemiński and Kobro's theory of sculpture is one of the most elaborate of our century, and the 15 or so sculptures that illustrate it—all by Kobro—are among the most astonishing. Following the "law of organicity," the theory begins with the difference between painting and sculpture:

> The painting has natural limits that are determined by the dimensions of the canvas. It cannot go beyond its natural limits. This in why the construction of the painting takes its limits as a point of departure. . . . A sculpture, on the other hand, does not have such natural limits, defined a priori. Hence the natural law must be for a sculpture not to enclose itself within a volume, but to unite with the totality of space, with the infinite space. The union of the sculpture with space, the saturation of space by the sculpture, the fusion of the sculpture in space and its link with it constitute the organic law of sculpture.[71]

Since it does not have "limits that would exist prior to its conception,"[72] a sculpture must be considered as a part of space, must exhibit the same characteristics as space. In exactly the same way that a figure, in one of Strzemiński's "architectonic" paintings, must be in an "undecidable" relationship with the ground of the painting (a positive/negative relationship), and consists only in the "motivated" division of the surface of the painting, a unist sculpture must divide and shape interior as well as exterior space. For Kobro, "the most important problem" in the entire history of sculpture is

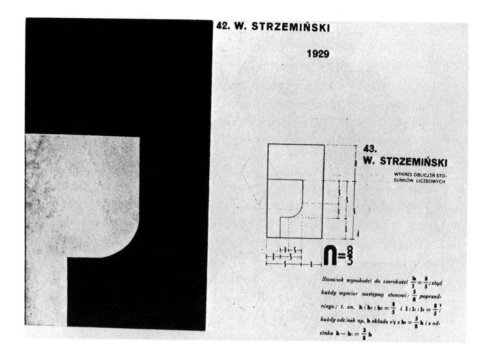

55. *Władysław Strzemiński, proportional scheme of an* Architectonic Composition, *now presumably lost. From Strzemiński and Kobro,* Composition of Space: Calculations of a Spatio-Temporal Rhythm, *1931. Photo Museum Sztuki.*

the relationship between the space contained within the sculpture and the space situated outside the sculpture. Aside from this fundamental problem, the following issues are relatively secondary: the static or dynamic character of the sculpture, the predominance of line or of volume, the use or nonuse of color, the handling in lights and shadows or in masses. From the solution given to this principal problem will stem both the type of sculpture and the solutions found for the secondary questions.[73]

I shall not try here to retrace the extremely complex typology of sculpture proposed by the theoreticians of unism from antiquity onward (Egyptian sculpture: a volume-sculpture, which does not raise the issue of exterior space; gothic sculpture, which reaches a union with that portion of exterior space contained within the limits of architecture; baroque sculpture, at last, where "the limit of form is the limit of the zone of influence of its dynamic forms," and which reaches a union with that portion of exterior space contained within this "limiting limit").[74] Again, despite the odd terminology, art historians would learn a lot from their analyses. But more important here is Strzemiński and Kobro's insistence upon "union with space." The issue is to avoid what Rosalind Krauss has called "the logic of the monument"—a commemorative logic that "distinguishes sculpture from the ongoing phenomena of daily life" and plunges the viewer "into a state of passive contemplation that cuts him off from the concerns of everyday life."[75] Why would anyone want to avoid this logic, when it has already demonstrated its effectiveness? Because it denies that sculpture inhabits the same space as the viewer, that is, the space of our experience in the world. Thus: "Unist sculpture does not produce sculptures. Unist sculpture sculpts space, condensing it within the limits of its sculptural zone [see fig. 56]. The unist sculpture, based upon the organic unity of sculpture and space, does not want the form to be a goal in itself, but only the expression of spatial relationships."[76]

Even if she subscribed to the ideology of transparency that defines, as Krauss demonstrated, a good portion of the constructivist production,[77] Kobro did not employ the axes of spatial coordinates as a grid conceived as the sign of a universal language. Even if unism conceived space as one of the a priori categories of our sensibility, it was always concerned with the space of our experience:

> The union of man and space is the action of man in that space. We come to know space through our actions. The vectors traced by the actions of man in space are: the vertical station of man and every object, the horizontal of the environment that he encounters on both sides, and the depth, before him, of forward movement.[78]

56. *Katarzyna Kobro,* Space Sculpture, *1925 (1967). Painted steel and wood, 50 × 78 × 56 cm (19⅝ × 31³/₁₆ × 22 in.). Reconstruction with use of the recovered fragment by Boleslaw Utkin and Janusz Zagrodzki, 1967. Museum Sztuki, Łodz. Photo of the museum.*

Space is, according to Kobro and Strzemiński, homogeneous and infinite, in a state of constant equilibrium (an equilibrium that is neither dynamic, based on movement, nor static, based on weight—that is, on a type of movement).[79] As a result, every dynamic form will subtract itself from space and reintroduce the logic of the monument. Moreover, every figure is necessarily dynamic because it is opposed, as center and foreign body, to the homogeneity of surrounding space: "The sculpture must not be a foreign body in space, nor the center that dominates illicitly the rest of space. It must create the prolongation of space. If sculpture is to be united with space, the fundamental laws of space must govern its construction."[80]

With the exception of her six earliest sculptures, made before 1925 and influenced by suprematism and Russian constructivism (figs. 57, 58),[81] all of Kobro's work is composed of open planes, orthogonal or curved; the intersection of these planes

57. *Katarzyna Kobro,* Suspended Composition 1, *1921 (1972). Fiberglass, epoxide resin, metal, and wood, 20 × 40 × 40 cm (7⅞ × 15¾ × 15¾ in.). Reconstructed by Boleslaw Utkin in 1972. Museum Sztuki, Łodz. Photo of the museum.*

58. *Katarzyna Kobro,* Abstract Sculpture 1, *1924. Glass, metal, and wood, 72 × 17.5 × 15.5 cm (28⅝ × 6⅞ × 6¹/₁₆ in.). Museum Sztuki, Łodz. Photo of the museum.*

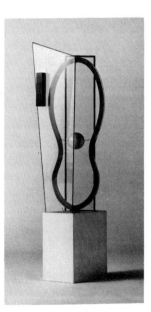

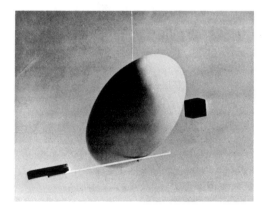

is supposed, according to the theory, to render space visible ("the division of space, the interruption of its continuity, the partial closing of one of it parts, all that renders it visible, plastic, for us, for space is by itself ungraspable and almost unperceivable").[82] These planes, whose division and articulation were determined according to a constant proportional system (the same one used by Strzemiński in his "architectonic" paintings), were conceived as materializations of the axes of the space of our experience: "The lines of space are continued in those of the sculpture";[83] or else "each part of space that is not filled can be transformed into a sculptural shape."[84] But if Kobro had stopped here, nothing would have distinguished her work from constructivism in general, except for a rigor of mathematical specification (which has allowed the reconstruction of several lost works [see figs. 59, 60]). The real inventiveness of her work lies in the two methods she employed to prevent her sculptures' being perceived as figures in space—two methods based on an extreme syntactic disjunctiveness.

The first is the use of polychromy to destroy the "optical unity," which would separate the sculpture from space; contrary to unist painting, unist sculpture must include the harshest contrasts possible (hence the use of primary colors—the only way to avoid the constitution of chromatic harmonies that would read as separate unities).[85] Contrasting with the formal arrangement of the sculpture, the disposition of colors causes it to explode in three dimensions: not only are two sides of a single plane painted different colors, but each color is also distributed noncontiguously in the three dimensions of depth, width, and height. A long quotation of Strzemiński and Kobro's text deserves to be made here, for it gives a very precise description of the works themselves:

> Because of their different color intensity, we cannot see all the various planes at once. . . . We do not unite adjacent colors but those that bear the same amount of energy. Thus we do not attempt to diversify the various forms by color but to lay a given color on various planes of the sculpture, perpendicular to one another and separated from the other color planes. . . . Each color creates within the sculpture new spatial forms, more and more numerous, that fit into each other. The spatial forms, related by the given common color, hinge and create many "corridors" that link them together and with the exterior space. . . . We have thus a system of spatial forms created by color. This system is analogous to the system of forms of the sculpture itself [prior to the application of color], with one important fact however: both systems do not overlap. . . . In this

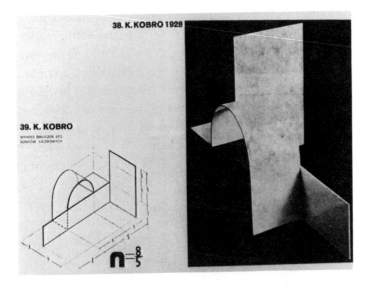

59. Katarzyna Kobro, proportional scheme of a Space Composition
3. From Strzemiński and Kobro, Composition of Space: Calculations
of a Spatio-Temporal Rhythm, *1931. Photo Museum Sztuki.*

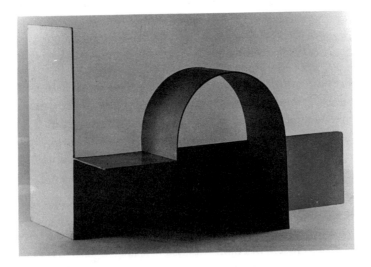

60. Katarzyna Kobro, Space Compositon 3, *1928. Painted steel, 40 ×
64 × 40 cm (15³/₄ × 25³/₁₆ × 15³/₄ in.). Museum Sztuki, Łodz. Photo
of the museum.*

manner the extreme diversity of spatial partitions is emphasized in unist sculpture: they are independent from one another and yet create through their connections an incalculable diversity of links between the sculpture and space. The arrangement of the sculpture's forms determine intersections that make space concrete and "corridors" that give to the sculpture the internal unity of the spatial phenomenon, linking it to space. The same happens for each color used.[86]

True, Kobro made few polychrome sculptures (if the number of surviving works is any indication). But the reason this system of optical disjunction is so effective in her work—in, for example, *Space Composition 4* (1929; fig. 61), one of her masterpieces and in my opinion one of the most extraordinary works of twentieth-century sculpture—is that it was grafted onto another disjunctive principle used to greatest advantage in her white sculptures such as, for example, *Space Composition 5* (1929–30; fig. 62), another highly successful work. This second method (to which the coloristic syntax is "analogous," as is stated in the quotation just made) takes into account, perhaps for the first time explicitly in the history of sculpture, the duration of aesthetic experience: in unist theory, sculpture, unlike painting, is an art that mobilizes *time:*

> The spatiotemporality of the work of art is related to its variability. We call spatiotemporal the spatial changes produced in time. Those variations are functions of the third dimension, of depth, which, although momentarily hidden, nevertheless reveals its existence while transforming the appearance of the work of art, the appearance of each form, in creating variability; when the spectator moves, certain forms present themselves, others hide; the perception of these forms changes constantly.[87]

Wanting to stage the "transformation of depth into breadth," to render visible that invisible object which is depth ("wherever we stand to observe the work of art, depth is always hidden from us"), to solicit the spectator's movement, Kobro made sculptures in which no elevation can be inferred from any other. As we circulate around her best sculptures, what was negative (empty) becomes positive (full), what was line becomes plane or point, what was straight becomes curved, what was wide becomes narrow. An entire stream-of-consciousness novel would be necessary to describe the transformations that occur as we circulate around the two works mentioned above. And while her theory participates in the contructivist ideology of transparency, Kobro's sculptural practice undermines that ideology, as David Smith would later do in using the same disjunctive language.[88] Rather than presupposing the existence of

61. Katarzyna Kobro, Space Composition 4, *1929. Painted steel, 40 × 64 × 40 cm (15¾ × 25³⁄₁₆ × 15¾ in.). Museum Sztuki, Łodz. Photo of the museum.*

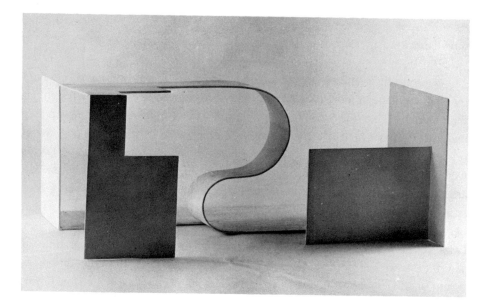

62. *Katarzyna Kobro,* Space Composition 5, *1929–30. Painted steel, 25 × 64 × 40 cm (10 × 25³/₁₆ × 15³/₄ in.). Museum Sztuki, Łodz. Photo of the museum.*

a generative core or spine, the rationality of which would be immediately intelligible (an image of our clear consciousness, to refer again to Rosalind Krauss's analysis of contructivism), these sculptures have the opacity of material objects, whose space they cohabit (the base has been eliminated). But unlike objects whose meanings are discovered through use, Kobro's sculptures treat our experience in the world in an abstract manner—without finality. Although we can apprehend them physically (measuring their variability as we move around them), neither the naked eye nor intellection is sufficient to comprehend them. The philosophical foundation of unism was phenomenology, albeit implicitly, as it will later be for minimalism, this time explicitly: "the form of existence produces the form of consciousness."[89]

Despite the radicality of their works, however, despite the unprecedented intelligence of their theory, Strzemiński and Kobro clung to one principle that pulled their work back into the orbit of metaphysics at the very moment they believed they had escaped from it. This is the principle of unity, which underpins their "law of organicity" and the essentialism of modernism as a whole. Strzemiński and Kobro were fully aware of the difficulties involved in breaking with a secular tradition ("we are still thinking baroque," they would say); they believed they could do so by deconstructing, through their elaborate strategy, the arbitrariness of composition. Yet, because they never abandoned the ancient concept of the unity of the work of art (which goes back at least to Vitruvius), and although they never used it in a traditional way, their work represents one of the subtlest consolidations of that tradition (as would later that of the American artists of the '60s, done according to the same premises minus the utopia).

As I wrote above, the essential question of modernism was that of motivation: "What is the mode of existence of the work of art once its expressive function has been discarded?" The answer was: "This existence is real as soon as the work of art if plastically self-sufficient and does not seek a transcendental justification, outside of itself." This "law of organicity" rests upon a fundamental naturalism (and, as might have been noted, the adjective "natural" appears frequently in the texts of unism): the naturalism of "creation," of *sui generis* production as opposed to reproduction.[90] The unist picture "is (exists) in itself." The claims of this form of naturalism are perfectly summarized by Jacques Derrida in his warning against a metaphysical reading of Mallarmé's conception of the mime: "Since the mime imitates nothing, represents nothing, opens up in its origin the very thing he is tracing out, presenting, or producing, he must be the very movement of truth. Not, of course, truth in the form of adequacy between the representation and the present of the thing itself, or between the imitator and the imitated, but truth as the present unveiling of the present: mon-stration, manifestation, production, *aletheia.*"[91] As Derrida demonstrates, nothing of the sort happens in Mallarmé's mimology, which thus constitutes a remarkable exception. For this type of naturalism is endemic to modernism as a whole. It guided the insatiable quest for motivation that the whole modernist enterprise represents; as such it commands the current "failure" of modernism as it commanded Strzem-iński and Kobro's jettisoning of their unist principles, no matter how far they went in their attempts to reduce the arbitrary. Mallarmé was right: *Un coup de dés jamais n'abolira le hasard.*

Piet Mondrian, *New York City*

In his article on Piet Mondrian's New York works, published in 1974, Joseph Masheck very judiciously analyzes the particularity and the newness of *New York City* (fig. 63) in relation to preceding works. He notes a more aggressive kind of flatness, an all-over effect of compression to a single plane. According to Masheck, this effect is

> partly accomplished by differentiating the densities and overlaps of the separate grids and by overloading the system with more identity than differentiation, so as to control the spatial weave. Thus, the three grids, composed of different numbers of lines all equal in width (15 yellow, 4 blue, 4 red) weave in and out, or avoid weaving, with no apparent governing principle, except perhaps the idea that there should be a lot more yellow than blue or red, both to weigh against them in value and to identify the grid more closely with the pigmentally white ground.[1]

Later in the same article, Masheck pursues the remainder of the variation to which Mondrian devoted himself: the "four blue and red bands assert both sameness and difference (1 vertical blue, 3 horizontal; 2 vertical red, 2 horizontal), balance and asymmetry. Meanwhile, a multitude of yellow-and-yellow intersections tightens the surface, and the overall sameness of the yellow grid enhances the differentiation of red from blue."[2]

The association between *New York City*'s all-over structure and the play that unfolds within it relative to difference and identity is very pertinent but is not specific enough, in my opinion. On the one hand, *all* of Mondrian's neoplastic works are constituted by an opposition between the variable (position, dimension, and color of the planes) and the invariable (right angle, the so-called "constant rapport"). On the other hand, the type of identity produced in *New York City* relies on *repetition*, a prin-

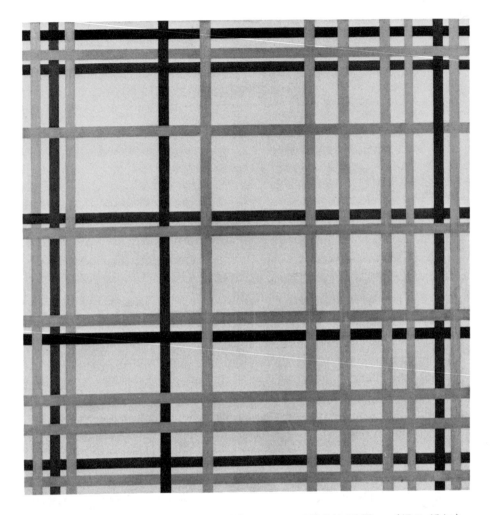

63. Piet Mondrian, New York City, *1942. Oil on canvas, 119.3 × 114.2 cm (47 × 45 in.). Musée National d'Art Moderne, Centre Georges Pompidou, Paris. Photo of the museum. The painting was entitled* New York City *when exhibited by Mondrian in 1942 (the title was changed to* New York City I *after his death, much later, when the unfinished paintings of the same series began to appear on the market). Throughout this essay, I will use the original title.*

ciple that, we know, explicitly governs a whole range of paintings predating neo-plasticism. *New York City* differs from the "classic" neoplastic works, as well as from the 1918–19 modular paintings with which it seems to have a good deal in common. It is, in part, because he never discusses this last point that Masheck doesn't entirely grasp the amplitude of the reversal that Mondrian effected in his New York works.

In fact, as James Johnson Sweeney realized quite early, one must go back to the 1917 works, which gave rise to modular grids for the two years that followed, in order to understand what happens not only in *New York City* but also in the two Boogie-Woogie paintings.[3] Everyone is aware of the extraordinarily rapid evolution of Mondrian's work during the years immediately preceding the foundation of neo-plasticism: under the influence of Bart van der Leck, he adopted the colored plane and the black dash on a white background as elements of his composition for the two *Compositions in Color, A* and *B* (1917, Seuphor 290–291).[4] Mondrian, who had not yet found a means of perspicuously relating these diverse elements (which are the result of a cubist disjunction between line and color), tied both plane and dashes together by way of an optical dynamism, based largely on their superimposition. The immediate consequence was to make the background recede optically. The next step was the five *Compositions* (also in 1917), all entitled *"With Colored Planes"* (Seuphor 285–289). Here all superimposition was eliminated, as well as all "line." In the last two of these canvases, the background itself is divided without remainder into planes of different shades of white. The colored rectangles (less numerous) are on the way to alignment. In spite of this, the rectangles fluctuate and, consequently, the background is hollowed out behind them.

It is at this point that the linear structure reappears, in three 1918 works, two of which have been lost.[5] There is no longer any white "background" and the rectangles, even more in alignment than before, are all bordered by grey lines. However, although the grey or white planes, less numerous than the others, cannot be taken as "background" in the painting, the rectangles still fluctuate; they are still individualized. At this point Mondrian introduced the all-over modular grid, which has the advantage of diminishing, or better still, of equalizing any contrast, preventing any individuation and abolishing the figure/background opposition. But this abolition, far from accentuating the painting's flatness, annihilates the surface of inscription with an overwhelming assault of optical flickers owing to the multiplication of lines and intersections. It re-creates an effect of illusory depth where the aim was to rule out that possibility. Little by little, Mondrian abandoned the modular grid (it took him two years to drop it completely) because, first, it did not fulfill the function for which he had intended it, fixing the surface in its integrity once and for all, without hierarchy; and, second, it exalted rhythm and repetition, which were inseparable from symmetry for Mondrian at that time; it exalted the "natural."

Neoplasticism was born out of this double rejection. And it is from a return to these two highly contradictory symbolic forms (depth and repetition) that *New York City* was composed. In describing the all-over structure of the painting, Masheck correctly observes the dialectic of repetition/symmetry that most critics, following Mondrian himself, have compared to the musical rhythm of boogie-woogie.[6] However, by ignoring the question of depth (or by only mentioning it in passing), Masheck blocks his own appreciation of the inaugural gesture this painting produced, which is why he all but excludes the unfinished canvases of *New York City II* (fig. 64) and *III* and *Victory Boogie-Woogie* from Mondrian's oeuvre.[7]

However, there are some excuses for this (and Masheck's article remains to date one of the best on Mondrian's later period). In fact the artist himself did not speak explicitly, anywhere in his later writings, about any sort of *return* to a pre-neoplastic problematic of depth. Conversely, "A New Realism," the fundamental article Mondrian was writing while painting *New York City* and which he meticulously polished on the same day as the opening of his first American exhibit (where the painting reigned supreme), clearly and concisely unveils important changes occurring in his ideas of rhythm and repetition.[8] Indeed, if the first theoretical texts of 1917–18 contradict the painter's then-current modular practice, they also very specifically anticipate the neoplastic style (and show that the module could never be more than a temporary solution). For Mondrian, rhythm is the subjective part of composition,

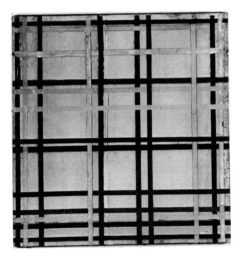

64. Piet Mondrian, New York City II *(unfinished), 1942–44. Charcoal, oil, and colored paper tapes on canvas, 119.3 × 114.2 cm (47 × 45 in.). Kunstsammlung Nordrhein-Westphalen, Düsseldorf. Photo Walter Klein.*

the relative ("natural," particular) element that must be interiorized, neutralized by the constant nonrepetitive opposition of plastic elements; it is by this means that we may attain the universal, the balance, repose, and that the tragic can be abolished.[9] It wasn't until 1927—not coincidentally in connection with jazz—that rhythm was given a positive value. Not limited or formal, the "free rhythm" of jazz is universal, not particular. By a kind of theoretical hocus-pocus, which is more common than we would generally believe, Mondrian dissociated rhythm from repetition, which remained "individual" (the oppression of the machine or biological limitation).[10] In the early thirties, the immobility of repose, then associated with symmetry, but also with "similitude" or repetition, was laid aside little by little on behalf of the notion of dynamic equilibrium (which first appeared in 1934).[11] The immediate plastic translation of this notion was as follows: lines, until that time considered secondary in relation to planes (their only function being the "determination" of those planes), became the most active element of composition.[12] Mondrian quickly began to assign a destructive function to the line. We can see how closely these theoretical adjustments parallel the evolution of his painting: "the rectangular planes (formed by the plurality of straight lines . . .) are dissolved by their homogeneity and rhythm alone emerges, leaving the planes as 'nothing.'" Written in 1930, in an article responding to Tériade's accusation of decorativeness in neoplasticism,[13] such a statement corresponds to everything that was woven around the "double line" from 1932 onward, as well as to explanations later furnished in both his autobiography ("Toward the True Vision of Reality") and his correspondence with Sweeney. The multiplied intersections of lines destroyed the static, monumental entity of the planes, abolishing them as rectangles and as form.[14]

The next step was to be the abolition of line as form by "mutual oppositions," which he explicitly attempted in his New York works. (It is noteworthy that in New York Mondrian didn't want to hear about lines, asking those who claimed to see them in his work in progress to point them out to him.)[15] Nonetheless, this ultimate destruction was only feasible once the possibility of repetition was fully accepted. In "A New Realism," Mondrian stated that "the plurality of varied and similar forms annihilates the existence of forms as entities. Similar forms do not show contrast but are in equivalent opposition. Therefore they annihilate themselves more completely in their plurality" ("NR," p. 349). Only syncopated repetition is capable of simultaneously destroying the "objective" expression of forms or elements of form (that singular, individual quality, independent of our perceptions, that makes a square a square and not a circle or a rhombus) and their "subjective" expression, the gestaltist transformation of these forms by our subjective vision that necessarily recreates other limitations.[16] If we fail to perceive the double movement of the strategy set forth by Mondrian in this text, we run the risk of missing the specificity of his New York works, particularly *New York City*. We also run the risk of not understanding why Mondrian magnifies the all-over optical perturbations with a violence unequaled since his 1918–19 grids, whereas he is very careful not to organize his canvas according to a regular weave. We run the risk of not understanding that the famous "if we cannot free ourselves, we can free our *vision*" speaks also of a painting that would be entirely free of the tragic that perception necessarily entails in that it always seeks to impose an order, a particular structure, a "limitation," a stability upon the free rhythm of the visual facts that confront it:[17] to liberate our vision is also to accept that we no longer master it. And it is obviously this vertigo, this *fading* that informs the aporetic braiding and the shallow depth of *New York City*.

Masheck's analysis isn't just insufficiently specific—it is also incomplete. At any rate, it seems to me to rely on assumptions that closer observation proves to be unwarranted. To take a crucial example, Masheck makes a passing remark in a footnote that one of the strips is narrower than the others (the second vertical yellow strip from the right). His conclusion that the strip "looks accidentally narrower" is a strange testimony to a certain level of ignorance of Mondrian's microscopic precision in his working method, but the statement is consistent with my earlier criticism of Masheck's article. For this "exception" relies on the opposition that the entire work produces and in a way abolishes, namely, the opposition between fictive depth ("optical") and real depth (thickness). If Mondrian allows himself this exception, perhaps it is to signal that he has finally conquered the menace of an illusionist hollowing out of the surface, telling us, in a sense, "this strip is more slender than the others; however, it is impossible for you to read it as more distant."

It would be unfair to forget that Masheck observes the "literal superimposition," in *New York City* that, according to him, allows Mondrian to avoid the optical flickers from which the earlier compositions (containing a heavy density of black lines) suffered. (The superimpositions are for Masheck the *Aufhebung,* the resolution of the earlier oscillations.) It would also be unfair not to mention his allusion to the problem of real depth, when Masheck notes that the width of the strips is equal to the thickness of the stretcher. But this is really a red herring that allows Masheck to avoid those questions directly posed by the unfinished works that use adhesive tape and, more subtly, by *New York City*. For in this painting Mondrian insists on retaining the sculptural quality of its unfinished state when it (like its companions) was no more than a braided field of overlapping tapes and therefore superimposed not only the "immaterial" optically colored grids, but the actual strips of tape as well, each endowed with a certain thickness (which ultimately projected shadow) and with upper and "under" surfaces. Even though Masheck briefly mentions the more assertive, more pictorial texture of the New York works, he does not notice that in *New York City* each strip possesses an individual facture and that when two identically colored strips intersect—as they did in the unfinished pictures—they do not do so indifferently. In fact, the braided effect, as Robert Welsh has already observed, is "an effect heightened by the subtly felt directions of the brushstrokes, which typically continue the movement of one line at the expense of that which it bisects, although this practice is applied with no apparent system."[18]

No apparent system: what does this really signify? (And let us note here that Welsh used a similar expression to the one Masheck used when he spoke of the colored braiding.) Is there a system, hidden from view? Must we search for some secret geometry in this painting that would be the abstract equivalent of the hidden symbolism that all the iconologists work themselves to death trying to uncover in all the art of the past? Certainly not, and it is well known that Mondrian loathed any axiomatization of his art and that he repeated throughout his life that he worked not by calculation, but by intuition.[19] It goes without saying that this picture—like the classical neoplastic paintings in general—does not come under the heading of systemic or programmed art. But if it is not systemic, isn't it, in some way, systematic? Isn't there a system functioning within it, entirely apparent, whose goal is to prohibit any stasis or fixing of perception in a systematic assurance? In fact, even these terms are somewhat crude, and to understand what happens in this painting (as well as what differentiates it from the modular paintings), we must introduce an opposition, for example between system (binary) and structure (tertiary)—or between woof and warp. We wonder if perhaps Mondrian is not the first painter to accomplish this "pas de trois" that Hubert Damisch has recently discussed,[20] not so much because of the braid of three primary colors (that triad is not new) as because in this painting the "exceptions" not only bore holes in the system through and through, they infinitize it; they cause it to slacken. (Here again, "exception" isn't quite right because it presumes that the rule is a given: to think in terms of exception is to think in terms of system and contrast. But no other, better term comes at once to mind.)

I have already indicated that *New York City* is, in a way, a sort of definitive victory over geometrical apriorism: in this painting a nonmodular repetition is invented, a grid becomes undone. Here, Carl Holty's memories are useful since they show that Mondrian was tempted for a moment to find a mechanical solution to the problem raised by this painting:

He complained about the "banality" of the corners of the original layout. He had varied the overlapping of the colored strips mechanically at first ("because [I] like to be logical"), placing red above blue, yellow above red, red above yellow in their respective corners. As he used only three colors, the fourth corner was embarrassing for a time. After giving the matter some thought, Mondrian decided that the logical process governing the layout was not binding on him in the further development of the picture. He proceeded to adjust the sections of the long colored strips (planes) to relate not only to each other but to the canvas as a whole, and disregarded the earlier disposition and variations.[21]

It is useless to state that the problem of the corners might have been easily resolved in such a mechanical fashion if Mondrian had kept a fourth color, namely black, as he did in *New York City II* (unfinished). This is a question of deliberate renunciation, and this renunciation depends on the painting's extraordinarily complex structure.

Suppose we take the yellow grid, which, but for six crossings, lies "above" the red and blue grids: the horizontal yellow strips "dominate" the verticals by texture at all but three intersections. But there is an exception in this binary system (above and beneath), an exception within the exceptions, an undecidable moment (the intersection of the second yellow horizontal from the top and the third yellow vertical from the left). Is it chance that this is the most isolated yellow intersection of the whole canvas, the one furthest from any other, the one that may claim to rival what Charmion Von Wiegand dubbed "the red cross" in the lower left third of the painting? Doesn't Mondrian want to express—here, in this very spot, more visible as detail because it is more isolated, more contrasting—the exception that transforms the binary opposition into a "pas de trois"? (Not only does the horizontal not dominate, the intersection is flat, level.) As for the six exceptions to the mere "appearance of system" (to speak as Masheck might), namely, the tendency of yellow to be laid out on top, isn't it remarkable that these exceptions are found either at the periphery or close to the "red cross," as if to assert a precedence of that element that a moment later is repudiated? If the primacy of yellow had not been breached, close to the edges of the painting, wouldn't the yellow lines that frame the composition on three sides have seemed to squeeze it, giving it a peculiar form, a static, systemic, definitive optical basis?

A photo of Mondrian in his studio showing *New York City* in an unfinished state (fig. 65) confirms that all of these exceptions are thought out. (This photo must have been taken in early September of 1941, since Mondrian had already begun to replace the colored tapes with paint.)[22] On the one hand, insofar as we can determine, all the yellow lines appear to be of equal width; on the other, the changes to come relate to all the areas I have mentioned. First, let us consider the "red cross"; in the unfinished state as in the final version, the vertical lay on top of all the horizontals in the upper section of the canvas (it is impossible to tell if it lay on top of the upper red horizontal), but it was constantly cut in the lower section by the yellow horizontals. As for the horizontal forming the "red cross," it passed underneath all the yellow verticals. This is entirely different in the finished version of the painting. The "red cross" is reinforced on three sides (and only three; in order that there be "structure," not "system," there must be interplay): toward the top and the left, passing over the nearest yellow horizontal and vertical; and toward the bottom, because the third yellow horizontal from the bottom is placed considerably lower. The only side of the "red cross" that is not accentuated is the right, where the vertical of that "undecidable" yellow crossing passes above it. As for this last intersection, which I shall call the "yellow cross" to simplify the matter (another inappropriate term that I only use here as a shortcut),[23] it is, given the identity of color, impossible to know what was happening "facturally," but there, too, we see that its precedence is accentuated in the final version of the painting. While Mondrian was interested in freeing the vertical of his "red cross" by the transformations I have noted, he decided, here, on the contrary, to correct his initial composition in an inverse sense and to make the red vertical pass underneath the horizontal of the "yellow cross." As for the exceptions of the periphery, three were added (on the left, the blue horizontal crossing over the first yellow vertical; then, as I have already mentioned, the horizontal of the "red cross" passing over the second yellow vertical; and, at the bottom, the vertical of the "red cross" passing over the lower yellow horizontal). Since the photo cuts off the painting we cannot know whether the exception at the right is a late addition (the red vertical near the edge of the painting that crosses over the horizontal of the "yellow cross"); and because the photo is in black and white, we cannot determine what happened to its red and blue overlaps of a similar value. We can, however, affirm that of the six exceptions to the global system of colored superimposition in the finished painting, only one, situated at the periphery, is visible in the photo of this stage of the work. This shows that it was not until relatively late, after beginning to paint the strips, that Mondrian was, on the one hand, driven to make the weaving of his composition more complex (to make it a braiding) and, on the other hand, to assign it a precise, structural function.

Von Wiegand gives us the following account: "I asked him if using the colored lines was not more difficult because the varied intensity of red, blue and yellow does

65. *Emery Muscetra,* Piet Mondrian in His Studio, *New York, September (?) 1941. Photo Sidney Janis Gallery, New York.*

not maintain the surface plane as easily as the black lines. He was aware of that but confident of finding proper solutions."[24] The solution was obviously the braiding, and the reversal Mondrian brought about in this painting informs this enigma: the transformation of a procedure of contrast (superimposition, which had indeed hollowed out the surface of his paintings in 1917) into an agent of flatness. This sort of reversal, as Clement Greenberg has so skillfully demonstrated, was already at work in the cubist collage. (In fact, it comprised its inaugural revolutionary act, and it is not surprising that a certain number of critics have insisted on the collagelike aspect of the unfinished *New York City* paintings.)[25] However, I believe that there is something different occurring. I would even say that in *New York City,* Mondrian definitely breaks with cubism (or with whatever cubist influence remained in his art), and it is surely not by chance that Mondrian refers explicitly to cubism (in his letters to Sweeney) in order to discuss the series of destructions that led him to do the New York works. More precisely, the chain reaction that he exposed (destruction of space by planes, of planes by lines, of lines by repetition) is supposed to explain "*why* [he] left the cubist influence."[26]

All of Mondrian's texts dealing with cubism, including Sweeney's "interview," say the same thing: cubism "has not accepted the logical consequences of its own discoveries," it has remained an abstraction *of* something, never having become fully abstract. This immediately places neoplasticism in the position of logical heir, the appointed dauphin in the line of "steady evolution" toward "the abstract expression of pure reality." But if most of the writings insist on the figurative character of cubism, Mondrian remarks that it has remained "basically an abstraction" (which means of course that it was not of itself abstract) because cubism was seeking above all to *express* space or volume (not, as we shall see, to *determine* space or volume). The two aspects of the problem are obviously linked, but everything seems as though Mondrian didn't realize this until that moment when he returned to a particular cubist usage of superimposing planes that he had abandoned after 1917, a certain construction of the surface of inscription *above* the material support surface.

Greenberg, in his analysis of the cubist collage, shows that Braque and Picasso were attempting to dissociate literal surface (that of the support) from depicted surface (that of the colored, or noncolored, planes) in order to introduce a minimum of three-dimensional illusion between the two. He also demonstrates how their surface of inscription became temporarily aporetic, denied and affirmed, simultaneously and in turn, until a suspended vibrato immobilized its ambivalence. Greenberg indicates as well how when they found themselves constrained to rep-

resent spatial relations (that is, illusion) only schematically and so to speak semiot-
ically they were also forced to return to representation—namely, to groupings of
independent forms functioning as silhouettes—since only large concatenated planes
could maintain the integrity of the picture surface.[27] I believe that it is precisely here
that the criticism of cubism in Mondrian's later work intervenes, or at least this is the
point where he once again takes up the dialogue with cubism that he had interrupted
with the advent of neoplasticism. Indeed, Greenberg himself notes that Picasso
invented a solution (with his reliefs) that allowed him to escape the optical dilemma
(decorative flatness/illusionist hollowing); but, faithful to an ideological model of
pictorial quality as resolved contradiction, he immediately placed the spatial literality
of these constructions into the domain of sculpture where, according to him, they
heralded the ideal he then held of that art—that sculpture be as pictorial as possible.
In a word, Greenberg absolutely shunned any comment on their quality as objects,
or on their opacity. From a painting becoming sculpture, he evoked a sculpture that
remained painting.[28]

   To say it briefly (but I shall return to this momentarily), in *New York City*, Mondrian recovers that impenetrability, that *nonopticality* of cubist relief, while instantly
avoiding any form being able to take root there or getting caught up in the woof of
the painting. If we agree to read this canvas as a critical reprise or an eradication of
cubist principles, we understand why Mondrian here abandons (for the first time but
one) the cubist dissociation of color and line.[29] We also understand why he sternly
considered his "classic" neoplastic works at this same time as being still too conspicuously *drawn*. (Dissociation always produces a hierarchical effect in favor of
drawing. This is Cézanne's lesson, and Matisse's, and Newman's, and, I would venture, the late Mondrian's as well. All of them wished to sketch in color.) Finally, to
understand *New York City* not as postcubist but as anticubist is to understand why
Mondrian so obstinately sought to annihilate contrast, that essential element of cubism, to de-semanticize contrasts by means of the all-over repetition (since "similar
forms do not show contrast, but are in equivalent opposition"). At the same time, at
least if we refuse to abide by Greenberg's postcubist reading, it is also to understand
a little of what links Pollock to Mondrian's late period.

Regarding Mondrian, Naum Gabo reports that

he was against space. Once he was showing me a painting. . . . "My good-
ness!" I said, "Are you still painting that one?" I had seen it much earlier.
"The white is not flat enough," he said. He thought there was still too
much space in the white, and he denied any variations of colour. His ideas

were very clear. He thought a painting must be flat, and that colour should not show any indication of space. . . . My argument was, "You can go on for ever, but you will never succeed."[30]

As Virginia Rembert has observed, this discussion, which occurred in the late thirties, immediately recalls Greenberg's famous remark regarding the impossibility of absolute flatness: "the first mark made on a canvas destroys its literal and utter flatness, and the result of the marks made on it by an artist like Mondrian is still a kind of illusion that suggests a kind of third dimension."[31] Unfortunately, Greenberg ends the debate by adding, "only now it is a strictly pictorial, strictly optical third dimension," and he seems to believe, against all evidence, that this new type of illusion was the effect Mondrian desired. Nonetheless, Greenberg's affirmation was not always thus. We can even say with Rembert that in this 1961 text he reversed his own position on Mondrian's art, the one to which he laid claim at the time of the painter's death. Didn't he write, just after Mondrian's death, that "his pictures . . . are no longer windows in the wall, but islands radiating clarity, harmony and grandeur—passion mastered and cooled, a difficult struggle resolved, unity imposed on diversity. Space outside them is transformed by their presence?"[32] For the time being, I shall dismiss the metaphorical geography. At this moment, Greenberg insisted on the physical presence of these paintings, which he opposed to the Albertian illusionism of the "window in the wall." In such a way, he notes their quality of inscribed objects in the real space of the room at a time when this essential characteristic of sculpture was not yet the hydra of literality that modern sculpture (for him) owed itself to destroy.[33]

Thanks again to Rembert, we know that this text was informed by an extraordinary article by G. L. K. Morris, published a year earlier in the *Partisan Review,* a journal of which both he and Greenberg were among the major editors. "Relations of Painting and Sculpture" is a modern version of the *paragone* of the Italian Renaissance (and Morris makes explicit reference to the well-known positions of both Michelangelo and Leonardo da Vinci). The era was one of redefinition. While in "Towards a New Laocoon." published three years earlier, Greenberg radicalized Gotthold Lessing's discourse (which dealt especially with literature) by characterizing the "essence" of each art by the propriety of its means, Morris examined the different types of relationships between painting and sculpture in history. Of the four categories he separated in his sequence of illustrations, each including a work of ancient and of modern art, without a doubt the most provocative is the category of "paintings conceived in terms of sculpture": a Mantegna is reproduced beside a Mondrian.[34] Of course, Morris is not in the least attempting to suggest that it is a question here of similar matters. On the contrary, his entire analysis rests on the initial assertion that modern art (since Cézanne) first had to renounce any desire to imitate the effects of sculpture in painting. But according to Morris, since cubism we have been witness to certain exchanges of function: sculptures are conceived as paintings, even though they may be in motion (Calder); paintings imply a literal tactility. The cubist collage was still rather reticent on this level:

> It is Mondrian, however, who goes farthest toward giving us sculpture,—although the word "object" might better characterize one of his canvases. Mondrian's paintings preclude any possibility of entrance at all; the very frame (set behind the canvas surface) pushes the area forward instead of letting the spectator into the wall. I find highly significant the contention which Mondrian once put forward verbally, that mural painting was "wrong." It is wrong for him indeed because he would not have his pictures a *part* of anything; they are free objects which one can touch and move around, as much a part of the world as any statue; they remain the strongest examples yet conceived of painting projected as sculpture. Previously the sculptural traditions had presented forms *inside* the painting realized in sculptural terms. But Mondrian gives us a thing in itself,—and here we have something entirely new, a fragment of the modern world, concise, compact and complete. I do not infer that Mondrian is the only one to propose this new conception; he has merely presented it with the least compromise and perhaps the sharpest sensibility.[35]

Incidentally, the other example Morris offers is comprised of Jean Arp's paintings and collages ("the only 'pure' besides neoplasticism," according to Mondrian).[36] More important for our discussion is the fact that the illustration Morris chose (and he had known Mondrian's work for a lengthy period: he had bought one of the artist's paintings as early as 1936) is a New York work and not a "classical" neoplastic painting. More precisely, it is true, it was one of those works begun in Europe, completed in New York, and presented by Mondrian with two dates (1939–42) at the time of his first one-man show at the Valentine Gallery.[37] One might find my entire argument weakened by the fact that Morris did not illustrate his article with *New York City,* which was also presented at that same exhibit. But it could be here a question of a deliberate act: his text appeared at the time of Mondrian's second showing at the Valentine Gallery, in January and February of 1943, where *Broadway Boogie-Woogie,* unquestionable an "optical" regression in relation to what Morris wanted to demonstrate, held the place of honor. Now in a way, *Broadway Boogie-Woogie* arises from *New York City.* If indeed Morris had the chance to see Mondrian's second New

York exhibit before publishing his article, he probably would have preferred to reproduce a painting from the artist's work that represented his progressive inclination toward a sculptural tendency rather than *New York City* which was, in a sense, its conclusion (but which comes off badly in black and white). Furthermore, certain characteristics of *New York City* foreshadowed the temporary negation of this sculptural tendency (with *Broadway Boogie-Woogie,*) before its final reaffirmation constituted by the unfinished *Victory Boogie-Woogie.* This is, of course, only conjecture: the important thing is that Morris considered Mondrian's New York works as participants in the order of object or sculpture and that Greenberg, far from speaking at that time about a new type of "purely optical" illusion, adopted the same point of view.

Everything occurred as though, in New York, Mondrian had at last taken into account Gabo's remark on the ineluctableness of spatial illusion in his earlier neoplastic works. It is as though he had judged these paintings in the same way Greenberg did, twenty years later, but, far from appreciating their optical spatiality, he had wanted to return to the origin of the problem in order to find a radical solution. This question had undeniably preoccupied him for quite some time. It has often been noted that from the thirties onward, his black lines were almost inlaid, engraved into the white surfaces. For Mondrian, it was visibly a matter of counterbalancing the optical hollowing effect of the white accentuated by the black lines. At the same time, the lacquered, shiny black aspect of the lines in opposition to the radiant matte quality of the white prevents those lines from being perceived as shadows. Another indication of the artist's preoccupation is the frame, whose usage Morris emphasizes in Mondrian's work, the zigguratlike frame that itself is of greater and greater importance from the thirties on (and one day it will be necessary to analyze to what extent the two evolutions are parallel: that of the material embedding of the black lines and that of the setup of the frame). We know from Sweeney's "interview" that Mondrian himself considered his frames as an essential contribution: "So far as I know, I was the first to bring the painting forward from the frame, rather than set it within the frame. I had noted that a picture without a frame works better than a framed one and that the framing causes sensations of three dimensions. It gives an illusion of depth, so I took a frame of plain wood and mounted my picture on it. In this way I brought it to a more real existence.[38]

In the case of both lines and frame, sculptural models were at Mondrian's disposal. (By this, I mean theoretical models and not examples to be imitated.) Around 1930, Jean Gorin realized his first neoplastic reliefs, whose hollowed lines (often white on white, thus shadowed) pleased Mondrian enormously. Mondrian said, "It goes farther than my work, which in the end remains *tableau*."[39] As for the famous remarks about the frame, they were directly associated in Mondrian's mind with the sculptures of his friend Harry Holtzman. Shortly after having sent to Holtzman a first version of those remarks, Mondrian wrote the following:

> Today Sweeney has asked me to lunch again and still asked some questions. I gave him some notes for the right understanding of some points and explained a little why I brought the canvas *on* the frame instead of *in* it. Then I wrote, "In recent three-dimensional works of Harry Holtzman we see the 'picture' still more from the wall brought into our surrounding space. In this way, the painting *annihile* [annihilates] literally the volume and becomes more real."[40]

Here again, Mondrian found Holtzman's columns more "modern" than his own paintings.[41]

But it is of primary importance that, in the first place, in both cases, Mondrian associates these three-dimensional works much more with architecture than with sculpture, and, in the second, that he was never tempted to pursue such a path.[42] For sculpture as such has the bad habit of constituting itself as figure against the surrounding space, which thus functions as background. Having no predetermined limit, sculpture is only conceivable from a neoplastic viewpoint as inscribing itself in an architectural space that it articulates (thereby avoiding the figurative menace).[43] Such is not the problem of the *tableau*, which is *necessarily* limited and which functions, according to Mondrian, as a "substitute for the ensemble." In short, it is not sculpture that Mondrian is after. He is seeking the sculptural in painting: he strives to give to his works, which are autonomous entities, the literal quality of an object that will render them optically impenetrable. To make sculpture per se would, for Mondrian, have been a renunciation. It would have meant siding with Gabo. He remains a painter and wants to resolve the problem in painting.[44]

"In Mondrian's Neo-Plasticism the surfaces are flat, but all is not yet flat. The painter still seeks contrasts, he paints in evenly colored planes but doesn't understand the consequences of this set purpose," wrote Władysław Strzemiński in his fundamental text entitled "Unism in Painting" in 1928.[45] In a sense, this is to say more or less the same thing Gabo (or Greenberg) would later say with one basic difference: Strzemiński's believed (or claimed to believe) in the possibility of an absolute pictorial flatness. However, Strzemiński's remark helps us understand the specificity of Mondrian's New York works. *New York City*'s flatness has a great deal to do with a neutralization of contrasts, as I have already mentioned. But here, Mondrian adopted a strategy rigorously opposed to the one Strzemiński had earlier adopted in his monochromes. (The monochrome settles nothing. No limit stops it from optically opening onto infinity.) Instead of suppressing all contrast, Mondrian multiplied contrasts, *just as Seurat had done.* We know that Mondrian did go through a neoimpressionist phase and that, under Jan Toorop's influence, he practiced Seurat's technique. This occurred about 1908. However, in all his first writings on color, it is not Seurat he mentions, but Cézanne. In his 1942 autobiography, when he wrote that "the first thing to change in [his] paintings was color," he was referring to the impressionists, Vincent Van Gogh, Kees Van Dongen, the Fauves. Not to Seurat ("T," p. 338).[46] Mondrian does mention pointillism in "A New Realism," right after a vehement protest against the then-current interpretation of abstract art as an "expression of space" (a late version of his dialogue with Gabo). Space should not be expressed, said Mondrian; it should be *determined,* articulated, destroyed as such, as receptacle, as void. It should be caught up in a network of oppositions from which it is inseparable. "To express space" is already to make it a peculiarity, a background from which forms raise themselves. "In the course of culture, space determination is not only established by structure and forms, but even by the mechanics of painting (brushwork, color-squares or points—impressionism, divisionism, pointillism). It has to be emphasized that these techniques deal with space-determination and not with texture. The expression of texture is the establishment of the natural aspect of things. Space-determination destroys this aspect" ("NR," p. 350). Although Mondrian's remark is not too clear (especially at a time, as all have noted, when he was adopting a more pictorial brushwork than in his "classical" neoplastic phase),[47] it is extraordinary that he refers to Seurat, among others, to illustrate his concept of determination of space.

What did Seurat do? As Jean Clay has superbly demonstrated in an article where he compares Seurat to Pollock and Pollock to Mondrian, Seurat worked on the superimposition of similar elements in an overall disposition: "The work process allies itself with a bombardment of discrete unities distributed in layers that articulate themselves on the one or more layers already laid down. It is because texture is constituted by 'relatively homogeneous' distinct elements that the work appears to us as an ordered superimposition of layers. The pigmentary mass 'unfolds' itself in a certain number of imbricated strata that, between them, offer sufficient similitude to form a system." Clay then returns to Pollock: "Pollock's 'contrapuntal' painting . . . is equally representative of this ordered articulation of distinct elements. . . . When the capacity for articulation fell short, Pollock's skeins ran together, formed blotches—

the networks, formerly interlaced, became clotted into an opaque, viscous mass."[48]
I shall return to Pollock, but I want here to follow Clay in analyzing depth as articulation in Mondrian's New York works. We have seen that in *New York City* Mondrian
abandoned contrast founded on a cubist dissociation of color and drawing. It is far
from the case, however, that he wanted to undo all differences in an absolute
"unism." On the contrary, Mondrian believed, as did Seurat, that it is only possible
to determine space by articulating it: "Opposition requires separation of forms,
planes or lines. Confusion produces a false unity," he wrote in "A New Realism"
("NR," p. 349). Hence the clear but also complex definition of intersections in *New
York City,* including tone-on-tone intersections—which is what Mondrian meant by
determination. Hence the desire to avoid all optical mixing (contradictory, certainly,
to the goal Seurat was after). Holty tells us, most probably speaking of *Victory Boogie-
Woogie,* that Mondrian "did not want the colors to 'harmonize' but to remain distinct
as forces. Too often, little blue areas next to yellow ones caused the effect to be green,
or reds and blues gave the effect of violet or purple. The object was to find the proper
intervals to prevent this 'weakening' of the color and to preserve its original strength
brought to life by oppositions."[49] I have said elsewhere that Mondrian had invented
a new type of color relation, nonchromatic, but founded nonetheless on the radicalization of atomism in Seurat's work: relations of quantities of intensity and weight,
not of tints and tones. However, I shall correct myself on one point. If color order
is always given at the outset in neoplasticism (the three so-called primary colors),
there are still variations in tints from one work to another in his "classical" period,
for the simple reason that before *New York City,* Mondrian's atoms (indivisible,
incompressible elements) were not yet the discrete, similar unities that articulated
themselves in the painting (the colored strips), but were the colors themselves, or
rather the colored tripartition given prior to its formal actualization in the painting.
In other words, in "classical" neoplasticism, the conceptual atom had not yet found
a rigorous plastic "translation." And this slippage between the colored a priori and
the necessity of a formal "equilibrium" gradually discovered, or constructed, in the
act of painting compelled Mondrian to make chromatic adjustments, even though he
then already tended to consider his colors as separate, absolute entities.[50] In the
famous remark Mondrian made in New York, "I always want to overbalance things,"
a statement usually quite rightly read as a denunciation of the static equilibrium in
his earlier neoplastic works, we can also see a lament precisely about the coloristic
fine-tuning he had been obliged to practice. He must indeed still have been striving,
in *New York City,* to find the perfect tone for each color, but that tone was ideally to
be independent of the overall color harmony of the painting. (And I believe that all

the color work of neoplasticism reached for this goal that remained unattainable as long as the formal ideal was governed by what Mondrian called "static equilibrium.")

In a rather strange text written about the time Mondrian definitively abandoned his practice of modulating white tones, he brought up the problem of color in a discussion of the nature of egoism. He stated that it was possible to view egoism in a positive fashion, a fact that traditional ethics, riddled with hypocrisy, was incapable of understanding. The color of neoplasticism furnished a good example of such an egoism founded on equality: "Neo-Plastic . . . gives each color and noncolor its maximum strength and value; and precisely in this way the other colors and noncolors achieve their own strength and value, so that the composition as a whole benefits directly from the care given to each separate plane."[51] We can easily see that the concept of mutual reinforcement of colored intensities is still indebted to an aesthetic of contrast. (Mondrian was never to renounce this idea, but in New York he would accentuate it to the point of dialectically transforming it into its contrary.) Nonetheless, the intrusion of color by way of egoism, in this text dealing with the social implications of neoplasticism, demonstrates that Mondrian was attempting even then to formulate an "achromatic" theory of color, to find an articulation of colors that would borrow nothing from the natural order, that would be, in a word, absolutely abstract.

I have said that one of Mondrian's main fears was optical mixing ("confusion produces a false unity"), which is perhaps why he was loath to speak about Seurat as one of his predecessors in the realm of color. Holty states that Mondrian complained of the radiance of the yellow in *Broadway Boogie-Woogie* when he saw the painting hanging in the Museum of Modern Art.[52] In fact, this problem had already occurred to him when he was working on *New York City.* Von Wiegand noted the following in her journal: "He showed me that yellow against white was making the background appear yellow by reflection and it [this painting] was not therefore so pure as the 'classical' one [a painting begun in London] where the yellow rectangle in the lower left was defined by the black line." Von Wiegand added, "Then we noticed that the reflection of sunset was casting a warm yellow glow on the paintings, which changed them and softened their colors."[53] Unfortunately for Mondrian, the sun wasn't the only cause. It would be pointless to deny that, in *New York City,* yellow and white intermingle ever so slightly. This intermingling is even cited by Masheck as an agent of the painting's flatness. I would say an involuntary agent because an optical one. (We should note that oddly enough a yellow-white mingling is the only kind Mondrian allowed himself during his "classical" neoplastic period, with the unicum that constituted his 1933 diamond painting with yellow lines.) But Mondrian's disappointment before *Broadway Boogie-Woogie* at the Museum of Modern Art may well be the debt he had to pay for a particular fetishizing of modern life. He had never liked the flickering of the gas lighting in his Parisian studio; in New York, the electrical lighting fascinated him with its evenness, its disengagement from natural rhythm, and its "abstraction." He painted at night. We can easily imagine the yellow and the contrast of yellow/white reacting differently by daylight and by electric light (one being white, the other yellow). I don't know what the lighting was like at that time in the Museum of Modern Art, but Holty tells us, according to Rembert, that the colors in *Broadway Boogie-Woogie* "had looked clearer and more distinct in the small space of Mondrian's studio than in the larger gallery at the museum, where the yellows appeared to bleed-off against the whites and a desirable crisp effect was lost."[54] Furthermore, it is that gentle coloration that Greenberg objected to in the painting when he saw it at the museum, going so far as to see impure colors in it (orange and purple), only to correct himself a week later, explaining his error by the new usage of greys in the painting.[55] (Several times during Mondrian's years as a painter, the artist complained of the changes his canvases underwent when they were illuminated in a way other than that used in his studio. In one of his earliest writings, for this very reason, he proposed that his canvases be painted in the very spot where they were to be hung.)[56]

Returning to *Broadway Boogie-Woogie*, we find that optical mixing is omnipresent. The intensity of the colors is subsumed in a generalized tone. From this point of view, it is the work closest to Seurat: a fusion is at work whose primary cause, according to Greenberg, is the small grey squares. That seems at first to be a curious interpretation, in the sense that most critics see in the grey squares a way of avoiding direct contrasts of primary colors and of "correcting," or, rather, of determining the optical oscillations generated at the intersecting nodes of *New York City* (by effects of simultaneous contrast).[57] But it is fundamentally a valid interpretation: in attempting to correct what still remained of "opticality" in *New York City,* Mondrian relinquished the sculptural, that literally "tactile" braiding, that determination of space—and consequently only accentuated opticality as such. In fact, two "optical" effects were at work: the oscillations at the line intersections and the illusionist hollowing out of the surface. (Both are secondary effects, which is why one is such a good way to contain the other.) While in *New York City* the first effect, oscillation, had been used by him to render the second, hollowing out, impossible, in *Broadway Boogie-Woogie* Mondrian attempted to integrate the oscillation as a *given* (that is, not any more as an effect) into his composition, but this attempt at once reinforced rather than suppressed the hollowing out. In the unfinished state of *Victory Boogie-Woogie* (whose superimpositions and oscillations are much more violent than those in *Broadway Boogie-Woogie* and whose white planes come forward as never before in Mondrian's painting); in the feverishness with which Mondrian "destroyed" the near-finished state of this painting in his latter days, to Sidney Janis's bitter regret; in that compulsion to heap tiny bits of paper upon other tiny bits of paper, I see a sort of frantic, impossible struggle against "opticality" for the "liberation of our vision."[58]

This strategy of destruction is more clearly at work in *New York City,* and I need not add that I do not comply with any reading that sees *Broadway Boogie-Woogie* as a sort of salvage of this painting or that sees *Victory Boogie-Woogie* as a failed version of it.[59] As Christian Bonnefoi has stated, it is a matter of first destroying the entity of the surface in order to be able to reinvent the surface as an instance, to be able to produce it and no longer consider it as a given.[60] We know about Erwin Panofsky's famous demonstration: perspective foreshortenings of the various "proto-Renaissances" have nothing to do with the monocular perspective of the Italian Renaissance, because they imply an aggregative space conceived as a simple receptacle, as a residue of what is not material body, the only substantial entity. In order for the perspective of the Renaissance to become possible, the art of the High Middle Ages had to renounce, under Byzantine influence, all ambitions of creating spatial illusion.

> So [Panofsky states], when romanesque painting reduces body and space to the surface, in the same manner and with the same consistency, this transformation imprints, for the first time, really, a definite seal on the homogeneity of body and space, in changing their former, loose optical unity into a solid and substantial one. Henceforth body and space are soldered together for better or worse and consequently when body again frees itself from the ties that link it to the surface, it cannot grow without the space increasing as well.[61]

In other words, for the painting's surface to be optically denied by the construction of perspective, for the window to open out on the world, this surface would first have had to be defined as an entity, it would have had to be geometrically constituted as a finite, homogeneous field. (Meyer Schapiro says that same thing by placing the question in a larger historical context, without falling into the perspectivist teleology characteristic of Panofsky: "The new smoothness and closure made possible the later transparency of the picture-plane, without which the representation of three-dimensional space would not have been successful.")[62] It is as though in New York Mondrian wanted to travel in reverse along the path that had led, in Mantegna's epoch five centuries earlier, to that piercing—that annihilation—of the painting's plane.

Everything happened as if he had realized at that time that to destroy this illusionism, this weight of tradition that entraps us, he had to destroy what had made it possible, namely the unity, the homogeneity of surface at work in Byzantium. (Indeed, it is obviously not by chance that he refers precisely to Byzantine art in his late writings, in order to note how his painting differs from it ["T," p. 340].)[63] The only way to establish the surface's optical impenetrability, its opacity, was to contest its material identity, the geometric cohesion that had been the condition for its annihilation. It is impossible to annihilate (make transparent) what does not exist as such (surface entity). Only a literalization of volume (braiding) can destroy spatial illusion.

In a dense and enigmatic text from his youth, Walter Benjamin defined painting in this manner: "Painting—An image has no background. Besides, one color is never superimposed upon another but rather appears at the very most in its medium. This is perhaps also hard to make out, and so one could not in principle for most paintings distinguish whether a color is closest to the foreground or furthest in the background. But this question is pointless. In painting there is neither background nor is there graphic line." Opposed to this is the category of drawing:

> Graphic line is determined in opposition to surface . . . In fact, graphic line is coordinated with its background. Graphic line designates the surface and thereby determines it by coordinating it itself as its background. Conversely there is a graphic line only on this background; this is why, for example, a drawing that entirely covered its background would cease to be a drawing altogether. The background thereby occupies a definite and, for the sense of a drawing, indispensable position; this is why within graphics two lines can determine their relation to each other only in relation to the background—a phenomenon that demonstrates with particular clarity the difference between graphic and geometric line.[64]

Must we deduce from this that *New York City* participates in the category of drawing since colors are superimposed on other colors? (But is it possible to establish other than by fragment, in detail, "whether a color is closest to the foreground or furthest in the background"?) Are there even graphic lines in this work? And if we admit for a moment that the colored strips are lines, is the relation between two lines uniquely determined by reference to their common background? *Is there a background in New York City?* Benjamin continues: "Graphic line confers an identity upon its background." Isn't that the opposite of what occurs in this painting? A series of questions pointing to the fact that with *New York City* a new category is invented, beyond painting and drawing.

To read Benjamin's text, we must refer to the circumstances of its composition. Written in the fall of 1917, "Über die Malerei oder Zeichen und Mal" was conceived as a response to a letter from Gershom Scholem, a letter about cubism, "although it was hardly mentioned."[65] For Benjamin it was a question of refuting the avant-gardist boast that cubism was an art completely estranged from pictorial tradition. It was also a question "of first outlining a universally valid conceptual foundation for that which we understand painting to be" (*B*, 1:173).[66] However, in wanting to demonstrate that a cubist painting and a painting by Raphael belong to the same sphere, that of painting and not of drawing, Benjamin conceded that he had omitted the analysis of what separated the two (*B*, 1:154).[67] Such was Benjamin's starting point. In his correspondence relating to this text, he cited Picasso's *Dame à l'éventail.* (The precise reference is unclear.)[68] We should note that he did not refer to the cubist collage, a silence not without significance, since it is highly possible that the problems laid bare by the collage bothered Benjamin a great deal as he began to elaborate his ideas on the opposition between painting and drawing. It may even be possible that these problems were the source of his interest in such a question, since this text immediately follows another, far more concise, written during the summer of 1917, which Benjamin considered indispensable to the proper understanding of his ideas. He summarized the substance of the earlier text to Scholem, not having the written copy at hand: "Allow me to add this important complementary remark: from the point of view of man, the level of drawing is horizontal; that of painting, vertical" (*B*, 1:167). Indeed, it is in this manner that he distinguishes between painting and drawing in "Malerei und Graphik." Certainly, according to Benjamin, there are some drawings that we may consider as we do paintings, on a vertical plane (for example, one of Rembrandt's landscapes), but there are others that cannot be placed vertically "without missing their true significance" (for example, children's drawings). "One could speak of two sections of the world's substance: the longitudinal section of painting and the transverse section of some drawings. The longitudinal section seems to be representative; it somehow contains things; the transverse section is symbolic, it contains signs."[69] If I think that the cubist collages were perhaps at the origin of Benjamin's reflections, it is because in those collages there was for the first time an attempt at a certain horizontalization of the pictorial plane, a sort of logical short circuit, the invention of a new category. It was an attempt that the cubists were forced to abandon. That is why the cubists were obliged to remain at the level of figuration and why Benjamin took only their paintings into account, and perhaps rightly so, wanting to demonstrate that finally they belonged to the same category as Raphael's paintings.[70]

I believe that this horizontalization of painting, this passage to the symbolic order of drawing in painting, is what is at work in *New York City,* and it is, in a sense, what earlier caused the impossibility of directly applying Benjamin's insights in "Über die Malerei oder Zeichen und Mal" to the painting. There may already be a tendency toward "the transverse section of some drawings" in Mondrian's work that came directly out of cubism. Many critics have noted this; among them are Leo Steinberg, who called *Pier and Ocean* (1915) a forerunner to what he named the "flatbed" in sixties art; and Svetlana Alpers, who spoke of a map in relation to this painting.[71] Others have remarked that if the cubists blurred their compositions on three sides, steadily maintaining the central figure on the support constituted by the lower limit of their paintings, Mondrian gnawed at his composition by haziness on all four sides at once.[72] Still others say that the blinkings of the 1918 diamond modular composition were inspired by a starry sky (which is to say an isotropic space).[73] But what is at stake in all these accounts is no more than a very uncertain tendency broached by the elaboration of neoplastic principles (and by the concept of static equilibrium) which depended entirely on gravitational sentiment, on man's upright position on earth. This last point even served as the essential argument in Mondrian's famous critique of Theo van Doesburg's use of oblique lines, which presupposes, according to Mondrian, an eye liberated from the human body: neoplasticism is "the true and pure manifestation of cosmic equilibrium from which, as human beings, we cannot separate ourselves."[74]

Obviously, something quite different happened in New York. Since his years in Paris, Mondrian had certainly worked at his paintings on a table, as though drawing.[75] But it was only with *New York City,* by using adhesive tapes, that this process moved into the painting. Why? Because each colored strip is an atom (indivisible: it is applied all at once) and because the atom is immediately laid out from edge to edge. It immediately governs the surface exactly like Pollock's networks (he worked with his canvases on the floor) and no longer requires putting the painting on an easel after every placement to verify its effect (or, to be more precise, no act of verification can concern any unit smaller than a whole line dividing the painting from edge to edge). Everything goes very quickly when one is no longer "balancing," when one is no longer obliged to weigh *everything,* when each stroke is all or nothing. All his observers have noted the rapidity with which Mondrian placed his strips of adhesive tape. (Von Wiegand, describing one of Mondrian's work sessions, spoke of the humming of "his intent mental activity, to which his steps and movements were an accompanying ritualistic dance."[76] This remark again reminds us of everything we know about Pollock's method.) Von Wiegand also evokes "the geometric rhythm of city traffic seen from above" when discussing *New York City,*[77] and this maplike metaphor will be reused constantly—remember that Greenberg, too, discussed Mondrian's painting in geographic terms. In short, in Mondrian's later works, there is a deliberate battle against gravitation—just as there is in Pollock's great *drippings.* This does not mean, in one case as in the other, that these works are reversible . . . try it and see! (Absolute reversibility assumes either monochromes or symmetry, the latter a form that had to wait until the sixties and Frank Stella's work to be definitively separated from the idea of decoration.) Painting, as opposed to some drawings, continues to be viewed from a vertical position. It is necessary to take this into account in the composition phase if one wants to liberate one's painting from any gravitational feeling. It is true that all the *New York City* works are higher than they are wide, as opposed to *Broadway Boogie-Woogie,* which is square. The small drawing that is like the first conception of this series shows that Mondrian has at first envisioned a more vertical format (which would make *New York City III*—the only one of the three that is distinctly vertical—the first of the series).[78] What does this signify? It means that Mondrian was only able to return to a square format (a very rare occurrence in his work, let it be noted) after having found a more structural means of attaining antigravitation with *New York City.* It has often been observed that he used fewer and fewer horizontal formats (and practically none at all after the thirties), as though he wanted to avoid at all costs the landscapelike connotations that were linked to his traditional concept of static equilibrium (the horizon line). It is also well known that he didn't like his paintings to be too "Gothically" vertical, finding them "tragic." Besides, it is certain that he was completely aware of the difference in value of horizontal and vertical lines (verticals always seem longer), which is why Mondrian generally accorded them less width. In a way, the equal width of the strips in *New York City* demonstrates that he felt sure enough of himself to no longer need such an artifice to counter the verticality of his painting. His return to the square in *Broadway Boogie-Woogie* shows that he no longer feared the ghost of the natural horizon. This completely contradicts Kermit Champa's reading of that painting. In *Broadway Boogie-Woogie,* Champa saw some sort of triumph of verticality, seeing in the *New York City* series signs foretelling this triumph. (On the one hand, the finished *New York City*—our painting—has more horizontals that verticals; on the other, as Masheck has noted, *Broadway Boogie-Woogie* was the first painting to contain more broken verticals than broken horizontals.)[79]

In the past few pages, I have often referred to Pollock (and it is not insignificant that it was Mondrian who discovered him, in a way, or who at least persuaded Peggy Guggenheim that Pollock's painting was something fundamental: "the most exciting painting that I have seen in a long, long time, here or in Europe").[80] I have also noted that Clay was careful to characterize a certain number of common elements between Pollock and Mondrian's New York painting. (These include the "all-over," depth as articulation, the impossibility of the observer's visual control over the general effect of the work's field. We could also mention the sense of detail, which Clay noted in relation to Pollock and which would also apply to *New York City* as it would to *Broadway Boogie-Woogie,* to say nothing of *Victory Boogie-Woogie.*) I believe that Mondrian's later works participate in the fundamental shift that Rosalind Krauss intuited in Pollock's work, in his method itself which assumes a break between painting a canvas (on the floor) and seeing it (on the wall) and which necessitates an operation of reading. "Certainly this break, this double movement—the rough experience on the floor; the deciphering on the wall—is reiterated in the observer's experience in front of the hung and finished painting. In fact we *can* look at Pollock's paintings as arising from pure optical sensation. But to view them in this way—following his early critics—proves that we possess none of the keys essential to understanding them."[81] In the same way, an "optical" interpretation of Mondrian, conceived in the assurance of immediate perception, cannot account for his New York paintings.

For it is undoubtedly the dominance of Greenberg's interpretation of Pollock (undeniably the best of its era) that led Steinberg to exclude this artist from his definition of the "flatbed."[82] Perhaps the same is true of Mondrian's later work, which should have interested Steinberg a great deal more than *Pier and Ocean. New York City* is one of the first "flatbeds," one of the first examples of the horizontal reversal that Steinberg considered in quasi–Lévi-Straussian terms as a passage from nature to culture in Robert Rauschenberg's art: "palimpsest, canceled plate, printer's proof, trial blank, chart, map, aerial view. Any flat documentary surface that tabulates information in a relevant analogue of his picture plane—radically different from the transparent projection plane with its optical correspondence to man's visual field."[83] Steinberg says that the "flatbed"—transverse section, symbolic—arises from action, as the verticality of the picture plane in the Renaissance arose from vision. There is a fundamental difference—a gulf, however small—between representing action and fulfilling it. Mondrian had this to say relative to the works of his youth: "Even at this time, I disliked [painting] particular movement, such as people in action" ("T," p. 338). Regarding free rhythm and dynamic (universal) movement, he wrote in one of his American texts that plastic art "creates *action* by the tension of the forms, lines, and the intensity of the colors—and in this is its force."[84]

Sculptural thickness (braiding), nonchromatic color relation (atoms), anti-gravitation (all-over): such is the conceptual, plastic "pas de trois" achieved by Mondrian in *New York City,* which is a painting, but also a diagram, a battle plan against the "longitudinal" section of representation. When Holty asked him why he kept repainting *Victory Boogie-Woogie* instead of making several paintings of the different solutions that had been superimposed on this canvas, Mondrian answered, "I don't want pictures. I just want to find things out."

66. Barnett Newman, Onement I, *1948. Oil on canvas, 68.5 × 40.6 cm (27 × 16 in.). Collection Annalee Newman, New York. Photo courtesy Annalee Newman.*

"On his birthday, January 29, 1948, he prepared a small canvas with a surface of cadmium red dark (a deep mineral color that looks like an earth pigment—like Indian red or a sienna), and fixed a piece of tape down the center. Then he quickly smeared a coat of cadmium red light over the tape, to test the color. He looked at the picture for a long time. Indeed he studied it for some eight months. He had finished questing."[1] With such words, vested in the neutral tone of historical narrativity, Tom Hess describes the event of what he called, and rightly so, Barnett Newman's "conversion": the "interruption" of process in the act of painting *Onement I* (fig. 66); the long, slow afterthought about this abrupt act; and the final conclusion of this rumination with the apparition of *Onement II* and *Be I,* which represent the actual sanction of the "conversion." Newman had "finished questing." Questing for what? one might ask. But anyone familiar with Newman's numerous statements will have the answer at the tip of his tongue: questing for his proper subject matter ("If we could describe the art of this, the first half of the twentieth century, in a sentence, it would read as the search for something to paint").[2] Yet if one is to take Hess's interpretation of *Onement I* seriously—as "a complex symbol, in the purest sense, of Genesis itself"—one cannot fail to wonder if anything at all is new here, for Newman had already been committed to that subject matter, to such an interrogation of the origin. It even seems to have been, right from the start (at least for the body of work that has not been destroyed), the only subject matter that he ever conceived for his painting.

"In 1940, some of us woke up to find ourselves without hope—to find that painting did not really exist," that painting "was dead," recalls Newman in a tribute to Pollock. "The awakening had the exaltation of a revolution. It was that awakening that inspired the aspiration . . . to start from scratch, to paint as if painting never existed before."[3] The search for a new beginning, for a new origin of painting, led directly to a thematics of the Origin. Think first of the "automatic" drawings of 1944–

67. Barnett Newman, Gea, *1945. Mixed media on paper, 71 × 56 cm (28 × 22 in.). Collection Annalee Newman, New York. Photo courtesy Annalee Newman.*

68. Barnett Newman, Genesis—The Break, *1946. Oil on canvas, 61 × 68.5 cm (24 × 27 in.). Private collection. Photo Pace Gallery.*

45, with their imagery of germination (one of them is called *Gea* [fig. 67], i.e., earth),[4] then of his canvases of 1946 and 1947: *The Beginning, Genesis–The Break* (fig. 68), *The Word I* (fig. 69), *The Command, Moment, Genetic Moment:* the titles of most of them refer directly to the dawn of the world as it is conveyed in the mythology of the Old Testament (the command, the word, the break that separated dark from light and gives rise to the possibility of life). It is true that there are some exceptions *(Pagan Void, Euclidian Abyss, Death of Euclid),* but the attack against abstract art and geometry that this second series of titles invokes is no less related to a certain idea of creation, even if it is not directly the myth of Genesis with which Newman is involved in the contemporary canvases.

If the subject matter is not new, are we then to say that with *Onement I* Newman "found a form" for this subject matter? But would not this suppose a sort of disjunction between the two, an anteriority of the subject matter itself, whose a priori spiritual essence would have only been waiting to be clothed in the appropriate body? Everything we know about Newman's method goes against such a supposition.

69. *Barnett Newman, The Word I, 1946. Oil on canvas, 122 × 91.5 cm (48 × 36 in.). Collection Annalee Newman, New York. Photo courtesy Annalee Newman.*

It is true that he speaks somewhere of the "pure idea," and this has often misled commentators ("For it is only the pure idea that has meaning. Everything else has everything else"),[5] but we should not fail to notice that this famous statement was made prior to the "conversion," prior to the traumatic discovery that suspended the production of *Onement I* in an interrupted but definitive gesture, prior to the succeeding months of reflection that filled with an intense labor of thought the blank, the void left by this suspension. Later in his life, that is, *after* this heuristic experience, Newman always disassociated himself from the notion of a pure idea. For example, in a statement dated January 1950 and obviously written for his first one-man show, he says that his paintings "are not abstractions," nor do they depict some "pure idea," adding that "there are specific and separate embodiments of feeling, to be experienced, each picture for itself," and this *specificity* is precisely what the notion of a pure idea waiting for its form would preclude.[6] His distrust of Mondrian's "purism" has everything to do with his belief that the Dutch painter's mode of working was "dogmatic" and that his paintings illustrated an idea that had been fixed once and for all, existing a priori in a pure presence to itself before being actualized in a work. For Newman, Mondrian's canvases were enlargements of sketches or diagrams conceived as the simple translation of a rationale, and Mondrian's art was the model he had to fight, to overcome. Hence his insistence upon working *alla prima,* intuitively ("The fact is, I am an intuitive painter, a direct painter. I have never worked from sketches, never planned a painting, never 'thought out' a painting before");[7] hence his total repudiation of geometry ("It is precisely this death image, the grip of geometry that has to be confronted. In a world of geometry, geometry itself has become our moral crisis").[8] It does not matter that on these matters Mondrian was much closer to Newman than the latter could have known at the time (he too never worked from sketches, never "thought out" proportions in his canvases; he too rebelled against the current assimilation of his art to a kind of pure geometry); what matters is Newman's constant dictum that if it is the meaning of his art that is his essential concern, this meaning does not lie in anything prior to its embodiment in a painting.

But how are we to reconcile the fact that, in the case of *Onement I,* its subject matter seems to have preexisted in such works as *Command* or *Genesis—The Break,* with Newman's denial of the very possibility of such an anteriority in almost all his statements following the "conversion?" The answer is simple: the "conversion" is or rather results from the discovery of this impossibility. "Creation" is indeed the subject matter of his work as much before as after the "conversion," but the meaning of "creation" is different in those various instances (its semantic richness is greater in the later versions, where it seems to encompass the more limited meaning of the prior ones as its condition of possibility). As far as meaning is concerned, that is, as regards both Newman's conception of meaning and its mode of actualization, *Onement I* represents the "dividing line" in his career, to use another of his phrases.

But what is so different, say, between *Moment* (fig. 70), painted in 1946, and *Onement I?* There is, instantly perceivable, a radical break between the two, but what is the nature of this break? Both are relatively small vertical and rectangular canvases whose overall expanse is divided symmetrically by a central vertical band of lighter color. The fact that in *Onement I* the contrast between the "band" and the "ground" is only formulated in terms of value (cadmium red light against cadmium red dark) while in *Moment* this contrast is further accentuated by a shift in the color scale (a band of pale yellow opposed to a brownish ground) does not seem to be the central issue (all works in Newman's "postconversion" career will show an interest in the different behavior of hue and value contrasts). What seems to be at stake here is the difference in treatment of the "ground" in this unlikely pair: while the field of *Onement I* is painted as evenly as can be (it was initially conceived only as

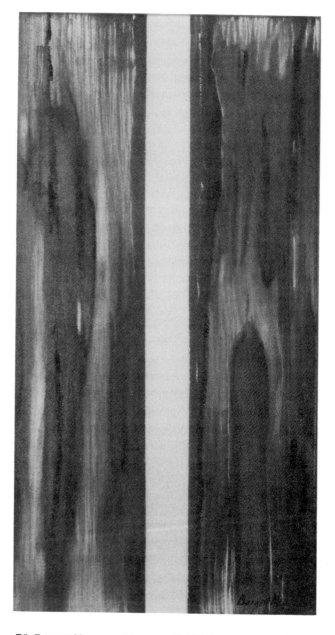

70. *Barnett Newman,* Moment, *1946. Oil on canvas, 76.2 ×
40.6 cm (30 × 16 in.). Tate Gallery, London. Photo courtesy
Annalee Newman.*

a "prepared ground"), in *Moment* we are confronted with a differentiated field that functions as an indeterminate background and is pushed back in space by the band— the band functions as a *repoussoir,* much like the stenciled letters in an analytical cubist canvas. The laterality of the field that is enunciated by the symmetry is undermined by an illusion of shallow depth. As Newman would later say of this work and his other paintings of the time (with the exception of *Euclidian Abyss),* it gives a "sense of atmospheric background," of something that can be conceived "as natural atmosphere."[9] Or, as he would also say later: he had been "manipulating space," "manipulating color" in order to destroy the void, the chaos that existed before the beginning of all things.[10] As a result, what he produced was an *image,* something that was not congruent with but *applied* to its field, that had existed in his imagination before it was painted on the canvas and thus could pretend to extend beyond its limits—something that has no adherence to its support (conceived as a neutral receptacle) and could have been worked out previously in a sketch (as indeed it was). *Onement I,* Hess reports, was to look something like *Moment:* "Newman was about to texture the background; then he would have removed the tape and painted in the stripe inside the masked edges."[11] To "texture the background" and to "paint in" the stripe is precisely what Newman renounced in *Onement I,* and it took him eight months to understand what this renunciation meant for his art.

No wonder. It is still as difficult for us to understand the nature of this radical break as it was for Newman at the time. A clue might be given by one of his statements, "The Ideographic Picture," which was written prior to the "conversion," between the painting of *Moment* and the interruption of *Onement I.* In that text, which contains the previously cited sentence about the "pure idea," Newman is at pains to define a new type of picture: it should not be a design nor "a formal 'abstraction' of a visual fact, with its overtone of an already-known nature," which is how he saw Mondrian's paintings, but it should convey a sense of shape akin to that of the Kwakiutl artist—shape as "a living thing," as "a vehicle for an abstract thought-complex." The new painting should be *ideographic*—and Newman refers to the dictionary to give some precision to his thought: the ideograph is a "character, symbol or figure which suggests the idea of an object without expressing its name," the ideographic is that which represents "ideas directly and not through the medium of their names." Leaving aside the question of the name, which points to an apparent contradiction in Newman's oeuvre, as he seems to have been vastly involved in the titling of his paintings (even calling two of his canvases *The Name),* one should nevertheless pay some attention to his resort to the dictionary at this juncture. For what does the phrase "ideographic picture" mean if not that the picture *itself* must "represent ideas directly"—i.e., be an analogon or a symbol of the idea it represents.[12] *A la lettre,* it means that the painting should not *contain* ideographs but rather should itself *be* an ideograph. A radical program indeed (the abolition of the opposition containing/ contained), which Newman certainly had no means to achieve when he was painting *Genesis—The Break,* or even *The Word, The Command,* and *Moment* (these works contain ideographs, symbols of the idea—the idea of creation—they are not ideographs themselves, they do not *look* like the idea of creation).

Onement I does. In what sense exactly? In that it does not contain, strictly speaking, anything. Not that it is empty, on the contrary: there is a field, and this field asserts itself as such. There is the field, which is given through its stark symmetrical division by a zip, and this sheer elemental division, because this is the sole "event" of the canvas, functions like the initial split that the Old Testament described as the break originating the world. Although it is a simple vertical "line" (hence a ready-made sign that preexisted in some absent stock of signs that—like all linguistic symbols—could be convoked and used at leisure), the meaning of the dividing zip depends entirely on a co-presence with its referent and/or the context of its actual utterance (as is true only of the type of sign known as "indexes"): its meaning lies entirely in its *co*-existence with the field to which it refers and which it measures and declares for the beholder. If *Onement I* is an ideograph, it is of a special kind, which emphasizes a certain circularity between the signification of the sign and the actual situation of its enunciation, like "I," "You," but also like "Now," "Here," "Not There—Here" (and one will have recognized some of the names given by Newman to his later works). In other words, it is what the linguists call a *shifter* (which combines the quality of the symbol and of the index), and I would say that this particular mode of being is shared by many of Newman's successful "postconversion" paintings. Like all previous paintings by Newman, *Onement I* is concerned with the myth of origin, but for the first time this myth is told in the present tense. And this present tense is not that of the historical narrative, but an attempt to address the spectator directly, immediately, as an "I" to a "You," and not with the distance of the third person that is characteristic of fiction. It is thus that *Onement I* fulfills the goal Newman set for his works, that of giving a "sense of place" to its beholder.

How does Newman achieve this? Above all, by the conspicuous use of symmetry. A comparison of *Onement I* with *Moment* again proves extremely helpful: both paintings are symmetrical, but while in *Moment* the differentiation of the background prevents any sense of lateral reduplication, and hence of assertion of the field itself, in *Onement I* the total bilateral reversibility of the painting prevents any possible dissociation between "image" and "field" (thus the sense of "totality" that Newman claimed as the main effect he searched for in his work: "Instead of working with the remnants of space, I work with the whole space").[13] In *Moment,* the symmetry is a matter of composition, it is the type of symmetry that Newman will later dislike in Ingres's *Apotheosis of Homer* or in Veronese's *Wedding Feast at Cana.*[14] In *One-ment I,* the symmetry is the essential means used by Newman to preclude the possibility of any vestige of traditional composition—and it is certainly on this matter that Newman's enterprise departs most radically from that of Mondrian.[15]

But one has to scratch further here, and it is worth looking at the two occasions when Newman spoke directly about the issue. The first occurs in a short catalogue essay written for an exhibition of Northwest Coast Indian painting at the Betty Parsons Gallery in 1946. Speaking about the characteristic bisection of all living things in this art, Newman concludes that the concern of the artists, "however, was not with the symmetry but with the nature of organism; the metaphysical pattern of life." Then, to the best of my knowledge, the issue of symmetry reappears only at the end of his life, in his "interview" with Schneider: if he disliked the *Wedding Feast at Cana* or the *Apotheosis of Homer* because they were symmetrical, he loved Uccello's *Battle* precisely because it was symmetrical. To be able to fully grasp this paradox, we should read the full unfolding of his stream-of-consciousness monologue.[16] Suffice it to say that while in the first case symmetry related to the "nature of organism," to the "metaphysical pattern of life," in the second it relates to man, hence to scale, totality, colorlessness (drawing), all-overness ("nothing to scrutinize," evenness of light), and apodictic evidence ("you get it or you don't").

The first thing to retain in this late statement of Newman's is what links it to the early ("preconversion") one: symmetry is not an issue in itself, it is concerned with life (a surprising enough departure from the tradition of abstract art, which always associated it with death). Yet there is a gap between the two statements. What was at first only the symbol of a theme, of a "pure idea" (organicity, life) has become, via the introduction of man, the locus of a whole range of associations that together define Newman's enterprise.

Are we then to subscribe to the existential and humanistic reading that has often been given of Newman's work, to the great discontent of all those who are inclined, like Greenberg or Judd, to a "purely formal" interpretation of his work? In a certain sense, yes, but in a certain sense only (nothing is more ridiculous than the interpretation of the zip as a surrogate for the human erect figure, and in that sense I remain extremely skeptical about the alleged influence of Giacometti).[17] For what is the perception of bilateral symmetry, indeed, if it is not, as Maurice Merleau-Ponty has remarked, that which constitutes the perceiving subject as an erect human being, if it is not what solidifies for us the immediate equivalence between the awareness of our own body and the always-already-given orientation of the field of perception?[18] "One wonders what would be the *self* in a world where no one knew about bilateral symmetry," writes the French psychoanalyst Jacques Lacan.[19] The implied answer, perhaps, is that it, the self, would *not be,* at all. Certainly the self would not partake of being-in-the-world, and the world would not be human, for we cannot dissociate *being* from *being situated.* The orientation of space, the orientation in space, which is transmitted by what Merleau-Ponty calls a "prepersonal" or "prehistorical" tradition (that of our body), is always-already a determination of our experience as being-in-the world. "Finally," writes Merleau-Ponty, "far from my body's being for me no more than a fragment of space, there would be no space at all for me if I had no body."[20]

Thus if the meaning of *Onement I* can be coined as that of the creation of a world, it is because this world is a world-for-us, neither the "objective" world described by mathematics and physics nor a kind of mythic space that one could describe in the past tense, that one could thematize with symbols and ideographs: the creation here is synonymous to *our* birth-to-the world, to our constitution as selves ("the self, terrible and constant, is for me the subject matter of painting"). But in choosing to actualize in *Onement I* something like an "originary perception"—the very constitution of a perceptual field via the declaration of its bilateral symmetry—something that only our own embodiment can give us access to, Newman did not anthropomorphize his painting. Despite the strong anthropomorphic connotations carried by any symmetrical configuration, it would be wrong, I think, to read *Onement I* as a kind of cryptic portrayal of man as such: one could perhaps say that about the art of the Kiawkiutl artists that interested Newman, as did an ethnologist like Claude Lévi-Strauss,[21] but it would confuse levels to do so here. Newman's painting does not depict man, even "abstractly," it pursues a sort of phenomenological inquiry into the nature of perception, that is, into that which in itself makes something like a man possible. And if he pursues this inquiry in painting, it is both because he is concerned with painting the origin and because painting is, like all art, ultimately dependent on perception.

Let us remain for a few more lines, however, in this connotative field, for it might be helpful to check the "phenomenological" reading I am proposing here of Newman's work (one has to note, just in passing, that I am not assuming that he ever read Merleau-Ponty's masterwork, the *Phenomenology of Perception:* I am content with stressing the quasi-simultaneity of their enterprises).[22] The seventeenth-century French philosopher Pascal had this to say about symmetry: "Symmetry. In anything one takes in at a glance; based on something that there is no reason for doing differently; and also based on the face of man. Whence it comes that we only desire symmetry in breadth, and not in height or depth."[23] The notations about the instantaneousness of the awareness of symmetry as well as its apodictic character are in line with what I have been attempting to say so far (one might even say that Newman felt at the time that not only was there "no reason for doing differently" to eradicate traditional compositional balance, there was nothing else to do).[24] But if I am more interested here in the remark about the grounding of symmetry in human figure, it is not for itself, but for what it leads to: symmetry as an essential condition of our perception, and not as the abstract law that mathematicians analyze, refers to a lateral dimension of the world. It presupposes the vertical axis of our body as the dividing vector of our visual perceptions, of our situation in front of what we see. It thus implies the nonreversibility of a top and a bottom as much as our being situated in or engaged with the world implies our erect human posture.[25]

This, I believe, is one of the lessons Newman drew from *Onement I* during his interruption of eight months, and which he tried to investigate further in some of his paintings of 1949, the most productive year of his entire career. The four canvases of this year in which he uses a horizontal "zip" constitute a deliberate attempt to pin down this issue (and, by the same token, to find a shortcut to liberate himself from the "plea" of bilateral symmetry).[26] But I see the attempt as a "failure"—and Newman must have seen it that way, as he did not revert to this problematic until 1951, that is, after having found other ways to depart from symmetry. (In a sense, however, it is absurd to speak of a "failure" here: not only is the "failure" entirely relative, but Newman's attempt was both logical and necessary—for what it foreclosed and what it opened in the future of his art. For the sake of brevity, though, let us keep the word "failure," but between quotation marks.)

Now, why a "failure"? Because in *Argos,* in *Dionysius* (fig. 71), and in the small untitled painting done at the same time, and no matter how hard Newman calculated their placement so as to undercut this effect, one of the two horizontal "zips" that each of these pictures "contains" reads like a horizon (and it is not always the same in a given canvas: the reading fluctuates, attaches itself now to this, now to that "zip"). The pictorial field is negated as a whole, the background recedes and the painting reads like an abstract landscape. None of those canvases is symmetrical, as if Newman knew that the nonisotropy of the top and the bottom would have condemned any symmetrical division to the same fate (that of making the field tilt in space, so to speak), but the counterbalance of weights with which he tried to combat this topological difference of value between top and bottom amounted to the kind of com-

71. Barnett Newman, Dionysius, *1949. Oil on canvas, 175.2 × 122 cm (69 × 48 in.). National Gallery, Washington. Photo courtesy Annalee Newman.*

positional rhetoric he had scorned in Mondrian's art. *Horizon Light* (fig. 72), perhaps the last of those horizontal canvases, reverts to symmetry and to a single horizontal "zip." Not that the "zip" is symmetrically placed in the field, but that it is itself vertically divided in its center by a radical shift in hue and value: not only does this fail to regain the wholeness of the field achieved in *Onement I,* but the "zip" itself seems to tilt in space, and the contrast between verticality and horizontality seems to bring Newman's art even closer to that of Mondrian. The conclusion Newman reached at this point is that there is no way to escape the fact that the perceptual space is originarily governed by nonisotropy in one direction and by symmetry in the other: both conditions, which are to one another like a verso to a recto of a piece of paper, are due to the fact that it is our body that perceives and not some mechanical and objective device.[27] When he returns to a top/bottom relationship, he emphasizes this point with a vengeance. In *Day before One,* the two "zips" are symmetrically disposed along the top and bottom edges of this eleven-foot-high canvas, yet they certainly do not look like mirror reflections of one another (the strong value contrast between the two is not the *cause* of this effect of a nonidentity; I would say rather that it hides, hence renders more mysterious and active, the subtlety of the effect

72. Barnett Newman, Horizon Light, *1949. Oil on canvas, 77.5 × 184 cm (30½ × 72½ in.). University of Nebraska, Lincoln Art Galleries, Sheldon Memorial Art Gallery. Gift of Mr. and Mrs. Thomas Sills. Photo of the museum.*

under the boldness of its declaration): "we only desire symmetry in breadth, and not in height or depth," or, as Newman would say, "all my paintings have a top and a bottom."[28]

Now, if we cannot escape those primary conditions of our visual perception that I just mentioned, it does not follow that we are taken merely to timelessly confront them—to confront, that is, the pure moment of the origin, as if in autistic isolation. We are compelled to move on, so to speak (and if the "mysteries of life" are the subject matter of his art, as Newman often claimed, those mysteries cannot be entirely subsumed in the flash of the origin). Again, 1949 is a fascinating year in Newman's production, as in it he explores the world of possibilities that *Onement I* had opened, and particularly how the apodictic evidence of this painting could give way to less assertive statements, to less triumphant feelings. It all happens as if, after having verified that evidence in a few other canvases (*Onement III, Onement IV, End of Silence*) and having definitively crystallized it in the injunctive *Be I* (again, the birth of the self to the world), he had tried with a fury to find other modes of declaration of the wholeness of the canvas than the one he had so successfully invented in *Onement I*. The simple enunciation of bilaterality was not to be discarded from his vocabulary (it remained the tenor of many canvases until the end of his life, although never again with a single zip dashing through its center, except in *Onement V* and *VI* and the second version of *Be I*), but he obviously did not want to be confined to it.

Because *Abraham* (fig. 73) still makes use of bilateral symmetry without declaring it (the right edge of the "zip," which becomes a plane, is congruent with the central axis of the painting), as if Newman did not want to relish its perceptual privilege, it could be read as a transitional work. I believe, on the contrary, that it is a major breakthrough, that this canvas opens for Newman a new paradigm that will immediately govern a flurry of other works (the most immediate of which is *By Two,* of the same year). For what does he accomplish here? Precisely because he used a symmetrical division but managed to destroy its power by the most subdued lateral displacement, he makes us aware that "nothing is more difficult than to know precisely *what we see,"*[29] that our perception is necessarily ambiguous and aporetic, that, precisely because we are oriented in the world, we cannot ever reach once and for all anything we perceive: *Abraham* is only partly symmetrical, and the discrepancy between its left and right sides is enough to radically undermine for us the actual perception of this quality. There is no way in which we can read the left and the right edges of the black "zip" as having simultaneously the same value. More than that, those different values have no means to be fixed, each will shift constantly as our gaze scans laterally across the canvas.

After *Abraham,* a whole range of Newman's production seems to have been involved in a radical attack against any kind of assurance that we might falsely attribute to our perception. All that he said about the necessity to "transcend" format and size in order to achieve "scale" (and, in the case of *Chartres and Jericho,* about his wish to destroy the triangle as an object) is directly related to his sense that the context entirely determines one's perception: he struggled against geometry precisely because in its faith in essential properties of figures, it seems to ignore this basic fact of experience (and again, on that matter, Newman is a lot closer to Mondrian than he believed). Thus if it is not altogether wrong to disclose secret symmetries in some of his works, as Tom Hess was at pains to do, it is largely counterproductive to do so, just as it is totally irrelevant to seek to define any system of proportion that he might have used. For Newman himself invariably labored to destroy the a priori certainty displayed by such diagrammatic modes of division (the only proportions that he thought of consciously are those of each of his canvases as a whole, in order to build the stretcher, but he could not do that before having a vague idea of what he wanted to achieve with the canvas in question, an idea that of course would have to be modified when he would be confronted with the actual canvas).

But *Abraham* does not only represent a break with the mere declaration of the anthropomorphic structure of symmetry; it is the first instance where Newman directly confronts an issue that the "conversion" of *Onement I* had allowed him to

73. Barnett Newman, Abraham, *1949. Oil on canvas, 210 × 87.6 cm (82¾ × 34½ in.). The Museum of Modern Art, New York. Philip Johnson Fund. Photo of the museum.*

dismiss altogether, that of the structure figure/ground, which constitutes, as much as our being situated, the basis of our perception. In *Onement I,* the bilateral division performed by the zip gave it immediately the status of a deictic: it declared the space it was congruent with, asserted its field of inscription without functioning as a *repoussoir.*[30] But how was a similar zip going to perform in a different situation? Certainly Newman did not want to abandon the sense of totality that he has been able to invent in *Onement I!*

Let us look for a moment at another painting, which I take to be anterior to *Abraham: Concord* (fig. 74). There are two reasons for my chronological reasoning. The first is that in *Concord* Newman still did not depart from pure bilateral symmetry: what he achieved here is a mere deemphasis of the axis of symmetry by doubling the zips and pushing them away, still symmetrically, on each side of it. The axis itself is not marked, but its virtuality is certainly not enough to cancel its power, on the contrary. Simply, the symmetry we perceive is not so much that of the field per se but that of the relationship of the two zips within the field. The second reason, which could be a consequence of this different use of symmetry, is that Newman seems to have attempted in *Concord* a return to the type of differentiated background that he had abandoned after *Moment,* as if he wanted to see, after having managed to invent a radically new sense of "wholeness," if he could retain this sense even in adverse conditions. Unfortunately, although *Concord* is probably one of his most seductive canvases (and maybe partly because of that, as Newman was always opposed to hedonism), I would say that he "failed" (note again the quotation marks). Due to the cursiveness of the brushstrokes whose traces seem to pass beyond the zips, and to the highlights on the zips that give them an almost metallic gleam, as if they were poles in the round, this is one of Newman's most "atmospheric" paintings. But again, this "failure" taught him that he could not prevent looking seriously into the whole question of the figure/ground opposition. I believe that he became extremely aware of the difficulty, which is perhaps why he used such a minimal color-value differentiation in *Abraham* (black on black), but his confidence must have grown immensely after the completion of the latter, for not a single painting of this extraordinary year reverts to such a minimalism in values (one would have to wait for white-on-white canvases like *The Name II* and *The Voice,* of 1950, to find such minimal contrasts in his work). At any event, after this inaugurating moment, he does not seem to have had any fear of the strongest contrasts imaginable—as his predilection for the black and white combination demonstrates.

To perceive is first of all to perceive a figure against a ground (this is the basic definition of perception). But the ground is not a given: it is indeed what we must

74. Barnett Newman, Concord, *1949. Oil and masking tape on canvas, 228 × 136 cm (89¾ × 53⅝ in.). The Metropolitan Museum of Art, New York. George A. Hearn Fund, 1968. Photo of the museum.*

preconsciously construct differently each time we are solicited to perceive. If such is the structure of perception, how could it be possible to prevent a pictorial field from becoming a ground against which the figures will solidify as figures and which they will push back? Newman's stroke of genius is to have understood that perception is made of a constant synthesis of different levels, and that to prevent this annihilation of the pictorial field as background, he would have to set some of those levels in irreconcilable opposition to one another. His strategy was to emphasize the intentional nature of the perceptual field by urging us to shift from our preconscious perceptual activity (or the "normal" preconscious level of perception) to a conscious one, and at the same time to prevent this consciousness from crystallizing in any definite way. Specifically, the function of the zip is radically altered once it is not placed on the axis of symmetry of the canvas: it functions as a landmark that we are urged to fix, as a pole to which we could attach our gaze in the way in which Turner attached himself to the mast of a ship during a tempest.[31] But to fix it would mean to isolate it completely from the global field, to ask ourselves what we see there, and in doing so to lose the ground on which is based our perception as a whole, i.e., the spatial reference of our body. Willing to become pure vision, we would lose what constitutes the total structuration of our vision. We cannot both fix the zip and look at the painting at the same time, and it is precisely upon this impossibility that Newman based the dazzling effect of his canvases.[32] In this way, he paradoxically laid bare one of the most traditional conventions of painting, a convention that lies at the base of the narrative tradition of this art, namely, the dissociation between the perceptual field (which is radically transformed when we pay attention to and try to fix one of its elements) and the pictorial field (whose elements solicit our attention). It is as if Newman succeeded in isolating this condition, as one isolates a chemical element, in stripping it from the realm of narrative, so to speak, and in making it one of the most significant means of his art (his statement that his "paintings are neither concerned with the manipulation of space nor with the image, but with the sensation of time" points to this among other things).[33] Newman's move seems to have gone this way (although he certainly would not have formulated it so): if the pictorial field is prevented from functioning like a permanent ground, if the canvas is divided in such a way that in looking at a zip we are solicited by another one farther away, hence are constantly in the process of adjusting and readjusting the fundamental figure/ground opposition, never finding a moment of repose when this structure could coalesce, then the only factual certitude that we will be able to grasp will be the lateral expanse of the canvas, the pictorial field as such. I believe that this, the basis of Newman's sense of scale, is what he discovered while painting *Abraham*. To be sure, there is no second zip in this canvas, but the very width of the single black band that cuts it across is enough to achieve the effect I have described: its two edges never solicit us simultaneously long enough for it to solidify as a figure (and it is not by chance that *By Two* immediately followed: it functions almost like a verification of what Newman had just discovered).

Most multi-zip canvases of the 1950s and 1960s would, I believe, sustain my demonstration, all the more since Newman added the parameter of color to his vocabulary of ambiguity, making the vast expanses of color of his canvases fluctuate in such a way that we have to renounce the possibility of ever controlling them perceptually. As an example, however, I would take *The Moment I* (fig. 75), for in its stark unity it presents a pristine occurrence of the effect I am trying here to describe. *The Moment I* is a ten-foot-wide, 102-inch-high horizontal rectangle of bare canvas that is split on its right side by two zips of saturated lemon yellow. Partly aided by the oily halo that surrounds the zips (more visible on the one closer to the center, which for the sake of brevity I shall call the "central" one), an immediate effect of simultaneous contrast occurs: a violet shadow emerges, as imprecise as any effect of this kind. Such effects are not as common as one might expect in Newman's work, but here it constitutes one of the most evident means by which he achieves this destabilizing of perception (or rather, the demonstration of the fundamental ambiguity of our perception) that is, I have been claiming, one of the tenets of his art. Looking at *The Moment I,* then, we start by noticing the quasi-impossibility of fixing, of isolating from its ground, any of the yellow zips. But scanning across the surface, we notice as well what is almost an incapacity *not to* try to fix the central one, necessarily more "powerful" than its companion as it controls a larger expanse of bare canvas. In the course of our repeated attempts to do so, always to be denied any final possession of this zip (the violence of the simultaneous contrast functions almost as an impenetrable obstacle here), we might be seduced by the possibility of considering the interval between the two zips as if it were itself a sort of extremely broad zip (we would then gladly rest on the assurance of our perception and maybe be able to hold a figure that we could weigh against a ground). But no, this will not do either: the lateral thrust of our gaze across the creamy color of the canvas is too strong to leave us in peace at that. And this for two reasons: the first, which is obvious, is that the two zips are off center to the right, leaving a large untouched zone at the left, which cannot but summon our gaze; the second one is more subtle, although we sense it at once: the area comprised between the right zip and the right edge of the canvas (that is, on the other side of the imaginary maxi-zip we are eventually trying to construe) is of the same dimension as the one comprised between the two yellow zips. This

75. *Barnett Newman,* The Moment I, *1962. Oil on unprimed canvas, 258 × 306 cm (101½ × 120⅜ in.). Kunsthaus, Zurich. Photo courtesy Annalee Newman.*

very duplication, with its play on the fragility of similarity and difference (of the *difference between* similarity and difference), prevents any isolation of the zone on which we were trying to zero in. Thus the call of the central zip greets us again, and we find ourselves back at the beginning of our search for something to perceive (to measure against a ground) or to fix (to isolate from that ground).

The Moment I dates from 1962, but the kind of structure I have just attempted to describe governs most works following *Abraham*. But his interrogation of the figure/ground opposition also led to other possibilities, successively presented in the first and second of his one-man shows. The first was that of having the painting itself perform the zooming in on the zip: in the six skinny vertical canvases of 1950, the visual field far exceeds the pictorial field, but as there is virtually no ground against which any zip might be claimed as a figure, we return to the type of wholeness invented in *Onement I* (albeit differently), that of the pure adequation of the image to the field. The second solution, inaugurated in the splendid *Vir Heroicus Sublimis,* is that of the very large canvases, where, on the contrary, the pictorial field far exceeds the visual field—at least if one obeys Newman's injunction to look at these paintings "from a short distance."[34] In a way, this last solution is only a radicalization of the type of effect that I have described in *The Moment I,* as witnessed by a very beautiful photograph that shows a man whom I take to be Newman himself and a female companion only a few inches from the surface of *Cathedra.* The lady is obviously busy trying to fix the white zip that splits the vast dark blue field, while "Newman," farther away from the zip, is only feeling its lateral call across the expanse of color. To analyze properly the nature of this radicalization, one would have to discuss anew the whole issue of the sublime, which seems at first so much to contradict Newman's desire to give a "sense of place" to the beholder of his works, but I obviously will have to postpone this issue for some other time, for some other place.

I would like rather to concentrate, in conclusion, on a third solution to the figure/ground question that appears for the first time in one of the elongated "shaped canvases" of 1950, the fourth untitled painting of that group (fig. 76). The canvas constitutes an obvious commentary on *Onement I:* it uses the same colors and is ostensibly symmetrical. Two dark red "zips" of equal size, each limited by a different side of the canvas, flank a lighter and wider field of double width; or one might also say: a bright red "zip" divides a field of dark red whose extension is drastically cut by the limits of canvas. The zip has become a plane, and in doing so has rendered utterly undecidable the very terms of the opposition figure/ground. The sequel to this positive/negative aporia will be *The Way I* (fig. 77), in which the lateral symmetrical

76. Barnett Newman, Untitled (Number 4),
*1950. Oil on canvas, 188 × 15.2 cm (74 ×
6 in.). Collection Mr. and Mrs. I. M. Pei,
New York. Photo courtesy Annalee
Newman.*

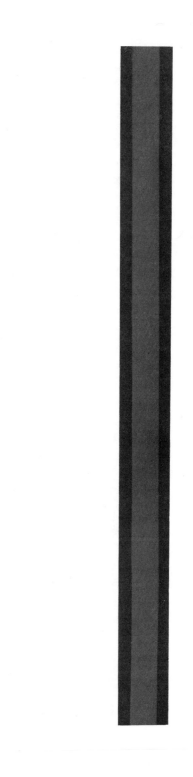

"zips" themselves have gained so much width that their existence as zip is wholly undermined, and Newman will be interested again in this obtrusively ambiguous structure until the end of his life (from *Primordial Light* [1954] to *The Way II* [1969], via *Profile of Light*, *Voice of Fire*, and *Now II* [1967], among other works). But I find it quite remarkable that in this case too Newman felt a definite urge to depart from symmetry. It all started, according to him, with the painting of *Who Is Afraid of Red, Yellow and Blue I* (fig. 78) (although one could say again that this is already announced by the lateral displacement and the widening of the zip in *Abraham*: in a sense *The Gate* [1954], which uses the type of displacement of bilateral symmetry seen in *Abraham,* but this time with planes, as in the works just mentioned, would point to such a filiation). "I did have the desire that the painting be asymmetrical and that it create a space different from any I had ever done, sort of—off balanced," writes Newman.[35] He then became immersed in a coloristic problem that led, as is well known, to his discovery that he could at last confront without fear Mondrian's dogma of the primaries. But, if we want momentarily to leave aside the issue of color (not that I think we should take too seriously Newman's anticoloristic stance—the famous "I am always referred to in relation to my color. Yet I know that if I have made a contribution, it is primarily in my drawing"[36]—but for the sake of clarity), we will have

77. Barnett Newman, The Way I, *1951. Oil on canvas, 101.6 × 76.2 cm (40 × 30 in.). National Gallery of Canada, Ottawa. Photo of the museum.*

78. *Barnett Newman,* Who Is Afraid of Red, Yellow and Blue I, *1966. Oil on canvas, 190.5 × 122 cm (75 × 48 in.). Collection Mr. and Mrs. S. I. Newhouse, Jr., New York. Photo courtesy Mrs. Newhouse.*

to turn to other canvases deriving from this new shift in his work, namely *White and Hot* (1967; fig. 79), an untitled painting of 1970 (fig. 80), and above all *Anna's Light* (1968; fig. 81) which combines with this new structure the huge size of *Vir Heroicus Sublimis* (it is, in fact, the largest painting Newman ever realized, measuring nine by twenty feet).

Those three paintings have in common a central field of color flanked by two asymmetrical white areas respectively bordered by the right and left limits of the canvas. One of these white areas is narrow—if it were not at the edge one would see it as a zip, and even as it is one is tempted to do so—while the other is larger but nevertheless infinitely narrow in comparison to the color field it delimits, hence denied any definite status for our perception (its narrowness or width is measured against the two other elements of the canvas, which give simultaneous and contradictory answers). The fact that those white areas are on the border of the canvas and are asymmetrically displaced (unlike what happens in *Now I* and *II,* for example) raises immediately the issue of our ability to take in the limits of the canvas. This is an important issue for Newman, whose large-size canvases emphasize that we do not cease to incorporate those limits in our perception even when they cease to be in

79. Barnett Newman, White and Hot, *1967. Oil on canvas, 213.4 × 182.9 cm (84 × 72 in.). The Saint Louis Art Museum, Gift of Mr. and Mrs. Joseph Pulitzer, St. Louis. Photo of the museum.*

our visual field (seeing *Noon Light* in a restorer's studio, unstretched and pinned flat on a board like a frog bound to be dissected, I realized there is no way to be able to look at a Newman without interiorizing those limits). In fact, looking at those three canvases, we immediately start to work on trying to define, for ourselves, their beginning and their end. In doing so, of course, we try to compute instinctively their center, but that is precisely what their asymmetry will forbid us to achieve: the off-centered color field will jump with our gaze either on one side or the other, will either try to push over the narrow white area with the help of the large one or vice versa. We try then to compute the center of the colored field alone, but here it is the nonidentity of the white areas, each pulling toward it or away from it the virtual axis we are trying to define, that will undermine our attempt: the lack of coincidence of those two centers prevents us from being able to grasp either of them. In the end, we will only be left with the sheer sense that this color area occupies *a* space with the solidity of a metal plate, but will have to renounce finding out *which* space exactly: we see that it is there (or rather "not there—here"), it confronts us forcefully, but we have no way of virtually absenting us from this *hic et nunc* to be able to conceptualize the nature of this confrontation.

80. Barnett Newman, Untitled, *1970. Acrylic on canvas, 197.8 × 152.4 cm (77½ × 60 in.). Collection Annalee Newman, New York. Photo courtesy Annalee Newman.*

It would seem at first that the red and white *White and Hot* and the blue and white untitled painting of 1970 function like a pair: in one canvas the larger white area is to the right, in the other to the left. Yet the different sizes of the two paintings indicate clearly that it would be altogether wrong to exhibit them as pendants (this would mean an attempt to reestablish some kind of symmetry, an attempt that would be doomed to failure). In fact, it is not by chance that *Anna's Light* was painted in the lapse of time that separates the two, for here Newman reverted to his greatest ally (largeness of scale) to give a final blow to the very possibility of a part-to-part relationship—that is, to achieve asymmetrically what he had achieved in *Onement I*, to address the spectator in the physicality of the present tense, as an "I" to a "You." But here Newman achieves this without resorting to the type of indexicality he had so successfully called upon in his "conversion" piece: the field is not simply declared by a zip that measures it for us. On the contrary, the colored field seems to move with us, to follow our gaze as a dog follows his master or the shadow our walking body. And, precisely because we cannot find its center (a situation that is almost opposite to what happens in *Onement I*), and hence do not manage to constitute it as a figure, it "moves" without ever leaving its base, reaffirming its instantaneous blast each time we try to distance ourselves from it.

The handling of color plays the same role in the three paintings (undercoats applied with a roller, final coat applied with a brush), but it is in *Anna's Light* that its function is most apparent: this last coat of red is shiny but slightly darker, which makes the hue modulate according to our distance from the painting and the way it is lit (the last coat is not evenly applied and there are areas where it does not seem to have been applied at all: when the canvas is brightly lit, those areas look darker from close up—as they are not shiny—and lighter from further away). These modulations are opposed to the sensuous color modulations one can find in the large canvases of the 1950s (think of *Vir Heroicus Sublimis,* whose unique red is constantly shifted by the color accents of the numerous zips, or of *Cathedra* and its deep blue). Those were part of the strategy of fixation/perception that I described earlier: like the zips, the modulations were constantly singularized but their singularity was constantly denied by the lateral spread of our perception. But here this opposition of fixation/perception seems abolished: we cannot even attempt to focus on anything but are constantly obliged to deal with the mere vastness of the whole red field, as a whole chunk of color. The modulations do not perform any more, as they did in the 1950s, like subtle accidents within a field, like a discrete solicitation of our gaze or an intimation to accommodate further, even if in the end we were denied this possibility. The shiny gloss, here and there, forestalls any desire for this sort of accom-

81. Barnett Newman, Anna's Light, *1968. Acrylic on canvas, 274.3 × 609.6 cm (108 × 240 in.). Kawamura Memorial Museum, Sakura (Chiba). Photo courtesy Annalee Newman.*

modation, and our gaze is not authorized ever to attempt to go beyond the surface of the canvas: as such, those modulations function as a sort of internal respiration of the field of color that has become as indivisible as one's own body. *Anna's Light* seems to me like the last major step Newman took in order to achieve the wholeness he wanted to achieve. In a way, this canvas is a direct answer to the puzzle raised by *Onement I:* how to free oneself entirely from part-to-part relationship without reverting to the pure laying out of the axis of symmetry, how to convey the essential discovery represented by the "conversion," that of the anchoring of perception within the "prehistorical" knowledge of our body without referring to the originary condition of its orientation in space. The red wall of *Anna's Light* shows that disorientation is as essential as orientation to our perception—and that disorientation could be achieved even without setting various levels of perception in mutual opposition. As such, it is one of Newman's most abstract canvases, and also one of his "fastest." Like *Onement I,* but with utterly different means, it assumes the existence of the instant, strives to suspend duration (which is impossible): such is, it seems to me, what separates most of Newman's art from minimalism (for what would his attachment to the word "zip" mean otherwise)? If *Onement I* represents the break of origin, *Anna's Light* expresses the flood of life made possible by this single flash.

The more closely you look at a word the more distantly it looks back.

—Karl Kraus

The question—despite its rhetorical flavor—must be asked at the very outset: why is it so hard to write about Robert Ryman's work? Aren't his paintings themselves—preeminently antiillusionist, flatly literal—all the explanation the viewer or critic needs to penetrate their ineffable silence? Don't they reveal what they're made of, proudly, with a kind of routine generosity, thereby cutting short any attempt at associative readings? Simply, don't they seem to suggest their own commentary, to define their own discursive terrain? And if we ask Ryman what we should see in his paintings on corrugated paper, whether, for example, we "should just see white gestures on a tan surface rather than skyscapes or studies of mist," he answers: "What the painting is, is exactly what [you] see: the paint on the corrugated and the color of the corrugated and the way it's done and the way it feels. That's what's there."[1]

Why is it so difficult then, for me and others, to approach his work and express our excitement about it? Isn't it tempting, but tediously elementary at the same time, to compile a list of "what's there" in a work of Ryman's, a recipe ("the way it's made"), a checklist? Isn't this what he as the artist invites us to do?

In Naomi Spector's lengthy essay on Ryman, she undertakes a systematic chronological description of Ryman's work from the point of view of process. Painstakingly, she establishes each painting as a procedural document, reconstructing Ryman's process of production in the smallest detail.[2] But how do I explain my hesitation to begin? Why this inertia instead of smartly stepping up to take my own turn as detective (the evidence: the paintbrush, the paint, the support) and insisting on my version of the facts?

It's not as if the historical development of the process itself isn't of primary importance, or that Ryman's inventiveness doesn't express itself in the making; it should be clear that in this sense he drives himself to experiment, and the story of these experiments never fails to interest me. Yet there is a certain innocence in the systematic decoding of the how-it's-done. Like the hunt for sources that used to take place in literary studies, or the search for the motif in art history (find the improbable valley that was the source of inspiration for this engraving by Seghers or this drawing by Claude Lorrain), the narrative of process establishes a primary meaning, an ultimate, originating referent that cuts off the interpretive chain. That is, an aesthetic of causality is reintroduced, a positivist monologue that we thought modern art was supposed to have gotten rid of: A (paintbrush) + B (paint) + C (support) + D (the manner in which these are combined) give E (painting). There would be nothing left over in this equation. Given E, ABCD could be deciphered, absolutely. By making the artist a kind of engineer who solves a problem of many parameters in his work (Ryman, the experimenter, does in fact often speak in these terms), the discussion of process in art is refitted to this heuristic mold. The object of this critical discourse then would seem to be: given the solution (the painter's "eureka"), find the problem.

Thus, pretending to believe that visual thinking functions only as anamnesis— recovering a section of Lost Time—the narrative account of process allegorizes painting without admitting it, or without realizing it is doing so, conceiving of the painting as a rebus. According to the process allegory, what we should see in *Empire* (1973; fig. 82) is not so much a canvas on which the subtle, white, all-over smoothness delineates three contiguous zones of fleecy horizontal bands, the intensity and rendering of each zone being scarcely distinguishable from one another, but a "reflection" of the "process of its creation";[3] viz., among other things, that three paintbrushes were used to make this painting, which is an index of the artist's heroic exertions. It isn't that I disapprove somehow of this sort of allegorization, or that I experience no pleasure—aesthetic pleasure, that is—in finding out that the painting's three bands correspond to the durability of the three paintbrushes. But does this mean that Ryman's is a world without qualities? That the White of *Empire* is not, to our senses, brilliant, hovering, vibrating, and materially dense, *before* it is seen as a *product?* before, that is, we could possibly worry about how it was produced?

Any attempt at commentary, especially when it addresses the visual "asceticism" of Ryman's paintings, even more when it examines them at very close range, becomes distanced from its object, or, rather, sees its object become distant. This is one of the meanings of the Kraus epigraph. The innocence of the process account stems from its believing itself capable of exhausting its object, of being able finally

82. Robert Ryman, Empire, *1973. Oil on linen, 244 × 244 cm (8 × 8 ft.). Collection Panza di Biumo, Varese. Photo courtesy of the artist.*

to state the truth about the truth, when it is in fact its object that exhausts it. The claim that the process account is essential is more interesting to me than the narrative itself, because it is precisely this claim that Ryman questions. The innocence of the process account is its failure to think about its own claims to primacy.

We know that Ryman sometimes makes prototypes of his paintings, that he discards many of them in the course of his work, that he is selective ("to obtain these thirteen panels Ryman worked on more than fifty," Barbara Reise wrote about the *Standard* series).[4] Does this mean that his choice is a function of the legibility of process in the completed work? Nothing could be less certain. Who would know, for example, looking at series *III, IV, V,* and *VII* (figs. 83, 84, 85, 86), whose titles correspond to the number of panels they contain, that the more or less identical panels were actually painted in groups of three?[5] And how *could* it be known, since except for the major exception of the first series (*III*), none of them is a multiple of three, nor is the total number of panels (nineteen), whether intended or not, divisible by three. Is this element of process then insignificant because it is concealed? No, because it generates (and thus "explains") the slight breaks in continuity, in the last three series, between the horizontal bands whose gestural rhythms extend from

83. Robert Ryman, III, *1969. Enamelac on corrugated paper. Three units, 152.4 × 152.4 cm each (5 × 5 ft.). Private collection. Photo courtesy of the artist.*

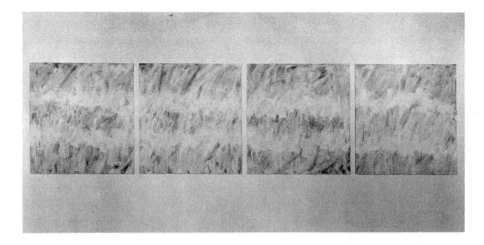

84. *Robert Ryman,* IV, *1969. Enamelac on corrugated paper. Four units, 152.4 × 152.4 cm each (5 × 5 ft.). Milwaukee Art Center. Photo courtesy of the artist.*

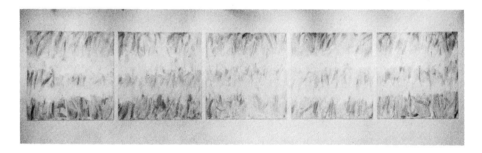

85. *Robert Ryman,* V, *1969. Enamelac on corrugated paper. Five units, 152.4 × 152.4 cm each (5 × 5 ft.). Collection Panza di Biumo, Varese. Photo courtesy of the artist.*

*86. Robert Ryman, installation, one-man show, 1969. Fishbach Gallery,
New York. Photo courtesy of the artist.*

panel to panel. But couldn't this slight discontinuity have been obtained by painting
these panels one by one? No, because the semiautomatic breadth of gesture corresponds to the entire width of the original surface existing as a sort of frieze (the
three panels that were initially juxtaposed extended over thirteen feet). Painting the
panels separately would cause excessive discontinuity, or, rather, discontinuity pure
and simple, which would signify nothing and be an empty sign, since it would not
be in opposition to the continuity it interrupts. Therefore, since this element of process is not insignificant, why isn't it expressed? Because process doesn't interest
Ryman *as such*. He attempts instead to construct a structure of oppositions: a paradigm. This is what the visual "asceticism" in his paintings is always ready to provide.
The structural paradigm—continuous/discontinuous—declined by the full series is
clearly legible: the procedural record has nothing more to teach us; it may even lead
to a concept of arithmetic accountability that is of as little value at this juncture as—
to repeat my metaphor—the "correct" motif of a Seghers engraving.

Another example is the *Stretched Drawing* (fig. 87), which demonstrates the
tension characteristic of all painting mounted on stretchers (the drawing was traced
first against a stretched canvas, then unmounted, then restretched). Barbara Reise
states that "[i]t is a 'drawing,' not a 'painting,' for dried paint—even on cotton canvas—cracks into non-adhesion during an accentuated stretching and restretching

87. *Robert Ryman,* Stretched Drawing, *1963. Charcoal pencil on cotton canvas, 38.1 ×
38.1 cm (15 × 15 in.). Collection of the artist. Photo courtesy of the artist.*

process. If Ryman were *only* 'into process,' he might have used paint and accepted its disappearance. . . ."[6] If he were a competent practitioner of Process art, as there was reason to believe, he no doubt would have chosen this solution, accompanying the result of his experiment with a caption detailing the course of events. The presence or absence of the work would simply be a record of the process, an index,[7] with no further exercise of the code, without recourse to a paradigm. But in fact we know that if he had undertaken such an experiment, Ryman would no doubt have considered the result a failure and would have destroyed it.

This drawing, then, instantiates *tension*—an institution ordinarily naturalized (taken for granted) in painting—declaring it a historical code rather than a natural fact. Yet it does so indirectly. If Ryman were to content himself with a frontal attack on the institution of tension, he would, like many painters working in France in the '70s, be satisfied by simply exhibiting his unstretched canvases in large sheets unrolled to the floor.[8] Choosing instead to set tension in contrast with its opposite, Ryman reveals the following aporia: which comes first, the stretching or the unstretching? The aporia itself leads to a historical investigation. That is undoubtedly the other sense of Kraus's aphorism: the closer you look at a word, the more echoes begin to reverberate from the sedimented strata of its historical, etymological dimension, the deeper the geological cut that opens up. Isn't it possible, for example, following Ryman, to read modern art according to this new oppositional axis—stretched/unstretched—and, on the basis of that point among others, to establish links between, say, Bonnard and Pollock (both of whom painted their canvases before stretching them)?

Finally, Ryman invests his paradigm with actual configurative power. We are tempted to say that the drawing was sketched on unstretched canvas; but can we in fact *say* that? The misshapen square that we see is not a *sketch*. It is not first and foremost the product of a freehand drawing. Nor even simply of the act of stretching, unstretching, and restretching the canvas. But of the intervals between them. Now, the narrative of process is strictly additive, for it can never recapitulate more than one successive set of acts; it cannot reveal how the work stages their proliferation. Making the work the objective complement of a series of transitive actions (squeezing the paint, stretching the canvas, etc.), the process account refuses to believe in the enigma of the work's potential intransitivity.[9]

Returning, then, to the initial question: why do I find it so difficult to write about Ryman? Isn't it enough to describe and analyze not the process itself but the process of the process (not *tension,* but the stretchedness of the unstretched stretch)? This is exactly where the difficulty lies. We know that all of modern culture is characterized by a loss of innocence regarding what we call the means of expression, and that the entire modernist enterprise can be read along the axis of this reflexivity. That this is taken for granted today is the result of its articulation in what we call the theory of modernism. That it suddenly solidified, excluding from the pictorial pantheon all but a very exclusive group of artists, should not diminish the breadth of the qualitative leap it effected in critical discourse over the past forty years. If it seems to be accepted as a given today that the old masters, whatever they may have said, were much more concerned with painting than they were with history, literature, theology, or psychology, this perception is as much due to the efficaciousness of this theory as it is to the emergence of abstract painting, for which for many years the discourse of reflexivity alone was able to provide a theoretical base.[10] Today's rush to deny the reflexive nature of the modern sensibility, to challenge the acquired knowledge of modernist critical practice, and at the same time, under the pretext of correcting the abuses of this criticism, simultaneously to represent all of modern art as a gigantic historical error and a terrorist mystification—all of this has only symptomatic importance. There will always be those who equate Bouguereau and Ingres, who prefer late de Chirico to early, who say that all the trouble started with Manet. That they are speaking very vociferously today and want us to think they are getting their revenge is only cant perpetrated in the name of history in order better to erase it. The same applies to practice: the antimodernist (mistaken for postmodernist) reaction reflected in the dominant trend in current exhibitions (the schoolboy pranks of the Italian "trans-avant-garde," the Sturm-und-Drang-ing of so-called German neoromanticism—even though it was precisely German romanticism that sowed the seeds of modern reflexivity) is only an epiphenomenon. It is nevertheless true that the historical revisionism I have referred to, like the return to the figurative order we are now witnessing, are both symptoms of the crisis of modernist discourse today. "I approach printmaking in the same way that I approach painting, from the point of view of working with the basic possibilities of the medium," says Ryman, modernist in spite of himself.[11] Is there anyone who doesn't see that this way of speaking is no longer enough? that it is vacuous because it applies in various ways to everything of importance that modern art has ever produced?

Eighteenth-century connoisseurs, responding to Titian's *sprezzatura* and the debate over the best distance from which to see his paintings, began to "look at the painter's handiwork closely, admire his touch and the magic of his brush," to prefer the sketch to the completed painting because it reveals the making of the work, insinuates the spectator into the studio, makes available in secret of the gods.[12] The artist's skills were evaluated by measuring the distance between effect (the resemblance of a portrait, for example) and the means used to achieve that effect (a tangle of gestures). The sudden interest in brushstroke came from an opposition, a discrepancy: a paradigm. And undoubtedly it was this sensualist probing by the connoisseur that finally led to the theory of modernism. But strangely enough, as Jean Clay has remarked, neither Clement Greenberg nor his followers bothered very much with the material process of constructing a work of art.[13] If they were never really interested in the pictorial process, it was because they saw no difference between the painter's formal intention and its realization, its visualization. So Clay continues, "It's as if, when speaking of Ryman, 'modernist' categories were grafted onto the pictorial components that Greenberg himself had avoided. 'Essence' would no longer reside in the ever greater coincidence between a delimited two-dimensional support and its painted surface, but in the specific qualities of texture, brushstroke, affixing elements, stretcher bars, etc., everything constitutive of painting itself, in its very *nature*."[14] And we have seen that Ryman himself speaks in these terms.

Greenberg's interpretation of art since Manet defines the modernist program as being engaged in the elimination of nonessential conventions. What hasn't been eliminated has to be motivated, has to have a logical place in the pictorial order. So far so good. But Ryman, starting from the same premises (there is something like a pictorial absolute),[15] shows that scarcely has a pictorial element been examined— given a motivation by virtue of its formative process—when that which was withdrawn as being arbitrary and unmotivated returns to threaten elsewhere.

A given division of the canvas is determined by the shape of the frame and the choice of paintbrush. Except, how is the paintbrush chosen? where does the frame itself come from? and outside the frame, for example, what is the source of the light that illuminates it? The paintbrush depends on the size of the canvas, but what determines the size of the frame? No requirement seems any longer to take precedence over any other, and when the painting—whew!—interrupts this infinite regress (Roland Barthes's favorite game of hand-over-hand), what is there except this residue of arbitrariness that modernism (the reductiveness of modernism) would have liked to eliminate?[16]

Valéry remarked, "The forms: I think that I think that I think . . . I dream that I dream etc. . . . are limited to only two real states of remove."[17] I would say that Ryman has attempted to paint that he paints that he paints; that he has always wanted, by means of an excess of reflexivity, to outflank the tautological reflexiveness in which modernism has been locked. Further, his success is due not to having attained that literally unthinkable reflexivity, but to the fact that every failure of his audacious attempt removes him further from his object, driving him to produce objects that are increasingly enigmatic and indeterminable. In a sense each of his paintings revives Poe's statement about the *mise en abyme*: "Now, when one dreams, and in the dream, suspects that one is dreaming, the suspicion *never fails to confirm itself,* and the sleeper is almost immediately roused. Thus Novalis is not mistaken in saying that *we are close to awakening when we dream we are dreaming.*"[18] That is, in this instance, by trying to solve the enigma, by trying to think painting, we always arrive, literally, at the same object or the same absence of object. This is what Ryman demonstrates again and again: there is a threshold of reflexivity beyond which the record is erased.

I have placed this text under the sign of Karl Kraus. If I may be permitted one last literary reference, I will return to him. Walter Benjamin writes of Kraus, "He, 'merely one of the epigones that live in the old house of language,' has become the sealer of its tomb. . . . No post was ever more loyally held, and none ever was more hopelessly lost."[19] In relation to modernism, Ryman is in the same position that Kraus occupies in relation to the German language: standing guard at its tomb, like any sentry, he holds an untenable position. He is perhaps the *last modernist painter,* in the sense that his work is the last to be able graciously to maintain its direction by means of modernist discourse, to be able to fortify it if necessary, but above all radically to undermine it and exhaust it through excess.

This detour by way of Kraus, with whom objectively speaking Ryman has very little in common, is not based solely on their parallel positions, but also on the similarity of their arsenals. We are aware of the extraordinary polemical force of Kraus's writing, the untiring, devastating rage that sustained him in his solitary editorship of *Die Fackel.* Benjamin shows that "in a world in which the most shameful act was still the *faux pas*"—the Vienna of 1900—Kraus was effective polemically because "he distinguishes between degrees of the monstrous."[20] In this sense he set for himself a criterion—*tact*—"whose destructive and critical aspect" he brought into play. "It is a theological criterion," Benjamin continues, "for tact is not—as narrow minds imagine it—the gift of alloting to each, on consideration of all relationships, what is socially befitting. On the contrary, tact is the capacity to treat social relationships, though not departing from them, as *natural,* even as paradisiac relationships, and so not only to approach the king as if he had been born with the crown on his brow, but the lackey like an Adam in livery."[21] What does Kraus make of this notion of tact? He does not use it to rise to the sacred, to its theological kernel, but to "dismantle the situation, to discover the true question the situation poses, and to present this in place of any other to his opponents,"[22] knowing full well there is absolutely no hope of escaping history, which he conceives of as an apocalypse. If Kraus treats social relations without "departing from them as natural relationships," it is in order better to capture that very nature in its own trap, better to read, under the "natural," the presence of history.

And what of Ryman? Doesn't he demonstrate extraordinary tact concerning all the institutions of the act of painting, as well as a destructive tact that drives each of them back to its problematic condition? His criterion remains, certainly, theological (his essentialist manner of naming Painting, Engraving), but like Kraus, doesn't he refuse to set limits in his quest of law? In the same way that Kraus, the guardian at the tomb of language, knew that "mankind is losing the fight against the creaturely world,"[23] Ryman also realizes that when the norms of painting are put to the test, what is arbitrary will have the last word. This is perhaps the source of the charm of his paintings, as it is of the difficulty one has in writing about them.

"His reflection has contributed greatly to pushing back the frontiers of the pictorial field," Stephen Rosenthal writes of Ryman.[24] I would say that, with respect to modernism, Ryman (perhaps without realizing it) works with a lethal delicacy; that simply reflexive discourse cannot be carried on with regard to his work; that in forcing reflexivity to reflect on itself he has moreover—quite simply—indicated the limits of our critical discourse more than he has pushed back those of his art, unless in the sense of a distancing of his object that is ever more irrevocable.

IV Archaeology

Painting: The Task of Mourning

> [*My paintings*] *are about death in a way:*
> *the uneasy death of modernism.*
>
> —Sherrie Levine

Nothing seems to be more common in our present situation than a mille-narianist feeling of closure. Whether celebratory (what I will call manic) or melancholic one hears endless diagnoses of death: death of ideologies (Lyotard); of industrial society (Bell); of the real (Baudrillard); of authorship (Barthes); of man (Foucault); of history (Kojéve) and, of course, of modernism (all of us when we use the word postmodern). Yet what does all of this mean? From what point of view are these affirmations of death being proclaimed? Should all of these voices be characterized as the voice of mystagogy, bearing the tone that Kant stigmatized in *About a Recently Raised Pretentiously Noble Tone in Philosophy* (1796)? Derrida writes:

> Then each time we intractably ask ourselves where they want to come to, and to what ends, those who declare the end of this or that, of man or the subject, of consciousness, of history, of the West or of literature, and according to the latest news of progress itself, the idea of which has never been in such bad health to the right and the left? What effect do these people, gentile prophets or eloquent visionaries, want to produce? In view of what immediate or adjourned benefit? What do they do, what do we do in saying this? To seduce or subjugate whom, intimidate or make come whom?[1]

Each time, which means that there is no generic answer to this question: there is no single paradigm of the apocalyptic, and no ontological inquiry about "its" tone. Because the tone of their writings is so different, it would be particularly misguided, and perverse, to connect Barthes to Baudrillard; Foucault to Bell, Lyotard to Kojéve—but it is done in the theoretical potpourri one reads month after month in the flashy magazines of the art world. Derrida's proviso, *each time,* means that in each instance one must examine the tone of the apocalyptic discourse: its claim to be the pure revelation of truth, and the last word about the end.

I will focus here on a specific claim: that of the death of painting, and more specifically, the death of abstract painting. The meaning of this claim is bounded by two historical circumstances: the first is that the whole history of abstract painting can be read as a longing for its death; and the second is the recent emergence of a group of neoabstract painters who have been marketed as its official mourners (or should I say resurrectors? But we will see that it is the same). The first circumstance leads to the question: when did all of this start? Where can we locate the beginning of the end in modern painting—that is, the feeling of the end, the discourse about the end, and the representation of the end? The existence of a new generation of painters interested in these issues leads to the question: is abstract painting still possible? In turn, this question can be divided into at least two others: is (abstract, but also any other kind of) *painting* still possible? and is *abstract* (painting, but also sculpture, film, modes of thought, etc.) still possible? (A third thread of the question, specifically apocalyptic, would be: is [abstract painting, but also anything, life, desire, etc.] still possible?)

The question about the beginning of the end and the question about the (still) possibility of painting are historically linked: it is the question about the (still) possibility of painting that is at the beginning of the end, and it is this beginning of the end that has been our history, namely what we are accustomed to name *modernism.* Indeed the whole enterprise of modernism, especially of abstract painting, which can be taken as its emblem, could not have functioned without an apocalyptic myth. Freed from all extrinsic conventions, abstract painting was meant to bring forth the pure *parousia* of its own essence, to tell the final truth and thereby terminate its course. The pure beginning, the liberation from tradition, the "zero degree" that was searched for by the first generation of abstract painters could not but function as an omen of the end. One did not have to wait for the "last painting" of Ad Reinhardt to be aware that through its historicism (its linear conception of history) and through its essentialism (its idea that something like the essence of painting existed, veiled somehow, and waiting to be unmasked), the enterprise of abstract painting could not but understand its birth as calling for its end. As Malevich wrote: "There can be no question of painting in Suprematism; painting was done for long ago, and the artist himself is a prejudice of the past."[2] And Mondrian endlessly postulated that his painting was preparing for the end of painting—its dissolution in the all-encompassing sphere of life-as-art or environment-as-art—which would occur once the absolute essence of painting was "determined." If one can take abstract painting as the emblem of modernism, however, one should not imagine that the feeling of the end is solely a function of its essentialism; rather it is necessary to interpret this essentialism as the effect of a larger historical crisis. This crisis is well known—it can be termed industrialization—and its impact on painting has been analyzed by the best critics, following a line of investigation begun half a century ago by Walter Benjamin.[3] This discourse centers around the appearance of photography, and of mass production, both of which were understood as causing the end of painting. Photography was perceived this way by even the least subtle practitioners. ("*From today painting in dead*: it is now nearly a century and a half since Paul Delaroche is said to have pronounced that sentence in the face of the overwhelming evidence of Daguerre's invention.")[4] Mass production seemed to bode the end of painting through its most elaborate *mise-en-scène*, the invention of the readymade. Photography and mass production were also at the base of the essentialist urge of modernist painting. Challenged by the mechanical apparatus of photography, and by the mass-produced, painting had to redefine its status, to reclaim a specific domain (much in the way this was done during the Renaissance, when painting was posited as one of the "liberal arts" as opposed to the "mechanical arts").

The beginnings of this agonistic struggle have been well described by Meyer Schapiro: the emphasis on the touch, on texture, and on gesture in modern painting is a consequence of the division of labor inherent in industrial production. Industrial capitalism banished the hand from the process of production; the work of art alone, as craft, still implied manual handling and therefore artists were compelled, by reaction, to demonstrate the exceptional nature of their mode of production.[5] From Courbet to Pollock one witnesses a practice of one-upmanship. In many ways the various "returns to painting" we are witnessing today seem like the farcical repetition of this historical progression. There were, it is true, simple negations: for instance, van Doesburg's *Art Concret* (the dream of a geometric art that could be entirely programmed) and Moholy-Nagy's *Telephone-paintings*. But it is only with Robert Ryman that the theoretical demonstration of the historical position of painting as an exceptional realm of manual mastery has been carried to its full extent and, as it were, deconstructed. By his dissection of the gesture, or of the pictorial raw material, and by his (nonstylistic) analysis of the stroke, Ryman produces a kind of dissolution of the relationship between the trace and its organic referent. The body of the artist moves toward the condition of photography: the division of labor is interiorized.

What is at stake for Ryman is no longer affirming the uniqueness of the pictorial mode of production vis-à-vis the general mode of production of commodities, but decomposing it mechanically. Ryman's deconstruction has nothing to do with a negation (contrary to what most of its readers think, what is called deconstruction has very little to do with negation per se. Instead, it elaborates a kind of negativity that is not trapped in the dialectical vector of affirmation, negation, and sublation). Ryman's dissolution is posited, but endlessly restrained, amorously deferred; the process (which identifies the trace with its "subjective" origin) is endlessly stretched: the thread is never cut.

If I insist on Ryman, it is because in his art the feeling of an end is worked through in the most resolved way. Although he is claimed by some as a postmodernist, I would say he is more accurately the guardian of the tomb of modernist painting, at once knowing of the end and also knowing the impossibility of arriving at it without working it through. Asymptotically, his paintings get closer and closer to the condition of the photograph or of the readymade, yet remain at the threshold of simple negation. His position is difficult to maintain, yet it is perhaps, historically, the most cogent one.[6] To understand this, we must look again at the historical development that preceded him. "If we could describe the art of this, the first half of the twentieth century, in a sentence, it would read as the search for something to paint; just as, were we to do the same for modern art as a whole, it must read as the critical preoccupation of artists with solving the *technical* problems of the painting medium. Here is the dividing line of the history of art," writes Barnett Newman, reminding us of Schapiro's insistence on the importance of touch, texture, and gesture.[7] But the paradox here, brilliantly enunciated by Thierry de Duve, is that the modernist opposition to both traditional painterly finish and the mechanical (which were fused by academic art of the late nineteenth century) bore within itself the stigmata of the mass-produced:

> Although tin or copper tubes were already in use in England at the end of the 18th century for the preservation of watercolor, it was only around 1830–1840 that tubes of oil paints began to be available on the market. . . . For John Constable or the Barbizon painters to leave their studio and paint outside, directly from nature, the availability of tubes of paint was a prerequisite. One cannot imagine them carrying along the bulky equipment that the preparation of paint on the premises would involve. Certainly, pleinairism was one of the first episodes in the long struggle between craftsmanship and industrialization that underlies the history of "Modernist Painting." It was also one of the first instances of an avant-

garde strategy, devised by artists who were aware that they could no longer compete, technically or economically, with industry; they sought to give their craft a reprieve by "internalizing" some of the features and processes of the technology threatening it, and by "mechanizing" their own body at work.[8]

It is this internalization of the mass-produced that led to Duchamp's disgust for paintings and his invention of the readymade. ("Let's say you use a tube of paint; you didn't make it. You bought it and used it as a readymade. Even if you mix two vermillions together, it's still a mixing of two readymades. So man can never expect to start from scratch; he must start from readymade things like even his own mother and father."[9]) The historical condition of modern painting as a return of the repressed is also exposed in Seurat's art (Duchamp's favorite), and then deconstructed—not negated—in Ryman's. Industrialization first produced a reaction within modernist painting that lead to the emphasis on process—but this reaction had only become possible through the incorporation of the mechanical within the realm of painting itself. Seurat's art marks the moment that this condition is recognized. After him, a long period of analytical decomposition followed—the strongest moment probably being Pollock—which culminated in a conscious incorporation of the mechanical in painting and a reversal of the original reaction to industrialization. Painting had reached the condition of photography. Ryman is the key figure in this historical development, but he has been backed up by a host of related practices in the 1970s.[10]

Even at the outset, industrialization meant much more for painting than the invention of photography and the incorporation of the mechanical into the artist's process through the readymade tube of paint. It also meant a threat of the collapse of art's special status into a fetish or a commodity. It is in reaction to this threat that the historicism and essentialism of modernism was developed. There is a tendency in America to believe that Clement Greenberg was the first advocate of the modernist teleology. On the contrary, as I have mentioned, the work of the first abstract painters was guided by the same teleology. It therefore seems more telling here, no matter how eloquent Greenberg's discourse has been, to seek the absolute beginning of such a construct: in other words the "beginning of the end." It seems that the first proponent was Baudelaire who conceived history as a chain along which each individual art gradually approached its essence. Nobody has better perceived the function of the threat of industrialization in Baudelaire's work than Walter Benjamin. The greatness of Baudelaire, according to Benjamin, is to have recognized that the fetishistic nature of the commodity-form (analyzed by Marx at the same time) was the threat that capitalism posed to the very existence of art. "When things are freed from the bondage of being useful," as in the typically fetishistic transubstantiation accomplished by the art collector, then the distinction between art and artifact becomes extremely tenuous. This tension lies, according to Benjamin, at the core of Baudelaire's poetry.

Except for the Italian essayist Giorgio Agamben, it has been little recognized how much the famous chapter of Marx's *Capital* on the fetishistic nature of the commodity, its "mystical" or "phantasmagoric character," owes to the German philosopher's visit to the Great Exhibition in London in 1851 where industrial products were given the kind of auratic presentation previously reserved for works of art:[11] "By means of this exhibition the bourgeoisie of the world is erecting in the modern Rome its Pantheon in which to exhibit with proud self-satisfaction the gods it has made to itself. . . . [It] is celebrating its greatest festival."[12] According to Marx, the fetishistic character of the commodity, what he called its "metaphysical subtlety," is grounded in the absolute repression of use value and of any reference to the process of production, or the materiality of the thing. And if Agamben is right in pointing at the connection between Marx's fundamental analysis and his visit to the London fair, then another connection brings us back to Baudelaire: Courbet's one-man show, in the bungalow he had built for this purpose next to the Beaux-Arts section of the Exposition Universelle in Paris in 1855, which contained among other works his famous *Studio* where Baudelaire is portrayed. As is well known, eleven works by Courbet had been accepted by the exhibition committee—and not minor ones—but he was dissatisfied with the way they were displayed: not exhibited together, but dispersed among an undifferentiated mass of hundreds of paintings exactly as, in the next building, machines and machine-made products were exhibited, competing for the gold medal. "I conquer freedom, I save the independence of art"[13] are the words Courbet used to explain the motivation of his parasitic show of some forty works, which he managed to install only six weeks after the inauguration of the fair and to maintain until it closed five months later. With these words, Courbet characterized what is for me the first avant-garde act, an act of defiance against the ever-growing realm of the commodity.

The universal commodification under capitalism is what, according to Benjamin, Baudelaire's genius was to perceive as the terrifying and endless return of the same. I cannot go deeply into Benjamin's extraordinarily complex analysis in this essay, but only note that beginning with Baudelaire's startling characterization of the writer as a prostitute, Benjamin sees the poet's successive identifications with the rag-picker, the flaneur, the bohemian, the dandy or the "apache," as the adoption of heroic roles bearing the stigmata of commodification: roles that were doomed to failure and were superseded by Baudelaire's final phantasmagoria, his conception of the new. Benjamin writes, "This villification that things suffer by their ability to be taxed as commodities is counterbalanced in Baudelaire's conception by the inestimable value of novelty. Novelty represents an absolute that can neither be interpreted [as an allegory] nor compared [as a commodity]. It becomes the ultimate entrenchment of art."[14] The shock of the new, in other words, is an expression that derives from Baudelaire's aesthetics. But there is more to it: Baudelaire sees modernity, the value of novelty, as necessarily doomed by the inevitable process by which the novel becomes antique. The quest for the absolute new in art becomes a moment that can never stop, endangered as it is by its devolution into the realm of interpretation or comparison. "But once modernism has received its due," writes Benjamin, "its time has run out. Then it will be put to the test. After its end, it will become apparent whether it will be able to become antiquity."[15] This is the banal process that was called *recuperation* in the 1960s, but has been better analyzed since then as an effect of the simulacral.

This urge toward the new, which is at the core of the historicist teleology of Baudelaire, is doubly a myth, both because of the immanent perishability of novelty, and because novelty is the very guise that the commodity adopts to fulfill its fetishistic transfiguration. Baudelaire indeed saw the connection between fashion and death, but he did not recognize that the absolute new he searched for all his life was made of the same stuff as the commodity, that it was governed by the same law as the market: the constant return of the same. Benjamin recognized this blind spot of Baudelaire's: "that the last defense of art coincided with the most advanced line of attack of the commodity, this remained hidden to Baudelaire."[16] Needless to say it also remained unseen by the numerous avant-garde movements that followed him. We must recognize, however, that the insistence on the integrity of specific media that occurs in every art of the last quarter of the nineteenth century was a deliberate attempt to free art from its contamination by the forms of exchange produced by capitalism. Art had to be ontologically split not only from the mechanical, but also from the realm of information—it had to be distinguished from the immediate transitivity of information that amounted to a general leveling of every fact of life. Mallarmé is certainly the most articulate on this point, and his awareness formed the basis of his theory against the instrumentalization of language by the press. If he insisted on the materiality of language, if he claimed that the poet must remunerate language, if he spoke of the intransitivity of language, it was because he tried to advocate a mode of exchange that would not be abstract, nor based on a universal interchangeability through the medium of a single general equivalent, nor reified in a mystifying fetish split off from the process of its production. I would say that although few artists were as consistent as Mallarmé and Baudelaire, one can certainly read the whole history of avant-garde art up to World War I as following in their wake.

There were many reasons for a shift in the situation of the art object to occur around World War I, and I would be a fool to claim one or two events as the origin of a complex set of transformations that were sometimes abrupt, sometimes gradual. But to pursue my thread concerning the market, I would like to consider two pivotal events: the famous sale of the Peau d'Ours, which occurred on March 2, 1914; and Marcel Duchamp's invention of the readymade, already mentioned, which happened at around the same time (I take his *Porte-bouteille* of the same year as more to the point than his *Roue de bicyclette* of 1913, which still involves, although ironically, a compositional procedure). The sale of the Peau d'Ours marked the astonishing discovery that far from being laughable, the avant-garde art of the past—novelty as antiquity—was highly profitable as an investment. Not only works by Gauguin, Vuillard, or Redon were sold at very high prices, but also paintings by Matisse and Picasso. It was discovered, in short, that investment in contemporary painting was much more profitable than the typical investments of the time, including gold and real estate. Needless to say, the speculative logic that emerged from this sale (buy today the Van Goghs of tomorrow because the new will become antiquity) was to shape the entire history of the twentieth century art market.

Now Duchamp. His readymades were not only a negation of painting and a demonstration of the always-already mechanical nature of painting. They also demonstrated that within our culture the work of art is a fetish that must abolish all pretense to use value (i.e., the readymade is an art object through its abstraction from the realm of utility). Furthermore, the readymade demonstrated that the so-called autonomy of the art object was produced by a nominalist institution (the museum or art gallery) that constantly buried what Marx called the point of view of production under the point of view of consumption (as the ethnologist Marcel Mauss noted once, "a work of art is that which is recognized as such by a group").[17] Finally, and more importantly, Duchamp's act presented the art object as a *special* kind of commodity—something that Marx had noted when he explained that "works of art properly speaking were not taken into consideration" in his account, "for they are of a special nature."[18] Having no use value, the art object does not have any exchange value per se either—the exchange value being dependent on the quantum of social work necessary for its production (Seurat demonstrated this *ad absurdum* through his desire to be paid *by the hour*). What Duchamp was keen to observe is that works

of art—as much as oyster pearls or great wines (other examples given by Marx)—
are not exchanged according to the common law of the market, but according to a
monopoly system maintained by the entire art network, whose keystone is the artist
himself. This does not mean that the exchange of works of art is beyond competition
or any other manifestation of the law of the market, but that their sometimes infinite
price is a function of their lack of measurable value. Value in the art world is determined by the "psychological" mechanisms that are at the core of any monopoly system: rarity, authenticity, uniqueness, and the law of supply and demand. In other
words, art objects are absolute fetishes without a use value but also without an
exchange value, fulfilling absolutely the collector's fantasy of a purely symbolic or
ideal value, a supplement to his soul.

Duchamp's discovery led him to a range of experiments meant to reveal the
mechanisms of the art network: I only need mention his 1917 *Fountain*, his various
appearances as a transvestite, and his *Chèque Tzank* of 1919, all of which pointed to
authenticity as the central theoretical construct on which the art network is based.
In Duchamp's wake, artists like Daniel Buren as well as Cindy Sherman and Sherrie
Levine have analyzed the nature of authenticity. This analytical strategy has often
been characterized as the "deconstructive tendency" of postmodernism, yet I am not
entirely confident with this labeling (which does not diminish at all the interest I
have for such practices). In so far as I interpret Duchamp's art as a negation, I interpret his heirs as explicating and radicalizing his negation. Or rather, if one wants to
stay with the term deconstruction, I would say that Duchamp and his heirs are deconstructing one aspect of what they negate (painting): specifically the imaginary aspect
of painting, which these artists consistently associate with its fetishistic nature
(deconstruction means also the sense of inescapability from closure). But there
remain, if I am allowed to borrow *metaphorically* the Lacanian terminology, two
other aspects of painting that must be considered: the real and the symbolic.

Both the Peau d'Ours sale and Duchamp's invention of the readymade had the
potential to spawn a kind of cynical conservatism: if the new was doomed to its transformation into gold by the market, and the work of art was by its very nature an absolute fetish, then it might seem that the avant-garde's ideology of resistance was
obsolete. In fact, such a cynical position was undertaken by what is called the *return
to order,* which started with Picasso's *Portrait of Max Jacob* in 1915 but which
became a massive phenomenon in the 1920s with Pittura Metafisica in Italy and the
Neue Sachlichkeit in Germany. These movements share a lot with the neoconser-
vative brand of postmodernism that has recently emerged (whether it's called new
wild, neo-romantik, trans-avanguardia, or whatever), as Benjamin Buchloh has bril-

liantly demonstrated.[19] The market itself induces this kind of cynicism.[20] The cynical attitude, however, was not the only one available. The feeling of the end could also be reclaimed by a revolutionary aesthetics. This is what happened in Russia, where artists immediately responded to the situation created by the events of October 1917. In a revolutionary situation, art cannot but sever its ties with the market and its dependence upon the art institution: it seeks to reestablish its use value and to invent new relationships of production and consumption: it breaks with the linear, cumulative conception of history and emphasizes discontinuity. In other words, in such situations art can open up a new paradigm, something that was eloquently advocated by El Lissitzky in the brilliant lecture he delivered in Berlin, in 1922, about "The New Russian Art."[21]

Of all of these gestures of the Soviet avant-garde, one of the most significant is Rodchenko's exhibition, in 1921, of three monochrome panels, which he later described with these words, "I reduced painting to its logical conclusion and exhibited three canvases: red, blue and yellow. I affirmed: It's all over. Basic colors. Every plane is a plane, and there is to be no more representation."[22] If Rodchenko's gesture is important, it is not because it was the "first" monochrome—it was not the "first" nor the "last"—and not because it was the first "last picture" (not only does Duchamp's readymade better deserve this title, but, as we have seen, in a way all modernist abstract paintings had to claim to be the last picture). If Rodchenko's gesture was so important, as Tarabukin saw when he analyzed it in *From the Easel to the Machine*, it was because it showed that painting could have a real existence only if it claimed its end; Rodchenko's "meaningless, dumb and blind wall . . . convinces us that painting was and remains a representational art and that it cannot escape from these limits of the representational."[23] Rodchenko's painting needed to attain the status of a real (nonimaginary) object, which meant its end as art. Again we are confronted with a negation—not a deconstruction—which accounts, according to me, for what must be called the failure of the productivist program in painting that followed Rodchenko's gesture logically (the dissolution of the artist's activity into industrial production). Or, to use again the terminology I borrowed before, Rodchenko deconstructed only one aspect of painting: its pretense to reach the realm of the real—a deconstruction that was carried out again, and further elaborated, by minimalism in the 1960s.

Rodchenko's was still not the only alternative to Duchamp's negation, nor to cynicism. In August 1924, shortly before he broke with the Dutch movement, Mondrian published his last article in the magazine *De Stijl*. Entitled "Blown with the

Wind," it is a denunciation of the *return to order* that was invading the galleries and had almost led him, three years earlier, to abandon painting altogether. He writes:

> If artists now reject the new conception, critics and dealers reject it even more strongly, for they are more directly exposed to the influence of the public. The sole value of abstract art, they openly assert, was to raise the level of naturalistic art: the new was thus a *means,* not a *goal.* [And here I intervene to mention Picasso's remark to a baffled Kahnweiler that his neoclassical works of the *return to order* period were *better* than those of his precubist naturalistic period. Back to Mondrian's text. This is, he writes,] an open denial of the essence of the new, which was to *displace and annihilate* the old. They too swing with the wind and follow the lead of the general public. Though quite understandable, this is temporarily disastrous for the new, for its essential nature is thus *lost from sight.*

I give you this long quotation for its insistence on the momentary nature of the *return to order* phenomenon: the whole article is suffused with a kind of optimism that would sound utterly incomprehensible if the role of the new were not laid down at the end of the article:

> Abstract art can evolve only by *consistent development.* In this way it can arrive at the *purely plastic,* which Neo-Plasticism has attained. Consistently carried through, this 'art' expression [the quotation marks are Mondrian's] can lead to nothing other than its *realization in our tangible environment.* For the time will come when, because of life's changed demands, 'painting' will become absorbed in life" (again, the quotation marks are Mondrian's).[24]

For anyone who is familiar with the voluminous writings of Mondrian, this sounds typical, and indeed, as I already noted, the myth of the future dissolution of art into life is one of his most frequent themes. Far from being a compulsive quest of the absolute new, structurally doomed to failure, as in Baudelaire's formal teleology, Mondrian's affirmation of the new is geared toward a definite *telos,* that of the advent of a classless society, where social relationships would be transparent and not reified, and where there would be no difference between artists and nonartists, art and life. The new art must be, within itself, the model and augury of such a liberation: this future liberation, or socialist state, is envisioned through the principle of neoplasticism, of which neoplastic art can only be a "pale reflection," albeit the most advanced possible at the time. This principle, which Mondrian also called the "general principle of plastic equivalence," is a sort of dialectic whose action is to dissolve any particularity, any center, any hierarchy. Any entity that is not split or constituted by an opposition is a mere appearance. Anything that is not determined by its contrary is vague, particular, individual, tragic: it is a cipher of authoritarianism, and it does not take part in the process of emancipation set forth by the "general principle of equivalence." Hence the complicated task that Mondrian assigns the painter is the destruction of all the elements on which the particularity of his art is based: the destruction of colored planes by lines; of lines by repetition; and of the optical illusion of depth by the sculptural weave of the painterly surface. Each destructive act follows the previous one and amounts to the abolition of the figure/ground opposition that is the perceptual limitation at the base of our imprisoned vision, and of the whole enterprise of painting. There is no doubt that Mondrian sets a task of the highest order for art: he prescribes a propaedeutic role. Painting was for him a theoretical model that provided concepts and invented procedures that dealt with reality: it is not merely an interpretation of the world, but the plastic manifestation of a certain logic that he found at the root of all the phenomena of life. In an article he wrote under the shock of the Nazi-Soviet mutual nonaggression pact, Mondrian says: "The function of plastic art is not descriptive. . . . It can reveal the evil of oppression and show the way to combat it. . . . It cannot reveal more than life teaches, but it can evoke in us the conviction of existent truth";[25] "the culture of plastic art shows that real freedom requires mutual equivalence."[26]

Arthur Lehning, an anarchosyndicalist leader of the 1920s, said that his friend Mondrian was a child in politics, and nothing could be more evident.[27] However, this naiveté, which appears to have been the only possible alternative to Duchamp's negation and to the cynical strategies of the *return to order* in Western Europe, should not blind us to Mondrian's remarkable position. One is struck by the fact that he never felt any compulsion toward the monochrome, which could easily have provided, so it seems, the kind of absolute flatness he was striving for. But as an iconoclast readymade, the monochrome could not have functioned for him as a tool to deconstruct painting or more specifically to deconstruct the order of the symbolic in painting (of tradition, of the law, of history). Mondrian felt that within the economic abstraction engendered by capitalism, painting could only be deconstructed abstractly, by analyzing, one after the other, one against the other, all of the elements that (historically) ground its symbolic order (form, color, figure/ground opposition, frame, etc.). This painstaking formal analysis was for him the only way painting could reach its own end. Because it was conceived of as an abstract model, painting could resist the abstract commodification that is the fate of every (art) object; it had to postpone its own dissolution into the real until the symbolic order on which it is grounded had been "neutralized." Painting was therefore engaged in the necessarily interminable task of this neutralization. It might seem strange to speak of Mondrian, whose system of thought owed so much to Hegel's dialectic, in terms of deconstruction, yet unlike any dialectician he never expected any leap, never paid any tribute to the modern ideology of the *tabula rasa:* he knew that the end of painting had to be gained by hard labor.

But is the end ever to be gained? Duchamp (the imaginary), Rodchenko (the real), and Mondrian (the symbolic), among others, all believed in the end—they all had the final truth, all spoke apocalyptically. Yet has the end come? To say no (painting is still alive, just look at the galleries) is undoubtedly an act of denial, for it has never been more evident that most paintings one sees have abandoned the task that historically belonged to modern painting (that, precisely, of working through the end of painting) and are simply artifacts created for the market and by the market (absolutely interchangeable artifacts created by interchangeable producers). To say yes, however, that the end has come, is to give in to a historicist conception of history as both linear and total (i.e., one cannot paint after Duchamp, Rodchenko, Mondrian; their work has rendered paintings unnecessary, or: one cannot paint anymore in the era of the mass media, computer games, and the simulacrum).

How are we to escape this double bind? Benjamin once noted that the easel painting was born in the Middle Ages, and that nothing guarantees that it should remain forever. But are we left with these alternatives: either a denial of the end, or an affirmation of the end of the end (it's all over, the end is over)? The theory of games, used recently by Hubert Damisch, can help us overcome this paralyzing trap. This theory of strategy dissociates the generic *game* (like chess) from the specific performance of the game (Spassky/Fisher, for example), which I will call the *match.*[28] This strategic interpretation is strictly antihistoricist: with it, the question becomes "one of the status that ought to be assigned to the *match* 'painting,' as one *sees* it being played at a given moment in particular circumstances, in its relation to the *game* of the same name."[29] Such questioning has the immediate advantage of raising doubt about certain truisms. Is the "alleged convention of depth"—rejected by the pictorial art of this century because, according to Greenberg, it is unnecessary—necessarily of the order of the *match* more than of the *game?* Or rather, should we speak of a modification of this convention within the *game?* Without thereby becoming a theoretical machine encouraging indifference, since one is obliged to take a side, this strategic approach deciphers painting as an agonistic field where nothing is ever terminated, or decided *once and for all,* and leads the analysis back to a type of historicity that it had neglected, that of long duration. In other words, it dismisses all certitudes about the absolute truth upon which the apocalyptic discourse is based. Rather, the fiction of the end of art (or of painting) is understood as a "confusion between the end of the game itself (as if a game could really have an end) and that of such and such a match (or series of matches)."[30]

One can conclude then that, if the match "modernist painting" is finished, it does not necessarily mean that the game "painting" is finished: many years to come are ahead for this art. But the situation is even more complicated: for the match "modernist painting" was the match of the end of painting; it was both a response to the feeling of the end and a working through of the end. And this match was historically determined—by the fact of industrialization (photography, the commodity, etc.). To claim that the "end of painting" is finished is to claim that this historical situation is no longer ours, and who would be naive enough to make this claim when it appears that reproducibility and fetishization have permeated all aspects of life: have become our "natural" world?

Obviously, this is not the claim of the latest group of "abstract" painters, whose work, as Hal Foster has rightly remarked, has been presented as either a development of appropriation art (which is supported by the presence of Sherrie Levine in the group) or as a swing of the pendulum (the market having tired of neoexpressionism was ripe for a neoclassical and architectonic movement: the "style" after the "shout," to make use of an old metaphor that art criticism proposed to distinguish between two tendencies within the realm of abstract art: one whose emblem was Mondrian and the other, Pollock).[31] The work of this recent group of painters wishes to respond to our simulacral era, yet paradoxically in their very reliance upon Jean Baudrillard, emphasized by Peter Halley who frequently writes critically about these issues, they all admit that the end has come, that the end of the end is over (hence that we can start again on another match; that we can paint without the feeling of the end but only with its simulacrum). As Foster writes, "In this new abstract painting, simulation has penetrated the very art form that . . . resisted it most."[32] Starting with a critique of the economy of the sign in late capitalism, Baudrillard was driven, by the very nature of his millenarianist feeling, to a fascination for the age of the simulacrum, a glorification of our own impotence disguised as nihilism. It seems to me that although the young artists in question address the issue of the simulacral—of the abstract simulation produced by capital—they have similarly abandoned themselves to the seduction of what they claim to denounce: either perversely (as in the case of Philip Taaffe who refers to Newman's sublime while he empties it of its content); or unconsciously (as in the case of Halley who seems to believe that an iconological rendering of simulacra—through his pictorial rhetoric of "cells" and "conduits"—could function as a critique of them). Like Baudrillard, I would call them manic mourners. Their return to painting, as though it were an appropriate medium for what they want to address, as though the age of the simulacral could be represented, comes from the feeling that since the end has come, since it's all over, we can rejoice at the killing of the dead. That is, we can forget that the end has to be endlessly worked through, and start all over again. But this, of course, is not so, and it is in flagrant contradiction to the very analysis of the simulacral as the latest abstraction produced by capitalism (perhaps this illusion is rooted in the abuse of the term postindustrialism, whose inveterate inadequacy to describe the latest development of capitalism has been exposed by Fredric Jameson).[33] Appropriation art—the "orgy of cannibalism" proper to manic mourning—of which this movement is obviously a part,[34] can then be understood as a pathological mourning (it has also its melancholic side, as noted by Hal Foster about Ross Bleckner and Taaffe in their fascination for the "failure" of op art).[35] Bleckner writes about Taaffe: "Dead issues are reopened by this changed subjectivity: artists become transvestites and viewers voyeurs watching history become less alien, less authoritarian."[36] I would correct the latter assertion this way: ". . . viewers watching oblivion become more alien, more enslaved." For "simulation, together with the old regime of disciplinary surveillance, constitutes a principal means of deterrence in our society (for how can one intervene politically in events when they are so often simulated or immediately replaced by pseudo-events?)."[37]

Yet mourning has been the activity of painting throughout this century. "To be modern is to know *that which is not possible any more,*" Roland Barthes once wrote.[38] But the work of mourning does not necessarily become pathological: the feeling of the end, after all, did produce a cogent history of painting, modernist painting, which we have probably been too prompt to bury. Painting might not be dead. Its vitality will only be tested once we are cured of our mania and our melancholy, and we believe again in our ability to act in history: accepting our project of working through the end again, rather than evading it through increasingly elaborate mechanisms of defense (this is what mania and melancholy are about) and settling our historical task: the difficult task of mourning. It will not be easier than before, but my bet is that the potential for painting will emerge in the conjunctive deconstruction of the three instances that modernist painting has dissociated (the imaginary, the real, and the symbolic). But predictions are made to be wrong. Let us simply say that the desire for painting remains, and that this desire is not entirely programmed or subsumed by the market: this desire is the sole factor of a future possibility of painting, that is of a nonpathological mourning. At any rate, as observed by Robert Musil fifty years ago, if some painting is still to come, if painters are still to come, they will not come from where we expect them to.[39]

"What does it mean for a painter *to think?*"(p. 59)—this is the old question to which Hubert Damisch has returned in connection with the art of this century, and which he alone in France seems to take seriously. Not only what is the role of speculative thought for the painter at work? but above all what is the mode of thought of which painting is the stake? Can one think *in* painting as one can dream in color? and is there such a thing as pictorial thought that would differ from what Klee called "visual thought"? Or again, to use the language current some ten years ago, is painting a theoretical practice? Can one designate the place of the theoretical in painting without doing violence to it, without, that is, disregarding painting's specificity, without annexing it to an applied discourse whose meshes are too slack to give a suitable account of painting's irregularities? Nowhere in Damisch's book are there broad examinations of the idea of "the pictorial." Instead there is, in each instance, the formulation of a question raised by the work of art within a historically determined framework, and the search for a theoretical model to which one might compare the work's operations and with which one might engage them. This approach simultaneously presupposes a rejection of established stylistic categories (and indirectly an interest in new groupings or transverse categories), a fresh start of the inquiry in the face of each new work, and a permanent awareness of the operating rule of painting in relation to discourse. For Damisch's question is also, as we shall see: what does the painter's pictorial thought mean for one who has undertaken to write?

Damisch's book stands alone in France, as it is resolutely opposed to: (1) the stamp-collecting approach of traditional art historians, whose veritable terror of the theoretical has gradually turned their texts into the gibberish of documentalists and antiquarians—in the sense that Nietzsche gave this word (with very few exceptions, twentieth-century art has remained untouched in France by this ravenous sort of discourse, empirical at best, and with nothing of history about it except the name); (2)

the ineptitude of art criticism, a form of journalism all the more amnesiac for having constantly to adapt itself to market trends; (3) that typically French genre, inaugurated on the one hand by Baudelaire and on the other probably by Sartre, of the text *about* art by a literary writer or philosopher, each doing his little number, a seemingly obligatory exercise in France if one is to reach the pantheon of letters or of thought.

While Damisch's book exposes the fundamental incompetence of the first two prevailing discourses (demonstrating to the historians their refusal to ask themselves about the type of historicity of their subject; teaching the critics the necessity of discovering what it is that calls into question the certitude of their judgments), it is in relation to the third and absolutely hegemonic kind of text that his lesson seems to me most important. Why? Because Damisch teaches us above all to rid ourselves of the stifling concept of *image* upon which the relation of this kind of text to art is founded—arrogant, ignorant, predatory texts that consider painting a collection of images to be tracked down, illustrations to be captioned.

One example: Jacques Lacan, usually so attentive to the signifier when language is at stake, is reproached for having invoked "abstract models from the start" when faced with François Rouan's braidings (Lacan's everlasting Borromean knots) rather than examining "on the evidence" the detail of the fabric (pp. 280–281). Not that Damisch has anything against abstract models in themselves; he simply says that the work produces them by itself for anyone who takes the trouble to notice, and that in this case neither Rouan's painting nor the theory of knots gains anything by the demonstration in the form of a priori advice from the eminent psychoanalyst.[1] Nor is it that Damisch becomes the prosecutor trying to pin down all the scornful remarks that characterize the discourse of his contemporaries on the subject of art. There is little of polemics in *Fenêtre jaune cadmium,* which consists of essays written between 1958 and 1984. Or rather there is a *polémique d'envoi,* as one speaks of a *coup d'envoi,* a "kickoff," which governs, if not the whole book, at least the texts of the first and second parts, entitled respectively "L'Image et le tableau" and "Théorèmes."

The Perceptive Model

Although they may seem somewhat foreign to anyone reading them today, the pages Damisch devotes to Sartre are decisive, and I would say today more than ever. These concern Sartre's thesis that there is no such thing as aesthetic perception, the aesthetic object being something "unreal," apprehended by the "imaging conscious-

ness." This thesis, from Sartre's *L'Imaginaire*, states that, in Damisch's words, "a portrait, a landscape, a form only allows itself to be recognized in painting insofar as we
cease to view the painting for what it is, materially speaking, and insofar as consciousness steps back in relation to reality to produce as an image the object represented" (p. 67). Such a thesis would at best hold true for a type of illusionistic
painting that, assuming it had existed at all, would only have existed at a particular
moment in history. That Sartre's aesthetic is an aesthetic of *mimesis,* in the most traditional sense of the word, is neither difficult nor fundamentally useful to demonstrate, although it may have had a considerable stake in its time. What is important
about Damisch's text is that he takes this aesthetic to be emblematic in developing
his polemic in an essay on an "abstract" painter, one of the most complex of them,
namely Mondrian. For is not only that what Sartre calls "the imaging attitude" blinds
our literati and philosophers to the rupture constituted by "abstract painting," it is
also this "imaging attitude" that still today governs studies by the majority of art historians, for the most part Americans, who take an interest in this kind of painting. If
dissertations abound that would make Malevich's *Black Square* a solar eclipse, Rothko's late works stylized versions of the Pietà and Deposition, or Mondrian's *Broadway Boogie-Woogie* an interpretation of the New York subway map, it is because the
kind of relation to art denounced by Damisch is not only very much with us but, in
the current hostility to theory, stands a good chance of becoming absolutely dominant. Damisch's text shows us, however, that we don't have to search for "une femme
là-dessous" (a woman underneath) in order to remain tied to the system of interpretation of which Sartre was the eponym. One has only to be inattentive to the specificity of the object to be led back to this system; hence Damisch's interest in the detail
of the signifier, the texture of the painting, everything that, according to Sartre, insofar as it is real, "does not become the object of aesthetic appreciation."[2]

   The case of Mondrian is symptomatic. How many purely geometric readings
(indifferent to the medium of expression), how many interpretations resulting from
blindness to the paintings' subtle games have given rise to the pregnant image of a
grid imposed upon a neutral background? As early as this formidable text of 1958,
and from the point of view of his controversy with Sartre, Damisch sees in Mondrian
a painter of the perceptive aporia, precisely the opposite of the "geometric abstraction" genre of which he is supposed to be the herald. For the first time, so far as I
know, the enterprise of *destruction* carried out by the Dutch painter was understood
as a concerted operation governing every detail of his painting. In order to comprehend, for example, the abandonment of all curves, there is no need to get mixed
up in the theosophical nonsense with which the artist's mind was momentarily

encumbered. It is because the line has the function of destroying the plane as such that it will have to be straight:

> The interdiction of any other line but the straight corresponded to the experiential fact that a line curving inward on a canvas or piece of paper defines "full" or "empty" spaces, which the imaging consciousness is irresistibly led to consider for themselves to the detriment of the line that serves as their pretext. Mondrian's paintings are made to counter such impulses and to hinder the movement whereby an unreal object is constituted from the tangible reality of the painting, the eye being ceaselessly led back to the painting's constituent elements, line, color, design. (p. 69)

Damisch's thesis is rigorously anti-Sartrean: in opposition to the "imaging consciousness," which necessarily has as its purpose the constitution of an image, he sees in Mondrian's canvases, in Pollock's, in Picasso's *Portrait of Vollard,* each with its own modality, "an ever-reversed kaleidoscope that offers to *aesthetic perception* a task both novel and without assignable end . . . the 'meaning' of the work consisting precisely in this swarming and ambiguous appeal" (p. 78). Or again: "If the painter has chosen to prohibit the imaging consciousness from giving itself free rein . . . it is for the purpose of awakening in the spectator the uneasiness with which the perception of a painting should be accompanied" (p. 71). Now, this task of the painter is the stake of his art; it is what makes his canvas a specific theoretical model, the development of a thought whose properly pictorial aspect cannot be circumvented:

> One cannot give way to reverie in front of a Mondrian painting, nor even to pure contemplation. But it is here that there comes into play, beyond the sensorial pleasure granted us by Sartre, some more secret activity of consciousness, an activity by definition without assignable end, contrary to the imaging activity which exhausts itself in the constitution of its object. Each time perception thinks it can go beyond what is given it to see toward what it would constitute as meaning, it is immediately led back to the first experience, which wants it to falter in constituting that white as background and this black as a form. *(Ibid.)*

I would call this theoretical model introduced by Damisch *perceptive,* but by antiphrasis, because for the painters studied it is a question in each case of "disturbing the permanent structures of perception, and first of all the figure/ground relationship, beyond which one would be unable to speak of a perceptive field" (p. 110, in connection with Dubuffet). With the exception of one or two texts, especially the one of 1974 on Valerio Adami in which a positive evaluation of the concept of image and of Sartre's aesthetics is hinted at, all the articles in *Fenêtre jaune cadmium* insist on this point: "Painting, for the one who produces it as for the one who consumes it, is always a matter of perception" (p. 148). And all the examples chosen (except for Adami and Saul Steinberg) assign to modernity the preliminary task of confusing the figure/ground opposition, without the assurance of which no perception could establish itself in imaging synthesis. It is this "perceptive model" that allows Damisch not only to compare Pollock and Mondrian but also to establish the ambiguity of the figure/ground relationship as the very theme of the American painter's interlacings and to reject as particularly unproductive the divide that some have tried to enforce between Pollock's great abstract period, that of the all-over works of 1947–50, and his so-called figurative canvases of 1951 and the years that followed. Likewise, Dubuffet's great period (the 1950s) is deciphered, by direct appeal to Merleau-Ponty, as an essential moment in this history of perceptive ambiguity:

> By treating the figures as so many vaguely silhouetted backgrounds whose texture he strives to decipher and—conversely—by carrying his gaze toward the less differentiated backgrounds to catch their secret figures and mechanics, this painter has restored to the idea of form its original meaning, if it is true that form cannot be reduced to the geometric outline of objects, that it is bound up with the texture of things, and that it draws simultaneously on all our senses. (p. 117)

The phenomenological theme of the original unity of the senses often returns in Damisch's writing, but it would be vain to see in these studies an application of Merleau-Ponty's theory. And this is not only because this recurrent theme is seriously questioned with regard to Fautrier (p. 134) or because the criticism of "pure visibility" is reoriented through psychoanalysis (pp. 262–263), but also because phenomenological apprehension in Damisch opens onto a second model, copresent with the first.

The Technical Model

In opposition to the "optical" interpretation that has been given to Pollock's all-over paintings by leading American formalist critics (Greenberg, Fried), an interpretation that partakes in a certain way, but much more subtly, of Sartrean unreality,[3] Damisch proposes from the start a reading that I would call *technical*. It begins (but this also applies to the texts on Klee, Dubuffet, or Mondrian) with an insistence on the real space set in play by these canvases (of course, it is always a question of countering the Sartrean imaginary or unreality). From this deliberately down-to-earth, ground-level apprehension flows a quite special attention to the process of the work as a place of formation, prior to its effects. Against the deliberately obfuscating attitude of the art historians, always ready to erase ruptures, Damisch establishes a chronology, or rather a technical logic, of invention: it would be wrong to see in the gesturality of *The Flame* (1937), or in the scribbled margins of *Male and Female* (1942) and *She-Wolf* (1943), the preliminary signs of Pollock's great art. In the first case, "the touch enlivens paint, a matter that still remains alien to it," while "Pollock's originality will later consist precisely in connecting so closely the gesture deployed on the canvas with the paint it spreads there that the latter will seem to be its trace, its necessary product" (p. 76). In the second case, we are dealing only with a borrowing, from Max Ernst or Masson, if you like: "The invention takes place, indeed, at the decisive moment when the painter raised this process, dripping—which after all had been only a means of 'padding'—to the dignity of an original principle for the organization of surfaces" (ibid.). For there is technique and technique, or rather there is the epistemological moment of technique, where thought and invention take place, and then there is all the rest, all the procedures that borrow from tradition or contest it without reaching that threshold that it is a question of designating—the reason that one can say of technique "indifferently, that it matters and does not matter for art" (p. 94).

It is by remaining at the elementary level of the gesture, of the trace, that Damisch discovers this threshold in Pollock, first in connection with *Shimmering Substance* (1946), where "each touch seems destined to destroy the effect born of the relation between the preceding touch and the background" (p. 78), then in the great all-over works of 1947–50: "Lines that plow the canvas through and through, in a counterpoint that no longer develops in width but *in thickness,* and each of which has no meaning except in relation to the one that precedes it—each projection of color succeeding another as though to efface it" (p. 80). This reading marks a beginning, first of all because it is the only one that makes it possible to understand the manner in which Pollock was working against surrealism (it is impossible in his case to speak of automatism, despite appearances: cf. p. 85), then because it points to the very place where Pollock's painting abandons, or rather destroys, the order of the image, "which is reduced to a surface effect, without any of the thickness that is the particular quality of painting," as Damisch says later on regarding Francois Rouan (p. 296).

Damisch is rapidly led, in Pollock's work, to make this category of *thickness* in the order of technique (which has since been reexamined by others alerted by his text)[4] the equivalent of the figure/ground confusion (to which it is linked) in the order of perception. From then on it becomes one of the essential question marks of Damisch's inquiry, functioning almost as an epistemological test in his discourse. The reemergence of the hidden undersides in Dubuffet (p. 114), the exchanges of position between outer surface and underside in Klee (p. 213), the interweavings of Mondrian and later of Rouan—all of these become theoretical models that *demonstrate* the painting of this century just as perspective demonstrated that of the Renaissance. It is therefore no accident that the book appears under the sign of *Le Chef-d'oeuvre inconnu*; the essay devoted to the novel provides the subtitle to the collection: "The Undersides of Painting."

> If one is to believe Frenhofer, it looks as though painting should produce its full effect only insofar as it proceeds, in its most intimate texture, from a predetermined exchange of positions that would be the equivalent of a kind of weaving in which the threads would go up and down alternatively, the same strand passing now above and now below, without the possibility of being assigned a univocal sign. (p. 16)

Frenhofer's name is invoked in no less than five texts in this collection in addition to the one devoted to the "philosophical study" of Balzac ("whoever writes proceeds in a way not dissimilar to one who paints, using a quotation that he had first singled out for completely different purposes, to start out on a new *development,* in every sense of the word" [p. 258]). Far removed from recent romanticist interpretations,[5] the Frenhofer of Damisch has been, from his first texts, the emblem of a conversion, the signal of invention—with Cézanne ("Frenhofer, c'est moi") and, one should add, Seurat—of a new thickness that would no longer borrow from the old academic recipes:

> And if one wants modernity in painting to be signaled by the replacement of the superimposition of preparations, of underpainting, glazing, transparencies, and varnish, by another craft based on flatness, the juxtaposition of touches, and simultaneous contrast, how can we not see that the problem of the "undersides" will only have been displaced or transformed, painting having necessarily kept something of its thickness, even if it were aiming only at surface effects? (p. 37)

Here, from the beginning, a metaphor intervenes to help us see that this *technical* model is irreducible to the *perceptive* model as it was earlier described, although it is its corollary: that of the figure inscribed on the chessboard, "in its full spaces as in its empty ones, but in the superimposition and overlapping of its layers as well" (p. 158), *inaccessible as such to pure vision*. The work on the thickness of the plane is for Damisch a technical model par excellence, because it implies a knowledge and a speculation (p. 279): we are dealing, as close as possible to the paint, with one of the most abstract—in its topological background—inventions of the pictorial thought of this century. "Without recourse to theory or to mathematics, a painter may very well come to formulate, by means all his own, a problematic that may later be translated into other terms and into another register (as happened in its time with perspective)" (p. 288). It is because he acknowledges that painting can provide theoretical models that Damisch will be able to single out in Pollock the moment of thickness and from then on rewrite a portion of the history of modern art.

The Symbolic Model

It is fashion nowadays to ask oneself about the ways and means by which the passage from painting to the discourse that takes it over is supposed to operate—if not about the end of this transference. It is even one of the most frequent commonplaces in our artistic and literary culture, a *topos* from which very few escape who, without claiming to be "art critics" (that is behind us), make it their profession, if not their work, to write about painting or about painters. Without remembering that this question, which one would like to see preceding any commentary, has already been decided by culture, which is at all times responsible for organizing the game, distributing the roles, and regulating the exchanges between the two registers of the visible and the readable, between the painted and the written (or the spoken), the seeing and the hearing, the seen and the heard. If this question today professes to be such, and a question to which culture, our culture, would not furnish a ready-made answer, it is still culture, our culture, that will have wanted it that way, and that always makes us ask it all over again. (p. 186)

If the numerous passages that Damisch devotes in this collection to the relation between painting and discourse avoid as much as possible the cliché that he denounces, it is partly because he demonstrates that his text can only belong to it. Like the Foucault of *This Is Not a Pipe,* whose analyses he anticipates as early as 1960, Damisch likes to draw a historical map of the connections between practices. Here he stresses the extent to which the mode of relation of painting to discourse has become in this century, thanks to abstraction and structural linguistics, a particularly necessary stumbling block in the analysis. It is because he considers painting a key to the interpretation of the world, a key neither mimetic nor analogical, but, as for science or language, *symbolic* (more in Cassirer's sense than Lacan's), and because he assigns to painting a cultural task equal to and different from the discourse that deals with it, that the archaeological or epistemological reading takes an unexpected turn in Damisch, as though finding in certain pictorial advances theorems of anthropological mutations.

Many pages in *Fenêtre jaune cadmium* concern the relations that mathematics and painting maintain at the symbolic level, whether it is a question of the role of mimesis in algebraic invention (p. 51) and notation (p. 196) or the common ground (projective plane) on which geometry and perspective construction work (p. 295). Furthermore, it is probably after having successfully shown how the invention of pictorial perspective in the Renaissance anticipated by two centuries the work of mathematicians on the notion of infinity[6] that Damisch was tempted to pursue the transserial inquiry into modern times. The long article on Paul Klee's *Equals Infinity* (Museum of Modern Art, New York), which compares the 1932 painting with the discoveries of Cantor and Dedekind on the power of the continuum, sufficiently shows the interest as well as the difficulty of a thought in which,

> beyond the accepted division of labor, the inherited separation of the fields of knowledge and significance, the *differences* among the practices known as "art," "science," "mathematics," and "painting" cease to be thought of in terms of exteriority in order to be thought of—whatever one understands thereby—in terms of relations of production, i.e., of *history*. (p. 215)

Partly because this is not my field, I prefer to leave it and insist instead on one of the symbolic models developed by Damisch for the art of this century, a model that moreover has the particular feature, according to Bataille, of ripping the frock coat philosophy gives to what exists, the "mathematical frock coat." One will recognize here the famous definition, given in *Documents* in 1929, of the *informe*, a term, again according to Bataille, *that serves to declassify*. Among the references that return at several points in this book (Frenhofer, Alberti, Ripa, and others), there is one that I consider emblematic of the reading that I am here seeking to circumscribe: it is those pages devoted by Valéry to Degas in which Valéry observed, in Damisch's words,

> that the notion of form is changed—if not cast in doubt altogether—by the projection onto the vertical plane of the canvas of the horizontal plane of the floor, which no longer functions as a neutral and indifferent background but as an essential factor in the vision of things, and can—almost—constitute the very subject of the painting. (p. 111)

Already in the essay devoted to Dubuffet in 1962—anticipating by a few years Leo Steinberg's invention of the concept of the *flatbed* picture plane in connection with Rauschenberg as well as more recent studies—the confusion of the vertical and horizontal proposed by one side of modern painting was taken for an essential mutation, participating, if you like, in a critique of optics, whose importance is yet to be measured.[7] This model includes Dubuffet's twin desires "to force the gaze to consider the painted surface as a ground viewed from above, and at the same time to erect the ground into a wall calling for man's intervention by line or imprint" (p. 112); Pollock's *grounds,* "an area, a space of play, attacked by the artist from all sides at once, which he did not hesitate to penetrate in person and which . . . put up a physical resistance to him" (p. 149); Saul Steinberg's *Tables* (p. 231), but I would be tempted to say of these, contrary to Damisch, that they do not come "directly into the inquiry," and are among "those that proliferate in its wake"(p. 130). Even Mondrian's work, as I have tried to show elsewhere,[8] touches on this symbolic model, this taxonomic collapse, this overturning of oppositions—especially between representation and action—on which our whole Western aesthetic is founded. Damisch probably had an intuition of this, since for him the study of Mondrian's work is "an invitation to *create* under its most concrete aspects" (p. 72). The revelation of this model is one of the most fruitful points of Damisch's book. From cubism to minimalism, from the abstraction of the 1920s to that of the '50s and '60s, I would almost go as far as to point to all the high points of modern art as verifications of this discovery, as demonstrations of its validity.

The Strategic Model

Shortly before his death, "and as though in passing," Barnett Newman confided to Damisch "that everything he had been able to do had meaning only in relation to Pollock's work and *against* it" (p. 154). I like to think that Damisch recalled this remark when he read Lévi-Strauss's *Voie des masques*, and that from long knowledge of this kind of secret, then from its sudden emergence as evidence, a fourth model emerged in Damisch's text, a *strategic* model.[9] Like chess pieces, like phonemes in language, a work has significance, as Lévi-Strauss shows, first by what it is not and what it opposes, that is, in each case according to its position, its value, within a field—itself living and stratified—which has above all to be circumscribed by defining its rules. Lévi-Strauss's condescending remarks about art historians, unable, in his opinion, to understand the structural or rather the strategic nature of signification, are not strictly deserved, at least if one considers art history in its earlier phases and not for what it has largely become today. As we know, Wölfflin conceived the baroque paradigm as incomprehensible unless measured against the classical; and Riegl demonstrated in a thick volume how the *Kunstwollen* of sixteenth- and seventeenth-century Dutch art was at first negatively defined in relation to that of Italian art of the same period. Such readings are, in any case, commonplace in *Fenêtre jaune cadmium* (see, for example, the comparisons between Pollock and Mondrian) and have the merit of no longer taking seriously the autonomy of what is called style. Likewise, since strategy means power stakes, there are many observations in this book on the history of the artistic institution in its relation to production, whether it has to do with the role of criticism, the museum, the market, the public, or even the relationship (fundamentally changed since Cézanne, p. 123) that the painter maintains with his or her canvas.

But the interest of the strategic model does not reside so much there as in what it allows us to think historically of the concepts revealed by the other models as well as the ties that they maintain among themselves. One will notice, by the way, that this fourth model was not born directly from a confrontation with the works themselves: it does not immediately take account of pictorial invention itself, of the status of the theoretical in painting, but of the conditions of appearance, of what establishes itself between works; it finds itself with respect to the other models in a second, metacritical position, and this is why it allows us to ask again the question of the pictorial specificity (of invention) and survival of painting, without getting stuck once more in the essentialism to which American formalist criticism had accustomed us. "It is not enough, in order for there to be painting, that the painter take up his brushes again," Damisch tells us: it is still necessary that it be worth the effort, "it is still necessary that [the painter] succeed in demonstrating to us that painting is something we positively cannot do without, that it is indispensable to us, and that it would be madness—worse still, a historical error—to let it lie fallow today" (p. 293).

Let us again take the strategic metaphor par excellence, that of chess: Damisch uses it to clarify his historical point. Let us suppose that Newman and Pollock are opponents. How can we determine in their moves what is of the order of the match, belonging in particular to its new although replayable developments, and what is of the generic order of the game, with its assigned rules? One can see what is displaced by this kind of question, such as the problem of repetitions that had so worried Wölfflin:

> It is certain that through the problematic of abstraction, American painters [of the abstract expressionist generation], just as already in the 1920s the exponents of suprematism, neoplasticism, purism, etc., could nourish the illusion that, far from being engaged merely in a single match that would take its place in the group of matches making up the *game* of "painting," they were returning to the very foundations of the game, to its immediate, constituent *données*. The American episode would then represent less a new development in the history of abstraction than a new departure, a resumption—but at a deeper level and, theoretically as much as practically, with more powerful means—of the match begun under the title of abstraction thirty or forty years earlier. (p. 167)

The strategic reading is strictly antihistoricist: it does not believe in the exhaustion of things, in the linear genealogy offered by us by art criticism, always ready, unconsciously or not, to follow the demands of the market in search of new products, but neither does it believe in the order of a homogenous time without breaks, such as art history likes to imagine. Its question becomes "one of the status that ought to be assigned to the *match* 'painting,' as one *sees* it being played at a given moment in particular circumstances, in its relation to the *game* of the same name" (p. 170)—and the question can be asked about any of the models (perceptive, technical, and symbolic) described above, as well as about the relations they maintain among themselves at a given moment in history.

Such questioning has the immediate advantage of raising doubt about certain truisms. Is the "alleged convention of depth"—rejected by the pictorial art of this century because, according to Greenberg, it is unnecessary—necessarily of the order of the "match" more than of the game (p. 166)? Also, concerning what Damisch observed of the "undersides of painting," should we not rather consider that a series of displacements will have modified their role (the position on the chessboard)? And is it not the same for the convention of "chiaroscuro" (ibid.)? Without thereby becoming a theoretical machine encouraging indifference, since on the contrary one has to take a side, the strategic approach has the advantage of deciphering the pictorial field as an antagonistic field where nothing is ever terminated, decided once and for all, and of leading the analysis back to a type of historicity that it had neglected, that of long duration (to which the symbolic model par excellence also goes back). Hence Damisch's supremely ironic attitude toward the apocalyptic tone adopted today concerning the impasse in which art finds itself, an impasse to be taken simply as one of the many interrupted matches to which history holds the secret.[10]

> The problem, for whoever writes about it, should not be so much to write about painting as to try to do something *with* it, without indeed claiming to understand it better than the painter does, . . . [to try to] see a little more clearly, thanks to painting, into the problems with which [the writer] is concerned, and which are not only, nor even primarily, problems of painting—if they were, all he would have to do would be to devote himself to this art (p. 288).

Because he considers painting a theoretical operator, a producer of models, because he agrees with this statement by Dubuffet given as a quotation—"painting may be a machine to convey philosophy—*but already to elaborate it*" (p. 104), and because he means in his work to receive a lesson from painting, Hubert Damisch offers us one of the most thoughtful readings of the art of this century, but one that also remains as close as possible to its object, deliberately situating itself each time at the very heart of pictorial invention. For what the perceptive, technical, and symbolic models aim primarily at demonstrating are the mechanisms of this invention, and what the strategic model takes account of is its mode of historicity.

Notes

Introduction: Resisting Blackmail

I am grateful to several colleagues and friends for their helpful comments in the final preparation of this introduction, particularly Werner Hamacher, Herbert Kessler, and Angelica Rudenstine.

1. Aloïs Riegl perfectly characterizes a kind of intellectual blackmail in his critique of positivism: "I do not share the view that a knowledge of monuments alone already constitutes the alpha and omega of art-historical knowledge. The well-known, dubious, and loud-mouthed argument, 'What, you don't know that? Then you don't know anything at all!' may have had a certain validity in the period of materialistic reaction to Hegelian overestimation of conceptual categories [this refers to the work of Gottfried Semper]. In the future we will have to ask ourselves in regard to every single reported fact, what the knowledge of this fact is actually worth. Even the historical is not an absolute category, and for the scholar, not only knowing per se, but also the knowing-how-to-ignore certain facts at the right moment may well have its advantage." ("Late Roman or Oriental?" [1920], tr. Peter Wortsman, in *German Essays on Art History,* ed. Gert Schiff [New York: Continuum, 1988], pp. 189–190.) On the issue of the "threshold of historicity" of any single fact, which puzzled neo-Kantian historians in Germany at the end of the last century, cf. my essay "Kahnweiler's Lesson," below.

2. The violence of the debate concerning the writings of Paul de Man's youth, and the amount of coverage it received even outside academia, are unfortunately a sign that the antitheory blackmail is gaining strength in this country. For a close look at the pros and cons in this issue, cf. *Responses: On Paul de Man's Wartime Journalism,* ed. Werner Hamacher, Neil Hertz, Thomas Keenan (Lincoln and London: University of Nebraska Press, 1989). At the same time, a similar "affair" (bringing about the same hysteria and similar arguments) emerged in France, where the antitheoretical pressure has been triumphant for a decade. This "affair," concerning Heidegger, was launched in 1986 by the publication of Victor Farias, *Heidegger et le nazisme* (Paris: Verdier), despite the fact that this book did not bring forth much new information, and added its share of mistakes and mystifications. Farias's pamphlet received an enormous media coverage (daily newspapers, radio, TV), whose general tone was hysterical. Three main arguments were repeated ad nauseam: (1) Heidegger's philosophy as a whole is Nazi philosophy; (2) philosophy is of no use if it cannot prevent one from becoming a Nazi; (3) philosophy, of any kind, always leads to totalitarianism. The mediocrity of such claims, and their extraordinary public effect, prompted major French philosophers and intellectuals to retort. Both Jacques Derrida and Philippe Lacoue-Labarthe wrote articles, then books, on the question of Heidegger and politics, but Jean-Luc Nancy, Maurice Blanchot, Emmanuel Levinas, and many others also intervened in the debate. (For a summary of the "affair," see the dossier presented by Arnold I. Davidson in *Critical Inquiry* 15, no. 2 [Winter 1989], pp. 407 ff.)

3.   Thomas Pavel, *Le mirage linguistique: Essai sur la modernisation intellectuelle* (Paris: Editions de Minuit, 1988). See especially pp. 44–57, where Lévi-Strauss's structural analysis of the myth of Oedipus is mocked (Pavel makes sure that the reader is informed, at the outset, that this famous analysis, reprinted later in *Structural Anthropology I,* dates from the same year [1955] as Chomsky's *The Logical Structure of Linguistics Theory*).

4.   Cf. "Writer, Artisan, Narrator," a memoir on Barthes's pedagogy, *October,* no. 26 (Fall 1983), pp. 27–33.

5.   Of the massive "poststructuralist" *Kunstliteratur,* to use the word coined by Julius von Schlosser, only Barthes's texts seemed to us genuinely unaltered by the kind of arrogance we saw everywhere else. He himself was a "Sunday painter" and was thus aware of the difficulties lying behind the very act of painting; furthermore, he always stressed his lack of qualifications on the matter, his amateurism, and never pontificated.

6.   Roman Jakobson, "On Realism" (1921), English tr. Karol Magassy, in Ladislav Matejka and Krystyna Pomorska, eds., *Readings in Russian Poetics: Formalist and Structuralist Views* (Cambridge, Mass.: MIT Press, 1971), p. 38.

7.   To be noted in passing: my lack of sympathy for the term "poststructuralism"—due both to the use of the prefix "post-" which I always hold to be a symptom of blackmail by fashion, and to the homogenization of contradictory voices it entails—might be a function of my lack of distance toward the critical field it is supposed to map.

8.   Cf. "The Antidote," *October,* no. 39 (Winter 1986), pp. 129–144. Haacke's comment on *On Social Grease* first appeared in Yve-Alain Bois, Douglas Crimp, and Rosalind Krauss, "A Conversation with Hans Haacke," *October,* no. 30 (Fall 1984), p. 33.

9.   P.N. Medvedev/M.M. Bakhtin, *The Formal Method in Literary Scholarship* (1928), English tr. Albert J. Wehrle (Baltimore and London: Johns Hopkins University Press, 1978), p. 49. Although the book appeared under the name of Medvedev, it is generally thought today that Bakhtin was its main, if not sole author. This question remaining hanging (hence my use of "they" and "their"), and quite in keeping with Bakhtin's sense of the dialogic, the translator and editor of the book ingeniously decided to use both their names united by a slash, thus forming a single name, to designate its authorship (cf. Wehrle's introduction, pp. ix–xxiii).

10.   Ibid.

11.   Clement Greenberg, "Modernist Painting" (1961), rpt. in Gregory Battcock, *The New Art* (New York: Dutton, 1966), p. 110.

12.   For Greenberg's emphasis on the "empirical and the positive," cf. for example "The New Sculpture" (1958 version), rpt. in *Art and Culture* (Boston: Beacon Press, 1961), p. 139; for a parallel between modernism and "modern science," cf. "Modernist Painting," pp. 107–108. To be honest, the Russian formalists themselves identified momentarily with positivism, as Medvedev/Bakhtin noted, quoting Eikhenbaum (*The Formal Method,* pp. 179–180, note 10).

13.   Greenberg's actual phrase, in a passage of the essay "American-Type Painting" where he is discussing Rothko, is: "like Newman (though it is Rothko who probably did the influencing here), he seems to soak his paint into the canvas to get a dyer's effect." Infuriated, and justifiably so for he had always insisted on the "solid," heavy, direct quality of his paint," Newman immediately wrote to Greenberg and asked him to correct the essay. Despite Newman's protest, Greenberg did not alter this sentence, which appears as it stands in the 1958 version of the text, republished in *Art and Culture,* p. 225.

14.   *The Formal Method,* p. 47.

15.   Roland Barthes, *Empire of Signs* (1970), English tr. Richard Howard (New York: Hill and Wang, 1982), pp. 28–29.

16.   Sergei M. Eisenstein, "In the Interest of Form" (1932), French tr. Luda and Jean Schnitzer, in *Au-delà des étoiles,* ed. Jacques Aumont (Paris: UGE, 1974), p. 234.

17.   Ibid., p. 239. Later in the text Eisenstein writes: "Form is first of all ideology. And ideology cannot be rented. Nature did not make provision for distribution centers of ideology to rightful owners" (pp. 240–241).

18. Ibid., pp. 235–236.

19. Ibid., p. 236.

20. Roland Barthes, "On *The Fashion System* and the Structural Analysis of Narrative" (1967), interview with Raymond Bellour, English tr. Linda Coverdale, rpt. in *The Grain of the Voice* (New York: Hill and Wang, 1985), pp. 50–51.

21. Cf. *The Formal Method,* pp. 14–15, 23, and 26–27.

22. Both essays have appeared in English in Matejka and Pomorska, *Readings in Russian Poetics,* pp. 66–78 and 79–81.

23. Roland Barthes, "Digressions" (1971), interview with Guy Scarpetta, English tr. in *The Grain of the Voice,* p. 115. The word "scientiste," used by Barthes, should not be translated by "scientist"— Barthes had absolutely nothing against science—although I am not aware of an English equivalent ("scientistic scholar?"). A "scientiste," in French, means someone who reveres the codes and signs of science more than science itself. "Scientisme," as such, has much to do with pseudoscience (the red herring of the "fourth dimension," for example, is a typical "scientiste" myth).

24. Cf. Roland Barthes, *Criticism and Truth,* tr. Katrine Pilcher Keuneman (London: Athlone Press, 1987), pp. 52 ff. The word was in fact explicitly borrowed by Barthes from H. Hécaen and R. Angelergues, *Pathologie du langage* (Paris: Larousse, 1965), p. 32.

25. Cf. Michael Ann Holly, *Panofsky and the Foundations of Art History* (Ithaca and London: Cornell University Press, 1984), p. 159. The 1932 article was entitled "Zum Problem der Beschreibung und Inhaltsdeutung von Werken der bildenden Kunst" [On the Problem of the Description of Works of Art and of the Interpretation of their Content]. It repeats word for word several passages from *Hercules am Scheidewege* [Hercules at the Crossroads], published by the Warburg Institute in 1930. This section of the current essay, devoted to Panofsky, is taken from a review I wrote of Holly's book ("Panofsky Early and Late," *Art in America,* July 1985, pp. 9–15).

26. Cf. Holly, *Panofsky,* p. 233, note 6. The 1955 version is entitled "Iconography and Iconology: An Introduction to the Study of Renaissance Art." For the relevant passage, cf. *Meaning in the Visual Arts,* p. 31.

27. Quoted in Holly, *Panofsky,* p. 169.

28. Erwin Panofsky, preface to the French edition of *Studies in Iconology* (*Etudes d'iconologie,* tr. Claude Herbette and Bernard Teyssèdre [Paris: Gallimard, 1967], p. 3), retranslated from the French. I am grateful to Herbert Kessler for having pointed to my attention Panofsky's last-minute renunciation of the iconography/iconology opposition.

29. Erwin Panofsky, "Introduction," *Studies in Iconology: Humanistic Themes in the Art of the Renaissance* (New York: Oxford University Press, 1939), p. 8.

30. Cf. *Etudes d'iconologie,* tr. Herbette and Teyssèdre, p. 23, note 1.

31. Not until the publication of Svetlana Alpers's *The Art of Describing: Dutch Art in the Seventeenth Century* (Chicago: University of Chicago Press, 1983) was the ability of Panofskian iconology to deal with the specificity of nonallegorical Dutch art even questioned. In fact, as Alpers remarks in a comment on the title of one of Panofsky's best-known essays, "The History of Art as a Humanist Discipline," Panofsky's entire enterprise was "grounded in Renaissance assumptions about man and art" ("Is Art History?," *Daedalus,* Summer 1977, p. 6). It is thus hardly surprising that, with the exception of *Die deutsche Plastik des elften bis dreizehnten Jahrhunderts,* published in Munich in 1924 and still not available in English, and of *Gothic Architecture and Scholasticism* (New York: Meridian Books, 1957), everything he wrote on medieval art is full of privative or negative connotations. Even an extraordinary study like *Renaissance and Renascences in Western Art* (Stockholm, 1960), which concerns almost exclusively the pre-Renaissance period, does not depart from this mode. On this point, cf. Jean Molino, "Allégorisme et iconologie: Sur la méthode de Panofsky," in *Erwin Panofsky,* coll. Cahiers pour un temps (Paris: Centre Georges Pompidou, 1983), pp. 27–47, and Jean-Claude Bonne, "Fond, surfaces, support (Panofsky et l'art roman)," ibid., pp. 117–133.

32. Barnett Newman, "Letter to the editor," *Art News,* September 1961, p. 6.

33.   Erwin Panofsky, "Three Decades of Art History in the United States," in *Meaning in the Visual Arts* (1955; rpt., Chicago: University of Chicago Press, 1982), p. 329. The subtitle of this essay, more akin to its content, is "Impressions of a Transplanted European." It was first published in 1953 under the simple title "The History of Art" in a volume entitled *The Cultural Migration: The European Scholar in America.*

34.   Ibid., pp. 329–330.

Matisse and "Arche-drawing"

1.   Jack Flam, *Matisse on Art* (New York: Phaidon, 1973), p. 73; hereafter cited in the text as Flam. For the still untranslated writings, I refer to Dominique Fourcade, ed., *Henri Matisse: Ecrits et propos sur l'art* (Paris: Hermann, 1972), hereafter abbreviated as *EPA.* The date following most references is the date of publication, not only for Matisse's articles, but also for remarks reported by others when they were presumably published soon after being made; no date is given when there is no way of knowing, even approximately, when the statement was made. Since what I am proposing in the next few pages is a close reading of "Modernism and Tradition," I shall dispense with references for shorter quotations from it.

2.   Translating the expression "into color and design" back into French, an expression that occurs in Alfred Barr's English translation of a radio interview, Dominique Fourcade renders it as "en termes de couleur et de forme," which clearly reveals the problems the French language has with the concept. But he quite rightly notes that the English is probably at fault: "Par le dessin et la couleur serait sans doute plus proche de la terminologie habituelle de Matisse [*Through color and drawing* would undoubtedly be closer to Matisse's usual terminology]" (*EPA*, p. 189, note 49).

3.   Furthermore, in order to express his contempt for a priori modes of plastic reasoning, Matisse refers explicitly to "design," which was called at the time "industrial art": "There are no rules to establish, let alone practical recipes, otherwise what you're doing is industrial art" (speaking to Diehl in 1943, *EPA*, p. 195).

4.   As Roger Benjamin observed, the excuses with which Matisse feels obliged to begin the "Notes" of 1908 are in part designed to counteract Maurice Denis's verdict, repeated at the time by the majority of critics, Gide amongst them, according to which his art suffered from an excess of theory (*"Notes of a Painter": Criticism, Theory and Context, 1891–1908* [Ann Arbor: UMI Research Press, 1987], pp. 166–167, 191–195, and passim). But it would be a mistake to see this as nothing more than cold calculation or rhetorical coquetry: cf. Fourcade's excellent note devoted to Matisse's ambivalence concerning writing, *EPA,* pp. 309–310, as well as the various entries under the heading "écrivain" (writer) in the book's index.

5.   On Gustave Moreau, the Louvre, and outdoor painting (*pleinairisme*), cf. the remarks assembled by Jacques Guenne in 1925 (Flam, p. 65), Pierre Courthion in 1931 (Flam, p. 54) and Gaston Diehl in 1954: "It was almost revolutionary of him to be teaching us the museum route at a time when official art, devoted to the worst pastiches, and contemporary art, drawn toward outdoor painting [*pleinairisme*], both seemed to be conspiring to turn us away from it" (Diehl, *Henri Matisse,* 1954, English tr. Agnes Humbert [New York: Universal Books, 1958], p. 7, trans. modified). On Matisse and Moreau, cf. Benjamin, *"Notes of a Painter,"* pp. 21–48 and passim.

6.   Moreover, Derain's name, along with those of other "fauves," appeared very rarely not only in Matisse's writing, but in his conversation. In 1949, he was to openly state to Duthuit that "to tell you the truth, the painting of Derain and Vlaminck did not surprise me, for it was close to the researches I myself was pursuing. But I was moved to see that these very young men had certain convictions similar to my own" (Georges Duthuit, *The Fauve Painters* [1949], English tr. Ralph Manheim [New York: Wittenborn, 1950], p. 30).

7.   "How grateful I am to Courbet for reorienting me in the Louvre!," a remark reported in Walter Pach, *Queer Thing, Painting* (New York: Harper, 1938), p. 122.

8. Matisse's copies, which have impressed all historians, play a determining role in the way in which he "settles" his relationship to the tradition. On this point (and on the copy exhibitions organized by Félix Fénéon at the Bernheim-Jeune gallery in 1910), cf. Roger Benjamin, "Recovering Authors: The Modern Copy, Copy Exhibitions and Matisse," *Art History* 12 (June 1989), pp. 176–201.

9. Quoted by the "Editors" in the preface to the original edition of Duthuit (*Les Fauves* [Geneva: Les Trois Collines, 1949], p. 10). This preface does not appear in the American edition.

10. Diehl, *Matisse,* p. 22.

11. I have slightly modified Flam's translation, which gives "spirit" instead of "mind" here. The French text reads: "Alors on part dans la brousse; pour se faire des moyens plus simples qui n'étouffent pas l'esprit" (*EPA,* p. 94).

12. Raymond Escholier, *Matisse from the Life* (1956), English tr. Geraldine and H.M. Colville (London: Faber and Faber, 1960), p. 43.

13. Pierre Schneider quite rightly notes that the references to the Orient become increasingly frequent in Matisse's remarks and writing, to the detriment of references to the other "great totemic figures" in the autobiographical notice of 1930: several years later, he mentions only Cézanne and the Orientals; in 1947, the "revelation" is imputed solely to the Orientals (Pierre Schneider, "The Revelation of the Orient," *Matisse,* English tr. Michael Taylor and Bridget Stevens Romer [New York: Rizzoli, 1984], p. 155).

14. Not "a" definitive impulse, as Flam translates, and which would indeed be more in keeping with what Matisse says of Cézanne elsewhere.

15. "Questions to Matisse: 'Wherein do you consider that Cézanne can have influenced your researches? Is it possible to associate him with the idea of using pure colors?' Answer: 'As to pure colors, absolutely pure colors, no. But Cézanne constructed by means of relations of forces, even with black and white'" (in Duthuit, *The Fauve Painters,* p. 26).

16. I have replaced "means" by "possibilities," which is the exact translation of the original French.

17. I shall continue to make frequent reference to "Modernism and Tradition," but not in any systematic way: my detailed examination of the text ends here. After the explanation of the break with divisionism, and the appeal to tradition mentioned above, one finds: (a) a declaration of optimism concerning the artistic production that the period has in store; (b) a statement on the artistic morality of risk taking; and (c) the anecdote on Vauxcelles's "baptism" of fauvism, followed by the already-mentioned critique of the label. As for the passage concerning divisionism, which I shall come back to, I leave aside one of its more obscure aspects, for it seems to me that Matisse is almost maliciously leading the reader astray here: Seurat's "great innovation" is not initially presented as having to do with color, but as "the simplification of form to its fundamental geometrical shapes." This is the only time in the entire theoretical corpus left to us by Matisse that he declares his interest in divisionism in these terms. I see it as a "contamination" of what Matisse has to say in this text and everywhere else concerning the very inseparability of drawing and color. Not that Seurat had nothing to teach him on "geometric deformation" (as it was then called), but it would be a mistake to see it as the essential aspect of what Matisse picks up from neoimpressionism. Moreover, "Modernism and Tradition" goes on to deal with the division of colors, in other words with what he otherwise finds more important (and which was specific to Seurat, "deformation" being, on the contrary, shared by the various currents reacting to impressionism).

18. Catherine C. Bock, *Henri Matisse and Neo-Impressionism, 1898–1908* (Ann Arbor: UMI Research, 1981).

19. "To arrange [one's] sensations and emotions" says the English text of "Modernism and Tradition" (Flam, p. 73). But Matisse used Cézanne's phrase often enough to suspect that "organiser [ses] sensations et émotions" was the French original.

20. Pierre Schneider, "Une saison décisive," *Cahiers Henri Matisse,* no. 4 (1986), Musée Matisse, p. 16. This notebook constitutes the catalogue of an exhibition entitled *Matisse: Ajaccio-Toulouse, une saison de peinture,* held in 1986 at the Musée Paul Dupuy in Toulouse and in 1986–87 at the Galerie des Ponchettes in Nice.

21.   Letter dated June 6, 1898, and published by Schneider, "Une saison décisive," pp. 12–14. Matisse's letter to Evenepoël, which must have preceded by a few days the mailing of the four sketches, has disappeared, but Evenepoël in his horrified response cites the painter's own words on the epilepsy, words that he must have found especially appropriate since he repeats them a week later, after Matisse visited him in Paris, in a letter to his father dated June 15 (ibid., p. 11). Evenepoël's letter to Matisse is a particularly important document, since it reveals a Matisse already seeking to deploy violently contrasting colors even before his reading of Signac's treatise ("this tablecloth with its emerald-green reflections and its human figure green on one side, red on the other, as if lit by an apothecary's jars," ibid., p. 13). Which amounts to saying that Matisse, whose self-doubt is legendary, must have been particularly happy to find in Signac a guide for "the organization of his sensations."

22.   *La Revue blanche,* vol. 16, no. 118, May 1, 1898 (chaps. 1 and 2); no. 119, May 15, 1898 (chaps. 3 through 6 inclusive). The last two chapters did not appear until July, after Matisse had returned to Corsica, but they contain, respectively, a collection of citations, from Charles Blanc to Ogden Rood and Ruskin (all authors whose authority is meant to bolster the theory presented in the preceding chapters), and a response to the various criticisms leveled at divisionism: the essential elements of the theoretical message are contained in the first six chapters. The text was reprinted in book form in 1899 (Éditions de la Revue Blanche).

23.   I owe this observation on the relative similarity between the importance that Goupil's book (*Manuel général de la peinture à l'huile,* 1877) had had for Matisse in 1889–90 and that of Signac's treatise in 1898–99 to Bock, *Matisse and Neo-Impressionism,* p. 14. On Goupil and Matisse, cf. Benjamin, *"Notes of a Painter,"* pp. 9–11 and passim, and Flam, pp. 18–19.

24.   For the function of Signac's historical overview, I refer the reader once again to Catherine Bock's study (*Matisse and Neo-Impressionism,* pp. 1 and 15).

25.   "By juxtaposing in bold, squarish strokes the various elements of hues broken down into their component parts, without concern for imitation or deftness, Cézanne came closer than either Monet or Renoir to the impressionists' methodical *division*" (Paul Signac, *De Delacroix au néo-impressionnisme,* ed. Françoise Cachin [Paris: Hermann, 1964], p. 105). According to statements made to Diehl, it was during his stay in Toulouse (absorbed in his reading of Signac) that Matisse decided to buy Cézanne's *The Bathers* [*Trois Baigneuses*] from Vollard, a work he kept until 1936, at which time he donated it to the Musée du Petit Palais (*EPA,* p. 134, note 103 to the letter Matisse wrote for the occasion to Raymond Escholier, reproduced ibid., pp. 133–134, and in Flam, p. 75). Certainly, Matisse had been exposed to Cézanne's work from at least the time of the presentation of Caillebotte's legacy to the Luxembourg, if not before, judging by certain remarks he made (cf. the note Dominique Fourcade devotes to this question, *EPA,* p. 81, note 10), but one cannot fail to be struck by the coincidence. Furthermore, as Benjamin notes (*"Notes of a Painter,"* p. 66), it is not entirely impossible that Matisse arrived in Paris in time to see Cézanne's second personal exhibition, organized by Vollard from May 9 to June 10, 1898 (sixty or so works). In fact, we know that he was in Paris before June 15 (letter from Evenepoël to his father), and, as it happens, that he stayed at least through June 26 (letter from Jules Flandrin cited by Benjamin, *"Notes of a Painter,"* p. 263, note 90). Whatever the case, whether he bought the picture because, in the terms laid down by Signac, he liked the brushwork, or, on the contrary (since the purchase was no doubt not made before his return to Paris in early 1899), in order to use it as a guide in his rejection of divisionism, in both cases his admiration for Cézanne would have been stimulated by his discovery of neoimpressionism.

26.   Cf. Bock, *Matisse and Neo-Impressionism,* pp. 21–29.

27.   In his diary, Signac makes the following observation concerning Seurat's canvas: "It is too divided, the brushstrokes are too small . . . the work . . . gives it an overall grayish tone" (cited by Cachin in her introduction to *De Delacroix au néo-impressionnisme,* p. 21). Corresponding to this, in the treatise itself, we have the important distinction between the principle of division and the pointillist technique that Signac strongly advises against, especially for larger works: "the comple-

mentary colors, which are amicable and mutually exalting if opposed, become hostile and destroy each other if mixed together, even optically. Opposed, a red surface and a green surface stimulate each other, but red dots mixed with green dots yield an overall gray, colorless effect" (ibid., p. 108). This passage is important since it shows that—even though it is advocated everywhere else in the treatise—Signac no longer believes in the fiction of "optical mixing" (which is perfectly logical given the size attained by his "mosaic-like" brushstrokes at that time). It is strange to notice just how readily the fauve (or rather, postfauve) Matisse, who would so exasperate Signac, could have subscribed to these lines. If Matisse did not heed the warning at the time of reading the treatise, it was because he had not yet experienced this weakening of color intensity through what Signac calls pointillist "niggling" (*pignochage*).

28. Bock, *Matisse and Neo-Impressionism,* p. 28.
29. Schneider, "Une saison décisive," p. 17.
30. Cited in Bock, *Matisse and Neo-Impressionism,* p. 37.
31. The works in question are *Still Life with a Purro I* [*Nature morte au Purro I*], *Place des Lices, Saint Tropez,* and *View of Saint Tropez* [*Vue de Saint-Tropez*]. Most historians have remarked that this last canvas is almost a pastiche of the famous views of the Estaque by Cézanne. However, as Jack Flam quite rightly observes, the color in *Place des Lices* is "that of a Cézanne seen through the eyes of Gauguin" (Jack Flam, *Matisse, the Man and His Art, 1869–1918* [Ithaca and London: Cornell University Press, 1986], p. 110). As Bock notes in relating its major points, it is in July 1904 that Emile Bernard's famous article on Cézanne appears in *L'Occident,* in other words, just before Matisse's second conversion to divisionism, and it is more than likely that Matisse discussed it with Signac (Bock, *Matisse and Neo-Impressionism,* pp. 64–65). In any case, Signac certainly owned a copy of the review, since a year after the text appeared, Matisse asked him to copy a few lines of it for him (Schneider, *Matisse,* p. 44). Schneider also notes that Matisse read the letters that Cézanne wrote to Camoin in 1902 (ibid., p. 152, note 17).
32. On the numerous opportunities Matisse had to see divisionist works between 1899 and 1904, cf. Bock, *Matisse and Neo-Impressionism,* pp. 57–58.
33. Maurice Denis, "La réaction française," *L'Ermitage,* May 15, 1905, rpt. in *Théories 1890–1910,* 4th ed. (Paris: Rouart et Watelin, 1920), p. 196.
34. Maurice Denis, "De Gauguin, de Whistler et de l'excès de théories," *L'Ermitage,* Nov. 15, 1905, rpt. in *Théories,* p. 208.
35. The canonical text concerning "transposition" is already to be found in the 1908 "Notes" (without naming the canvas, Matisse discusses the transformation of *Harmony in Red* [*La Desserte rouge*] of the same year, where the background had initially been green, then blue, concluding with these words: "I am forced to transpose, and it is why it is sometimes felt that my picture has been completely changed when, after successive modifications, the red has succeeded the green as the dominant color"; Flam, p. 37, translation slightly modified). The metaphor of the chess game will appear later on, but in most instances in order to illustrate the idea that in such cases it is the "same sensation" that is "differently presented": "The difference between the two canvases is that of two aspects of a chess-board in the course of a game of chess. The appearance of the board is continually changing in the course of the play, but the intentions of the players who move the pawns remain constant" ("Modernism and Tradition," Flam, p. 72; cf. also the entry "chessboard" [*échiquier*] in the index of *EPA*). Jack Flam has unearthed a color photograph of *Harmony* when it was still *in blue,* which demonstrates that if the final version is "the same painting," it is precisely because it is not the same in appearance: the passage from blue to red in the ordering of the color necessitated a certain number of adjustments in the register of the composition (in order to produce the same effect with different means, the latter have to be employed differently): cf. Flam, *Matisse, the Man,* p. 231. In conclusion, let us note that Matisse will go on to impressively illustrate his intentions in the series of eight canvases painted in 1947, ending with the extraordinary *Le Silence habité des maisons,* all eight on the same motif, but each one with a different color range (reproduced in color by Matisse in *Verve,* vol. 6, nos. 21–22, no pagination). On color transposition in Matisse, cf. Jean-

Claude Lebensztejn, "Les textes du peintre" (1974), rpt. in *Zig Zag* (Paris: Flammarion, 1981). This text is still the best study concerning the different aspects of Matisse's use of color.

36.   "For me, the revolutionary character of Seurat is that he was the very first painter to have created pictures whose matter is perfectly homogeneous: the small marks which convey color are the same as those that convey line and space." Meyer Schapiro made this observation in the course of a discussion that followed a paper by Guy Habasque on simultaneous color contrast at a colloquium on color organized by the Centre de Recherches de Psychologie Comparative in May 1954 (*Problèmes de la couleur* [Paris: SEVPEN, 1957], p. 251).

37.   Diehl, *Matisse,* p. 22, translation slightly modified.

38.   Bock, *Matisse and Neo-Impressionism,* p. 77.

39.   Unfortunately, this passage from the French edition of Diehl's book (*Henri Matisse* [Paris: Tisné, 1954], p. 28) was omitted from the American edition.

40.   The canvas was shown for the first time at Matisse's personal exhibition at the Druet gallery in March-April of 1906 (Bock, *Matisse and Neo-Impressionism,* p. 89). In a letter to Simon Bussy, dated September 19, 1905, Matisse writes of this canvas: "I've obtained an extension from the Salon d'Automne and I must hurry to finish in time. As I am painting in dots, it is rather a long process, especially since they don't always come out right the first time" (Schneider, *Matisse,* p. 188).

41.   Letter of January 14, 1906, quoted in Alfred Barr, *Matisse, His Art and His Public* (New York: Museum of Modern Art, 1951), p. 82. According to Schneider, who rectifies the weird "Augustin" found in Barr's version (changing it to Anquetin), the original letter is said to be missing (*Matisse,* French ed. [Paris: Flammarion, 1984], p. 273, note 3). Schneider's translators put "Augustin" back in his version of the quotation and proceeded to fiddle with the footnote, which then became incomprehensible.

42.   Letter of July 14, 1905, cited by Schneider in *Matisse,* p. 98. See the French version of this book (same pagination) for the original text.

43.   John Rewald, "Extraits du journal inédit de Paul Signac, 1894–1895," *Gazette des Beaux Arts,* July-Sept. 1949, p. 102. Cited by Bock, *Matisse and Neo-Impressionism,* p. 69.

44.   Bock, p. 145, note 53.

45.   Cf. Dominique Fourcade and Isabelle Monod-Fontaine, exhibition catalogue of *Henri Matisse, Dessins et sculpture* (Paris: Musée National d'Art Moderne, 1975), p. 30; and Schneider, *Matisse,* p. 242. Flam remarks that Vauxcelles criticized the painting in these terms when it was presented to the Indépendants: "when one executes a work, one must leave nothing to chance; to enlarge a lovely sketch by squaring up is an error" (*Matisse, the Man,* p. 489, note 7), which would tend to indicate that Vauxcelles, who knew Matisse, saw the cartoon in the artist's studio (on the relations between Matisse and Vauxcelles, on the whole quite cordial, cf. Benjamin, "*Notes of a Painter,*" pp. 99–113 and passim).

46.   There is currently no way of verifying this fragile hypothesis. Nevertheless, if one compares the experiment of the two *Le Luxe* canvases with that of the two versions of *The Young Sailor [Jeune marin]* that Matisse painted in 1906, there is a noticeable similarity in the differences between the two members of each pair. In the second *Young Sailor,* for example, not only are the Cézanne-like "passages" eliminated in favor of monochromatic planes, but the proportions of the sailor's body are more massive (cover more surface area) than in the first picture. One thing, however, distinguishes the two pairs (a major difference that disrupts the similarity between the differences): the *Young Sailor* canvases do not have exactly the same format, whereas Matisse held rigorously to this condition for the two *Le Luxe* canvases. Is this in order to force himself to be more rigorous in his "demonstration"? In this case, returning to the cartoon, a practice he had apparently abandoned almost two years earlier, would have proved to be almost necessary.

47.   Diehl, *Matisse,* p. 22, trans. modified.

48.   It would be highly presumptuous of me to provide a "summary" of Jacques Derrida's problematic in *Of Grammatology* (1967, English tr. Gayatri C. Spivak [Baltimore: Johns Hopkins University Press, 1976]), and pursued since in his many works, if only because the very notion of a

"summary," which presupposes anteriority, a transcendence of the "idea" with respect to its "expression," is seriously undermined in Derrida's work. Nevertheless, despite the fact that "deconstruction" has become one of the major theoretical models taught in universities, especially in the United States, I do not want to seem priggish to the reader who might not know what I'm talking about. Here is what the reader who is interested in the analogy I'm tracing needs to know: According to Derrida, starting with the first great texts of western metaphysics, speech has been privileged as constituting language in its essence, while (phonetic) writing has been seen as a mere reproduction, speech's useful but imperfect double. Western phonocentrism rests on a hierarchization in which the voice is seen as "immaterial," intimately connected to consciousness (to the logos, to truth), and writing as the tragic but inevitable debasement of the purely intelligible into the sensible, of the "idea" into the body and matter. This hierarchization forms the basis of western metaphysics (which Derrida calls "logocentrism"), and, in particular, the basis of all the oppositions constituting it (signifier/signified; expression/content; body/soul, etc.). Phonetic writing, however, is a myth (writing has never been a simple transcription of living speech), and speech itself, far from being pure self-presence, is entirely governed by the system of differences that make up a language. There is therefore a differential principle "prior" to the speech/writing division, a "*différance*" (difference/deferring) constituting every sign (including vocal signs) as a trace or a mark: it is this "originary" principle, "prior" to the oppositions of western metaphysics, that Jacques Derrida calls "arche-writing."

49.   Quoted in Louis Aragon, *Henri Matisse: A Novel* (1971), English tr. Jean Stewart (New York: Harcourt Brace Jovanovich, 1972), vol. 2, p. 308.

50.   Cf. the entry "quantity" (*quantité*) in the index of *EPA*. To my knowledge, Lebensztejn is the only one to have dealt directly with this question, noting a parallel between Matisse's theory and that of Albers (*Zig Zag*, pp. 188–193). But, for reasons that will be outlined later, unlike me, he in no way sees it as the principal axis of Matisse's innovation. An extremely rich comparative study could be done on Matisse and Albers, whose *Interaction of Color* is undoubtedly one of the century's most intelligent texts on color. I shall note only two aspects in passing: the little experiment on simultaneous contrast that Matisse performs on his dentist (Aragon, *Matisse: A Novel*, vol. 2, pp. 255–256), and the following fragment from a letter to Pallady concerning the colors in *The Rumanian Blouse* [*La Blouse Roumaine*]: "A vermillion red which, combining with its neighboring colors, took on the depth and adaptability of a Venetian red (so why didn't I use a Venetian red to start with? Because its reactions on its neighbors are less intense)" (dated December 7, 1940 by Schneider, *Matisse*, p. 382, note 7).

51.   Matisse had written "*par des voisinages*," which is difficult to translate. Flam renders it as "by their relationships," which is too general. "*Par leur voisinage*," in the singular and with a definite article, would clearly be "by their neighborhood," but Matisse uses both the indefinite article and the plural form: this implies that "voisinage," referring to an action, is the substitute for a substantified verb that does not exist in French, hence my decision to render it as "neighborings."

52.   Quoted in Aragon, *Matisse: A Novel*, vol. 1, p. 138. I replaced "sections" with "compartments," a key word in Matisse's theory, which is used in the French original.

53.   The vocabulary of color fluctuates greatly. During the Signac period, *teinte* (hue) more often than not designates color proper (red or blue hues) and *ton* (tone) the value the painter gives to it by means of the gradations from black to white. Like numerous painters, Matisse frequently uses these terms interchangeably, and his statements reveal no terminological rigor on this point.

54.   Reported by Pierre Dubreuil, one of Matisse's pupils: Diehl, *Matisse*, French edition, p. 42. Dubreuil's memoir about Matisse's classes has unfortunately been omitted in the American edition.

55.   This importance of the limit also governs the particular attention Matisse gives to the orientation of the field: "Take a rectangular sheet of paper and a figure represented by a vertical—this vertical will produce an entirely different impression if the paper is held horizontally. In these two cases a reconstruction must be effected" (quoted in Duthuit, *The Fauve Painters*, p. 81).

56.   Contrary to his usual practice, and no doubt due to the imposing surface area of this decoration (which meant he had to rent a kind of garage in which to paint, and led him to use paper

cutouts to work on it), Matisse initially tried, unsuccessfully, to sketch his composition on a smaller scale: "whenever I attempted sketches of it on three canvases of a square meter each, I couldn't bring it off. Finally, I took three canvases of five meters, exactly matching the dimensions of the wall, and one day, armed with a charcoal pencil clamped to the end of a long bamboo, I set about drawing the whole thing at once. It was as if I were being borne along by some rhythm inside. I had the surface in my head" (quoted in Diehl, *Matisse*, p. 65, trans. modified).

57. Barnett Newman, "Introduction to *18 Cantos*" (1964), reprinted in Harold Rosenberg, *Barnett Newman* (New York: Abrams, 1978), p. 246. Newman may be the American painter that best understood this lesson from Matisse. Nor is it by chance that in the text I mention here Newman directly associates the question of scale with that of the relationship with the frame (he is discussing the series of lithographs entitled *Cantos,* where he makes several proofs of the same print, giving them a different margin each time). Nor is it surprising that American artists of the minimalist generation should have retained, above all, Matisse's conception of scale: cf. Jean-Claude Lebensztejn's interviews with Donald Judd and Frank Stella in *Art in America*, July-August 1975, pp. 71–75.

58. "I think that one day easel painting will no longer exist because of changing customs. There will be mural painting" (to Verdet, 1952, Flam, p. 143). Consider, for example, Pollock's declaration: "my painting does not come from the easel" (*Possibilities,* Winter 1947–48), and his interview with William Wright ("the direction that painting seems to be taking here [in New York] is away from the easel, into some sort, some kind of wall—wall painting," in Francis V. O'Connor, *Jackson Pollock* [New York: Museum of Modern Art, 1967], p. 81). Cf. also Clement Greenberg's important text entitled "The Crisis of the Easel Picture" (1948), reprinted in *Art and Culture* (Boston: Beacon Press, 1961), pp. 154–157. Let us note in passing that it is not by chance that both Newman and Pollock were always incapable of doing preliminary drawings for their canvases, and expressed their views on the subject on several occasions. Pollock says, for example, that "I approach painting in the same sense as one approaches drawing; that is, it's direct. I don't work from drawings" (interview with Wright in O'Connor, *Jackson Pollock*): it is this "direct" that is linked to what I am calling here "arche-drawing."

59. On the subject of the terminal character of the chapel at Vence, cf. also Flam, pp. 128, 149, and *EPA,* pp. 266, 270. Concerning relations of scale, Pierre Schneider insists more than once on the fact that the Cimiez apartment in which Matisse worked out his chapel had exactly the same dimensions as the building itself (see, for example, *Matisse,* p. 675).

My decision to exclude the "Nice years" from this consideration of the "Matisse system" is based on a periodization current in Matisse criticism subsequent to the retrospective organized by Pierre Schneider in 1970 (but already to be found in a statement made by André Lévinson in 1930: cf. Lebensztejn, *Zig Zag,* pp. 161–163). The idea of such a discontinuity has recently been contested by Dominique Fourcade and Jack Cowart in the exhibition they organized at the National Gallery in Washington in 1987, "Henri Matisse: The Early Years in Nice 1916–1930." Although I am the first to admit the necessity of not neglecting this period in Matisse's oeuvre, and although the exhibition showed that it was incomparably richer and more diverse than generally thought, I don't think that the common idea of a certain slackening and of a "return to order" over the course of this period in Matisse's career can be abandoned. Anyway, he was well aware of the break that the Merion *Dance* was engendering in his oeuvre: hard at work on the painting, he wrote to the organizer of his 1931 exhibition at the Georges Petit gallery (an exhibition in which his "Nice" works predominated) to convey his fear that this latest manifestation might be received as "a first class burial" (cited by Schneider, *Matisse,* p. 655, note 48).

60. Pierre Schneider reports that Matisse was disappointed at not receiving a commission for the World's Fair in 1937 (ibid., p. 177).

61. Father Marie-Alain Couturier cites the following declaration (although there is no way of determining from the context whether it was made by Picasso or Matisse): "I don't need any kind of special presentation. I paint so that my canvases can be presented in the open air. One day, they were exhibited in glasshouses owned by the City of Paris—it was perfect. I don't need walls to be

painted any special color" (*Se garder libre* [Paris: Cerf, 1962], p. 57). If the statement comes from Matisse, what we find here is an effect of the "overcompensation" he indulged in through reinforcing internal quantity relations.

62.   Dominique Fourcade, "'I think I've been able to say something with drawing,'" preface to the exhibition catalogue *Henri Matisse, Dessins et sculpture*, p. 23.

63.   Quoted by Barr, *Matisse*, p. 190. Here Matisse is talking about *The Gourds* [*Les Coloquintes*, 1916; Museum of Modern Art, New York], and he writes roughly the same thing in 1946 about *The Moroccans* [*Les Marocains*] of the same year ("Black Is a Color," Flam, p. 107). Cf. also his statements to Tériade in 1952 (Flam, p. 133), to Aimé Maeght and to Picasso (*EPA*, p. 202, note 64).

64.   According to Ernst Gombrich, this law goes back to Apelles; cf. his "The Heritage of Apelles" (1972), reprinted in the collection of the same name (Ithaca and London: Cornell University Press, 1976), pp. 3–18. I should like to thank Charles Dempsey for bringing this text to my attention.

65.   Quoted in Duthuit, *The Fauve Painters*, p. 86.

66.   Erwin Panofsky, *Idea*, English tr. Joseph J.S. Peake (Columbia: University of South Carolina Press, 1968). Commenting on this sentence from "Notes," Roger Benjamin sees in it the mark of an indebtedness to Puvis de Chavannes, who remarked to Emile Bernard that "before it is executed, my creation is almost always complete in my head" (*"Notes of a Painter,"* p. 199). Now, on this point, nothing could be further from Matisse than Puvis's thinking: "A work of art is never made in advance, contrary to the ideas of Puvis de Chavannes, who claimed that one could not ever visualize the picture one wanted to paint too completely before starting. There is no separation between the thought and the creative act. They are completely one and the same" (to Verdet, 1952, Flam, p. 143). It might be objected that in close to fifty years Matisse's theory could have changed, and no doubt it did, but not in this respect. In "Notes," too, he states that "the thought of a painter must not be considered as separate from his means" (Flam, p. 35, the end of the sentence being translated there as "pictorial means," which is far too restrictive).

67.   "The work is coming along. I hope to break down the wall around me and to be able to sing freely," he writes to Pierre Matisse in February 1940 (*EPA*, p. 183; he is referring to *The Rumanian Blouse*). On Matisse's recurring use of the metaphor of singing, cf. the entry concerning this subject (*chant*) in the index of *EPA*.

68.   Barr reproduces a preparatory sketch for one of these woodcuts (*Matisse*, p. 322), called *Seated Woman* [*Femme assise*] and entitled *Petit bois clair* (no. 318) in Marguerite Duthuit-Matisse and Claude Duthuit's catalogue raisonné of Matisse's prints (*Henri Matisse: L'Oeuvre gravé* [Paris, 1983], vol. 1, pp. 248–249). John Elderfield reproduces a preparatory sketch for *Seated Nude* [*Nu de profil dans une chaise longue (grand bois)*] in *Drawings of Henri Matisse* (New York: Museum of Modern Art, 1985), p. 185 (no. 15). This woodcut, which will be central to our discussion, is number 317 in the catalogue raisonné (vol. 1, pp. 246–247). Another brush and ink drawing of the same period, *Standing Nude, Drying Herself* [*Femme debout, se déshabillant*] (no. 11 in the exhibition *Matisse as a Draughtsman*, Baltimore Museum of Art, 1972), is so stylistically similar to the woodcuts that we can only agree with Victor Carlson when he hypothesizes that "it was intended to be a study for a woodcut which was never realized because of the artist's dissatisfaction with the tedium of the graphic process" (*Matisse as a Draughtsman*, p. 42). This last point reinforces my conviction concerning the dating of the woodcuts. We know that Matisse himself did not do the actual chiseling, but entrusted this long and boring task to his wife (cf. William Lieberman, *Henri Matisse, Fifty Years of His Graphic Art* [New York: Braziller, 1956], p. 19, note 3). The woodcuts may very well have been done *during* and *after* the painting of *Le Bonheur de vivre*, based on the drawings predating the picture. If Matisse didn't much care for this printmaking technique (apart from these three examples from 1906, we know of only one other woodcut, *Le Luxe*, dating from 1907 [no. 320 of the catalogue raisonné of Matisse's prints], whose composition is the inverted mirror image of the two paintings bearing the same name, which date from 1907 and 1908), it is because of the gap—in this case, especially pronounced—between conception and realization. What we have here is a paradox that is fairly typical of Matisse's dialectical evolution: in my opinion, the "Matisse system," which entirely

eliminates this gap, comes into being with these woodcuts that, at a purely technical level, are perhaps one of its ultimate manifestations. After this, the painter is able to compose "with his drawing so as to enter directly into the arabesque with the color" and to have done with all mediation.

69.   Cf. Josef Albers, *Interactions of Color* (New Haven: Yale University Press, paperback edition, 1970), pp. 72–73.

70.   *Still Life with Pineapple* is no. 72 in the exhibition catalogue *Matisse as a Draughtsman* (p. 164). A good color reproduction of the painting bearing the same title and date can be found in Aragon, *Matisse,* vol. 2, p. 341, and in issue number 21–22 of *Verve* (no pagination). The true painted equivalent of this drawing is *Black Fern* [*Intérieur à la fougère noire*], also dating from 1948, where we find a repetition of the speckled pattern (reproduced in the same issue of *Verve* and in Aragon, p. 340). Matisse uses speckling again in *The Necklace* [*Nu debout au collier*], a drawing dating from 1950 (Museum of Modern Art, New York) but this time with what is probably a humorous displacement: the dots are both constitutive of a pattern and a faithfully mimetic rendition, since they represent the pearls in the necklace and the grapes in the bunch the nude is holding in her hand (see the exhibition catalogue *Henri Matisse, Dessins et sculpture,* no. 154).

71.   Just after evoking "going off into the jungle" in order to escape the "house kept by country aunts" that divisionism then represented for him, Matisse declares to Tériade that "the influence of Gauguin and Van Gogh was felt then, too" (1929, Flam, p. 58, trans. slightly modified).

72.   Cf. Duthuit, *The Fauve Painters,* p. 28.

73.   According to Ellen Oppler, this retrospective had a considerable impact on Derain, who was still talking about it a year later: "It's almost a year since we saw Van Gogh, and, really, I'm constantly haunted by the memory I have of him. More and more I see the real meaning of his work" (letter to Vlaminck quoted in Oppler, *Fauvism Reexamined* [1969 dissertation, pub. New York: Garland Publications, 1976], p. 111; the relations between Derain's and Van Gogh's art are discussed in pp. 104–107).

74.   Cited in ibid., p. 107, note 3. (English tr. in *The Complete Letters of Vincent Van Gogh,* vol. 3 [London: Thames and Hudson, 1958], p. 478; trans. modified.) This letter to Emile Bernard, which had already been published by *Mercure de France* in 1893, is quoted in an article by Ad. van Bever, "Les aînés—un peintre maudit: Vincent Van Gogh," *La Plume,* June 1 and 15, 1905. As Oppler observes, it is unlikely that the fauves read this letter when it was first published, but "they would have seen, or at least heard about these excerpts published so soon after the retrospective at the Indépendants." It should be noted that Matisse later discusses the letters Van Gogh wrote to Emile Bernard with J. and H. Dauberville (*EPA,* note 71). As Jack Flam points out, at least one testimony, that of Walter Pach in 1938 (Pach, *Queer Thing, Painting,* p. 118), states that Matisse directly associated his liberation from divisionism *mainly* with Van Gogh's influence, which can only be an exaggeration (*Matisse, the Man,* p. 488, note 37).

75.   According to Hans Purmann, his escort during his trip to Bavaria in 1910 (to see the exhibition of Muslim art that was then drawing to a close in Munich), Matisse scandalized Hugo von Tschumi, then director of the Neue Staatsgalerie and an ardent defender of modern painting, by declaring his preference for Gauguin and even Redon over Van Gogh (Barr, *Matisse,* p. 109). But as Oppler remarks (*Fauvism Reexamined,* p. 111, note 2), his German hosts' extraordinary enthusiasm for Van Gogh would have incited Matisse to exaggerate.

76.   The drawing is no. 15 in the exhibition catalogue *Henri Matisse, Dessins et sculpture.* The painting is reproduced in color in Flam, *Matisse, the Man,* p. 127, as is the drawing (p. 128).

77.   Oppler, *Fauvism Reexamined,* pp. 129ff.

78.   Speaking to Sembat in 1913 (*EPA,* p. 47, note 10). I shall come back to *The Arab Café* later. On the purchase of the Gauguin, cf. Schneider, *Matisse,* p. 138. The painting is no. 422 in the catalogue raisonné of Gauguin's painted work by Georges Wildenstein (*Gauguin* [Paris: Beaux Arts, 1964], p. 164).

79.   For the Escholier version, cf. *Matisse, ce vivant,* (Paris: Fayard, 1956), pp. 134–135. Jack Flam translated the second and most important addition in his edition (Flam, p. 165, note 3).

80.   Quantity as profusion is banished, with the paradoxical exception of the canvases from the Nice period, generally seen as his least colorful (in other words, works that do not directly concern the "Matisse system" that I am attempting to outline here). On this point, cf. Pierre Schneider (*Matisse*, pp. 513–514), who observes that certain all-over effects in the Nice canvases are due to the very large number of colors disseminated in them. "Color is never a question of quantity, but of choice," Matisse says to Gaston Diehl, only *apparently* contradicting everything I have highlighted so far, since what Matisse actually disapproves of is the use of too many colors in the same canvas (quantity as profusion is quite logically opposed to quantity as quality, based on surface area: you cannot have both a myriad of hues *and* large, flat color planes). Matisse's statement to Diehl concerns Diaghilev's Ballet Russe, and more particularly Bakst's sets for *Scheherazade:* they "overflowed with color. Profusion without moderation. It looked like it was splashed about from a bucket" (Flam, p. 99; trans. modified). Elsewhere, he remarked that "it was magnificent, but without expression" (Flam, p. 116).

81.   Edmond Duranty, "Le Peintre Marsabiel," *La Rue,* first year, no. 8 (July 20, 1867), p. 6. This text is initially modified in 1872, when it becomes the first part of another short story entitled "La Simple vie du peintre Louis Martin," which came out in installments in *Le Siècle* (November 13, 14, 15, and 16; reprinted in *Les Séductions du Chevalier Navoni,* [Paris: Dentu, 1877]). Whereas the 1867 version was entirely devoted to Cézanne-Marsabiel, the latter, renamed Maillobert, is only a secondary character in the portrait of another artist whose character is largely based on Bazille. The text was finally reprinted with very slight changes under the title "Le peintre Louis Martin," published posthumously in *Le Pays des arts* (Paris: Charpentier, 1881), pp. 315–350.

I thank Michael Doran and Victor Merlhès for putting me on the Duranty trail by bringing *Le Pays des arts* to my attention (cited at length by John Rewald in 1936 in *Cézanne et Zola* [Paris: Editions Sedrowski], pp. 111–112). Intrigued by this late publication of a caricature of the "couillarde" period, at a time when Cézanne's art no longer had anything to do with the *impasto* of his youthful works, I made enquiries on the matter to Dianne Pitman, who has just finished a remarkable work on Bazille. I should like to thank her not just for providing the references of the previous texts, but for sending me copies of the different versions. (Cf. also Theodore Reff, "Cézanne and Poussin," *Journal of the Warburg and Courtauld Institute* 23 [1960], p. 163, note 99.)

82.   The sentence is printed as "un kilo de vert est plus vert qu'un demi-kilo [a kilo of green is greener than half a kilo]" in the exhibition catalogue *Gauguin et le groupe de Pont-Aven* (Quimper, 1950), in which several extracts of the Gloanec boarding house visitors' book are published (p. 63). I thank Victor Merlhès for sending me a copy of it. Noting that "it seems virtually certain that Cézanne knew of this text" by Duranty, Merlhès suggested to me that it is actually "possible that he may have picked up the expression attributed to him quite legitimately and started using it."

83.   Cf. the extract from "Diverses choses" published by Daniel Guérin in his anthology of Gauguin's writings, *Oviri: Ecrits d'un sauvage* (Paris: Gallimard, 1974), p. 176 (pp. 266 ff. of the original manuscript, Musée d'Orsay, Paris).

84.   Maurice Denis, "Cézanne," *L'Occident,* September 1907, reprinted in *Théories,* p. 253, and more recently with a critical apparatus by Michael Doran, in *Conversations avec Cézanne* (Paris: Macula, 1978), p. 173. Another version of the statement also appears in Maurice Denis's *Journal* in October 1906 (Paris: Editions La Colombe, vol. 2, 1957), p. 48, and in the impressive article entitled "Le Soleil," where Gauguin and Matisse are frequently discussed (*L'Ermitage,* December 15, 1906, reprinted in *Théories,* p. 222). As Oppler points out (*Fauvism Reexamined,* p. 316, note 1), it is highly likely that Cézanne never actually uttered this expression as it stands, and that what we are dealing with is probably an amalgamation of his and Denis's thought, which is quite symptomatic of Denis's agenda (he refers to Bernard's reminiscences when he cites this statement in 1906, but in fact it doesn't appear in them; by contrast, the passage from "Diverses choses" had just been published in the monograph on its author by Jean de Rotonchamp (*Paul Gauguin* [Weimar, 1906; new ed., Paris: Crès, 1925], p. 244).

85.   Gauguin, *Oviri,* p. 177.

86.   "Cézanne's " expression turns up several times in Gauguin's writings, as Victor Merlhès, to whom I owe these various references, points out. In the *Cahier pour Aline,* in 1893: "A kilo of green is greener than half a kilo. The young painter should give some thought to this so-called La Palissade. You'll perhaps understand why a tree trunk in a painting has to be bluer than it is in reality. The day that some idiot came up with this expression of comparison—it's a serving of spinach [*un plat d'é-pinards*]—painting faded for a good forty years" (facsimile edition by S. Damiron [Paris: Société des amis de la Bibliothèque d'Art et d'Archéologie de l'Université de Paris, 1963], p. 15). Then, in 1902, it turns up again in *Racontars de rapin,* this time in the context of a discussion on the minimum size of a painting in relation to the actual scene in nature: "mathematically, a kilo of green is greener than half a kilo. Therefore, proportionally speaking, a hundred thousand kilos of green in nature correspond to a milligram of green on your canvas. That's where the mathematics lead" (Paris: Falaise, 1951, pp. 68–69).

87.   This sentence appears in a fragment published posthumously in 1949 (*Oviri,* p. 27).

88.   Quoted in Duthuit, *The Fauve Painters,* p. 46.

89.   The origin of the falling out, which happened in December 1886, was perfectly trivial, but the antipathy would worsen over the years, and, as Sven Lövgren points out, would seal Gauguin's inability to benefit from what Fénéon might have taught him (*The Genesis of Modernism* [Stockholm: Almquist and Wiksell, 1959], pp. 96, 116–117). He was utterly unable to understand, for example, why in 1889 Fénéon characterized his work as tending "toward a goal analogous [to that of the divisionists], but through different practices." In numerous testimonies, Gaugin appears as the gallant knight of anti-divisionism, and this is how he presents himself in *Avant et après,* which also contains a biting remark about Signac: discussing Van Gogh, he writes: "When I arrived in Arles, Vincent was absorbed in the neoimpressionist school, and he was really struggling, which made him suffer" (*Oviri,* pp. 293–294). De Monfreid picks up the same idea in his reminiscences, when discussing Van Gogh: "He too had felt Gauguin's influence—Gauguin had rescued him from the aimless wanderings in which the pointillists had plunged him," ("Sur Paul Gauguin," *L'Ermitage,* vol. 3, December 1903, p. 269). We know that Gauguin was close enough to Seurat to pass on to him a so-called Turkish manuscript on painting, which he "cites" in *Avant et après,* and a copy of which was found in Seurat's papers (according to Merlhès, it was in fact a hoax perpetrated by Gauguin). Furthermore, in the famous "Notes synthétiques," today dated at 1884–85, which are greatly indebted, as are Seurat's theories, to *Grammaire des arts du dessin* by Charles Blanc, Gauguin advocates the division of colors (cf. *Oviri,* p. 24; these "Notes" were published for the first time in 1910). On the relations between Gauguin and Seurat, cf. also Mark Roskill, *Van Gogh, Gauguin and the Impressionist Circle* (Greenwich: New York Graphic Society, 1970), pp. 86–97.

90.   Quoted in Escholier, *Matisse from the Life,* p. 37, trans. slightly modified.

91.   This is why I cannot agree with Pierre Schneider's remarks on Matisse's "missed encounter" with Gauguin (Matisse is said to have appreciated Gauguin before Collioure but "it was the post-Collioure Matisse who, in complete good faith, was unable to recognize the importance that the canvases he had seen at Vollard's, and later at Georges-Daniel de Monfreid's, had had for him"; *Matisse,* p. 257).

92.   Signac, *De Delacroix au néo-impressionnisme,* pp. 108–109.

93.   It is true that he goes on to say that taking in the "overall effect," one can "move closer in order to study the play of colored elements, should one be interested in these technical details" (ibid., p. 111).

94.   Cf. notably *Racontars de rapin,* partially republished in *Oviri,* p. 263. Pissarro, for his part, disappointed by divisionism, whose procedures he had momentarily welcomed, is supposed to have said to Matisse: "it's like print [c'est comme de l'imprimerie]" (quoted in Duthuit, *The Fauve Painters,* p. 59, note 1). On this question, cf. Norman Broude, "New Light on Seurat's 'Dot': Its Relation to Photo-Mechanical Color Printing in France in the 1880's," *Art Bulletin* 56 (December 1974), pp. 581–589.

95.   Here again I must register my disagreement with Pierre Schneider, who claims that Gauguin's "tones remained local" (*Matisse,* p. 256).

96.   Bock alludes to this distinction between the division of the brushstroke and the division of color (without, however, referring to Gauguin) in order to show that what distinguishes Pissarro's inability to go all the way with the divisionist system from Matisse's defection is that Pissarro divides his brushstrokes without dividing his colors (since he places intermediate tones, transitions, between two points of contrasting color). "In fact, ultimately Matisse did just the opposite" (*Matisse and Neo-Impressionism,* p. 123, note 62).

97.   Lebensztejn, *Zig Zag,* p. 174.

98.   The three lithographs mentioned here are, in order, nos. 391, 393, and 402 of the catalogue raisonné of his graphic oeuvre (*Matisse: L'Oeuvre gravé,* vol. 2, pp. 5 and 11).

99.   The first pen drawing exploring the principle of economy, a veritable manifesto of modulation through quantity, is no doubt the study for *Marguerite reading* [*Marguerite lisant*] (Musée du Grenoble), a canvas that was first exhibited at the Salon d'Automne in 1906 (the drawing, which belongs to the Museum of Modern Art in New York, is no. 22 in the exhibition *Henri Matisse, Dessins et sculpture*). The assurance Matisse attains in this work (fig. 88)—foreshadowing by some twenty years the spectacular pen drawings of 1929–42—shows that the research carried out during the elaboration of *Le Bonheur de vivre* is henceforth an unshakable acquisition.

100.   "Order my thoughts [mettre de l'ordre dans mon cerveau]." Matisse uses this expression several times when discussing his excursions into the domain of sculpture, excursions that allowed him to "take a break from painting," even if painting remained his main concern ("I did it to order my sensations, to find a method that completely suited me. Once I'd found it in sculpture, it proved useful in my painting" (to Courthion, 1941?, *EPA,* p. 70, note 45). It is even more true of the relations between pictorial practice on the one hand and drawing and engraving on the other.

101.   Certainly, as Meyer Schapiro notes, the homogeneity of the brushstroke is entirely relative (going from minuscule pointillism to the longitudinal brushstroke). But, as Jean Clay puts it so well, "the equality is due not to the absolute identity of the constituent pigments but to the absence of polarities that would render a certain zone in the painting more dense. You have an irregular texture, but irregular in the same way throughout" ("Pollock, Mondrian, Seurat: la profondeur plate," in Hans Namuth, *L'Atelier de Jackson Pollock* [Paris: Macula, 1978], no pagination).

102.   Quoted by "The Editors" in their preface to the original edition of Duthuit (*Les Fauves,* p. 11).

103.   Lebensztejn, *Zig Zag,* p. 186. In 1942, Matisse tells Courthion that "when I use green, it doesn't mean grass, when I use blue, it doesn't mean sky" (*EPA,* p. 95, note 44). Commenting on this remark, Lebensztejn writes: "If the choice of colors doesn't matter, why not go back to the object's own colors, since it is their respective quantities that govern the harmony and bring out the color in all its force. Sky blue no longer signifies the sky, but blue. And this saturated blue is valid only through its harmony (in other words, its difference) with the neighboring greens and reds."

104.   The statement is all the more surprising in that the goldfish in the painting in question, *The Arab Café* (1913, Hermitage Museum, Leningrad) are not yellow at all but a dull ocher bordering on orange, at least in the reproduction I have seen (A. Izerghina, *Henri Matisse: Paintings and Sculptures in Soviet Museums* [Leningrad: Aurora, 1978], plate 50, and Flam, *Matisse, the Man,* p. 354). Like *Le Luxe II* and *Interior with Eggplant* [*Intérieur aux aubergines*], "the picture is painted in very fragile and easily erasable size colors, which make for a gentle mat surface. In 1962–63, after prolonged preparation, the paint layer of the canvas was painstakingly reinforced by the restorers" (Izerghina, p. 179). Rather than assuming any kind of carelessness on the part of the Russian restorers, then, the mistake can be attributed not to Matisse himself (he had only just painted the canvas when he described it to his interlocutor), but to Sembat's transcription of the statement.

105.   Signac, *De Delacroix au néo-impressionnisme,* p. 108.

106.   Matisse to Bonnard, on the occasion of Klee's death (letter of October 17, 1940, "Correspondance Matisse-Bonnard," annotated by Jean Clair, *Nouvelle Nouvelle Revue Française,* no. 211, July 1970, p. 97). Klee's statement is taken from his "Pedagogical Sketchbook" (1925), English tr. Sibyl Moholy-Nagy (New York: Praeger, 1960), p. 33. Klee's extremely complex theory would merit more than this brief mention. Let us nonetheless note that, unlike Matisse, he considers "instan-

88. Henri Matisse, Marguerite Reading [Marguerite lisant]*, 1906. Pen and black ink on white paper, 39.6 × 52.1 cm (15⅝ × 20½ in.). The Museum of Modern Art, New York. Photo of the museum.*

taneous" perception of a painting to be a calamity ("Does a picture come into being all at once? No, it is built up piece by piece, the same as a house. And what about the beholder: does he finish with a work all at once? Often yes, unfortunately" ["Creative Credo" (1920), in Paul Klee, *The Thinking Eye,* Notebooks, vol. 1 (London: Lund Humphries, 1961), p. 78]). His whole system rests on the notions of weight and movement (in Strzemiński's terminology, analyzed in an essay below, Klee's art would be "baroque" par excellence), and if he gives any consideration to the extension of a colored surface, it is for the most part after and independently of the "quality" (saturation) and "density" (value) of the color he has in mind (cf. "On Modern Art" (1924), in Robert Herbert, *Modern Artists on Art* [Englewood Cliffs: Prentice-Hall, 1964], pp. 79 ff.

107.   Quoted in Aragon, *Matisse,* vol. 1, p. 234.

108.   Quoted in ibid., p. 236.

109.   There is a color reproduction of the painting in Schneider, *Matisse,* p. 649, and in Aragon, *Matisse,* vol. 1, p. 252, here entitled *The Cloak.*

110.   On this issue, cf. my article, "Le futur antérieur—sur un tableau de Christian Bonnefoi," *Macula,* no. 5/6, 1979, pp. 229–233.

111.   Rosamond Bernier, "Matisse Designs a New Church," *Vogue,* Feb. 15, 1949, p. 132, trans. slightly modified. For another and similar account, cf. Gyula Brassaï, *Picasso and Co.*, English tr. Francis Price (London: Thames and Hudson, 1967), pp. 220–221. Matisse's statement to Brassaï about the film ends up this way: "I have never been so frightened as I was sitting there, watching my poor hand start out on the adventure, in slow motion, as if I had been drawing with my eyes closed." Immediately after this passage, Brassaï recalls Matisse's experiments with drawing with the eyes closed, comparing them to Picasso's exercises of the same kind around 1933. The photographer had in fact been the witness of such an experiment: "One day, in 1939, in his studio on the rue des Plantes, Matisse had done a drawing for me with a mask around his eyes. It was a head, drawn with a piece of chalk, almost in a single line. In this very expressive portrait, the eyes, the mouth, the nose, the ears all overlap, as they do in Picasso's deliberately distorted faces. Matisse was so enchanted with it that he asked me to take a photograph of him standing in front of the door on which he had drawn it. There can be little doubt that this particular work of Matisse now exists only in my photograph." Curiously enough, however, it is rather the extremely limited amount of distortion and overlap that strikes one when looking at the Brassaï photograph of this "blind drawing" (fig. 53 of his book), and I would say that it is on the contrary the confirmation that he controlled the surface even without the use of his eyes that made Matisse so proud of it.

112.   It is not by chance that I mention the possibility of a monochrome canvas here: its resurgence in the nineteen-sixties and seventies shows that one of the great problems for painters at the time was to escape the arbitrariness of division. For other solutions to the same problem (how to divide a surface without being "subjective"), cf. my "Le futur antérieur," and the essay on Strzemiński and Kobro below. Cf. also the interview with Christian Bonnefoi in *Macula,* no. 5/6, 1979, in particular pp. 217–218.

113.   To Pierre Courthion, quoted in Jean Guichard-Meili, *Matisse,* English tr. Caroline Moorehead (New York: Praeger, 1967), pp. 48–49.

114.   Cf. Barr, *Matisse,* p. 49; John Elderfield, *The Wild Beasts: Fauvism and Its Affinities* (New York: Museum of Modern Art, 1976), p. 20; and Schneider, *Matisse,* p. 121. Catherine Bock (*Matisse and Neo-Impressionism,* p. 127, note 19) develops a long note on this question, criticizing the way in which Matisse criticism as a whole reproduces Barr's position without discussion. For his part, Roger Benjamin insists on the very important role of Denis's critical discourse in Matisse's training ("*Notes of a Painter,*" passim). Whatever the case, certain of Vuillard's works from 1890–92, with their juxtaposed flat applications of pure color, are not all that remote from the audacities of fauvism, even if their color spectrum is very different (cf. Jean Clay, *Modern Art 1890–1918* [New York: Vendome Press, 1978], pp. 30–31).

115.   In the "Notes synthétiques," mentioned above: "Green alongside red does not yield a red-brown mixture, but two vibrant notes. Put some chrome yellow next to this red, and you have three notes that enrich each other and increase the intensity of the first tone, the green" (*Oviri,* p. 24).

116.   Ambroise Vollard, *Paul Cézanne* (1914), English tr. Harold L. Van Doren (New York: Frank-Maurice Inc., 1926), p. 126 (trans. slightly modified). Vollard adds whimsically: "The prospect made me tremble."

117.   Cited by Maurice Denis, "Cézanne," in *Conversations avec Cézanne,* p. 172.

118.   This is related to another of Renoir's questions, this time directed to Matisse, concerning color value: "So how do you do it, then? If I used a black like that in one of my pictures, it would stand out." "I wasn't able to find an explanation at first," says Matisse, "yet the explanation is quite simple: it comes from a combination of forces that make up the canvas; this is my generation's contribution" (to Courthion, 1941, cited by Dominique Fourcade, "Autres propos de Henri Matisse," *Macula,* no. 1 [1976], p. 102).

119.   In the long essay entitled "The New Art—The New Life: The Culture of Pure Relationships," begun in the late twenties and finished in 1931, Mondrian tries to explain what he means by "dynamic equilibrium." Discussing the way it manifests itself in real life (since neoplasticism sees itself as a form of realism), he seizes on the theory of deterrence: the arms race "will eventually abolish war; the very development of weapons will make it impossible" (*The New Art, The New Life: The Collected Writings of Piet Mondrian,* ed. Harry Holtzmann and Martin James [Boston: G.K. Hall, 1986], p. 262). Written in French, the text was only published in English, posthumously.

120.   These remarks can be aligned with Georg Schmidt's particularly fine description of Cézanne's work methods (1952): "Cézanne's first step consisted in disrupting the equilibrium of the empty surface by choosing a line in the motif—let's say a horizontal—and placing it on the top right of the canvas, for example: here you have the painting's first 'unfinished state.' To this horizontal line, he now opposes a vertical, also extracted from the motif, placing it at the bottom left: the vertical and the horizontal balance each other—this is the work's first 'finished state.' Then he starts over: a diagonal rising from left to right gives you the second 'unfinished state.' A diagonal in the opposite direction, rising from right to left, forms the work's second 'finished state.' After the painting has passed through many such stages, its linear scaffolding is solidly in place: in it, direction and counter-direction support each other as they multiply. The mature drawings offer—from 1872 on—countless magnificent examples of such 'finished states,' each one of them holding the possibility of an entirely new beginning." Cited by Adrien Chappuis, *Les dessins de Paul Cézanne au Cabinet des Estampes du Musée des Beaux-Arts de Bâle* (Olten and Lausanne: Urs Graf), pp. 15–16.

121.   Emile Bernard, "Souvenirs sur Paul Cézanne," *Mercure de France,* 1907, reprinted in *Conversations avec Cézanne,* p. 58. Bernard concludes by saying that "his way of working was actually like a form of meditation, brush in hand," which is again reminiscent of Mondrian (cf. his response to Carl Holty, who asked him why he ceaselessly reworked *Victory Boogie-Woogie* instead of making several paintings out of the various stages it had gone through: "I don't want pictures. I just want to find things out" (cited below in "Piet Mondrian, *New York City*").

122.   Cézanne, talking to Joachim Gasquet:

> I take my motif . . . (*he joins his hands together*). A motif, you see, is like this . . .
> ME: Like what?
> CÉZANNE: Like this . . . (*He repeats the gesture, spreading his hands, with all ten fingers apart, then brings them slowly together and joins them, interlocking and tightening them as he goes.*) That's what you have to achieve . . . If I go too high, or too low, everything is ruined. There can't be a single loose mesh, a single hole through which the emotion, the light, the truth might escape. I work on the whole canvas at once, if you see what I mean.

(*Cézanne,* 1921, reprinted in *Conversations avec Cézanne,* pp. 108–109.)

123.   Already quoted above, from Duthuit, *The Fauve Painters,* p. 26.

124.   On this point, cf. Lawrence Gowing, "The Logic of Organized Sensations," in *Cézanne: The Late Work,* ed. William Rubin (New York: Museum of Modern Art, 1977), pp. 57 ff. Cézanne condemns Gauguin's flat planes: "[Gauguin] didn't understand me . . . ; I never wanted and will never

accept the absence of modeling or shading; it just doesn't make sense. Gauguin wasn't a painter, all he did was produce Chinese images" (Bernard, "Souvenirs," *Conversations avec Cézanne*, pp. 62–63). For Cézanne, even the flat and unified surface of an object cannot be represented as it is. As Rivière and Schnerb put it, "A surface only seems to us even in tone and value because our eye moves to perceive it as a whole, and if the painter, to represent it, extends a coat of monochrome color over his canvas, he will reproduce it without truth" ("L'Atelier de Cézanne" [1907], reprinted in *Conversations avec Cézanne*, p. 88; English tr. in Judith Wescher, ed., *Cézanne in Perspective* [Englewood Cliffs: Prentice-Hall, 1975], p. 60, here slightly modified).

125. In 1896–97, in other words at the very time that Matisse was led to frequent him a great deal, Pissarro (who was also the mentor of both Cézanne and Gauguin) was advising young painters to work the canvas all-over: "Don't work bit by bit, but paint everything at once by placing tones everywhere, with brush strokes of the right color and value, while noticing what is alongside. Use small brush strokes and try to put down your perceptions immediately. The eye should not be fixed on one point, but should take in everything, while observing the reflections which the colors produce on their surroundings. Work at the same time upon sky, water, branches, ground, keeping everything going on an equal basis and unceasingly rework until you have got it. Cover the canvas at the first go, then work at it until you can see nothing more to add" (quoted by John Rewald, *The History of Impressionism*, revised edition [New York: Museum of Modern Art, 1961], p. 458). Bock insists on the effect that such advice could have had on Matisse in 1897–98, prior to his first encounter with divisionism (*Matisse and Neo-Impressionism*, pp. 11–12). She's probably right, but these remarks also indicate the extent to which Pissarro remains within an impressionist problematic; not just because of the divided brushstroke, but also because of the "perceptions" that have to be "fixed": the all-over approach is envisaged here only in relation to fidelity to the motif ("observe" everything). For it to take on a properly constructive value in Matisse would require both the lesson he learned from Cézanne and the desire for a "synthetic" art, completely disengaged from the impressionist framework to which divisionism was still tributary.

126. Diehl, *Matisse*, p. 65; trans. slightly modified.

127. Ibid., p. 14, trans. modified.

128. Lydia Delectorskaya, . . . *l'apparente facilité . . . Henri Matissse, Peintures de 1935–1939* (Paris: Maeght, 1986), p. 23.

129. Ibid., p. 28.

130. Matisse to Courthion: "Often one adds, one paints over, one completes something without touching the overall composition. I myself redo the composition every time. I never get tired. I always rely on the preceding state to help me begin again" (reported by Schneider, *Matisse*, p. 376). Moreover, Yvonne Landsberg's brother remembers that while doing his sister's portrait, "Matisse re-covered the whole canvas at each sitting" (cited in Barr, *Matisse*, p. 184).

There may have been another reason for this procedure, related to the role played by the whiteness of the material itself in Matisse's art from his divisionist period on: "Paint on a white canvas. If you put a tone unrelated to your motif on an already brightly colored surface you establish a false harmony that will give you trouble later on" (reported by Dubreuil, in Diehl, *Matisse*, French ed., p. 42). Certainly, he is discussing reusing an abandoned canvas here, but there is room for wondering whether in his daily practice of erasing with turpentine Matisse wasn't seeking to rediscover "the touching whiteness" of the bare canvas.

131. Schneider points out that before Derain's arrival in Collioure (in June), Matisse has as a companion a certain Terrus, a disciple of Signac (*Matisse*, p. 205).

132. A statement reported by Aragon in the form of indirect speech (*Matisse*, vol. 1, p. 138). The sentence immediately follows a remark by Matisse, this time reported in direct speech, on Rembrandt and modulation: "I said to myself that Rembrandt does not need to touch his paper to give it a certain quality: the first states of Rembrandt's etchings are very interesting in this respect, with their indications of quantities of paper enclosed and marked out" (translation slightly modified to retain the word *quantité* of the original). Pierre Schneider dates *The Siesta* from the summer of 1906 (*Matisse*, p. 382, note 22), basing his argument on the fact that Marguerite Duthuit-Matisse, who

appears in it on the balcony, did not arrive in Collioure until the summer of 1906. I wouldn't be overly bothered should *The Siesta* come after *Le Bonheur de vivre,* but it has to be admitted that, in its color register, this canvas is very close to the works of summer 1905 (the canvas is usually dated from 1905).

133.　Quoted in Schneider, *Matisse,* p. 216.

134.　Flam, *Matisse, the Man,* p. 164.

135.　To Courthion, reported by Schneider, *Matisse,* p. 242. On the critics' judgments concerning *Le Bonheur de vivre,* notably its "lack of [compositional] unity" (Morice, Vauxcelles), cf. Benjamin, *"Notes of a Painter,"* passim.

136.　Cf. Schneider, *Matisse,* p. 280.

137.　The quantity-quality equation is barely mentioned in the three important monographs devoted to Matisse (those of Barr, Flam, and Schneider). True, Schneider devotes a few paragraphs to it, but in my opinion misses the point: he notes for example that "the transition, the real transformation from a world of quality to a world of quantity, characteristic of the modern period on a variety of levels (economic, political, and social), made its first appearance in painting, with its extreme consequences, in the Merion Dance" (*Matisse,* p. 623, with an extremely puzzling reference to the Bauhaus, Le Corbusier, and "design"). Two pages later, Schneider discusses "Matisse's apprenticeship of the quantitative world," referring to the large stage backdrop that Matisse did in 1920 for Diaghilev's staging of *The Song of the Nightingale*: here, the "quantitative" is conceived simply in terms of size, not scale. A little later in the book, even though Matisse's instructions concerning this notion are perfectly clear when discussing the illustrations in his books, Schneider interprets the "quantitative" in the *Mallarmé* book (on which the painter was working at the same time as the *Dance*) as the passage from the intimacy and privacy of drawing to the public space of publishing (p. 628). The only time he mentions the role of proportion in the modulation of Matisse's drawing, Schneider dismisses the question in half a sentence (p. 574).

138.　On the tactical role of the illustrations here, meant to show that if Matisse is not a cold theoretician, he's a "reasonable" man and not a dangerous madman, cf. Benjamin, *"Notes of a Painter,"* p. 163. Inversely, and even though Apollinaire uses the word "reasonable," Matisse's interview with the poet a few months earlier had been illustrated with works that had caused a scandal at the Salon: in this case, it was a question of demonstrating that, contrary to what the Picasso circle was suggesting, Matisse was not lagging behind when it came to innovation (ibid., p. 130).

139.　Desvallières's introduction does not appear in Flam's *Matisse on Art*. I am using Roger Benjamin's translation here (*"Notes of a Painter,"* pp. 158, 160–161). On Desvallières's role as a critic, cf. ibid., pp. 133–149. In his commentary on Desvallières's introduction, Benjamin points out that the reference to romanesque art is part of a strategy of national rehabilitation: even if Matisse's buyers are Americans, Russians, or Germans, he is still one of us.

140.　I have occasionally modified Flam's translation. As these modifications concern minor points, I shall not point them out.

141.　On what opposes Matisse to Kandinsky, cf. Lebensztejn (who quotes the same passage), *Zig Zag,* pp. 186–187 (see in particular the note devoted to Aragon's incomprehension).

142.　Quoted in Aragon, *Matisse,* vol. 2, p. 308.

143.　Even the otherwise excellent book by Roger Benjamin, which (after an extremely involved analysis of its theoretical context) ends with a close reading of the "Notes," virtually ignores the quantity-quality equation. He mentions it only in relation to the question of "deformations" (discussing the dot whose size has to be increased, he refers to Desvallières on romanesque art), and only elucidates Matisse's stand against squaring with the use of the cartoon picked up from Signac (*"Notes of a Painter,"* p. 202). If Benjamin neglects this question, it is in part because of the very way in which he proceeds, that is, by dividing the text up into major themes that are then "contextualized." The method is not without its advantages, since it makes it possible to trace Matisse's borrowings from what was in the air at the time, but it inevitably masks the text's articulation, as I have tried to outline it.

144. The graphic work from 1941–42 is indeed phenomenal, especially the series of *Thèmes et variations*.

145. Lydia Delectorskaya, . . . *l'apparente facilité* . . . , p. 115.

146. Here again, I have replaced Flam's "spirit" with "mind."

147. Jacques Derrida, *Of Grammatology*, pp. 200ff.

148. "Au Beauty Parlour," *Traverses*, no. 7 (a special issue on make-up), February 1977, pp. 74–94.

149. The assumption of color as "the return of the repressed" in modernity had become a veritable cliché at the time Lebensztejn wrote his text (we see its most ridiculous effects, with all the "theoretical" woodenness it entails, in Marcel Pleynet's "Le Système de Matisse" (1971), English tr. Sima N. Godfrey in Pleynet, *Painting and System* (Chicago: University of Chicago Press, 1984), pp. 7–79, a text that, for its part, does its best to repress everything Matisse might owe to neoimpressionism. It goes without saying that Lebensztejn's contribution has nothing to do with the drone-like reiteration of this worn-out tune. Pierre Schneider also pursues Derrida's analysis of Rousseau and the secondary status of color (but without referring to it) (*Matisse*, p. 363).

150. Lebensztejn, *Zig Zag*, p. 178.

151. Jacques Derrida, *Positions* (1972), English tr. Alan Bass (Chicago: Chicago University Press, 1981), pp. 41–42.

152. This indifference toward a conflict that to him seems entirely artificial is perfectly evident in what he has to say about Ingres and Delacroix (the "draftsman" and the "colorist"). First, drawing: "Ingres and Delacroix, who seem so remote and even opposed, draw closer together to the extent that their works are considered from a distance. It seems obvious to me that they have the same sense of the arabesque. Trace the principal contours of *Massacre of Chio* and those of *Angelica*: your tracing will have an understandable meaning, the one derived from these two compositions. If, by contrast, you wanted to trace the contour of a scene painted by Titian, virtually nothing would remain. There you have an index of a very powerful link, perhaps created by the time in which these two painters lived, a link that their contemporaries, who thought of them as enemies, did not yet distinguish" (to Fels, 1929, *EPA*, p. 128, note 93). He then goes on to discuss color: "Today it is easy to see the similarities between them. Both expressed themselves through the *arabesque* and through *color*. Ingres, because of his almost compartmentalized and distinct color, was called 'a Chinese lost in Paris.' They forged the same links in the chain. Today only nuances prevent us from confusing them with each other" ("Observations on Painting," 1945, Flam, p. 100).

153. Letter of July 14, 1905, quoted in Schneider, *Matisse*, p. 98.

154. Here is Cézanne's statement in its entirety: "The planes fall on top of each other, which is where neoimpressionism came from, with its practice of circumscribing contours with a black line, a flaw that must be forcefully resisted" (letter to Emile Bernard, October 23, 1905, reprinted in *Conversations avec Cézanne*, p. 46). The majority of Cézanne criticism, after John Rewald, takes this remark to be a critique not of Seurat but of the "cloisonnisme" of Bernard, Anquetin, and later Gauguin. It is hard to see why Cézanne would make use of a term that has been constantly applied to divisionism since Fénéon's baptismal essay appeared in 1886: on the contrary, it seems to me that here he puts his finger on one of the most symptomatic paradoxes of divisionism. Furthermore, the reader will notice how reminiscent these "planes" that "fall on top of each other" are of what Matisse has to say: in a divisionist painting, "everything is treated in the same way," in other words, sensation is not "organized."

155. The divisionists themselves were aware of the hiatus between color and drawing in their paintings. Around 1896, Luce and Cross thought they had found a solution in coloring their thick contours, a solution later adopted by Signac in his watercolors (where the brushstroke is not divided). Matisse himself will adopt this procedure in his own watercolors, a technique with which he is not terribly familiar and which he seems to adopt exclusively during his second divisionist period, under the direct influence of Signac. It is as if he had realized that drawing in color solves nothing, since the question is merely slightly displaced: it was in trying to use color in drawing that he made the break I have discussed here.

Kahnweiler's Lesson

I would like to thank Orde Levinson, who is preparing an anthology of Kahnweiler's writings in English, for having pointed many texts to my attention, and for letting me use his unpublished translations.

1.   Daniel-Henry Kahnweiler, *My Galleries and Painters,* dialogues with Francis Crémieux, tr. Helen Weaver (New York: Viking, 1971), p. 74.

2.   Jacques de Gachons, "La Peinture d'après-demain (?)," *Je sais tout,* April 15, 1912, pp. 349–351; quoted at length in Werner Spies, "Vendre des tableaux: Donner à lire," in *Daniel-Henry Kahnweiler: Marchand, éditeur, écrivain,* exhibition catalogue, Musée national d'art moderne, Centre Georges Pompidou (Paris, 1984), pp. 17–44.

3.   Daniel-Henry Kahnweiler, *The Rise of Cubism,* trans. Henry Aronson (New York: Wittenborn, 1949), p. 13; originally published as articles in the Zürich *Weissen Blätter* in 1916, reissued as a collection in 1920. The first seeds of this text on cubism date from 1915, when Kahnweiler wrote the manuscript of *Der Gegenstand der Aesthetik,* not published until 1971 in Munich (Heinz Moos Verlag), and which bears the trace of his theoretical "apprenticeship" at Berne. The last three chapters of this book are dedicated to cubism and include a good section of what became *The Rise of Cubism.* I thank Orde Levinson for acquainting me with this text.

On the titling of cubist paintings by Kahnweiler, see William Rubin, "From Narrative to 'Iconic': The Buried Allegory in *Bread and Fruit Dish on a Table* and the Role of *Les Demoiselles d'Avignon,*" *Art Bulletin* 65 (December 1983), p. 618, note 13. The interview in *Je sais tout* reveals that Kahnweiler's obsession with "reading" started quite early on: "Oh! I know that the reading of the last works by Picasso and Braque is quite uneasy. As for me, I've been initiated. I witnessed the blossoming of these paintings. I know everything the artist wanted to put in. So, sir, this represents 'the poet' . . . —And this? . . . —A still life. It's one of the most perfect inventions by Picasso. There is, here, a violin, a fan, glasses, a manuscript whose pages are falling, a pipe . . . " (quoted in Spies, "Vendre des tableaux," pp. 28–29). Doubtless, Kahnweiler's titles were occasionally inappropriate, as Picasso wrote him from Ceret in June 1912, concerning a painting that Kahnweiler wished to buy from him: "I don't understand the title you gave it"; cited in *Donation Louise et Michel Leiris,* exhibition catalogue, Musée national d'art moderne, Centre Georges Pompidou (Paris, 1984), p. 166. Otherwise, *Bouteille de marc de Bourgogne, verre, journal* (1913) seems to be the only one of Picasso's paintings named by the painter. It includes on the back an inscription in his hand: "A bottle of Burgundian marc on a round table/a glass and a newspaper in the background/a mirror/1913/Picasso" (we note, however, that the "mirror" has disappeared); Pierre Daix and Joan Rosselet, *Picasso, The Cubist Years 1907–1916: A Catalogue Raisonné of the Paintings and Related Works* (Boston: New York Graphic Society, 1979), p. 297, no. 567.

4.   The final chapter of *Der Gegenstand der Aesthetik,* titled "Die Ausläufer des Kubismus" (The Offshoots of Cubism), already includes a critique of abstraction as hedonistic decoration, incapable of articulating a sense of space.

5.   Kahnweiler, *My Galleries and Painters,* p. 42.

6.   Ibid. On Kahnweiler's "negative publicity," see Spies, "Vendre des tableaux," p. 20.

7.   Kahnweiler, *My Galleries and Painters,* p. 22.

8.   Spies, "Vendre des tableaux," p. 33.

9.   The facts are well known and reported in detail in *My Galleries and Painters,* p. 50. Kahnweiler was in Rome the day war was declared. This was, for him, "an unspeakable laceration." As a German, he did not wish to fight for Germany; French by choice, he did not wish to take part in the butchery. The French government's sequestration of his possessions, his retreat to Switzerland, and, as a final blow, as late as 1921–23, the absurd liquidation of his collection in public sale by the state followed. On this grotesque episode of the Third Republic's cultural policy and its intentional nature, see Jeanne Laurent, *Arts et pouvoirs* (St. Etienne: CIEREC, 1982), pp. 116–120.

10.   Daniel-Henry Kahnweiler, "Die Grenzen der Kunstgeschichte," *Monatshefte für Kunstwissenschaft* 13, no. 1 (April 1920), pp. 91–97; French tr. in Daniel-Henry Kahnweiler, *Confessions esthétiques* (Paris: Gallimard, 1963), pp. 68–83. Shortly after, Erwin Panofsky also cited Georg Simmel's

article, "Das Problem der historischen Zeit" (in *Philosophische Vorträge* 12 [1916]; later published in Simmel, *Essays on Interpretation in Social Science,* ed. Guy Oakes [Totowa, N.J.: Rowman and Littlefield, 1980], pp. 127–144); see Panofsky, "Zur Problem der historischen Zeit" (1927), reprinted in *Aufsätze zu Grundfragen der Kunstwissenschaft,* ed. H. Oberer and E. Verheyen (Berlin: Verlag Bruno Hessling, 1974), pp. 77–83.

11.   See Spies's excellent article, "Vendre des tableaux," to which I owe a good part of what follows. See also Arnold Gehlen, "D.-H. Kahnweilers Kunstphilosophie," in *Pour Daniel-Henry Kahnweiler,* ed. Werner Spies (Stuttgart: Hatje, 1965), pp. 92–103. Gehlen and Spies justly compare Kahnweiler's position (well summarized in the sentence "Only the man who is intimate with the painting of his time sees truly, fully") with Fiedler's; for Fiedler, not only is art a means of knowledge (nonconceptual) of the real, but at the extreme only the artist is able to see truly works of art. Compare the pronouncement by Nietzsche quoted by Kahnweiler in *Der Gegenstand der Aesthetik,* p. 55: "Art only speaks to the artists. . . . The notion of the art lover is a mistake."

12.   Spies refers in his article to Apollinaire's irritated letter to Kahnweiler after learning of Kahnweiler's little interest in his book, *Les Peintres cubistes* ("Vendre des tableaux," p. 35).

13.   On the legend of Bergson as godfather to cubism, see Edward Fry, *Cubism* (New York: Oxford University Press, 1978), p. 67. More recently, Timothy Mitchell has tried to demonstrate that "Bergson's philosophy is as important to the development of Cubism as Schelling's Nature Philosophy was to German Romantic painting," which makes no sense unless one considers only, as does Mitchell, Jean Metzinger's minor cubism and his theory; "Bergson, Le Bon, and Hermetic Cubism," *Journal of Aesthetics and Art Criticism* 36 (Winter 1977), pp. 175–183. Kahnweiler never ceased to maintain his scorn for Albert Gleizes and Metzinger's book (*Du Cubisme,* 1912) and to insist on Picasso's small esteem for it; *My Galleries and Painters,* p. 43.

14.   Maurice Raynal, "Conception et vision," *Gil Blas,* August 29, 1912; reprinted in Fry, *Cubism,* p. 94.

15.   Rosalind Krauss has shown all the benefits that can be drawn from an invocation of Berkeley apropos of cubism in her review of the exhibition "The Cubist Epoch," *Artforum* 9, no. 6 (February 1971), pp. 32–38.

16.   Kahnweiler, *The Rise of Cubism,* p. 12. If Kahnweiler "effaced" almost all direct reference to Kant in *The Rise of Cubism,* it is noteworthy that Kant's name occurs much more frequently in *Der Gegenstand der Aesthetik,* at the same time that Kahnweiler was undergoing his philosophical apprenticeship. Here, Kahnweiler refers most frequently to the Kant of the *Critique of Judgment,* while later references more frequently concern the first two critiques. See also the "ideal library" Kahnweiler proposed to Raymond Queneau, in which only the *Critique of Pure Reason* and the *Critique of Practical Reason* appear; Raymond Queneau, "D.-H. Kahnweiler," in *Pour une bibliothèque idéale* (Paris: Gallimard, 1956), p. 156. (I thank Orde Levinson for this reference.) A rigorous analysis of Kahnweiler's Kantianism should examine the privilege granted the two first critiques over the third, and the link there may be between this (neo-Kantian) privilege and Kahnweiler's theory of perception, in that it contradicts certain of Kant's propositions in the *Critique of Judgment.*

17.   On the "unfinished" status of *Demoiselles d'Avignon,* see Leo Steinberg's refutation in "The Philosophical Brothel," *Art News* 71, no. 5 (September 1977), pp. 20–29, and no. 6 (October 1977), pp. 38–47 (reprinted in *October,* no. 44, Spring 1988, pp. 17–74); and the restatement by William Rubin contributing many documentary "proofs" in "From Narrative to 'Iconic,'" pp. 647–649.

Kahnweiler's 1929 text on Gris, included in the French version of *The Rise of Cubism,* ends on this note: "If, in the framework of the history of art, one of the essential aims of cubism consisted in the return to the unity of the work of art, in the desire to create not sketches, but autonomous and complete organisms, then no cubist pursued this aim with more success and spirit of continuity than Juan Gris. If, as we think, cubism was not only a discovery, a renewal, but also a return to the true traditions of painting, then it is to him above all that we owe it" (*Confessions esthétiques,* p. 51; I am quoting Orde Levinson's translation).

18.   Kahnweiler, *The Rise of Cubism,* p. 8. In the previous version of this essay, I had not posited that Kahnweiler had misunderstood Picasso's statement: it was my contention that it was one of

Picasso's witticisms, and that the critic, obsessed by the Kantian definition of space as an a priori category of sensibility, had taken it too seriously. A recent conversation with Leo Steinberg, however, has convinced me that I had myself misjudged Picasso's remark: probably made in 1909, as Steinberg suggested, it refers to Picasso's obsession with the difficulty of providing a direct access to depth, without the traditional code of foreshortening, associated with tactility (this obsession was first discussed by Rosalind Krauss with regard to the Horta landscapes in her review of "The Cubist Epoch," and is analyzed at great length in her essay "The Motivation of the Sign," read at a seminar on cubism at the Museum of Modern Art, New York, in November 1989, to appear in the second volume of the catalogue of the exhibition "Picasso and Braque: Pioneering Cubism," organized by William Rubin at the museum). Read in this context, the remark takes on a basic phenomenological dimension that is genuine to Picasso: as Leo Steinberg pointed out to me, the artist does not speak, like Kahnweiler, of the "position of objects in space" (*Rise of Cubism,* p. 8), but of "the distance between the tip of the nose and the mouth," that is, of the first sight the infant discovers and tries to control with his sense of touch. And it is not by chance that in his numerous heads of 1909, it is precisely for the relationship between the tip of the nose (the prow of the human body) and the mouth that Picasso tries the most numerous combinations. I am grateful to Leo Steinberg for having retrieved for me this quote from the usual clichés about cubism (the essence of the objects, etc.), where I thought it belonged.

19.   "What undoubtedly worried Gris in his friends' work was the complexity, the confusion of lines—only apparent, it is true, but troublesome for the reader of canvases that justly claimed to be representational and realistic. This smacked of the 'ambiguity' that he detested. His own contributions were clarity, purity and a hatred of falsehood. Picasso and Braque always proclaimed that they disdained tricks of brushwork; but, carried away by their emotions, they often yielded in spite of themselves to their technical gifts. Only Gris made his hand completely subservient to the will of his very clear mind." (Daniel-Henry Kahnweiler, *Juan Gris: His Life and Work,* tr. Douglas Cooper [London: Lund Humphries, 1947], p. 78.) The semantics of the whole passage indicates that Kahnweiler shares Gris's abhorrence or at least finds it justified.

20.   Alexandre Koyré, "La Dynamique de Nicolo Tartaglia" (1957); reprinted in *Etudes d'histoire de la pensée scientifique* (Paris: Gallimard, 1973), p. 117.

21.   French tr. in *confessions esthétiques,* pp. 81–82. For Erwin Panofsky's commentary on this text, criticizing Kahnweiler's reading of Riegl as too influenced by Worringer, see "The Concept of Artistic Volition" (1920), tr. Kenneth Northcott and Joel Snyder, *Critical Inquiry* 8, no. 1 (Autumn 1981), p. 24, note 7.

22.   Kahnweiler dated these two works incorrectly. He placed the first in spring 1910, whereas it dates from winter 1909–10, but particularly he dated *The Portuguese* (which he named *Joueur de guitare*) as summer 1910, while it is actually from 1911. His argument does not suffer from this, however, because although shifted in time, the logic of sequence is maintained.

When I write that Kahnweiler was the only critic to understand the evolution of cubism until Greenberg, I should immediately add the proviso: at least in the West. Indeed, while Western cubist criticism was usually pretty dim, some Russian critics and artists proposed in the teens formal interpretations that match easily those of Kahnweiler and Greenberg. There were also, it is true, the symbolist-expressionist and apocalyptical analyses of a Nikolay Berdyaev or a Georgy Chulkov, but those were counterbalanced by discussions of Picasso's and Braque's texture by Kasimir Malevich and David Burliuk, of Picasso's "tactility" by Yakov Tugendhold, and most of all by Ivan Aksenov's account of Picasso's pictorial and semiological inventions during his cubist phase, published in 1917 (Aksenov's lengthy analysis of *The Poet* [*Le poète*] of 1912 and its "combed hair," for example, surpasses anything Kahnweiler or Greenberg had to say on this matter). Fragments of Berdyaev's, Chulkov's, Tugendhold's, and Aksenov's texts are translated in English by P.S. Falla (in Marilyn McCully, *A Picasso Anthology* [Princeton: Princeton University Press, 1982], pp. 104–118). For more on Picasso's fortunes in Russia, cf. "Dossier: La Russie et Picasso," ed. Kristina Passuth, *Cahiers du Musée National d'Art Moderne,* no. 4 (April-June 1980), pp. 299–323. For more on cubism and Russia, cf. "Dossier: Le cubisme en Russie," ed. Kristina Passuth, *Cahiers du Musée National d'Art Moderne,* no. 2 (October-December 1979), pp. 278–327. There is a very simple explanation for the generally high quality of cubist criticism in Russia, and a hint is given by Tugenhold's text: while their Parisian counterparts had only on view the works of epigones of the movement—Braque and Picasso almost never exhibited their works publicly in Paris between 1909 and 1919—Russian artists and critics had on view the masterpieces of the Shchukin and Morozov collections. In Paris, except for Kahnweiler, a few intimate friends of Braque and Picasso, and the *habitués* of the Steins' salon, nobody could have had such a great firsthand knowledge of the art and issues at stake. The fact that cubism played a major role in the elaboration of the literary school of Russian criticism (see below) is undoubtedly related to this exceptional situation.

23. "Thus Picasso painted figures resembling Congo sculpture"; Kahnweiler, *The Rise of Cubism,* p. 8. This is all we find on African art and Picasso's "Negro" period in this text. On the other hand, the Ivory Coast mask is already associated with what Kahnweiler called the "open form" in Picasso's constructions, but in a rather elliptical manner. What engaged him especially at this time (and this interpretation seems more linked to the late phase of analytic cubism than to the constructions properly speaking) is the combination of "a scheme of forms and 'real details' (the painted eyes, the raffia hair) as stimuli" (p. 16). Already in *Gegenstand der Aesthetik,* Kahnweiler stated his admiration for African art ("I consider some of these styles, for instance the styles of the Ivory Coast and of Guinea in Africa, of New Caledonia in Polynesia, among the most sublime artistic expressions of mankind"; ch. 7, p. 40, quoting Orde Levinson's translation).

24. See Pierre Daix, "Il n'y a pas 'd'art nègre' dans *Les Demoiselles d'Avignon,*" *Gazette des beaux-arts* 76 (October 1970), pp. 247–270; and its refutation by Rubin at the time in "From Narrative to 'Iconic,'" pp. 632ff., and in his "Picasso," in the exhibition catalogue *"Primitivism" in Twentieth-Century Art: Affinity of the Tribal and the Modern* (New York: Museum of Modern Art, 1984), vol. 1, pp. 254ff.

25. Kahnweiler, *Gris,* pp. 75–76. "Negro Art and Cubism" appeared in English in *Horizon* 18, no. 108 (December 1948), pp. 412–420. I believe it is no accident that William Rubin, who organized the New York exhibition, found this text "confused and confusing"; *"Primitivism,"* vol. 1, p. 310. Brassaï's book of photographs, for which Kahnweiler wrote the preface, appeared in French in 1948 (Paris, Editions du Chêne) and in English in 1949 (*The Sculptures of Picasso,* tr. A.D.B. Sylvester [London, Rodney Phillips], unpaginated).

26. Kahnweiler, "Negro Art and Cubism," p. 412. Rereading Leo Steinberg's masterful essay on Picasso's *Three Women* after the publication of the current text, I realized the extent to which it had influenced me, albeit unconsciously, while I was writing these lines. The same distinction between what I call the morphological and the structural pervades the dense passage he devotes to the relationship between Picasso and African art (on the one hand, "superficial manifestations of striated hatchings or piewedge noses"; on the other, the discovery of "the ineluctable mutability of the makeable"). There is a major difference in our positions, however, in that Steinberg places this discovery, which he describes remarkably, within the first encounter of African art by Picasso, while I don't. Even if I agree with Steinberg that African art had a liberating function for Picasso and that "the energy he derived from it" remained at work throughout the entire phase of analytical cubism, I would say that the confidence he received from what I call his first encounter with this art did not imply yet a comprehension of the possibilities opened by its structural nature. (Cf. Leo Steinberg, "The Polemical Part," *Art in America,* March-April 1979, p. 125. The article constitutes an appendix to "Resisting Cézanne," *Art in America,* November-December 1978, pp. 115–133.)

27. Kahnweiler, preface to *The Sculptures of Picasso.*

28. James Johnson Sweeney, "Picasso and Iberian Sculpture," *Art Bulletin* 23 (September 1941), pp. 192–198.

29. On these points see Jean Laude, *La Peinture française (1905–1914) et "L'Art nègre"* (Paris: Klincksieck, 1968), pp. 257 and 262. In "Negro Art and Cubism," Kahnweiler distinguishes very clearly between the initial interest in masks (which are "reliefs") and the later interest in statuary (p. 417, note 2).

30.   I disagree here with Jean Laude, who cites André Breton with approbation: "'They have nothing in common with expressionist deformations,' André Breton correctly emphasized, in 1933, of the 1906–7 heads in *quart-de-brie*" (*La Peinture française*, p. 260). On the one hand, as both Leo Steinberg and Rubin have noted, it would be reductive to evacuate entirely the "savage" and (sexual) apotropaic connotations of the "Negro" heads of the right section of the *Demoiselles d'Avignon* and the works that followed. On the other hand, we should beware of confusing psychological inexpressiveness and antiexpressionism. Laude remarks, moreover, that Picasso's interest in African masks stemmed not only from their character of relief but from their psychological "emptiness," this interest being an issue, as well, of his difficulties at the time in his creation of the *Portrait of Gertrude Stein* and the solution he found in borrowing, for the writer's countenance, from Iberian sculpture (p. 251). The expressionist deformation of the mask functions as a sign of a refusal of psychological depth.

31.   For an illustration of the borrowings in which Epstein and Karl Schmidt-Rotluff indulged, see "*Primitivism*," vol. 2, pp. 397, 438–439.

32.   Kahnweiler, preface to *The Sculptures of Picasso*. I have corrected the "Wobé" of the original text to "Grebo," according to the attribution of these masks given by experts. William Rubin pointed out to me that, as he had noted in "*Primitivism*" (vol. 1, pp. 76–77, note 58), it was Picasso himself who told Kahnweiler about the Grebo/*Guitar* relationship. This does not impinge on the thrust of my argument, however, for such a piece of information would have been of no use for someone who had not previously understood the issues at stake.

33.   Rubin cites Salmon's account numerous times. "The images from Polynesia or Dahomey appeared to him as 'reasonable'" (André Salmon, "Petite histoire anecdotique du cubisme" [1912]; reprinted in Fry, *Cubism*, p. 82). However, Rubin minimizes its scope considerably in interpreting it as meaning "factual" or "tangible" and pointing out from this an affinity with the style of Picasso's "Negro" period ("tactile," "sculptural"), in opposition to the purely pictorial considerations of analytic cubism; cf. "*Primitivism*," vol. 1, p. 309, note 175.

34.   Kahnweiler, "Negro Art and Cubism," p. 419.

35.   Kahnweiler, preface to *The Sculptures of Picasso*.

36.   William Rubin, who found Kahnweiler's text "confused and confusing" (see note 25), created, in fact, a confusion regarding this notion in Kahnweiler's work. Kahnweiler associated "transparency" with the "superimposed planes" of Braque's and Picasso's painting in 1912, while Rubin believes that Kahnweiler associated it with the facets of analytic cubism, to which he finds an equivalent in the transparency of Antoine Pevsner's sculptures. Against the ideology of transparency, see Rosalind Krauss, *Passages in Modern Sculpture* (Cambridge, Mass.: MIT Press, 1981), esp. pp. 47–51, where cubist relief is interpreted as a war machine destined to sap the foundation of Western sculpture up to Rodin.

37.   Kahnweiler, preface to *The Sculptures of Picasso*.

38.   "Das Wesen der Bildhauerei" was first published in the Weimar review *Feuer* in November-December 1919 (vol. 1, nos. 2–3, pp. 145–156); French tr. in *Confessions esthétiques*, p. 99.

39.   Adolf von Hildebrand, *Das Problem der Form in den bildenden Künsten* (Strasbourg: Heitz, 1893); the American edition is *The Problem of Form in Painting and Sculpture*, tr. Max Meyer and Robert M. Ogden (New York: G. E. Stechert and Co., 1907), p. 113.

40.   The common view of Bernini's sculpture as arch-pictorial in that it is elaborated for a single point of view has recently and efficiently been disputed by Joy Kenseth ("Bernini's Borghese Sculptures: Another View," *Art Bulletin*, vol. 63 [June 1981], pp. 191–210). Rosso's art is still awaiting its revision.

41.   I have noted elsewhere the relation between Hildebrand's position and Greenberg's; Yve-Alain Bois, "The Sculptural Opaque," *Sub/stance* 31 (1981), pp. 23–48. It is never as clear as in Clement Greenberg's suppression in the second version of his essay "The New Sculpture," published in *Art and Culture* (Boston: Beacon Press, 1961), of the passage from the first version, published in *The Partisan Review*, where he assimilated modern sculpture to an object "as palpable and inde-

pendent and present as the house we live in and the furniture we use" (*Partisan Review* 16 [June 1949], p. 641. In other respects, Michael Fried was to take up again Greenberg's second position. It is not fortuitous that we encounter under Hildebrand's signature a condemnation of Canova's theatricality as radical as that by Fried of the theatricality of minimalism; see "Art and Objecthood" (1967), reprinted in Gregory Battcock, ed., *Minimal Art* (New York: Dutton, 1968), pp. 116–147. In truth, Fried's position is more complex and merits a longer development here. As he has himself indicated to me, his notion of anti-objecthood originated from a reading of Maurice Merleau-Ponty, and in particular of "Indirect Language and the Voices of Silence" (1960, rpt. in *Signs*, tr. Richard C. McCleary [Evanston: Northwestern University Press, 1964], pp. 39–83), which rests directly on Saussure. In his first text on Anthony Caro, from which a number of formulations were to be taken up again in "Art and Objecthood," Fried proposed three notions of anti-objecthood. The first is "syntactic" and implicitly Saussurian (Caro's sculpture functioning according to a system of differences), the second "optical" in Greenberg's sense (concerning the use of color in Caro's work), and the third more directly phenomenological, considering sculpture as bringing about a dialogue, by the indirect means of an abstract "gesturing," with the world in which our bodies move. See Michael Fried, "Anthony Caro," *Art International* 7, no. 7 (September 1963), pp. 68–72.

42. Clement Greenberg, "Collage," reprinted in *Art and Culture*, p. 79.

43. See Greenberg, "The New Sculpture" (second version): "Sculpture can confine itself to virtually two dimensions (as some of David Smith's pieces do) without being felt to violate the limitations of its medium" (*Art and Culture*, p. 143). An argument in favor of the "opticality" of sculpture follows.

44. See William Rubin, *Picasso in the Collection of the Museum of Modern Art* (New York: Museum of Modern Art, 1972), p. 207. *Still Life with Chair Caning* belongs to the series of oval still lifes begun after February 1, 1912 (publication of the booklet *Notre Avenir est dans l'air*, whose cover figures in three of these paintings; see Daix, *Le Cubisme de Picasso*, p. 278, nos. 463–466). It was finished before Picasso's departure for the south, as he mentioned it to Kahnweiler among the works remaining in Paris that he wished to keep (see *Donation Michel and Louise Leiris*, p. 167).

45. For a very clear distinction between the two, see Jean Laude, *La Peinture française*, pp. 368–371, where it appears that Picasso only realized a handful of "collages."

46. Edward Fry, review of Daix, *Picasso: The Cubist Years*, in *Art Journal* 41 (Spring 1981), pp. 93–95. According to Fry, who cites a number of documents, Picasso should have bought his Grebo mask at the time of a trip to Marseilles in August 1912, which is quite possible. This said, the fact that Picasso had possessed another Grebo mask (referred to by William Rubin to challenge the terms of this argument; Laude maintains in another connection that Picasso owned the second mask as early as 1910) shows rather that the question is not that of the date of purchase but of an "epiphany" that could have occurred much later, and for which we must seek evidence in the work, not in the circumstances.

Fry has recently expanded (and confirmed) his view on the chronology of events leading to the *Guitar* ("Picasso, Cubism, and Reflexivity," *Art Journal* [Winter 1988], pp. 296–310). The issue is particularly complicated by the confusion among scholars, including myself, between three versions of the sculpture: (1) A cardboard version that, as new evidence tends to indicate (notably correspondence between Braque and Picasso), was realized in Paris and dates probably from October 1912 (Picasso gave this work to the Museum of Modern Art in New York in 1971; after restoration it was exhibited and was reproduced in *Pablo Picasso: A Retrospective*, ed. William Rubin [New York: Museum of Modern Art, 1980], p. 156). (2) A "supplemented cardboard version," in which the previous version is incorporated in "a no-longer-existing-still-life ensemble," to use Fry's terms. This assemblage, first published by Apollinaire in *Soirées de Paris*, no. 18 (November 1913), p. 13, is dated by Fry to early 1913. (3) The metal (and better known) version, which I had chosen as an illustration for the first publication of the current essay. According to Fry, this third version, also given by Picasso to the Museum of Modern Art in 1971, could have been made as late as 1914. The confusion between these different versions does not alter my view according to which the *Guitar* played a major role in the invention of synthetic cubism, for the inventive moment rests indeed with the early cardboard version. But Fry criticizes me—and it is an important issue that some of my students did not fail to raise—for not having taken into account Braque's invention of the *papier collé*. According to Fry, the "*Guitar* is a reflexive transformation of the classical tradition of structure. But only at the level of mental procedure does it offer any suggestions for the reflexive transformation of pictorial illusionism. For Picasso, the pictorial equivalent of the Grebo mask was Braque's first *papier collé*, of September 1912" ("Picasso, Cubism, and Reflexivity," p. 300). Indeed, if the *Guitar* coincides with the inauguration of synthetic cubism, or even constitutes in itself this inauguration, one might wonder why it was Braque, and not Picasso, who created the first *papier collé*, and why Picasso, so prompt at "cannibalizing" any new "technical" discovery by Braque, would have waited a few months before investigating this new set of possibilities.

Furthermore, William Rubin has recently suggested that *Braque*, and not Picasso, had been the inventor of cubist constructions, producing paper sculptures perhaps already in 1911! The sequence of events, as unrolled by Rubin, turns out to be: (1) Braque's first paper sculptures (possibly realized in the summer and fall of 1911 in Céret along with *The Portuguese* and works that include simulated woodgraining, such as *Homage to J. S. Bach*, and brought back to Paris in January 1912); in Picasso's mind, the paper sculptures are associated with the nickname he gave to the artist (Wilbourg, from the aviator-inventor Wilbur Wright). (2) Picasso's first collage, *Still Life with Chair Caning* (Spring 1912). (3) Braque's first *papier collé*, *Fruit Dish and Glass* (realized in Sorgues while Picasso is in Paris, in early September 1912); Piccaso sees it when he briefly returns to Céret in mid-September. (4) Back in Paris, Picasso realizes his cardboard *Guitar* (October 1912), *then* his first *papier collé*. (This sequence of events is recapitulated in William Rubin, "Picasso and Braque: An Introduction," catalogue of the exhibition *Picasso and Braque: Pioneering Cubism* (New York: Museum of Modern Art, 1989), pp. 15–62.

How to reconcile this new chronology with my interpretation, and furthermore, what argument could I find to uphold my apparently ungenerous treatment of Braque? The question is too complex to receive an answer here (a serious comparison of Braque's and Picasso's *papiers collés* would be necessary), but several preliminary points may be suggested. First, let us remark that in Rubin's sequence there is no mention of the discovery of the Grebo mask (according to Fry, it should be situated in August 1912, prior to Picasso's first trip back to Paris and return to Sorgues where he is confronted with Braque's *papier collé*). Although Rubin does allude briefly to the Grebo mask in his text, and at greater length in a footnote where he discusses the present essay, its exclusion from the recapitulative sequence points to an apparent logical traffic jam: it is as if one could not at the same time have Braque as a "precursor" and African art as a catalyst. Secondly, as quoted by Rubin, Braque said to André Verdet: "I have to admit that after having made the *papier collé*, I felt a great shock, and it was an even greater shock for Picasso when I showed it to him." This "greater shock" indeed provides a clue, and, to my mind, reconciles the new chronology with my account of Picasso's theoretical discovery through his encounter with the Grebo mask. Indeed Fry himself, albeit unwillingly, gives the beginning of an answer: what differentiates Picasso's *papiers collés* from Braque's is precisely the level of the semiological investigation. In short, it is because Braque did not himself experience the Grebo mask "epiphany" that he never reached the abstract "level of mental procedure," to use Fry's phrase, that characterizes Picasso's works of 1912–13. And it is because he had had the experience of the epiphany that Picasso could see in Braque's *papier collé* much more than its author could have seen, notably, as is discussed later, that signs, because they are arbitrary, are oppositional and nonsubstantial. (As for Braque's paper constructions, Rubin excellently shows that they were far from raising such issues, and that Braque never considered them as much more than studio props to sort out pictorial problems: it would remain for a Tatlin to fully exploit their innovation, alluded to below.) Finally, as Braque himself insisted upon many times in his later years, the *papier collé* method, as elaborated as it may be, remained for him merely a means to dissociate color and drawing (something Picasso had achieved in painting during his stay at Cadaqués), not an investigation on the arbitrariness of the sign. This would explain why his *papiers collés* soon returned to a kind of neoclassical mode of composition. On the difference between Braque's and

Picasso's cubism, cf. my "Semiology of Cubism" in the second volume of the catalogue of the exhibition *Braque and Picasso: Pioneering Cubism*, to appear in 1991 (New York: Museum of Modern Art).

47.   Picasso himself casts some doubt on the historical importance of analytic cubism, in an interview with Kahnweiler:

> PICASSO: Cubism—the real cubism—was basically a horridly materialistic affair, a base kind of materialism.
>
> I: What do you mean by "real cubism"? What was measurable? What an engineer, as you said at the time, could have constructed from the pictures?
>
> PICASSO: No, not that—that was not so bad. No, I mean the imitation of the material form—you know, the objects represented from the front, in profile and from above. Basically, what Braque did. Gris thought about it, too, but he didn't go all the way. I well remember what I told them in the cubist room at the Indépendants, where there were some Gleizes and Metzingers: "I thought we'd enjoy ourselves a bit, but it's getting bloody boring again."
>
> . . . .
>
> I: So it's basically the so-called "analytic" cubism that you're condemning?
>
> PICASSO: Yes.

Daniel-Henry Kahnweiler, "Gespräche mit Picasso," *Jahresring 59/60* (Stuttgart: Deutsche Verlagsanstalt, 1959), pp. 85–86 (I thank Orde Levinson for having pointed this text to my attention; I am using his translation). There is no reason to suspect the account of the conversation, for Picasso's stance here goes directly against Kahnweiler's own preferences. The artist is certainly unfair with Braque as well as with his own work during the "analytic" period, and I would not let him have the last word on this matter. But the fact is that, as years went by, Picasso became more and more critical toward analytic cubism, and more and more laudatory of the synthetic *papiers collés* and constructions.

48.   On the contrary, the absence of *papiers collés* in the Museum of Modern Art's *"Primitivism"* exhibition seems a symptom of blindness issuing directly from a noncritical adherence to Greenberg's reading, a blindness even more astonishing in that the exhibition opened with the Grebo mask/1912 *Guitar* pair, which might have made us think that Kahnweiler's lesson had been understood.

49.   Carl Einstein, *Negerplastik* (Leipzig: Verlag der Wessen Bücher, 1915); French translation in *Médiations* 3 (Paris, 1961), pp. 93–113; see also Jean Laude's introduction, pp. 83–91. Certainly Einstein's interpretation, typical of German neo-Kantianism, insists much more on the shaping of space in African art than on the constitution of the figurative object, but we will see that it is precisely the inseparability of these two instances, once we have set aside the opposition figure/background, that Picasso discovered in African art. In fact, modeling is not completely foreign to African art (and is even rather important for the art of the Yoruba, the Baoulé, and Benin); however, the cubists, contrary to the fauves, and especially in the second phase of their interest in African art (discussed here), favored the austere and hieratic art of Sudanese cultures and of the Dogon, an art that took nothing from traditional modeling.

50.   On this point, see David Summers, *"Figure come Fratelli*: A Transformation of Symmetry in Renaissance Painting," *Art Quarterly*, n.s., 1, no. 1 (1977), pp. 66–69.

51.   Kahnweiler, "Negro Art and Cubism," p. 416. (This is also reported in his preface to *The Sculptures of Picasso*.) Daix writes, "Picasso confirmed to me that he had destroyed this still life or that he had made something else with it" (*Picasso: The Cubist Years*, p. 83), which seems perfectly plausible. The status of the slight relief in the *Violin* of the Pushkin Museum, which Daix deems very important, seems on the contrary very problematic to me (it is dated from the summer of 1912, but I would definitely put it before the *Guitar*, which is a further argument for dating the latter to the fall). Cf. Daix, ibid., pp. 104 ff. and 282 (no. 483).

52.   Conversely, Jean Laude is perfectly correct in writing that André Derain "did not draw all the consequences from his discovery" of African art when the painter described his visit to the "Musée nègre" of London (the British Museum) to Vlaminck in these terms: "It is therefore understood that relations of volume can express light or the coincidence of light with this or that form" (Laude, *La Peinture française*, p. 303).

53.   Werner Spies, "La Guitare anthropomorphe," *La Revue de l'art* 12 (1971), p. 91. Kahnweiler remarks also, in his preface to *The Sculptures of Picasso*, on the exacerbated pictorialism of this *Head of a Woman*.

54.   Kahnweiler, preface to *The Sculptures of Picasso*.

55.   Kahnweiler, *Rise of Cubism*, p. 10.

56.   On the circumstances of the editing of these two texts, see Jean-Louis Paudrat, "From Africa," in *"Primitivism,"* vol. 1, pp. 149–151. Einstein's book was doubtless written at the beginning of 1914 (its publication was slightly delayed by the war), Markov's book at the end of 1913 to the beginning of 1914.

57.   Vladimir Markov, *Iskusstvo negrov*, was translated and published in French by Jean-Louis Paudrat as "L'Art des nègres," *Cahiers du Musée national d'art moderne* 2 (1979), pp. 319–327. In his introduction, Paudrat gives some biographical information on Markov, resituates his work in the context of the period, and ends on Markov's conception of "montage" ("a dynamic assemblage of heterogeneous materials"), which he compares to the organizing principles of Picasso's *papiers collés* and Tatlin's *counter-reliefs*.

58.   See Einstein, *Negerplastik*, pp. 99–100. Markov cites Picasso's remark (reported by Yakov Tugendhold): "It is not the characteristics of these sculptures that interests me, it is their geometric simplicity" ("L'Art des nègres," p. 324).

59.   Spies, "Vendre des tableaux," p. 38. William Rubin recently suggested to me that Picasso's rediscovery of African art in 1912, at a moment when he was searching for a way out of the "hermetism" of the final phase of analytic cubism, must have reactivated many of the ideas he had conceived and then abandoned during his work on *Les Demoiselles d'Avignon* (that is, before analytic cubism), particularly that of the arbitrary nature of the sign. An extraordinary sketch for the "crouching nude" in his great painting, recently exhibited at the Picasso Museum in Paris (no. 63 of the catalogue of the exhibition *Les Demoiselles d'Avignon*), confirms this hypothesis. For what we witness in this study is a bust *in the process of becoming a head*. On this point, and on the traumatic effect of the *Demoiselles d'Avignon*, based on a deferral, cf. Yve-Alain Bois, "Painting as Trauma," *Art in America*, June 1988, pp. 131–140, 172–173.

60.   See M. O. Čudakova and E. A. Toddes, "La Première Traduction russe du *Cours de linguistique générale* de F. de Saussure et l'activité du Cercle Linguistique de Moscou," *Cahiers Ferdinand de Saussure* 36 (1982), pp. 63–91. The article retraces the diffusion of Saussure's book in Moscow, and analyzes the response of Russian linguists at the time of their confrontation with the Saussurian theory. Even before the (restricted) diffusion of the *Course* in Russia, Saussure's ideas were known by his student Sergei Karcevskij (ibid., p. 76). See Roman Jakobson, "Sergej Karcevskij," in *Selected Writings*, vol. 2 (The Hague: Mouton, 1971), pp. 517–521.

61.   Immediately after a passage on Karcevskij in the postface of the first volume of the *Selected Writings* (The Hague: Mouton, 1962), Jakobson wrote:

> Perhaps the strongest impulse toward a shift in the approach to language and linguistics, however, was—for me, at least—the turbulent artistic movement of the early twentieth century. The extraordinary capacity of these discoverers to overcome again and again the faded habits of their own yesterdays . . . is intimately allied to their unique feeling for the dialectic tension between the parts and the uniting whole, and between the conjugated parts, primarily between the two aspects of any artistic sign, its *signans* and its *signatum*.

See also on this point the interview with Jakobson published by Jean-Pierre Faye in *Le Récit hunique* (Paris: Seuil, 1967), where the linguist relates, "In 1913–14, I lived among the painters. I was the friend of Malevich" (p. 281). The best analysis of what cubist painting represented for Jakobson can be found in *What Is Poetry?* (1933–34):

> Why is it necessary to make a special point of the fact that sign does not fall together with object? Because besides the direct awareness of the identity between sign and object (A is A1), there is a necessity for the direct awareness of the inadequacy of that identity (A is not A1). The reason this antinomy is essential is that without contradiction there is no mobility of concepts, no mobility of signs, and the relationship between concept and sign becomes automatized. Activity comes to a halt, and the awareness of reality dies out.

(*Selected Writings*, vol. 3 [The Hague: Mouton, 1981], p. 750.) The Russian formalists' concept of *ostranenie* ("making strange") derives from this view of cubism as an enterprise of "disautomatization."

62. Roman Jakobson, "Structuralisme et téléologie" (1975), in *Selected Writings*, vol. 7 (Berlin, New York, Amsterdam: Mouton, 1985), p. 125.

63. Jakobson insisted many times on Baudouin de Courtenay's role as precursor; see "Jan Baudouin de Courtenay," *Selected Writings*, vol. 2, pp. 389–393. In the interview with Faye mentioned above, he even states that the linguist influenced Saussure, whom he knew quite well (*Le Récit hunique*, p. 276). N. Slusareva has shown that a great number of Russian linguists were struck, once acquainted with the *Course*, by the similarity between Saussure's ideas and those of their teacher; "Quelques considérations des linguistes soviétiques à propos des idées de F. de Saussure," *Cahiers Ferdinand de Saussure* 20 (1963), pp. 23–46, esp. 27–28. On Baudouin de Courtenay, see the critical edition of Saussure's *Cours de linguistique générale* by Tulio de Mauro (Paris: Payot, 1973), pp. 339–340. On Baudouin's participation in the meetings of the Union of the Youth, cf. the burlesque account given by Benedikt Livshits, *The One and a Half-Eyed Archer* (1933), trans. John Bowlt (Newtonville: Oriental Research Partners, 1977), pp. 203–207.

64. An excellent general view, taking into account the works proliferating after the appearance of the *Course* up to 1962, is given in Rudolf Engler, "Théorie et critique d'un principe saussurien: L'Arbitraire du signe," *Cahiers Ferdinand de Saussure* 19 (1962), pp. 5–65.

65. Handwritten notes cited by Engler, ibid., p. 59.

66. Handwritten note cited by de Mauro in his edition of the *Cours,* p. 440.

67. Ferdinand de Saussure, *Course in General Linguistics*, trans. Wade Baskin (New York: McGraw-Hill, 1966), p. 120. Rosalind Krauss was the first to cite this passage in connection with Picasso's cubist work, and specifically with the *papiers collés*; "In the Name of Picasso" (1981), reprinted in *The Originality of the Avant-Garde and Other Modernist Myths* (Cambridge, Mass.: MIT Press, 1985), pp. 23–40. Her interpretation of cubism by way of Saussure is situated in a poststructuralist perspective that I do not hold here, preferring to keep to the more classical structuralist aspects of Saussurian linguistics in order to trace a relation between it and cubism. The elements that we bring forward from cubist work are not exactly the same. It is therefore appropriate that we do not "need" identical aspects of the same theory. This removes nothing from the fact that I owe much to her interpretation.

As far as I know, the first critic to have traced a parallel between cubism and Saussure's linguistics is Pierre Dufour, in an excellent text in which he insisted, as I do here, on the difference between the referent and the signified, and on the radical break produced by synthetic cubism as far as the conception of the semiological nature of painting is concerned ("Actualité du cubisme," *Critique,* no. 267–268 [August–September 1969], pp. 809–825). Referring to this essay, Jean Laude elaborated on the analogy in a text entitled "Picasso et Braque 1910–1914: La transformation des signes," which contains many incursions into the problematics of the Russian formalists (*Le Cubisme,* ed. Louis Roux [Saint Etienne: CIEREC, 1971], pp. 7–28), and in "La Stratégie des signes," his preface to Nicole Worms de Romilly, *Braque, le cubisme: Catalogue de l'oeuvre 1907–1914* (Paris: Maegth, 1982), pp. 11–53. Pierre Daix referred also to the Saussurian model (more precisely as reinterpreted by Lévi-Strauss) in his *Picasso: The Cubist Years* (passim), albeit in a nonrigorous way. For a discussion of some of these essays in semiotic terms, see Wendy Holmes, "Decoding Collage: Signs and Surfaces," in *Collage: Critical Views,* ed. Katherine Hoffman (Ann Arbor: UMI Research Press, 1989), pp. 193–212. Unfortunately, Leo Steinberg's lecture on the parallel between Saussure and Picasso's cubism has remained unpublished. It was first delivered in March 1976 at the American Academy in Rome, two months later at the Grand Palais in Paris, and, each time in a revised version, in various institutions in America—culminating in a Guggenheim Museum address in 1985. While Steinberg, like the authors just mentioned, focuses on the Saussurian notion of the arbitrariness of the sign, he insists on the fact that this heuristic model is most appropriate to take into account Picasso's concern with "the data of three-dimensionality" (that which cannot but be encoded, for the canvas is flat, while the rendering of two-dimensionality does not require a semiotic transformation): it is there that the artist conspicuously explores "the availability of alternative modes." Steinberg's linguistic parallel does not end with Saussure's concept of the arbitrariness, however, although it depends upon it. In a lecture delivered in November 1989 at the Johns Hopkins University, entitled "The Intelligence of Picasso," he drew from the figures of rhetoric to characterize Picasso's devices (*hypallage*, for example, where the qualities of one object are transferred to an object associated with it, as in "green thumb" or "topless bar," offers an accurate description of the mechanism put to work in many cubist *papier collés* of 1914: a glass takes up the color and matter of the wooden table on which it rests). Finally, Steinberg showed that one of the main reasons for the efficacy of the linguistic model when one deals with cubism rests on the "isolation of predicates" that the spoken language and Picasso's art have in common (one cannot say with the same verbal sign that a glass is empty and where it lays on the table). By contrast, the iconic signs of mimetic painting are characterized by a fusion of predicates.

68.   The appearance of the word *positive* seems so strange here, at first reading, that we might be tempted to believe this an interpolation by the editors of the *Course*. For once, our suspicions are unfounded. The recent publication of students' notebooks that served as a basis for the edition of the *Course* shows that *positive* figures in three of these notebooks; Rudolf Engler, critical edition of the *Cours de linguistique générale*, vol. 1 (Wiesbaden: Harrassowitz, 1968), p. 272.

69.   Saussure, *Course*, p. 122.

70.   I cite this from the student notebooks published by Engler, *Cours*, p. 259, rather than from the *Course*, because the diagram, which shows very clearly that value is dependent on the paradigmatic relation and on the syntagmatic relation, was omitted by the editors of the *Course*.

71.   René Amacker, "Sur la notion de 'valeur,' " in *Studi saussuriani per Robert Godel* (Bologna: Il Mulino, 1972), p. 14. This text represents, to this day, the best explanation of this particularly complex notion.

72.   Saussure frequently uses the metaphor of a chess game. The example of the knight can be found on p. 110 of the *Course* (for other occurrences, see pp. 22 and 88ff.). Matisse, as well, had a predilection for this metaphor; see *Matisse on Art*, ed. Jack D. Flam (London: Phaidon, 1973), pp. 72, 137, and the essay "Matisse and Arche-Drawing" above.

73.   Student note cited by Amacker, "Sur la notion de 'valeur,' " p. 15. "Signification" appears in the place of "value" in the manuscript. I follow Amacker's correction here.

        This discussion is to be related to Kahnweiler's structural conception of history, as it is developed in "The Limits of Art History," and which derives from Simmel (determination for each historical configuration of the threshold of historicity beyond which an event is not historical) and from Riegl (relativity of the artistic value and of the historical value). In his "Modern Cult of Monuments" (1903), Riegl noted that even the least important object bears, aside from the historical information it conveys, an artistic value: "Every historical monument is also an art monument, because even a minor literary monument like a scrap of paper with a brief and insignificant note, apart from its historical value concerning the development of paper production, the evolution of writing and of writing instruments, contains a whole series of artistic elements—the form of the piece of paper, of the letters, and their composition. To be sure, these are such insignificant elements that for the most part we neglect them in many cases because we have enough other monuments that convey much the same thing in a richer and more detailed manner. But were this scrap of paper the only surviving testimony to the art of its time, we would consider it, though trivial in itself, an utterly indispensable artifact" (tr. Kurt Foster, *Oppositions,* no. 25 (Fall 1982), p. 2; translation slightly modified).

74.   Saussure, *Course,* pp. 115–116.

75.   Ibid., p. 133. The student notebooks read "limitation of arbitrariness in relation to the idea"; see Engler, *Cours,* p. 301.

76.   Ibid.

77.   Engler, "Théorie et critique," p. 10.

78.   Saussure, *Course,* p. 132. I have corrected the mistake of the American translator, who inverted the × sign with the + sign. With respect to "Teach × er," Saussure referred to a preceding passage of the *Course,* which seems particularly pertinent in relation to cubism as it concerns what the linguist calls the "syntagmatic solidarities": "Almost all units of language depend on what surrounds them in the spoken chain or on their successive parts. This is shown by word formation. A unit like *painful* decomposes into two subunits (*pain-ful*), but these subunits are not two independent parts that are simply lumped together (*pain + ful*). The unit is a product, a combination of two independent elements that acquire value only through their reciprocal action in a higher unit (*pain × ful*)"; pp. 127–128.

79.   The gravest error of the editors of the *Course,* aside from the addition of the little drawing of the tree in this chapter, was to have introduced a passage on the *unmotivated* character of the sign (figuring in a later lesson) in the passage concerning radical semiological arbitrariness, which must be distinguished from relative linguistic aribrariness. Their interpolation reads as follows: "The word *arbitrary* also calls for comment. The term should not imply that the choice of the signifier is left entirely to the speaker. . . . I mean that it is unmotivated, i.e., arbitrary in that it actually has no natural connection with [reality]" (pp. 68–69). This last word, an addition of the editors (cf. Engler, "Théorie et critique," p. 50), was corrected to "signified" by the translator, and rightly so. The arbitrariness of the sign absolutely does not concern, in Saussure's work, the relation between sign and referent but that between the signifier and the signified.

80.   Kahnweiler, preface to *The Sculptures of Picasso.*

81.   Student note in Engler, *Cours,* p. 261.

82.   Rather than compare Picasso's formidable sculpture, *Head [Tête]* (1930), which effects this transformation of mouth to vagina, with the Jukun mask, which relates to it vaguely from a morphological point of view, the organizers of the Museum of Modern Art "'Primitivism'" exhibit could have compared it to an object having only a structural connection with it, effecting the same type of metaphorization, inasmuch as this semantic transformation is well described by William Rubin in his introduction to the catalogue (vol. 1, p. 60). Picasso's *Tête* and the Jukun mask are reproduced in the catalogue, vol. 1, pp. 320–321.

83.   See Daix, *Picasso: The Cubist Years,* p. 303, nos. 594–598.

84.   Kahnweiler, preface to *The Sculptures of Picasso.*

85.   Leo Stein, *Appreciation: Painting, Poetry and Prose* (New York: Crown, 1947), p. 177; cited by Fry, *Cubism,* p. 39.

86.   Kahnweiler, preface to *The Sculptures of Picasso.*

87.   Paul M. Laporte has perceived, on the contrary, a great similarity between Hildebrand's theory of perception in his treatise and Braque's and Picasso's cubism. It is true that he only speaks in rather general terms of the works of these last, and that he keeps to "analytic" cubism, which accommodates itself very well to remarks on the inherent ambiguity in the perception of volume. Laporte never broaches the essential problem in Hildebrand's work that preoccupies us here, the relation between sculpture and real space. If we can admit in a strict sense a certain relation between Hildebrand's theory and analytic cubism (although this seems dubious and not very profitable), it still is impossible to elaborate such a relation for all of Braque and Picasso's production after the 1912 rupture that I have tried to describe. See Paul M. Laporte, "Cubism and Science," *Journal of Aesthetics and Art Criticism* 7 (March 1949), pp. 243–256.

While correcting the galleys of this book, I became aware of a letter from Kahnweiler to Gombrich, published by the latter, in which any link between Hildebrand and cubism, which Gombrich had also fantasized, is emphatically denied: "In my opinion the problems which Hildebrand treats—proximal and distant perception etc.—have nothing to do with the problem of cubism. . . . Do you think that Hildebrand's ideas are close to cubism? I would rather think the opposite." Quoted in E. H. Gombrich, "From Careggi to Montmartre—A Footnote to Erwin Panofsky's Idea," in *'Il se rendit en Italie,' Etudes Offertes à André Chastel* (Paris: Flammarion, 1987), pp. 670–671.

88.　Picasso's experiment was published for the first time in *Cahiers d'art* 25, no. 2 (1950), p. 282; see Daix, *Picasso: The Cubist Years*, p. 299, no. 578. Braque's sculpture is reproduced in Nicole Worms de Romilly, *Braque, le cubisme: Catalogue de l'oeuvre 1907–1914*, preface by Jean Laude (Paris: Maeght, 1982), p. 41.

89.　See Jean Laude, *La Peinture française*, p. 390, for a comparison between the reduced iconographic repertoire of cubism and the vocabulary of African art.

90.　In spite of his rich examination of the relation between African art and cubism during the years 1907–09, and in spite of his brilliant analysis of the characteristics of this art and the many points it had in common with the cubism of the following years, Jean Laude barely perceived the importance of the shock experienced by Picasso in 1912. Laude places the start of a more "profound" interest in this art in 1909, when Picasso had ceased to borrow directly from the forms of African art (ibid., p. 323); he therefore does not make the *Guitar* an inaugural moment in Picasso's work. His proposed formal and functional analysis of African art remains to this day, after that of Einstein, the richest; see esp. pp. 372–373, 382–388.

91.　Daniel-Henry Kahnweiler, "Entretiens avec Picasso," *Quadrum* 2 (November 1956), p. 74. The allusion to "Raynal's picture" is explained in this manner by Kahnweiler: "This concerned one of Picasso's pictures (from the year 1917) belonging to Maurice Raynal, a picture representing a guitar and painted with the use of sand."

92.　See André Salmon, *La Jeune sculpture française* (Paris: Societé des Trente, 1919), pp. 103–104:

> Some witnesses, already shocked by the things covering the walls, which they refused to call pictures because they were made with oilcloth, packing paper, and newspapers, said while pointing with superiority at the object to which Picasso had devoted the most thought and care:
> 　—What is that? Does that rest on a pedestal? Does that hang on the wall? Is it painting or sculpture?
> 　Picasso, dressed in the blue of Parisian artists, responded in his most beautiful Andalusian voice:
> 　—It's nothing, it's "el guitare!"
> 　And thus the watertight compartments were demolished. We were delivered from painting and sculpture, liberated from the imbecilic tyranny of genres. This is no longer this and that is no longer that. It's nothing, it's "el guitare!"

In his preface, Salmon claims that his book was ready to appear before the war.

93.　For Kahnweiler's theory of writing, which postulates a double origin of languages (pictographic from painting; alphabetic from mnemonotechnical signs), see *Gris*, pp. 35–46. Kahnweiler's conceptions, and the works to which he referred, have been made obsolete by more recent research. See I.J. Gelb, *A Study of Writing: The Foundation of Grammatology* (Chicago: University of Chicago, 1952), passim.

94.　See Kahnweiler, *Der Gegenstand der Aesthetik,* chap. 14, pp. 54–55.

95.　Ibid., chap. 3, p. 26. I quote Orde Levinson's translation here. Kant explicitly rejects "associations" in the formation of the judgment of taste; *Critique of Judgment,* tr. J.H. Bernard (New York: Hafner, 1951), pp. 77ff., but his point of view is not so removed from Kahnweiler's when he announces several times, as Michael Podro has noted, that aesthetic satisfaction can elude us on the one hand when we are confronted by too familiar objects and on the other hand when we are not familiar enough with the elements that we need to arrange, nor practiced enough in the unification of these elements; see Podro, *The Manifold in Perception* (Oxford: Clarendon Press, 1972), pp. 19–21.

96. Daniel-Henry Kahnweiler, "Le Véritable Béarnais" (1947), rpt. in *Confessions esthétiques*, p. 118.

97. Kahnweiler, *Gris*, p. 40.

98. Daniel-Henry Kahnweiler, "Le Sujet chez Picasso" (1951), rpt. in *Confessions esthétiques*, p. 131.

99. Daix, *Picasso: The Cubist Years*, p. 293, no. 542. On Picasso and Mallarmé, see Ronald Johnson's article, which records the occurrences of these references in his cubist work, "Picasso's Musical and Mallarméan Constructions," *Arts Magazine* 51, no. 7 (March 1977), pp. 122–127. On Mallarmé and cubism in general, see Laude, *La Peinture française*, p. 351; and Christopher Green, "Purity, Poetry and the Painting of Juan Gris," *Art History* 5 (June 1982), p. 182 and passim.

100. Apart from the text titled "Mallarmé et la peinture"(1948), rpt. in *Confessions esthétiques* (214–221), Kahnweiler insisted on the relation in his book on Juan Gris. See particularly *Gris*, pp. 90–91 and 130, as well as p. 46, note 1, on Apollinaire.

101. "Two days before, he had reproached me violently because I was attacking abstract art"; Daniel-Henry Kahnweiler, "Entretiens avec Picasso au sujet des Femmes d'Alger," *Aujourd'hui* 4 (September 1955), p. 12. See, for example, in *Juan Gris,* his attack against Mondrian. "Mondrian's so-called paintings are unfinished because there is no means of finishing them; they are not paintings, that is to say, writing. They never get beyond the preliminary stage, so they are a kind of decoration" (p. 118). For a critique of the notion of reading in Kahnweiler's work, see Spies, "Vendre des tableaux," pp. 40–41.

102. Cited by Laude, preface to de Romilly, *Braque, le cubisme,* p. 53. See also Gino Severini, "Symbolisme plastique et symbolisme littéraire," *Mercure de France,* February 1, 1916, pp. 466–476, which averts the traditional parallel between Mallarmé and impressionism in order to compare the "partitioning of ideas" of the poet with the "partitioning of form" of Braque and Picasso (esp. pp. 468–469); and Yakov Tugendhold's essay on the Picassos of the Shchukin collection (in McCully, *A Picasso Anthology,* p. 109). Tugendhold was an extremely francophile symbolist art critic (the essay appeared in *Apollon,* one of the main organs of the Russian symbolist movement), whose firsthand knowledge of Mallarmé's poetics far surpassed that of Severini. In his comparison between the poet's and Picasso's enterprises, he first posits a difference ("The guitar does not suggest to [Picasso] any sentimental or human analogy as it did to Mallarmé," a statement quite at odds with the recent anthropomorphic readings of Picasso's guitars alluded to above); then he stresses their common love for the vernacular, the raw material, as a contrasting means in a composition; finally, he insists on their "don quixotism." The parallel between Mallarmé's endeavor and Picasso's is also evoked by the French poet Pierre Reverdy. Unfortunately, the polemical nature of his text diminishes somewhat its implications: refuting the idea that modern poetry stems from painting, he insists on the fact that "when Picasso showed his first audacities, their works [those of Mallarmé and Rimbaud], *their spirit,* was in the mind of all." Immediately follows a passage where the cubist enterprise is identified with what poetry "had always been," which closes abruptly the issue ("Le cubisme, poésie plastique," *L'Art,* February 1919, rpt. in Pierre Reverdy, *Nord-Sud, Self-Defense et autres écrits sur l'art et la poésie* [Paris: Flammarion, 1975], p. 144).

103. Stéphane Mallarmé, *Oeuvres complètes* (Paris: Gallimard, 1945), p. 400:

> Evoquer, dans une ombre exprès, l'objet tu, par des mots allusifs, jamais directs, se réduisant à du silence égal, comporte tentative proche de créer: vraisemblable dans la limite de l'idée uniquement mise en jeu par l'enchanteur de lettres jusqu'à ce que, certes, scintille, quelque illusion égale au regard. Le vers, trait incantatoire! et on ne déniera au cercle que perpétuellement ferme, ouvre la rime une similitude avec les ronds, parmi l'herbe, de la fée ou du magicien.

The De Stijl Idea

1.   Theo van Doesburg, "Algemeene Inleiding," *De Stijl,* "Jubilee Number" (vol. 7, no. 79/84, 1927, pp. 2–9); English tr. by R.R. Symonds in H.L.C. Jaffé, *De Stijl* (London: Thames and Hudson, 1970), pp. 218–225.

2.   The chart recapitulating the "Principieele medewerkers aan De Stijl" was published in the "Jubilee number," pp. 59–62; cf. also Jaffé, *De Stijl,* pp. 224–225. In its original publication in *De Stijl,* the last column of the chart, following the one listing Brancusi for the years 1925–27, was empty so as to emphasize the availability of *De Stijl*'s columns to yet other members of the European avant-garde; this last column has been deleted in Jaffé.

3.   On the additive mode of minimalism, cf. Rosalind Krauss, *Passages in Modern Sculpture* (New York: Viking, 1977), pp. 243 ff., and "Lewitt in Progress" (1977), in *The Originality of the Avant-Garde and Other Modernist Myths* (Cambridge: MIT Press, 1985), pp. 245–258.

4.   Two other examples, both among the rare De Stijl realizations in the realm of "applied art," are Theo van Doesburg's 1917 stained-glass window triptych *Composition IV* (now in the collection of the Dienst Verspreide Rijkskollecties in The Hague, but initially in the stairwell of Wils's Haus Lange in Alkmaar), and his tile composition above the main entrance on the façade of Oud's *De Vonk Vacantiehuis* in Noordwijkerhout (1917–18, still in place). As for Mondrian, *Evolution* (1911) was once believed to be his only triptych; however, Joop Joosten has recently discovered a photograph indicating that *Composition in Color A, Composition in Color B,* and *Composition with Black Lines,* the first major paintings of 1917 (Rijksmuseum Kröller-Müller), were once symmetrically exhibited as a triptych (cf. Joop Joosten, "Painting and Sculpture in the Context of De Stijl," in *De Stijl, 1917– 1931: Visions of Utopia,* ed. Mildred Friedman [Minneapolis: Walker Art Center, 1982], p. 59).

5.   In the last issue of *De Stijl* ("Dernier numéro," January 1932, p. 48); English tr. by Martin James and Harry Holtzman, *The New Art—The New Life: The Collected Writings of Piet Mondrian* (Boston: G.K. Hall, 1986), p. 183.

6.   Cf. Joop Joosten, "Abstraction and Compositional Innovation," *Artforum* 11, no. 8 (April 1973), pp. 55–59, and Yve-Alain Bois, "Du projet au procès," in *L'Atelier de Mondrian,* ed. Bois (Paris: Macula, 1982), pp. 26–43.

7.   At the time of the first publication of this essay, Sjarel Ex discovered photographs of a few modular grids by Huszar, dating from the end of 1918, one of them particularly close to Mondrian's so-called *Checkerboard Composition in Dark Colors* and *in Light Colors,* dated slightly later. Ex quotes a letter from Mondrian to van Doesburg speaking of his surprise at Huszar's arrival at the same solution as his. Unlike Mondrian, however, Huszar was not able to integrate what he had learned from the grid in his later practice and soon returned to a strong hierarchization of the figure as opposed to the ground. Ironically, it is a grid painting of Huszar rather than by Mondrian that van Doesburg chose to discuss in *De Stijl,* pointing to the way in which, although perfectly modular, it exhibited a "constant changing of position and dimension," thus contrasting with the simple plaid composition to which it is compared ("Over het zien van de nieuwe schilderkunst" [On Looking at New Painting], *De Stijl* 2, no. 4 [February 1919], pp. 42–44; English tr. in Jaffé, *De Stijl,* pp. 127–130. Until Ex's discovery, Huszar's only published grid, now lost, was thought to be either a unicum in his pictorial production or a sketch for a stained-glass window; furthermore, it was supposed to derive from Mondrian's grid canvases. Cf. Sjarel Ex, "Vilmos Huszar," in Carel Blotkamp, ed., *De beginjaren van De Stijl 1917–1922* (Utrecht: Reflex, 1982); English tr. Charlotte and Arthur Loeb as *De Stijl: The Formative Years* (Cambridge: MIT Press, 1986); see especially pp. 97–102.

8.   Cf. Theo van Doesburg, "Van Natuur tot Kompositie" [From Nature to Composition], *De Hollandsche Revue* 24 (1919), pp. 470–476. The transformation of the "young woman" into a modular grid proceeded in eight stages. One cannot refrain from thinking that this is a *post factum* reconstruction and that, starting from the grid, van Doesburg gradually distorted its geometrical network to obtain the figurative "point of departure."

9.   At first sight, Vantongerloo seems to be in the same category as van Doesburg, claiming that his paintings and sculptures were the geometric result of algebraic operations. But I believe that

the "scientificity" of Vantongerloo's work was pure fantasy. The equations with which he titled his works have no perceptible relation to their formal configurations. As opposed to van Doesburg's arithmetic schemes, which were relatively simple, Vantongerloo's were much too complex to be effective (supposing that there is some basis for his claims). We certainly can view his works without taking these schemes into account. In fact, it is precisely this ineffectiveness that leads me to include Vantongerloo's work (at least his sculpture) as partaking of the "De Stijl idea."

10. Cf. Gerrit Rietveld, "Mondrian en het nieuwe bouwen," *Bouwkundig Weekblad,* March 15, 1955, p. 128. For him, stained glass was an *applied* art, an ornament added in the interstices of architecture, and by its very nature violated De Stijl's demands for elementarization and integration. In this article Rietveld confirms that he never met Mondrian, which casts some light on the power of van Doesburg as a link between the dispersed members of the movement.

11. Bart van der Leck, "Over schilderen en bouwen," *De Stijl* 1, no. 4 (March 1918), p. 37. See also van der Leck's "De nieuwe beelding in de schilderkunst," *De Stijl* 1, no. 1 (October 1917), pp. 6–7, and in the same issue J.J.P. Oud, "Het monumentale stadsbeeld," pp. 10–11. Those last two texts are translated into English in Jaffé, *De Stijl,* pp. 93–96. For a detailed account of the position of Mondrian during the early years of De Stijl, cf. Yve-Alain Bois, "Mondrian and the Theory of Architecture," *Assemblage,* no. 4 (October 1987), pp. 103–130.

12. For an exemplary study of this collaboration, as well as of the whole issue of De Stijl's abstract interior, cf. Nancy Troy, *The De Stijl Environment* (Cambridge, Mass.: MIT Press, 1983), passim.

13. Even the factory project, the one Mondrian preferred in Oud's oeuvre (though we should rather say the one he disliked the least) bears those very characteristics that cast it aside from the De Stijl canon (the symmetry of the massive art deco entrance; the serial repetition of the windows). And despite appearances, the 1923 small "semipermanent house"—Oud's most elegant building— and his 1925 *Café De Unie* are absolutely foreign to the principle of De Stijl: the first is entirely symmetrical (a fact concealed by the photographs published at the time); the second, entirely based on a modular repetition.

14. Cf. van Doesburg, "Aanteekeningen over monumentale kunst" [Notes on Monumental Art], *De Stijl* 2, no. 1 (November 1918), pp. 10–12 (English tr. in Jaffé, *De Stijl,* pp. 99–103.

15. For a full discussion of the Rosenberg exhibition, cf. Nancy Troy, *The De Stijl Environment,* pp. 75–81 and 97–121, and Yve-Alain Bois and Nancy Troy, "De Stijl et l'architecture à Paris," in *De Stijl et l'architecture en France,"* ed. Bois and Reichlin (Brussels: Mardaga, 1985), pp. 25–90 (especially pp. 36–51). This publication is the catalogue of an exhibition bearing the same title (held at the Institut Français d'Architecture, Paris, November-December 1985), for which I reconstituted, with the help of Nancy Troy, the 1923 show in its entirety.

16. Theo van Doesburg, "Dada en Feiten," *De Stijl,* "Jubilee Number" (1927), p. 56.

17. Artists have best understood the antifunctionalist nature of Rietveld's furniture. Thus I owe a great deal to the French painter Christian Bonnefoi's article "L'Inversion de la lisibility," in Hubert Damisch, ed., *Modern'Signe* (Paris: Corda, 1977), vol. 2, pp. 183–263, and to the American sculptor Scott Burton, who proposes a similar interpretation in his "Furniture Journal: Rietveld," *Art in America,* November 1980, pp. 102–108.

18. Gerrit Rietveld, "View of life as a historical background for my work" (1957), English tr. in Theodore M. Brown, *The Work of Gerrit Rietveld* (Utrecht: Bruna and Zoon, 1958), p. 162.

19. Cf. Charles Baudelaire, "La morale du joujou" (1853), in *Oeuvres Complètes,* ed. Y.-G. Le Dantec (Paris: Gallimard, 1961), p. 525.

20. It is not known if the photograph was made early (published at the instigation of Rietveld himself), although it would be in keeping with Rietveld's insistence on elementarization and (in this case through the standard sizes of all the wood) on the possibility of mass production. This photograph is reproduced in Daniele Baroni, *Gerrit Thomas Rietveld Furniture* (London: Academy Editions, 1978), p. 51.

Strzemiński and Kobro: In Search of Motivation

References to essays by Strzemiński and Kobro are given to their Western publication (either French or English). However, every quotation has been checked with the original Polish by Lilianna Sekula, which accounts for some modifications. I would also like to thank Mary-Alice Lee for her help in preparing the English version of this essay.

1. Frank Stella, quoted in Bruce Glaser, "Questions to Stella and Judd" (1966), in G. Battcock, ed., *Minimal Art* (New York: Dutton, 1968), p. 149.

2. The 1976 American tour of "Constructivism in Poland" (an exhibition initially organized in 1973 by the Folkwang Museum in Essen, Germany, and the Kröller-Müller Museum in Otterlo, Holland, jointly with the Museum Sztuki, Łodz, Poland, which holds most of the surviving works of Strzemiński and Kobro) was almost unnoticed. Its catalogue (hereafter cited as *CP*), which was available in English as early as 1973, still provides the best visual documentation of Strzemiński's and Kobro's work, and contains a vast anthology of their writings; its short but excellent critical texts are the work of Polish scholars. As far as I know, the short article Kate Linker wrote about Kobro is the only direct offspring of this exhibition in the American literature ("Katarzyna Kobro: Art/Architecture," *Arts Magazine,* October 1976, pp. 92–93), later followed by Merle Schipper's more generous account ("Katarzyna Kobro," *Women's Art Journal* 1, no. 2 [Fall 1980-Winter 1981], pp. 19–24). To that must be added Margit Rowell's short but excellent treatment of Kobro's work in the preface to the catalogue of the exhibition she organized at the Guggenheim Museum (*The Planar Dimension 1912–1932: From Surface to Space,* pp. 30–31); the mention of the "Kobro case" in Albert Elsen's overview of modern sculpture (*Modern European Sculpture 1918–1945: Unknown Beings and Other Realities* [New York: Braziller, 1979]); and Marcia Hafif's pious wish that we return to Strzemiński's principles ("Beginning Again," *Artforum,* September 1978, pp. 34–40). Not an impressive record. With one exception, the French situation is not much better: my own publication, in the first issue of *Macula* (1976, pp. 14–27), of a translation by Pierre-Maxime Jedryka of Strzemiński's brilliant text, "Unism in Painting," did not initiate a critical wave. The section concerning Polish constructivism in the exhibition catalogue *Présences polonaises* (Paris: Centre Georges Pompidou, 1983) consists of new and badly translated versions of the 1973 catalogue essays by Polish scholars. The recent article by Xavier Deryng, "Le 'Tableau absolu,' mythe des années 20: L'unisme de Strzeminski" (in *Les Abstractions I: La diffusion des abstractions, Hommage à Jean Laude,* ed. Louis Roux [Saint Etienne: CIEREC, Université de Saint Etienne, 1986], pp. 95–104), is utterly derivative. The exception I mentioned above is Andrei Nakov's book, *Abstrait/concret,* which appeared in 1981 (Paris, Transédition), and which I had unfortunately not read when the present essay first appeared. Although it only partly concerns the Polish avant-garde (most of the book being devoted to the Russian one), it provides some very useful information on Strzemiński's and Kobro's beginnings in Russia, and gives a convincing interpretation of Strzemiński's essentialism as a dialectical result of his polemics with Mieczysław Szczuka, who was competing with him for the leading position of the modern movement in Poland, and whose position could be called "productivist." The arrival in France, after the military coup of 1982, of one of the experts on Polish constructivism, Andrzej Turowski, might elicit a new interest in the matter (Turowski's masterly book on the subject, *Konstruktywizm polski* [Łodz, 1981], still awaits translation into a western language, although a book by the same author appeared recently with a chapter devoted to Strzemiński and Kobro: *Existe-t-il un art de l'Europe de l'Est* [Paris: Editions de la Villette, 1986]. Outside France and the U.S., a few publications must be taken into account. The most important is the catalogue of the Strzemiński exhibition at the Städtische Kunsthalle in Düsseldorf (March-April 1980), with an introduction by Turowski and the German translation of some of Strzemiński's texts. In 1985 Kettle's Yard Gallery (Cambridge, England) organized an exhibition entitled *Constructivism in Poland 1923 to 1936,* in conjunction with the Museum Sztuki in Łodz. Its small catalogue, again mostly due to Polish scholars (Stanisławski and Zagrodski), contains an anthology of texts, among them a text by Strzemiński and another by Kobro that had not hitherto been translated into English.

Two major Polish publications have recently enhanced our knowledge of the work of Strzemiński and Kobro. *Władysław Strzemiński—in memoriam,* ed. Janusz Zagrodzki (Ł odz: Sztuka Polska, 1988), is an anthology of texts by Strzemiński, memoirs, documents, and critical essays by Polish and western scholars (including a Polish translation of the present text). *Katarzyna Kobro—i kompozycja przestrzeni,* also by Zagrodzki (Warsaw: Państwowe Wydawnictwo Naukowe, 1984), is the first monograph devoted to the artist. Both books reproduce a quantity of documents and works hitherto unpublished, and both confirm, sad as it might seem, that the unist period marked the apogee of Strzemiński's and Kobro's production.

Finally, I would like to thank Pierre-Maxime Jedryka for having shared with me his knowledge of the art and theory of Strzemiński and Kobro. His master's thesis at the Ecole des Hautes Etudes en Sciences Sociales, completed in 1975, reinforced my conviction about their work, which had originated with the 1973 show.

While this book was in galleys, I came across another western publication and a dissertation. The first is *Tre Pionérer For Polsk Avant-Garde,* the catalogue of an exhibition held at the Fyns Kunstmuseum, Odense, Denmark, in 1985; it contains translations of texts hitherto unpublished in English, by Strzemiński and Kobro and by Henryk Stażewski, the third musketeer of the Polish avant-garde to whom this exhibition was also dedicated; another feature of this catalogue is a very useful essay of Lise-Lotte Blom on the Russian beginnings of Strzemiński and his relationship to cubism. As for Ursula Grzechca-Mohr's dissertation, *Kobro (Katarzyna Kobro-Strzemińska) und die konstruktivische Bewegung* (Münster, Kunsthistorischen Institut der Universität, 1986), I very much regret that I found it too late to be able to discuss it here.

3.   *L'Espace uniste,* ed. and tr. Antoine Baudin and Pierre-Maxime Jedryka (Lausanne: L'Age d'Homme, 1977). Henceforth cited as *EU.*

4.   There was always some confusion about the notion of "modernism," owing to the stiffening of the position of Greenberg, who confiscated the word during the '50s. One must distinguish between modernist theory in the narrow sense, the only one to actually take up the word—that is, Greenberg's and his followers' (a theory that in the end accepted only a few artists in the modernist pantheon)—and the modernist theory in the broad sense, which evaluates and isolates in modern art from impressionism onward its capacity of reflexivity and autodefinition. One must thus distinguish between the opposition to modernism in the narrow sense, minimalism's opposition in the '60s, for example (minimalist artists wanted to broaden the possibilities of artistic reflexivity that were defined in a too restricted way by Greenberg), and the current rejection of modernism in the broad sense, often grounded on a strict refusal of reflexivity as such.

5.   "The farther a society pushes the division of activities, the higher a level of culture it attains. It is then a question of conferring on art tasks appropriate to it. The romantic conception of art as a magical art implied the reunion of several arts while in fact it was subordinating them all to a literary thematics and didactics." Strzemiński, "Modern Art in Poland" (1934), in *EU,* pp. 139–140.

6.   Strzemiński, "a.r.2" (1932), in *EU,* p. 129.

7.   Strzemiński, "B = 2; to read" (1924), in *CP,* pp. 82–83.

8.   Cf. the remarkable text by Strzemiński, entitled "Functional Printing," in *CP,* pp. 111–113. Strzemiński, who was one of the masters of modern typography, took the question of medium specificity seriously: typography requires the greatest contrasts to fulfill its function, that is, the greater readability of a text (thus is necessarily "anti-unist," as he said in his discussion with Chwistek in 1934: cf. *EU,* p. 157). Starting from this idea, radically opposed to the Bauhaus notion of economy, Strzemiński realized a series of typographical compositions based on the poems of his friend Julian Przyboś. On Strzemiński as a typographer, cf. the catalogue of the exhibition "*Druk funkcjonalny*" by J. Zagrodzki (Ł odz: Museum Sztuki, 1975).

9.   Strzemiński, "Discussion" (with L. Chwistek, held in 1934, published in 1935), *EU,* p. 161 (tr. slightly modified).

10.   Strzemiński, "What Can Legitimately Be Called New Art" (1924), in *EU,* p. 57.

11.   Strzemiński, "Discussion," *EU,* p. 161.

12.   Strzemiński, "Aspects of Reality" (1936), *EU,* p. 177.

13.   Clement Greenberg, "Modernist Painting" (1961), rpt. in Gregory Battcock, ed., *The New Art: A Critical Anthology* (New York: Dutton, 1973), p. 110.

14.   Strzemiński: "The fatal attraction of the baroque is so strong that, reasoning in baroque terms, we are unaware of the fact, and we believe that we are free from this way of thinking," "Unism in Painting" (1927–28), in *CP,* p. 92 (tr. slightly modified).

15.   Ibid., p. 95.

16.   Strzemiński, "Modern Art in Poland," *EU,* p. 139.

17.   Strzemiński, "B = 2; to read," *CP,* p. 80.

18.   Ibid., p. 83 (tr. slightly modified).

19.   Strzemiński, "Modern Art in Poland," *EU,* p. 143 (tr. slightly modified).

20.   Ibid., p. 136.

21.   Strzemiński, "Aspects of Reality," *EU,* p. 178.

22.   Katarzyna Kobro, "Functionalism" (1936), in *CP,* p. 119 (tr. slightly modified).

23.   Strzemiński, "Modern Art in Poland," *EU,* p. 146 (tr. slightly modified).

24.   Ibid., p. 143.

25.   El Lissitzky, "New Russian Art," in Sophie Lissitzky-Küppers, *El Lissitzky: Life, Letters, Texts* (London: Thames and Hudson, 1968), pp. 330–340.

26.   Strzemiński, "Notes on Russian Art" (1922), in *EU,* pp. 50–51. Strzemiński seems at first totally unfair with regard to Rodchenko and Stepanova, especially since their achievement in the field of sculpture and of "design" respectively is not to be discarded that easily. On the contrary, I would hold that some of Rodchenko's sculptures are major objects in the production of this century. But elsewhere in the text Strzemiński praises the Obmokhu group, with whom Rodchenko was closely associated, and credits it for having raised the level of contemporary sculpture to that of modern painting ("the only nice consequence, albeit unpremeditated, of the autohypnosis of productivism"). Strzemiński left Russia in 1922, before Stepanova's first textile designs were known, and it is not certain that he would have reacted negatively to them. At any rate, as the rest of the text makes clear, it is the *pictorial* production of Rodchenko and Stepanova that he is dismissing here, and as far as I am concerned with a perfect right (with the exception of a handful of works, such as his triptych of monochromes signaling his farewell to painting [1921], Rodchenko's pictures are mediocre; Stepanova's are no better).

27.   "Expressionism may be defined as that trend that expresses feelings of a literary character (above all the feeling of confusion to which a mechanical world gives rise), using techniques that belong to every artistic movement of the past (including cubism and futurism). It is, if you will, an applied art (exploitation of the formal accomplishment of others)." Ibid., p. 42.

28.   Strzemiński, "Our Visual Potential" (1934), quoted by Antoine Baudin in his introduction to *EU,* "Avant-garde et constructivisme polonais entre les deux guerres: quelques points d'histoire," p. 28.

29.   The abrupt and apparently definitive halt to Kobro's career is usually attributed to the birth of a daughter, then to the war and the Nazi persecutions (the Nazis destroyed practically all of her sculptures), then to the postwar depression and Stalinist persecutions (Kobro died of illness in 1951, one year before Strzemiński). It is obvious that all these factors are relevant. I simply do not believe that they explain everything.

30.   On this issue, cf. in this volume the essays "Painting: The Task of Mourning," and "Ryman's Tact."

31.   Strzemiński, "Discussion," *EU,* p. 156.

32.   Strzemiński, "Aspects of Reality," *EU,* pp. 180–181. Antoine Baudin makes the connection with Arp in his introduction to the text, ibid., p. 181.

33.   Cf. Strzemiński, "Notes on Russian Art," *EU,* pp. 47–49.

34.   Strzemiński, "Modern Art in Poland," *EU,* p. 149.

35.   Strzemiński, "a.r.2," *EU,* p. 130.

36. Ibid., p. 129.

37. Strzemiński and Kobro, "Composition of Space, Calculations of Spatio-Temporal Rhythm" (1931), in *EU*, pp. 111–112.

38. Ibid., p. 112.

39. Strzemiński, "Discussion," *EU*, p. 160.

40. Strzemiński, "The Principles of New Architecture" (1931), in *CP*, p. 39. Quoting the last sentence of this passage, Baudin notes that it refers to a polemic between Strzemiński and the architect Szymon Syrkus, a polemic that would end with Strzemiński's break with the group *Praesens*, of which he was a most active member: during the preliminary work for the "Universal National Exhibition" of 1929, in Poznan, Strzemiński accused Syrkus of having plagiarized a sculpture by Kobro for his Fertilizer Pavilion, and of having "reduced its spatiality to a vulgar decorativism by filling the metallic skeleton" (cf. Baudin, "Avant-garde et constructivisme polonais," p. 22 and note 43).

41. Kobro, "Functionalism," *CP*, pp. 119–120.

42. Rietveld wrote, for example: "If, for a particular purpose, we separate, limit and bring into a human scale a part of the unlimited space, it is (if all goes well) a piece of space brought to life as reality. In this way, a special segment of space has been absorbed into our human system." ("View of Life as Background for My Work" [1957], English tr. in Theodore M. Brown, *The Work of G. Rietveld, Architect* [Utrecht: A. W. Bruna, 1958], p. 162; also quoted above in "The De Stijl Idea," where I insist upon De Stijl's antifunctionalism.) Rietveld's architectural theory is very similar to that of Kobro and Strzemiński.

43. On this issue, cf. my article, "A Picturesque Stroll around *Clara-Clara*," *October*, no. 29 (Summer 1984).

44. Strzemiński, "Modern Art in Poland," *EU*, p. 137.

45. Strzemiński, "a.r.2," *EU*, p. 130.

46. Strzemiński, "What Can Legitimately Be Called New Art," *EU*, p. 58.

47. Strzemiński, "Unism in Painting," *CP*, p. 92.

48. Strzemiński, "Modern Art in Poland," *EU*, p. 145.

49. Strzemiński, "What Can Legitimately Be Called New Art," *EU*, p. 57.

50. Strzemiński, "B = 2; to read," *CP*, p. 62 (tr. slightly modified).

51. Strzemiński, "Unism in Painting," *CP*, p. 91.

52. Cf. Michael Baxandall, *Giotto and the Orators* (Oxford University Press, 1971), particularly the third part, "Alberti and the Humanists: Composition."

53. Strzemiński, "Unism in Painting," *CP*, p. 91 (tr. slightly modified). Yves Klein's concept of the monochrome was based on the same antidialectic, antidualistic, antitheatrical premises: "Why not two colors in the same painting? Well, because I refuse to provide a spectacle in my painting. I refuse to compare and to put in play, so that some stronger elements will emerge in contrast to other, weaker ones. Even the most civilized representation is based on an idea of "struggle" between different forces, and the reader [*sic*] is confronted by an execution [*mise à mort*] in a painting, by a morbid drama by definition, be it a drama of love or hate." ("The Monochrome Adventure," unfinished manuscript, Part I, in *Yves Klein* [Paris: Centre Georges Pompidou, 1983], p. 172. The English translation of this text in the American version of this exhibition catalogue [Houston: Institute for the Arts, Rice University, 1982], p. 220, is too faulty to be of any use.) A similar tendency toward the rejection of all contrasts is at the base of Ad Reinhardt's art and theory, although his *Black Paintings* make clear that he never accepted the idea of a plain monochrome. His idea of "oneness" or "nonduality" is quite similar to that of Strzemiński, and the litany of negations that constitute his "Twelve Technical Rules" could almost have been signed by the theoretician of unism. (Obviously the Polish painter would not have subscribed to a dictum such as "no texture" or "no size," but slogans from "no brushwork" to "no chess-playing," through others such as "no sketching," "no form," "no design," "no color," "no time," and "no movement," would have met his approval. Cf. *Art as Art: The Selected Writings of Ad Reinhardt*, ed. Barbara Rose [New York: Viking, 1975], pp. 205–207.) Finally, to complete this short comparison between unism and the art of the '50s and '60s, the whole interview of Stella and Judd by Bruce Glaser (mentioned above) should be recalled: both artists insist on the need to "get rid of compositional effects" and of part-to-part relationships (or contrasts).

Judd's diatribe against what he calls ignorantly "the whole European tradition" could very well have been signed by Strzemiński: "All that art is based on systems built beforehand, a priori systems," etc. ("Questions to Stella and Judd," p. 151).

Since unism strove toward the elimination of all contrasts (as signs of "dramatic tensions," hence of "literature"), no art of the past could have been accepted in its pantheon, not to speak about its or our present. But Strzemiński's extremism, there again, provides a striking stylistic analysis of the art of Cézanne as "arch-baroque" (that is: as an art entirely governed by conflicting forces striving toward an equilibrium), an analysis that matches entirely that of Matisse (cf. the essay "Matisse and Arche-drawing" in this volume). The only difference between Strzemiński and Matisse on this point, of course, is that while the latter held Cézanne's energetic conception as a radical break and a model to emulate, the former described it as the climax of a long tradition to be fought.

54.   Strzemiński, "Unism in Painting," *CP,* p. 92.

55.   Ibid.

56.   Ibid., p. 91.

57.   It is well known that Greenberg's first major essay was entitled "Towards a Newer Laocoön" (*Partisan Review* 7 [July–August 1940], pp. 296–310), and Greenberg's debt to Kant is acknowledged in "Modernist Painting." On this issue, as well as the exclusion of temporality, cf. Bois, "A Picturesque Stroll."

58.   Strzemiński, "Unism in Painting," *CP,* p. 95. For entirely different reasons (he was himself a proponent of dynamism), Theo van Doesburg also criticized Mondrian, in 1930, in a notebook that was published posthumously, for the role of composition in his paintings ("the perfect harmony resulting from this pictorial discipline was deeply classical and if one disregards [*fait abstraction des*] the figures, a picture by Ingres or Poussin is identical to one by Mondrian"; *De Stijl,* last issue, 1932, p. 28). Strzemiński's two ideas are justified (Mondrian does not fully reach planarity; his art remains compositional), but they might not be as interrelated as he thought. There is certainly a thrust, in Mondrian's last period, to overcome planarity as such through an investigation of physical thickness: cf. in this volume "Piet Mondrian, *New York City,*" passim.

59.   Strzemiński, "Unism in Painting," *CP,* p. 90.

60.   Strzemiński, "Notes on Russian Art," *EU,* p. 46.

61.   "Because of its linear character, the form detaches itself from the painting and contrasts with the ground"; Strzemiński, "B = 2; to read," *EU,* p. 65. The English translation (*CP,* p. 83) omitted this sentence.

62.   Strzemiński, "Object and Space" (1928), in *EU,* p. 83. This passage was omitted in the English translation, *CP,* pp. 104–105.

63.   Strzemiński, "Unism in Painting," *CP,* p. 94.

64.   As noted by Pierre-Maxime Jedryka in the postface to *EU,* "Ellipses," passim.

65.   Strzemiński, "Discussion," *EU,* p. 156.

66.   Strzemiński, "Unism in Painting," *CP,* p. 94.

67.   Strzemiński and Kobro, "Composition of Space, Calculations of Spatio-Temporal Rhythm," *EU,* p. 123.

68.   Strzemiński, "a.r.2," *EU,* p. 131.

69.   Janusz Zagrodzki analyzed the use of the Fibonacci series, an essential means for the reconstruction of Kobro's works. ("Reconstruction of Katarzyna Kobro's Sculptures," in *CP,* pp. 55–56). It would be a lot easier (but pedantic) to analyze Strzemiński's "architectonic compositions" in the same way.

70.   Strzemiński, "B = 2; to read," *CP,* p. 83.

71.   Strzemiński and Kobro, "Composition of Space," *EU,* p. 86.

72.   Ibid., p. 87.

73.   Ibid., p. 85.

74.   Ibid., p. 97.

75.   Strzemiński, "Modern Art in Poland," *EU*, p. 149. For Krauss's analysis of the "logic of the monument," cf. "Sculpture in the Expanded Field" (1978), in *The Originality of the Avant-Garde and Other Modernist Myths* (Cambridge, Mass.: MIT Press, 1985), pp. 279–280.
76.   Strzemiński and Kobro, "Composition of Space," *EU*, p. 106.
77.   Cf. Rosalind Krauss, *Passages in Modern Sculpture* (New York: Viking, 1977), pp. 56–67. Krauss's vision of constructivism is somewhat partial, for she takes the work of Naum Gabo as the essential model (Rodchenko's wood sculptures of 1921, whose additive structure is very close to that of Carl Andre's minimalist works of the late '50s, could in no way be reduced to the "transparent" diagram of Gabo).
78.   Strzemiński and Kobro, "Composition of Space," *EU*, p. 104.
79.   "A summary analysis of the notion of weight is enough to reveal all the dynamism it contains" (ibid., p. 103).
80.   Ibid., p. 102.
81.   To my knowledge, only one of these early sculptures survives, but the team of Polish scholars working on unism at the Museum Sztuki in Łodz have been able to reconstruct another four from photographs, largely thanks to Kobro's rigorous system of proportions. The first one, not reconstructed, is a dense, quasi-cubist conglomerate of heteroclite objects and materials made in 1920, when Kobro and Strzemiński were living in Russia. The second, *Suspended Sculpture 1* (1921, reconstructed in 1972) looks like the translation into space of a painting by Malevich; the third, *Suspended Sculpture 2* (1921–22, reconstructed in 1971) reflects the esthetics of the Obmokhu group and resembles both a work by Medunetsky in the collection of the Yale University Art Gallery and Rodchenko's hanging sculptures (all works exhibited at the third Obmokhu exhibition in Moscow in May 1921). *Abstract Sculptures 1, 2, and 3* (all from 1924, the first one preserved, the last two reconstructed in 1972) are related to Naum Gabo's "transparent" constructivism, which has been analyzed by Rosalind Krauss (cf. note 77). Kobro's real genius did not appear until 1925, with *Space Sculpture*.
      Three things are worth noting here, concerning the relationship of Kobro's art to the production of the Obmokhu group: (1) In his "Notes on Russian Art," Strzemiński describes this relationship as that of a fellow-wanderer: "Close to them we find the most talented of these young artists, Kobro, whose suprematist sculptures are a phenomenon of European importance. Her works represent a true breakthrough, the conquest of still virginal values; they do not imitate Malevich's work but are parallel to it" (*EU*, p. 50). (2) In their "Composition of Space," Strzemiński and Kobro reproduce a work by Medunetsky (ill. 15). The work, now lost, is visible on one of the two photographs of the Obmokhu show just mentioned (cf. Christina Lodder, *Russian Constructivism* [New Haven: Yale University Press, 1983], p. 66; Lodder labeled this work *a* on the photograph). (3) The elements combined in the sculpture just mentioned, *Suspended Sculpture 2*, are in fact tools, as if Kobro's only answer to the productivist position advocated at the time (but not yet put into practice) by some members of the Obmokhu group was an esthetization of labor.
      Despite the obvious ties of Kobro with this group, one should not overestimate its impact on her work and imagine her a follower: she seems rather to have been open to the various trends of the Russian avant-garde, without any dogmatism. This explains, for example, why Strzemiński calls her work suprematist (before Kobro left Russia with Strzemiński, in 1922, she had been a member of the Smolensk branch of Unovis, the organization founded by Malevich), but according to Zagrodzki, she might also have studied with Tatlin at the Moscow Free State Artistic Studio in 1919 (*Katarzyna Kobro—i kompozycja przestrzeni*, p. 31).
82.   Strzemiński and Kobro, "Composition in Space," *EU*, p. 105.
83.   Ibid., p. 104.
84.   Ibid., p. 87.
85.   Ibid., p. 109.
86.   Ibid., pp. 107–108.
87.   Ibid., p. 115.
88.   Cf. Rosalind Krauss, *Passages in Modern Sculpture*, pp. 147–173.

89.   Strzemiński, "B = 2; to read," *CP*, p. 81. Of course, Strzemiński could not have read Husserl: I am just underlining a striking similarity.

90.   The most characteristic formulation of this type of naturalism is to be found in Jean Arp's rejection of the label "abstract art": "We don't want to copy nature. We don't want to reproduce, we want to produce. We want to produce like a plant produces a fruit, and not reproduce. We want to produce directly and not by way of any intermediary. Since this art doesn't have the slightest trace of abstraction, we name it: concrete art" ("Concrete Art" [1944], in *Arp on Arp*, ed. Marcel Jean, English tr. Joachim Neugroschel [New York: Viking, 1972], p. 139). The same idea is expressed virtually in the same terms by almost all the abstract artists of the first modernist wave, and I have quoted above Strzemiński's longing for "picture as organic as nature" ("Unism in Painting," *CP*, p. 92). However, five years later, answering a questionnaire sent by the French little magazine *Abstraction-Création* (no. 2, 1933), he and Kobro stressed the difference between artistic work and natural production. One of the questions was: "What do you think about the influence of trees on your work?" Kobro answered: "A tree possesses an inexact form, given by chance. Since I strive toward the concrete, trees have no influence whatsoever on my work" (p. 27). Strzemiński's reply was more elaborate: "Trees revealed to me what is not a work of art. The form of a tree stems from: (a) symmetry (in the shape and the distribution of leaves). This symmetry is the result of the cellular division of the plant. A painting does not grow, its cells do not go through the process of division, hence symmetry has no role to play there. (b) The fluid curvature of the shape of the stems and trunk, itself the result of the pressure of the wind, the direction of the sun (of light), and the spray of sap within the plant. These forces are not to be found in a picture, hence its form is different" (p. 40). Those remarks, however, do not weaken the fundamental naturalism of the unist position: they simply mark a growing caution of its advocates toward the natural metaphor, almost at the end of the unist adventure.

91.   Jacques Derrida, *Dissemination*, English tr. Barbara Johnson (Chicago: Chicago University Press, 1981), pp. 205–206.

Piet Mondrian, New York City

This article would not have been possible without the valuable help of the late Charmion von Wiegand and the late Harry Holtzman. Both let me quote from unpublished material in their archives. Finally, I would like to thank Michael Fried for his help with the present version of this article.

1.   Joseph Masheck, "Mondrian the New Yorker," *Artforum* 13 (October 1974), pp. 60–61.

2.   Ibid., p. 62.

3.   See James Johnson Sweeney, "Mondrian, the Dutch and *De Stijl*," *Art News* 50 (Summer 1951), p. 63. Meyer Schapiro made a similar remark, at about the same time, in his courses. (However, his article on Mondrian appeared much later. See "Mondrian," in Schapiro, *Modern Art, 19th and 20th Centuries: Selected Papers* [New York: Braziller, 1978], p. 256.)

4.   When I refer to a number accompanied by "Seuphor," it refers to the "catalogue by group" included in Michel Seuphor's book on the artist. See Seuphor, *Piet Mondrian: sa vie, son oeuvre*, 2d ed. (Paris: Flammarion, 1970).

5.   One of these paintings belongs to Max Bill (Seuphor 301), another was reproduced in *De Stijl* (2 [March 1919], plate 9), and a recently published photo of the third was found in Vilmos Huszar's papers and published by Ankie de Jongh, "Die Stijl," *Museumjournaal* 17 (Dec. 1972), p. 273.

6.   See Sweeney, "An Interview with Mondrian," in the exhibition catalogue *Piet Mondrian* (New York: Museum of Modern Art, 1948). This "interview" was in fact Sweeney's collage of letters Mondrian had sent to him as he was preparing a monograph on the artist. See also Sweeney, "Piet Mondrian," in this same catalogue (p. 13) and, among others, Robert Welsh's article "Landscape into Music—Mondrian's New York Period," *Arts Magazine* 40 (Feb. 1966) and Karin von Maur's "Mondrian and Music," in *Mondrian: Drawings, Watercolours, New York Paintings* (Stuttgart: Staatsgalerie, 1981), pp. 287–311.

7.   In a way, Masheck adopted Sidney Janis's position that *Victory Boogie-Woogie* had been ruined by Mondrian's "last minute" transformations. (See E. A. Carmean, Jr., *Mondrian: The Diamond Compositions* [Washington, D.C.: National Gallery of Art, 1979], p. 63.) Masheck goes so far as to say that this painting is "formidably muddled, so much so that only our knowledge that it was once finished allows us to consider it at all" (Masheck, "Mondrian," p. 65).

8.   The final version of the text of "A New Realism" was first published in Mondrian's *Plastic Art and Pure Plastic Art 1937 and Other Essays, 1941–1943* (New York: Wittenborn, 1945). It was reprinted in *The New Art—The New Life: The Collected Writings of Piet Mondrian*, ed. and tr. Harry Holtzman and Martin S. James (Boston: G. K. Hall, 1986), pp. 345–350; further references to this essay, abbreviated "NR," will be included in the text. Also see Virginia Rembert, "Mondrian, America, and American Painting" (Ph.D. diss., Columbia University, 1970), pp. 60–62 and p. 107 notes 44, 45.

9.   See Mondrian, "De Nieuwe Beelding in de Schilderkunst," *De Stijl* 1 (Feb. 1918), p. 44 and note 2; translated in Mondrian, *The New Art*, p. 39 and n. j. See also Mondrian, "De Nieuwe Beelding in de Schilderkunst," *De Stijl* 1 (Aug. 1918), p. 124, note 5; translated in Mondrian, *The New Art*, p. 57 n.j. I would like to thank Kathy Stein for her help with philological details.

10.   See Mondrian, "De Jazz et de Neo Plastic," *i 10—Internationale Revue* 1 (Dec. 1927), pp. 421–427; translated in Mondrian, *The New Art*, pp. 217–222.

11.   Concerning repose, which henceforth has a negative connotation, see Mondrian, "L'Art Réaliste et l'art superréaliste: La Morphoplastique et la néoplastique," *Cercle et carré*, no. 2 (April 15, 1930), no pagination. ("Equilibrium through equivalence excludes similarity and symmetry, just as it excludes repose in the sense of immobility." Translated in Mondrian, *The New Art*, p. 229.) The notion of dynamic equilibrium appeared in Mondrian's "Vraie valeur des oppositions," written in 1934 but first published in a Dutch translation in 1939. The original French text was published in *Cahiers d'Art* 22 (1947), pp. 105–108; translated in Mondrian, *The New Art*, pp. 283–285.

12.   "It is a great mistake to think that Neo-Plastic constructs rectangular planes set side by side—like paving stones. The rectangular plane should be seen rather as the result of a plurality of straight lines in rectangular opposition. In painting the straight line is certainly the most precise and appropriate means to express free rhythm." Mondrian, "L'Art réaliste et l'art superréaliste"; translated in Mondrian, *The New Art*, p. 231.

13.   Mondrian, "De l'art abstrait," *Cahiers d'Art* 6 (Jan. 1931), p. 43; translated in Mondrian, *The New Art*, p. 240. Tériade had attacked neoplasticism in "Hygiène artistique," *L'Intransigeant*, March 11, 1930. Mondrian had composed a response that the journal refused to publish. It appeared instead in *Cahiers d'Art*, minus its polemical section and any reference to Tériade's article. The complete, original version is translated in Mondrian, *The New Art*, under the title "Cubism and Neo-Plastic," pp. 236–261.

14.   For an analysis of Mondrian and the function of lines and their multiplication in his work during the thirties, see Welsh, "The Place of *Composition 12 with Small Blue Square* in the Art of Piet Mondrian," *Bulletin of the National Gallery of Canada*, no. 29 (1977), pp. 21–26.

15.   See Rembert, "Mondrian," pp. 144–145, note 22.

16.   I am summarizing pp. 346–348 of Mondrian, "A New Realism," *The New Art*.

17.   Mondrian, "Toward the True Vision of Reality," *The New Art*, p. 341; further references to this essay, abbreviated "T," will be included in the text.

18.   Welsh, "Landscape into Music," p. 35.

19.   For more information about Mondrian's antigeometry, see my "Du procés au projet" in *L'Atelier de Mondrian*, ed. Bois (Paris: Macula, 1982), p. 35.

20.   Hubert Damisch, "La Peinture est un vrai trois," *Fenêtre jaune cadmium ou les dessous de la peinture* (Paris: Seuil, 1984); see esp. pp. 289–290 and 301. Regarding the problematics of this book, see my review, "Painting as Model," below.

21.   Carl Holty, "Mondrian in New York: A Memoir," *Arts* 31 (Sept. 1957), pp. 20–21.

22.   Regarding a different photo taken by the same photographer—Emery Muscetra—at the same time, on the same spot, and published by Sidney Janis in 1941 (Janis, "School of Paris Comes to U.S.,"

Decision, Nov.–Dec. 1941, p. 89), see Rembert, "Mondrian," p. 102, note 35. The photograph reproduced here offers two advantages relative to the *Decision* photograph: it is clearer, and a larger portion of *New York City* is shown. It was reproduced for the first time in *50 Years of Mondrian* (exhibition catalogue, Sidney Janis Gallery, New York, Nov. 2–30, 1953). Charmion von Wiegand's unpublished diary tells us that after painting the "background" of *New York City* in white (entry for Aug. 1, 1941), Mondrian had begun to paint the yellow lines even before August 13. On September 9, Mondrian told von Wiegand that he had changed the two lower horizontal yellow lines two months earlier without yet having found a solution. On September 16, she remarked that the painting hadn't changed for a week. "I do like it best," Mondrian said. The painting is not mentioned again in the diary, Mondrian busying himself henceforth with reworking his London paintings to prepare for the exhibition at the Valentine Gallery. Perhaps the painting was then in its finished state.

23.   Mondrian insisted on this even in his earliest writings on neoplasticism: it is always a matter of destroying the cross by multiplying it.

24.   Margit Rowell, "Interview with Charmion von Wiegand," *Piet Mondrian, 1872–1944, Centennial Exhibition* (New York: Solomon R. Guggenheim Museum, 1971), p. 81.

25.   See especially Nancy J. Troy, *Mondrian and Neo-Plasticism in America* (New Haven: Yale University Art Gallery, 1979), p. 10.

26.   See Sweeney, "Interview," p. 16, and Sweeney, "Mondrian, the Dutch and *De Stijl*," p. 62.

27.   See Clement Greenberg, "Collage," *Art and Culture: Critical Essays* (Boston: Beacon Press, 1961), pp. 70–83. For a "nonoptical" reading of the cubist collage, see Rosalind Krauss, "In the Name of Picasso," *October*, no. 16 (Spring 1981), pp. 5–12. See also my essay "Kahnweiler's Lesson," above.

28.   This problematic was not yet established in "Towards a Newer Laocoön," published by Greenberg in 1940. Devoting a few lines to sculpture after a lengthy discussion of painting, Greenberg writes:

> Sculpture hovers finally on the verge of "pure" architecture, and painting, having been pushed up from fictive depths, is forced through the surface of the canvas to emerge on the other side in the form of paper, cloth, cement and actual objects of wood and other materials pasted, glued or nailed to what was originally the transparent picture plane, which the painter no longer dares to puncture—or if he does, it is only to dare.

Turning then to artists like Arp, who "escape eventually from the prison of the single plane," he says, "They go . . . from painting to colored bas-relief, and finally—so far must they fly in order to return to three-dimensionality without at the same time risking the illusion—they become sculptors and create objects in the round, through which they can free their feelings for movement and direction from the increasing ascetic geometry of pure painting" (*Partisan Review* 7 [1940], p. 309; rpt. in Greenberg, *Perceptions and Judgments, 1939–44*, vol. 1 of *The Collected Essays and Criticism*, ed. John O'Brien [Chicago: University of Chicago Press, 1986], p. 36). This liberty in relation to the pictorial order that Greenberg then assigned to sculpture was to be denied any significance by all his later writings.

29.   The only previous instance was the 1933 "diamond" painting with yellow lines at the Gemeentemuseum de La Haye (Seuphor 410).

30.   Naum Gabo, "Reminiscences of Mondrian," *Studio International* 172 (Dec. 1966), p. 292.

31.   Greenberg, "Modernist Painting," *Arts Yearbook*, no. 4 (1961), p. 106. See Rembert, "Mondrian," p. 125.

32.   Greenberg, "Art," *The Nation*, Mar. 4, 1944; rpt. in Greenberg, *Perceptions*, pp. 187–189.

33.   Regarding Greenberg's change of heart on the question of literality, see my article "The Sculptural Opaque," *Sub/stance* 31 (1981), pp. 23–48, esp. pp. 41–42.

34.   The other pairs of illustrations are a Bernini and a Calder for "sculptures conceived in terms of painting"; an ancient Greek statue and a sculpture in the round by Picasso for "sculptures that are entirely sculpture"; and a Byzantine mosaic and a synthetic cubist painting by Picasso for "paintings that are entirely painting" (G. L. K. Morris, "Relations of Painting and Sculpture," *Partisan Review* 10 [Jan.–Feb. 1943], illustrations between pp. 64–65).

35.   Ibid., pp. 69–70. We can relate what Morris says about the opposition *sculptural forms inside a painting* and *painting conceived as sculpture* to this idea of Wölfflin's that the more a represented object coincides with the field of the image, the more the painting is tactile, linear; the less it is picturesque, pictorial, the less it necessarily puts "opticality" to work: "Everyone knows that, of the possible aspects of a building, the front view is the least picturesque: here the thing and its appearance fully coincide. But as soon as foreshortening comes in, the appearance separates from the thing, the picture-form becomes different from the object-form, and we speak of a picturesque movement-effect." Wölfflin goes on to associate the picturesque charm with the illusion of movement. (See Heinrich Wölfflin, *Principles of Art History: The Problem of the Development of Style in Later Art*, tr. M. D. Hottinger, 7th ed. [New York: Dover, 1950], p. 25.) The question of total equivalence of the object and its field was "analyzed" in a programmatic manner by Jasper Johns in his series of flags, this equivalence causing painting to become object. If we envision Mondrian's work from the point of view of this tendency to "become object," we can understand the painter's interest in building facades seen head-on (1913–16), and what Mondrian himself had said about his early years. Speaking about his "Naturalist period," he said: "I never painted these things romantically; but from the very beginning, I was always a realist. Even at this time, I disliked particular movement, such as people in action. I enjoyed painting flowers, not bouquets, but a single flower at a time, in order that I might better express its plastic structure" ("T," p. 338). A complete study of the growing frontalization of the motif in Mondrian's work could spring from this point of view.
36.   Mondrian to Albert Roth, Nov. 1, 1931, quoted in Roth, *Begegnung mit Pionieren* (Basel and Stuttgart: Birkhäuser, 1973), p. 164.
37.   The painting in question does not appear in Seuphor's book. Reproduced in color in Ottavio Morisani's *Astrattismo di Piet Mondrian* (Venice: Neri Pozza, 1956), it was at that time in Gates Lloyd's collection in Washington. I am not certain of its dimensions nor of its precise date of composition. (Morisani gives 1939–42 as a date, but Rembert, who thinks it was part of Mondrian's first New York exhibition, dates it at 1939–40 [Rembert, "Mondrian," p. 302].)
38.   Sweeney, "Interview," p. 15.
39.   Mondrian to Jean Gorin, Jan. 31, 1934, "Lettres à Jean Gorin," *Macula* 2 (1977), p. 130.
40.   Mondrian to Harry Holtzman, June 1, 1942. Mondrian wrote this letter after Holtzman had created his two sculptures. For more on these important works, see Troy, *Mondrian and Neo-Plasticism in America*, p. 11, and Krauss, *Terminal Iron Works: The Sculpture of David Smith* (Cambridge, Mass.: MIT Press, 1971), p. 147, note 21. Also see Daniel Abadie's commentary in *Paris-New York* (Paris: Musée National d'Art Moderne, 1977), p. 441.
41.   On Jan. 9, 1942, von Wiegand recorded in her diary Mondrian's reaction after he had seen Holtzman's first column: "He told me that Holtzman was doing an interesting work—a kind of sculpture and painting—'He really is much more modern that I am—you will see—and he leans toward what I wrote about the end of art.'—'Most people hate that idea.' 'I know,' he said, 'it will come and Holtzman is less personal than I am, less traditional and nearer to architecture.'"
42.   Mondrian wrote to Gorin about one of his reliefs: "Nonetheless, a difficulty occurs: it should not have been exhibited as a 'tableau'—It's between a tableau and an architectural realization (so to speak), rather a 'plastic-aesthetic realization in our surroundings.'" Mondian then wrote in the margin of the letter: "It's true, a new form of painting may come out but, I believe, that would necessitate a very long preparation." The letter continues: "It's farther than my work, which still remains 'tableau' in essence—I already told you that, I think. They are two different values, which is one of the many reasons I prefer to do solo exhibits. Exhibiting with others gives rise to false comparisons" (Mondrian to Gorin, 31 Jan. 1934, *Macula* 2 [1977], p. 130. I have attempted here to keep Mondrian's punctuation and the peculiarities of his language).
43.   See the essay "Strzemiński and Kobro: In Search of Motivation," above.
44.   In his discussion with Georges Charbonnier, Giacometti perceived the problematic nature of the new category that Mondrian was trying to invent. The text is very keen but poorly articulated. Giacometti begins by presenting the problem of pictorial illusion and the impossibility of completely freeing oneself from it. (This is the same problem Gabo discussed.) But because he identifies

the semiological order with that of representation, he can only conceive of Mondrian's work as an impasse. However, while noting that Mondrian's painting does not escape the economy of the projective trace (the work being the imprint of its producer on canvas), he ends his text by making this a sort of experience-limit, giving it an interpretation that approaches Morris's:

> As for me, I am persuaded that painting is only that which is illusion. The reality of painting is the canvas. There is a canvas; that is reality. But a painting can only represent what it itself is not, namely, the illusion of something else. If you will, it seems to me that there is no great gulf between writing and painting. The signs of writing are only the signs of what they themselves are not. It is the same with painting. Take as an example abstract painting, or Mondrian. Mondrian wanted to abolish illusion and create an object in itself equivalent to any other object. He came to a sort of impasse. Mondrian is one of the painters I like the most, because I believe it is wonderful to have gone so far in a given direction. But the whole thing dead-ends. And yet Mondrian deluded himself: his painting is not at all an object in itself. It is altogether uniquely . . . the imprint of Mondrian on a canvas! In fact, Mondrian's painting almost became an object. He considered it, a bit, as such. But, really, I believe that Mondrian is coming from the domain of painting and entering into another realm.

(Georges Charbonnier, "Entretien avec Alberto Giacometti," *Le Monologue du peintre* [Paris: Julliard, 1959], pp. 169–170.)

45. Strzemiński, "L'Unisme en peinture," *L'Espace uniste*, ed. and tr. Antoine Baudin and Piérre Maxine Jedryka (Lausanne: L'Age d'Homme 1977), p. 80.

46. For more about Cézanne and color, see Mondrian, "De Nieuwe Beelding in der Schilderkunst," *De Stijl* 1 (Feb. 1918), p. 43; translated as "The New Plastic in Painting" in Mondrian, *The New Art*, pp. 38–39.

47. The expression "mechanics of painting," unusual for Mondrian, may refer to an article by Morris that appeared in *Partisan Review* ("On the Mechanics of Abstract Painting," Sept.–Oct. 1941, pp. 403–417). In fact, it is known that Mondrian hardly appreciated the article, perhaps because in that article Morris spoke of texture in terms the artist considered to be too traditional. See von Wiegand's diary, entry for Sept. 25, 1941.

48. Jean Clay, "Pollock, Mondrian, Seurat: la profondeur plate," in Hans Namuth, *L'Atelier de Jackson Pollock*, ed. Clay (Paris: Macula, 1982), no pagination.

49. Holty, "Mondrian in New York," p. 21. Unfortunately, we cannot discuss in depth the complex debate on color that occurred in the De Stijl group from 1917 to 1919 until Max Bill releases the correspondence between Mondrian and Vantongerloo. Echoes of this dialogue appear in Mondrian's correspondence with van Doesburg. (Both rejected Vantongerloo's theory founded on optical mixing and measuring the color "harmony" of a painting by the color created by the sum of its colors—this being, ideally, grey.) For a concise analysis of this problem, see Els Hoek, "Piet Mondrian," in Carel Blotkamp et al., *De Stijl: The Formative Years, 1917–1922*, trans. Charlotte I. Loeb and Arthur L. Loeb (Cambridge, Mass.: MIT Press, 1986), p. 62. In this context, it is interesting to note what van Doesburg says about his use of relief (hollow and relief) for the linear structure in some of his "decorations" of the Aubette in Strasbourg (1926–28): "The painting of the ceiling and the walls in the great hall on the first floor and in the cinema/ballroom was done in relief, for two reasons. First, because that way I managed a more defined surface and the super-brilliance of the colors was avoided and second, because the fusion of two colors was absolutely impossible" (Theo van Doesburg, "Notices sur l'Aubette à Strasbourg," *De Stijl* 8 [1928], p. 6).

For an analysis of Mondrian's system of color, as indebted to Seurat's, opposed to Matisse's, and clearly understood by Fernand Léger, see Bois, "Du Projet au procès," pp. 36–37. Marcel Duchamp was remarkably aware not only of Mondrian and Seurat's affinities but also of their departure from a purely optical, chromatic conception of color. He said in an interview with Alain Jouffroy, after having scorned impressionist, fauve, cubist, and abstract art for "stopping at the retina": "Their physical preoccupations: the reactions of color, etc., put the reactions of the gray matter in the background. This doesn't apply to all the protagonists of these movements. . . . Some men like Seurat or like Mondrian were not retinalists, even in wholly seeming to be so" (quoted in Alain Jouffroy, "Conversations avec Marcel Duchamp," *Une Révolution du regard* [Paris: Gallimard, 1964], p. 110). I am grateful to Rosalind Krauss for bringing this text to my attention.

50.　"You are the first person who has ever painted Yellow," Winnifred Nicholson told him one day. "He denied it but the next time I saw him, he took up the remark. 'I have thought about it and, it is so, but is merely because Cadmium yellow pigment has been invented'" (Winnifred Nicholson, "Reminiscences of Mondrian," *Studio International* 172 [Dec. 1966], p. 286).

51.　A first draft of "L'Art nouveau—la vie nouvelle: la culture des rapports purs" was completed in Dec. 1931 but remained unpublished during Mondrian's lifetime. See also "The New Art—The New Life = The Culture of Pure Relationships" in Mondrian, *The New Art*, p. 272.

52.　See Rembert, "Mondrian," p. 96.

53.　Von Wiegand unpublished diary, entry for Aug. 13, 1941.

54.　See Rembert, "Mondrian," p. 85.

55.　Greenberg, "Art," *The Nation*, Oct. 9, 1943, p. 416, and "Art Notes," *The Nation*, Oct. 16, 1943, p. 455; rpt. in Greenberg, *Perceptions*, pp. 153–154.

56.　Mondrian, "De Nieuwe Beelding in der Schilderkunst," *De Stijl* 1 (Jan. 1917), p. 31; translated in *The New Art*, p. 37. A letter dated May 16, 1917 to van Doesburg informs us that this idea came to Mondrian after deploring the alteration undergone by the *Compositions in Color A* and *B* when they were exhibited at the Stedelijk Museum in Amsterdam (unpublished letter in the van Doesburg archives, Dienst Verspreide Rijkscollecties, The Hague).

57.　See for example Welsh, *Piet Mondrian: 1872–1944* (Toronto: Art Gallery of Toronto, 1966), no. 112, p. 220.

58.　Regarding the optical flickers due to retinal afterimages and their importance in the modular Mondrians of 1918 as well as their multiplication in his work of the late thirties and forties, see Welsh, *"Composition 12,"* pp. 17–26, and Clara Weyergraf, *Piet Mondrian und Theo van Doesburg: Deutung von Werk und Theorie* (Munich: Fink, 1979), pp. 8–20.

59.　Kermit Champa ("Piet Mondrian's 'Broadway Boogie Woogie,'" *Arts Magazine* 54 [Jan. 1980], pp. 150–153), Masheck, and Rembert all consider *Broadway Boogie-Woogie* as a *resolution* of the *New York City* series. Curiously, Rembert doesn't appear to pay particular attention to Mondrian's loss of affection (which she notes) for this second-to-last painting. See Rembert, "Mondrian," p. 135.

60.　See three articles by Christian Bonnefoi: "A Propos de la destruction de la surface," *Macula* 3/4 (1978), pp. 163–169; regarding Mondrian, "Sur l'apparition du visible," *Macula* 5/6 (1979), pp. 205–209; and "Composition du retrait," *L'Atelier de Mondrian*, pp. 60–61.

61.　Erwin Panofsky, "Die Perspektive als 'symbolishe Form,'" *Aufsätze zu Grundfragen der Kunstwissenschaft*, ed. Hariolf Oberer and Egon Verheyen (Berlin: Bruno Hessling, 1974), p. 113. Regarding this matter, see Jean Claude Bonne's reading of Panofsky's text, "Fond, surfaces, support (Panofsky et l'art roman)," in *Cahiers pour un temps: Erwin Panofsky*, ed. Jacques Bonnet (Paris: Centre Georges Pompidou and Pandora Editions, 1983), pp. 117–134.

62.　Schapiro, "On Some Problems in the Semiotics of Visual Art: Field and Vehicle in Image-Signs," *Semiotica* 1 (1969), p. 224.

63.　Although Mondrian had already spoken of Byzantium in his 1917–18 writings, it is possible that New York's artistic intelligentsia influenced the renewal of his interest: we have seen that Morris spoke of Byzantine art in his article on sculpture and painting (see n. 34), and an article written much later by Greenberg ("Byzantine Parallels," *Art and Culture*, pp. 167–170) shows that the American artistic milieu had been interested in it for several decades.

64.　Walter Benjamin, "Über die Malerei oder Zeichen und Mal," *Gesammelte Schriften*, ed. Rolf Tiedemann and Hermann Schweppenhäuser, 6 vols. to date (Frankfurt am Main: Suhrkamp, 1974–), vol. 2, pp. 603–607. I would like to thank Peter Fenves for his meticulous translation of all passages of Benjamin's texts and letters quoted in this essay. It should be noted that Wölfflin distinguishes painting and drawing in a similar way in his *Principles of Art History*, published two years earlier: "Painting, with its all-covering pigments, on principle creates surfaces, and thereby, even where it remains monochrome, is distinguished from any drawing. Lines are there, and are to be felt everywhere, but only as the limits of surfaces which are plastically felt and modelled throughout by the tactile sense" (Wölfflin, *Principles of Art History*, pp. 41–42).

65.   This is what Benjamin himself stated in a letter to Gershom Scholem, Oct. 22, 1917 (Benjamin, *Briefe*, ed. Gershom Scholem and Theodor W. Adorno, 2 vols. [Frankfurt am Main: Suhrkamp, 1966], vol. 1, p. 154; further references to this work, abbreviated *B*, will be included in the text).

66.   This letter to Ernst Schoen dates from late 1917 or early 1918.

67.   In this same letter Benjamin adds, "The problem of cubism lies, from one point of view, in the possibility of a not necessarily *colorless* painting but rather radically *uncolored* painting in which linear structure [*der lineare Gebilde*] dominates the image [*das Bild*]—without, however, cubism's ceasing to be painting and turning into graphics" (*B*, 1:154).

68.   Theodor W. Adorno and Gershom Scholem, the editors of Benjamin's correspondence, tell us that this *Dame mit Fächer* was exhibited at the gallery Der Sturm in Berlin during the summer of 1917 and was the point of departure of Gershom Scholem's reflections (*B*, 1:156–157, note 3), but I was not able to identify the painting with certainty, although this would obviously cast some light on Benjamin's view of cubism. In his meticulous recension, George Brühl does not list any painting by Picasso as having been exhibited in Der Sturm after 1913 (Brühl, *Herwarth Walden und "Der Sturm"* [Cologne: Dumont, 1983], p. 264). Although titles are not the most reliable guides, since Picasso did not assign them himself, one may determine which painting Benjamin was referring to by examining four possibilities, all with similar titles, in the various catalogues raisonnés of Picasso's oeuvre up to 1917. *Femme tenant un éventail* (1908; Pierre Daix, *Picasso: The Cubist Years, 1907–1916* [Boston: New York Graphic Society, 1979], no. 168, p. 222) was apparently in the collection of Sergei Shchukin in Moscow at the latest in 1913. *Femme à l'éventail* (1909; Daix, no. 263, p. 239) apparently entered the Shchukin collection between 1913 and 1918, but it is unlikely that the Russian collector, who was buying directly from Kahnweiler in Paris, would have bought a painting as late as the fall of 1917—at a time when his country was in a complete political turmoil (for that matter, it is equally unlikely that he would have lent any works in his collection to the gallery Der Sturm, which, furthermore, was only functioning as a German showcase for Kahnweiler's stable—in other words, works exhibited were generally for sale). *Femme à l'éventail* (1910–18; Daix, no. 364, p. 258) is a work that Picasso had begun in Cadaqués in 1910 and is said by Christian Zervos to have reworked and finished only in 1918; and *Femme à l'éventail* (Zervos, *Pablo Picasso*, vol. 3, *Oeuvres de 1917 à 1919* [Paris: Cahiers d'Art, 1943], no. 21, p. 8) was painted in Barcelona during the summer of 1917. Of these four candidates, two have to be ruled out: the first (out of circulation too early) and the last (too late). The 1909 painting seems quite improbable, for the reasons mentioned above, but as a magisterial example of analytical cubism, preceding immediately the breakthrough of the work at Horta de Ebro in the summer of 1909, it is more in accordance with what we know of Scholem's reaction than any other works considered here. In his discussion with Scholem, Benjamin quotes the latter as having characterized cubism as "communicating the essence of the space that is the world in decomposing it" (*B*, 1:155). Another (remote) possibility would be that the 1910–18 canvas was exhibited before Picasso reworked it, or that the date given for this second working session, 1918, is wrong. This canvas, now in the collection of the National Gallery of Art in Washington, is one of the most "abstract" paintings by Picasso and participates in the vertical/horizontal reversal that is attempted in synthetic cubism. A letter sent to Scholem prior to his death regarding this matter remained unanswered.

69.   Benjamin, "Malerei und Graphik," *Gesammelte Schriften*, vol. 2, pp. 602–603.

70.   For a different usage of Benjamin's vertical/horizontal opposition, see Michael Fried, *Realism, Writing, Disfiguration: On Thomas Eakins and Stephen Crane* (Chicago: University of Chicago Press, 1987), p. 174. Fried himself remarks: "In short, Benjamin and I make somewhat different use of the same basic opposition between verticality and horizontality, but of course we are fundamentally concerned with different artistic phenomena, he with Cubism, I with Eakins."

71.   See Leo Steinberg, "Other Criteria," *Other Criteria: Confrontations with Twentieth-Century Art* (New York: Oxford University Press, 1972), p. 85, and Svetlana Alpers, *The Art of Describing: Dutch Art in the Seventeenth Century* (Chicago: University of Chicago Press, 1983), p. 258, note 23.

72.   See Carmean, *The Diamond Compositions*, pp. 20–21, and Clay, "Pollock, Mondrian, Seurat," no pagination.

73.   See Clay, "Pollock, Mondrian, Seurat," no pagination; Welsh, "*Composition 12*," p. 17; and Carmean, *The Diamond Compositions*, p. 24.

74.   Mondrian, "Le Home—La Rue—La Cité," *Vouloir*, no. 25 (1927); translated in Mondrian, *The New Art*, p. 210.

75.   Seuphor, *Piet Mondrian*, p. 158.

76.   Charmion von Wiegand, "Mondrian: A Memoir of His New York Period," *Arts Yearbook* 4 (1961), p. 62.

77.   Ibid., p. 61.

78.   The drawing in question was bought by the Musée National d'Art Moderne in Paris at the same time as *New York City*. The title that has been given to it is *New York City—Classical Drawing no. 6* (graphite on paper, 22.8 × 21 cm., inventory number M.N.A.M. Paris, AM 1984–271D). The unfinished *New York City III* is still in the collection of the Sidney Janis Gallery, New York.

79.   See Champa, "Piet Mondrian's Broadway 'Boogie Woogie,'" and Masheck, "Mondrian the New Yorker," p. 64.

80.   Jimmy Ernst, *A Not-So-Still-Life: A Memoir* (New York: St. Martin's–Marek, 1984), p. 241. Until now, the only known version of this anecdote was Peggy Guggenheim's. The publication of these memories by Max Ernst's son sheds a new light on Mondrian's interest in Pollock. Of course, it was not yet a matter of an *all-over dripping* (this is 1943), but I'd wager that a later painting would have fascinated Mondrian even more.

81.   Krauss, "Emblèmes ou lexies: le texte photographique," *L'Atelier de Pollock*, no pagination.

82.   Steinberg, *Other Criteria*, p. 84.

83.   Ibid., p. 88. Certainly there are authentic "flatbeds" before *New York City*, for example Ivan Puni's *Bains* (1915, Berninger Collection). See my "Malevich, le carré, le degré zéro," *Macula* 1 (1976), p. 47. But these were notable exceptions. For a discussion and development of the "flatbed" idea, see Krauss, "Rauschenberg and the Materialized Image," *Artforum* 13 (Dec. 1974), pp. 36–43.

84.   Mondrian, "Liberation from Oppression in Art and Life," written in 1939–40, first published in *Plastic Art and Pure Plastic Art*, pp. 37–48; reprinted in Mondrian, *The New Art*, p. 329.

Perceiving Newman

I would like to thank Michael Fried for reading this text and suggesting many editorial improvements.

1.   Thomas B. Hess, *Barnett Newman* (New York: Museum of Modern Art, 1971, p. 51).

2.   "The Problem of Subject Matter," quoted in Hess, *Newman*, p. 39.

3.   "Jackson Pollock: An Artist's Symposium; Part I," *Art News*, April 1967, p. 29.

4.   While making these drawings, and insisting on the difference between his own art and surrealism, Newman wrote: "[the new painter] is . . . engaged in a true act of discovery in the creation of new forms and symbols that will have the living quality of creation." From "The Plasmic Image," quoted in Hess, *Newman*, p. 38.

5.   "The Ideographic Picture," Betty Parsons Gallery, January–February 1947.

6.   Newman wrote a statement for each of his first two one-man shows, but only one is included in Hess's and Rosenberg's bibliographies, dated either 1950 or 1951. The only statement quoted by those authors is the second one, to which I will return (about the relationship of the beholder to large canvases). Hess and Rosenberg mistook it for the 1950 statement (although the latter dated it correctly in his bibliography, and although it would have made little sense to speak of "large pictures" then), but Lawrence Alloway related it accurately to Newman's second one-man show in his preface for the catalogue of the exhibition of the *Stations of the Cross* (Guggenheim Museum, 1966, note 12).

7.   Barnett Newman, in Dorothy G. Seckler, "Frontiers of Space," *Art in America*, Summer 1962, p. 83.

8.   Statement in the catalogue of "The New American Painting: As Shown in Eight European Countries 1958–1959," a touring exhibition organized by the Museum of Modern Art, New York, where it closed. The statement is not in Hess's or Rosenberg's bibliographies.

9.   Interview with David Sylvester, in *Abstract Expressionism: The Critical Developments*, ed. Michael Auping (Buffalo: Albright-Knox Gallery, 1987), pp. 143–144.

10.   In Seckler, "Frontiers of Space," p. 86.

11.   Hess, *Newman*, p. 57.

12.   Although his conclusions and his formulation are different from mine, and although he did not relate this idea to Newman's text for the "Ideographic Picture" exhibition, Gerard Sondag wrote some noteworthy pages about *Onement I* as being the first "symbol-painting" in Newman's oeuvre, and as radically suppressing the image. I thank him for letting me read his unpublished essay on abstract expressionism.

13.   In Seckler, "Frontiers of Space," p. 87.

14.   Cf. Pierre Schneider, "Through the Louvre with Barnett Newman," *Art News*, Summer 1969, pp. 38–39.

15.   In that sense, Newman's symmetrical paintings are a direct precedent to Noland's and Stella's works of the late 1950s and early 1960s, although their use of symmetry is more complex than that of a simple bilaterality (it is a rotational symmetry, hence their tendency to inscribe a center around which everything evolves rather than an axis defining a field). Both Stella and Judd, in their famous interview with Bruce Glaser, spoke eloquently of symmetry as a means to "get rid of compositional effects," and Stella as a means of declaring the surface of his canvases. Cf. Bruce Glaser, "Questions to Stella and Judd" (1966), reprinted in *Minimal Art*, ed. Gregory Battcock (New York: Dutton, 1968). Donald Judd, who tried to buy *Shining Forth (To George)*, paid his special tribute to Newman in 1964, although the text was only published in 1970 (reprinted in his *Complete Writings 1959–1970* [Halifax: The Press of the Nova Scotia College of Art and Design, 1975], pp. 200–202). Cf. also his comments in Jeanne Siegel, "Around Barnett Newman," *Art News*, October 1971, pp. 44–46 and 59–60. In most of those texts, Mondrian's type of compositional balance is taken as an example of what the use of symmetry enabled the artists in question to overcome.

16.   It reads: "Fantastic. Absolute totality. One image. I suppose this is so because the light is even from corner to corner. No spotlights—Courbet and Pissarro are like that. Monet, for instance, was always spotlighting theatrically, except in his late work. Hence his popularity." He pauses. "Physically, it is a modern painting, a flat painting. You grasp the thing at once. What a fantastic sense of scale!"

    "By scale, you don't mean size?"

    "It is beyond the problem of size. It looks big. The content and the form are inseparable: that's scale." He pauses again. "It is a strictly symmetrical picture. Hence its totality. It is like the symmetry of man. It has no color: it is beyond color. It is not black, not red. The color is pure light—nightlight, perhaps, but light. What bothers me is color as color, as material, as local. In Poussin, a pink is a pink."

    And the statement itself has a follow-up, when Newman discusses Courbet's *After the Hunt*: "This is the nearest thing to Uccello. There is nothing to scrutinize. You get it or you don't." (In Pierre Schneider, "Through the Louvre," pp. 35 and 71.)

17.   Hess was the first to refer to Giacometti's elongated sculpture, which Newman saw in New York in 1948, in a show that opened ten days before he "painted" or rather "interrupted" *Onement I*, but Hess himself cautioned against making too much of such a filiation. Recently, however, David Sylvester (who laid out the precise chronology) went as far as to claim that Giacometti was one of the two European artists who ever influenced Newman (the other being Matisse). To strengthen his argument, he referred not only to Hess but also to Irving Sandler's interpretation of the stripes as "figures, ravaged by space" whose "tremendous, eroded edges suggest vulnerable human touches, while their verticality evokes man's aspirations to the sublime, as in Still's pictures," in *The Triumph*

of American Painting: A History of Abstract Expressionism (London: Pall Mall, 1970), p. 190. (Cf. David Sylvester, "The Ugly Duckling," in Auping, *Abstract Expressionism: The Critical Developments*, p. 138.) Nothing seems to me more reductive than such an assimilation. It is as false as "this shrewd popularization of the big lie, that modern art isn't modern," which Newman pointed as the core of the criticism of Fry, Bell, and Read ("The Problem of Subject Matter," in Hess, *Newman*, p. 39). Newman is partly responsible for this confusion, in his insistence that his work is not "abstract"—but one has to realize that when he says that he means almost inevitably that it is not "abstracted from" nature, as he thought the work of Mondrian was. The association of Newman to Matisse, on the other hand, seems perfectly justifiable to me (cf. the essay "Matisse and 'Arche-Drawing,'" above).

18. Maurice Merleau-Ponty, *Phenomenology of Perception*, tr. Colin Smith (London: Routledge and Kegan Paul, 1962), p. 206.

19. Jacques Lacan, "De nos antécédents," in *Ecrits* (Paris: Seuil, 1966), p. 71.

20. Ibid., p. 102.

21. Cf. "Le dédoublement de la représentation dans les arts de l'Asie et de l'Amerique" (1944–45), reprinted in *Anthropologie structurale I* (Paris: Plon, 1958), p. 289. In this text, Lévi-Strauss explains the symmetry in the art of North American Indians, Maori, and archaic China by the fact that their culture is a "mask" culture, where tatooing was often a surrogate of the mask: in those cultures, the first surface to receive a pictorial sign is thus the human face. The idea goes back to Marcel Mauss, for whom the origin of painting lies in cosmetics. Cf. *Manuel d'ethnographie* (Paris: Payot, 1967), pp. 95–96; these lectures, given before World War II, were first published in 1947.

22. The *Phenomenology of Perception* was written during World War II and published in French in 1945 (the English translation appeared only in 1962). Newman's work has already been associated with phenomenology, notably by Donald B. Kuspit ("A Phenomenological Approach to Artistic Intention," *Artforum*, January 1974, pp. 52–53), and by David J. Glaser ("Transcendence in the Vision of Barnett Newman," *Journal of Aesthetics and Art Criticism*, Summer 1982, pp. 415–420), but in such a general way that I find it extremely difficult to relate it to his actual works.

23. Blaise Pascal, *Pensées*, tr. Martin Turnell (New York: Harper and Brothers, 1962), p. 416. "In anything one takes in at a glance" translates "Est ce qu'on voit d'une vue," which is fair enough, although "vue" does not only refer to the instantaneousness of a glance, but to the phenomenon of vision as such: symmetry as a condition of perception rather than as a quality of perceived objects.

24. The only other alternative would be a monochrome, a solution that never tempted Newman, although his interest in the sublime, that is in the nonrepresentable, could have led him to it, as it did other artists. I see in this refusal of the monochrome a confirmation of my reading of Newman's work as a fundamental inquiry about the nature of perception, for, as Merleau-Ponty wrote, "A really homogeneous area offering *nothing to perception* cannot be given to *any perception*" (*Phenomenology of Perception*, p. 4). Perhaps Newman felt that the monochrome represented an attempt doomed to failure: in order to perceive it, the beholder has to construct a visual field on the wall against which it immediately functions as a figure. Newman's rejection of Rauschenberg's *White Painting* of 1951 (consisting of seven white rectangle monochromes juxtaposed) should be read in the light of this phenomenon ("Emptiness is not that easy. The point is to produce it with paint," quoted in Harold Rosenberg, *Barnett Newman* (New York: Abrams, 1978, p. 59).

25. This nonreversibility is an essential issue in Merleau-Ponty's *Phenomenology of Perception* (cf. notably pp. 244–254).

26. It is only for the sake of brevity that I call "zips" the horizontal dividers of those canvases, as they do not function whatsoever like the vertical zips of Newman's usual format—hence my quotation marks. I will use the same device later with regard to the "dividers" that have become planes.

27. Of course, this "native" condition is culturally modified, notably by the predominance of the right hand in most societies and, in the West at least, by the left-to-right direction of writing and reading. Newman was fully aware of this phenomenon which he explores, I believe, in all the works where the symmetry is assessed by more complex means than the pure division of the canvas by its axis of symmetry. A canvas of 1949 is paradigmatic here (*Yellow Painting*), but this interest shows

constantly through the years (one of his last canvases, *Who Is Afraid of Red, Yellow and Blue II*, of 1967, not to speak of *Shining Forth (to George)*, is based on the same structure). See also the numerous works, to which I'll refer later, where the "zips" are symmetrically adjacent to the right and left edges of the canvas, eventually struggling to become planes themselves, as in *Noon Light*. On the issue of the cultural destabilization of bilateral symmetry and its effect on painting, cf. Heinrich Wölfflin, "Über das Rechts und Links im Bilde," in *Gedanken zur Kunstgeschichte: Gedrucktes und Ungedrucktes* (Basel: Benno Schwabe & Co, 1941), pp. 82–90, and Meyer Schapiro, "On Some Problems in the Semiotics of Visual Arts: Field and Vehicle in Image-Signs," *Semiotica* I (1969), pp. 223–242. Bernard Lamblin dealt in a phenomenological manner with the issue, which he linked to the problem of the expression of time in painting. Cf. *Peinture et temps* (Paris: Klincksieck, 1983), pp. 56–125.

28.   In Seckler, "Frontiers of Space," p. 86. In a conversation with Tom Hess held at the Guggenheim Museum (on May 1, 1966) at the occasion of the exhibition of the *Stations of the Cross*, Newman said he had to protest against a collector who had hung a painting of his upside down.

29.   Merleau-Ponty, *Phenomenology of Perception*, p. 58.

30.   On the essential function of the deictic in Newman's work, cf. Max Reithman, "Newman et Mondrian," *Artistes*, special issue no. 1, June 1984, pp. 50–67.

31.   "The only link I can realize with Turner is that when Turner strapped himself to the mast in an attempt to paint the storm, he was trying to do the impossible," said Newman in the conversation with Tom Hess at the Guggenheim Museum. I take this statement as a direct rebuttal against a common interpretation of Newman's "sublime" that tends to read his works as abstract landscapes (cf., in particular, Robert Rosenblum's "The Abstract Sublime," *Art News*, February 1961, pp. 38–41 and 56–58, where the connection to Turner is made).

32.   On this characteristic of attention and on the act of fixing, cf. Merleau-Ponty, in particular *Phenomenology of Perception*, pp. 225–226. While editing the present text, Michael Fried called to my mind his interpretation of Morris Louis's *Unfurleds* as similar in approach (cf. Michael Fried, *Morris Louis* [New York: Abrams, 1970], pp. 32–34), and indeed some of Newman's work and those particular canvases of Louis share a lot of characteristics (symmetry, large scale, etc.). Fried specifically spoke of the impossibility for the viewer to see both "banks" of the *Unfurleds* at the same time, hence to perceive a part-to-part relationship, and of the lack of distance of the beholder, which paradoxically produces a sense of the wholeness of the canvas. I do not think, however, that we are "compelled by that closeness to focus, to look, infinitely *beyond*" the zips as we are, according to Fried, with regard to the rivulets of color in Louis's canvases.

33.   "Prologue for a New Esthetic," quoted in Hess, *Newman*, p. 73. This statement has also to be read in the light of the interest for Newman of the sublime, which I can only mention here in passing. On this point, cf. Jean-François Lyotard, "L'Instant, Newman," in *L'Art et le temps*, ed. Michel Baudson (Brussels: Société des Expositions du Palais des Beaux-Arts, 1984), pp. 99–105.

34.   The whole statement greeting the visitors of his second one-man show, which I have already mentioned in passing, was: "There is a tendency to look at large pictures from a distance. The large pictures in this exhibition are intended to be seen from a short distance."

35.   Statement for *Art Now: New York*, vol. 1, no. 3, March 1969, n.p.

36.   In Seckler, "Frontiers of Space," p. 87.

Ryman's Tact

1.   Phyllis Tuchman, "Interview with Robert Ryman," *Artforum* 9, no. 9 (May 1971), p. 53.

2.   Naomi Spector, *Robert Ryman* (Amsterdam: Stedelijk Museum, 1974).

3.   Ibid., p. 24.

4.   Barbara Reise, "Robert Ryman: Unfinished II (Procedures)," *Studio International* 187, no. 964 (March 1974), p. 122.

5.   Cf. Spector, *Ryman*, p. 19.

6.   Reise, "Ryman: Unfinished II," p. 123.

7.   See Rosalind Krauss's text on the index (and photography as a model for abstract art in the '70s), "Notes on the Index" (1977), rpt. in *The Originality of the Avant-Garde and Other Modernist Myths* (Cambridge: MIT Press, 1985), pp. 196–219.

8.   This essay was written in 1981. At that time in France many painters of the Support Surface group or closely associated with it (Louis Cane, Daniel Dezeuze, Claude Viallat, etc.), where exhibiting unstretched canvases directly tacked on the wall and often unrolling to the floor. Those works were undoubtedly informed by the production of Dorothea Rockburne and of Alan Shields.

9.   There are many other examples of the interval. Jean Clay points out two: "It is like a work where Ryman will claim alternately to "uncomplete" something completed and complete something uncompleted [cf. Reise, "Ryman: Unfinished II," pp. 122ff.], the completion of the uncompleted taking on meaning only in that it raises the question of the uncompletedness of all paintings. Or the exhibition of a nakedly frameless painting: Ryman attaches a canvas to a wall, frames it with a broad brush stroke, pulls it off, and fixes it in another location. Covered with hairline cracks and chipped, the painted frame adheres to the wall, while the jagged outlines and curved edges of the work itself evidence the act of unframing. Even if a frame were supplied, it would never be more than an unframed-reframed painting" (Jean Clay, "La Peinture en charpie," in "Dossier Ryman," *Macula*, no. 3/4 [November 1978], p. 173).

10.   As can be ascertained from the introduction to these essays, I would not subscribe to such a sentence today, for it is too beholden to Greenberg's monism. Far from presupposing the existence of something like painting per se, purified of all heterogeneity, I would insist on the fact that the "concept" of painting is constantly changing. And, in keeping with the long Tynjanov/Jakobson excursus of the introduction, I would say that while at a certain point in history "painting" had eventually to encompass "history, literature, theology, or psychology," it came to be defined, during the modernist period, as having not an inclusive but an exclusive relationship toward these disciplines.

11.   Telephone interview of Robert Ryman by Nancy Tousley, in *Prints: Bochner, Lewitt, Mangold, Marden, Renouf, Rockburne, Ryman* (Toronto: Art Gallery of Ontario, 1974), p. 49.

12.   E. H. Gombrich, *Art and Illusion: A Study in the Psychology of Pictorial Representation* (New York: Pantheon, 1960), p. 199.

13.   Clay, "La Peinture en charpie," p. 171.

14.   Ibid., p. 183.

15.   In the brief text he wrote for the catalogue of the "Fundamental Painting" exhibition at the Stedelijk Museum in Amsterdam in 1975, Ryman himself speaks about an "absolute" in painting. More naively, at the very beginning of his career, Ryman painted what appeared to be a programmatic work (fig. 89). The painting, dated 1958, is untitled, but written, white on black, in the middle of a long horizontal rectangle that stripes its surface are the words: "The Paradoxical Absolute." Naive precisely because it makes a statement without constructing a paradigm, this painting implies belief in the immediacy of a paradox simply by virtue of its linguistic formulation.

16.   Thierry de Duve, assuming the relative irreproducibility of Ryman's paintings, clarifies some theoretical connections between them and photography and speaks about what there is of the auratic in them that is resistant to it ("Ryman irreproductible" [1980], rpt. in de Duve, *Ecrits Datés I 1974–1986* [Paris: La Différence, 1987], pp. 119–158).

17.   Paul Valéry, *Cahiers*, vol. 11 (Paris: Gallimard, 1974), p. 207.

18.   Edgar Allan Poe, "A Tale of the Ragged Mountains," in *The Complete Tales and Poems of Edgar Allan Poe* (New York: Random House, 1938), p. 683.

19.   Walter Benjamin, "Monument to a Dead Soldier," in "One-Way-Street," *One-Way Street and Other Writings*, tr. Edmund Jephcott and Kingsley Shorter (London: New Left Books, 1979), p. 79.

20.   Walter Benjamin, "Karl Kraus," in *Reflections*, tr. Edmund Jephcott (New York: Harcourt Brace Jovanovich, 1978), p. 244.

21.   Ibid.

22.   Ibid., pp. 243–244.

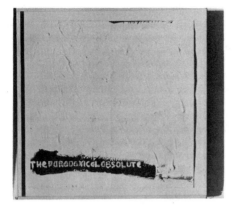

89. Robert Ryman, The Paradoxical Absolute, *1958. Casein on printed paper, 17.7 × 18.4 cm (7 × 7¼ in.). Collection of the artist. Photo courtesy of the artist.*

23.   Ibid., p. 245.

24.   Stephen Rosenthal, "Notes sur le procès pictural," in "Dossier Ryman," *Macula,* no. 3/4 (November 1978), p. 158.

Painting: The Task of Mourning

1.   Jacques Derrida, "Of an Apocalyptic Tone Recently Adopted in Philosophy" (1983), tr. John P. Leavey, Jr., *The Oxford Literary Review* 6, no. 2 (1984), pp. 22–23. This essay is a reading of Kant's pamphlet mentioned above.

2.   Kasimir Malevich, *Suprematism. 34 Drawings* (Vitebsk, 1920), English tr. in Malevich, *Essays on Art*, ed. Troels Andersen, vol. 1 (New York: Wittenborn, 1971), p. 127.

3.   I refer here to the critical work accomplished in the magazine *October* by Rosalind Krauss, Douglas Crimp, and Benjamin H. D. Buchloh; but also to Hal Foster's recent anthology of articles, *Recodings: Art, Spectacle, Cultural Politics* (Port Townsend, Wash.: Bay Press, 1985), and to various articles by Thierry de Duve.

4.   Douglas Crimp, "The End of Painting," *October*, no. 16 (Spring 1981), p. 75.

5.   See Meyer Schapiro, "Recent Abstract Painting," in *Modern Art: 19th and 20th Century (Collected Papers)* (New York: Braziller, 1978), pp. 217–219. The text appeared first under the title "The Liberating Quality of Avant-Garde Art" in *Art News* during the summer of 1957.

6.   Cf. the essay "Ryman's Tact," above. See also the excellent article by Thierry de Duve, "Ryman irreproductible" (1980), rpt. in de Duve, *Ecrits Datés I 1974–1986* (Paris: La Différence, 1987), pp. 119–158, which deals explicitly with Ryman's relationship with modernism and photography.

7.   Barnett Newman, "The Problem of Subject Matter," c. 1944, as quoted by Tom Hess in *Barnett Newman* (New York: Museum of Modern Art, 1971), pp. 39–40.

8.   Thierry de Duve, "The Readymade and the Tube of Paint," *Artforum,* May 1986, pp. 115–116.

9.   Marcel Duchamp to Katherine Kuh (1961), quoted in ibid., p. 113.

10.   See Rosalind Krauss, "Notes on the Index" (1977), reprinted in *Originality of the Avant-Garde and Other Modernist Myths* (Cambridge: MIT Press, 1984).

11.   Giorgio Agamben, *Stanze* (1977); French tr. Yves Hersant (Paris: Christian Bourgois, 1980), part two ("Dans le monde d'Odradek—Oeuvre d'art et marchandise"), p. 75.

12.   Karl Marx and Friedrich Engels, "Review—May to October [1850]," in Marx and Engels, *Collected Works*, vol. 10 (New York: International Publishers, 1978), p. 500. The original text was published, although not in its entirety, in the *Neue Rheinische Zeitung*, no. 5–6, 1850. The editors of the *Collected Works* ascribe the text to Marx (see ibid., p. 695, note 348).

13.   *Lettres de Gustave Courbet à Alfred Bruyas*, ed. Pierre Borel (Geneva: Editions Pierre Cailler, 1951), p. 87.

14.   Walter Benjamin, "Paris, Capital of the Nineteenth Century," second version (1939), in *Das Passagenwerk*, Gesammelte Schriften, vol. 5 (Frankfurt: Suhrkamp, 1983), p. 71.

15.   Walter Benjamin, "The Paris of the Second Empire in Baudelaire" (1938), English tr. in *Charles Baudelaire: A Lyric Poet in the Era of High Capitalism* (London: New Left Books, 1973), p. 81.

16.   Walter Benjamin, *Das Passagenwerk*, pp. 71–72.

17.   Marcel Mauss, *Manuel d'ethnographie* (1947), 2d ed. (Paris: Payot, 1967), p. 89.

18.   Karl Marx, *Oeuvres* (Paris: Gallimard, 1968), vol. 2, p. 1871.

19.   Benjamin H. D. Buchloh, "Figures of Authority, Ciphers of Regression," *October*, no. 16 (Spring 1981). (I am not so sure anymore that Picasso's *Portrait of Max Jacob* should be heralded as the point of departure of the vast movement of the "return to order." In fact, Picasso's irony there implies a distance that is very much in keeping with his cubist enterprise. I hope to be pursuing this angle in further studies.)

20.   See "Mythologies: Art and the Market," Jeffrey Deitch interviewed by Matthew Collings, *Artscribe International* (April–May 1986), pp. 23–26. Almost any assertion made in this interview with Deitch, a corporate art advisor, would require a commentary, starting with his denial of having a cynical position. Nevertheless, it provides valuable information on the present situation: while Marcel Duchamp could say in 1966 that "the museums are run more or less by the dealers" and that "in New York, the Museum of Modern Art is completely in the hands of the dealers" (Pierre Cabanne, *Dialogues with Marcel Duchamp*, tr. Ron Padgett [New York: The Viking Press, 1971]), we are now confronted by the omnipotence of the collector. He has made the dealer into a mere appendage of his own body: this is the situation that is well described in Deitch's interview.

21.   Reprinted in Sophie Lissitzky-Kuppers, *El Lissitzky* (London and New York: Thames and Hudson, 1968), pp. 330–340.

22.   Alexander Rodchenko, from the manuscript "Working with Maiakovsky" (1939), quoted in *From Painting to Design: Russian Constructivist Art of the Twenties* (Cologne: Galerie Gmurzynska, 1981), p. 191. On Rodchenko see also Benjamin H. D. Buchloh, *Niele Toroni—L'Index de la peinture* (Brussels: Editions Daled, 1985), pp. 40–42 (unpublished in English).

23.   Nikolai Tarabukin, *From the Easel to the Machine* (1923), English tr. in *Modern Art and Modernism: A Critical Anthology*, ed. Francis Frascina and Charles Harrison (New York: Harper and Row, 1982), p. 139. It is worth noting that Tarabukin was totally immersed in millenarianism: his major reference is Spengler's *Decline of the West*.

24.   Piet Mondrian, "De Huif naar den Wind," *De Stijl* 6, no. 6/7 (1924), p. 88. Translated in *The New Art—The New Life: The Collected Writings of Piet Mondrian*, ed. and tr. Harry Holtzman and Martin S. James (Boston: G. K. Hall, 1986), p. 181. For Picasso's remark, cf. Daniel-Henry Kahnweiler with Francis Crémieux, *My Galleries and Painters* (1961), English tr. by Helen Weaver (New York: Viking, 1971), p. 54.

25.   Piet Mondrian, "Liberation from Oppression in Art and Life" (1941), rpt. in *The New Art*, p. 323.

26.   Ibid., p. 327.

27.   Cf. Yve-Alain Bois, *Arthur Lehning en Mondriaan—Hun vriendschap en correspondentie* (Amsterdam: Van Gennep, 1984), p. 39.

28.   Cf. Hubert Damisch, *Fenêtre jaune cadmium* (Paris: Seuil, 1984), p. 167. I have slightly shortened here the discussion of Damisch's model, which was longer in the original version of the present essay, so as to avoid a redundancy with the following essay in this volume, "Painting as Model."

29.   Ibid., p. 170.

30.   Ibid., p. 171.

31.   One remembers the book by Michel Seuphor, *Le Style et le Cri* (Paris: Seuil, 1965), which helped to vulgarize such a critical distinction.

32.   Hal Foster, "Signs Taken for Wonders," *Art in America*, June 1986, p. 90.

33.   See Fredric Jameson, "Postmodernism, or the Cultural Logic of Late Capitalism," *New Left Review*, July–August 1984, pp. 53–92.

34.   "Orgy of Cannibalism" is an expression of Karl Abraham to characterize the manic state in "Esquisse d'une histoire du developpement de la libido basée sur la psychoanalyse des troubles mentaux" (1924). In this article, Abraham completes the famous but very short text by Freud on "Mourning and Melancholia." See Abraham, *Développement de la libido, Oeuvres Complètes*, vol. 2 (Paris: Payot, 1973), p. 293.

Dwelling on the early essays of Freud and Abraham, Melanie Klein shows how the feeling of triumph and omnipotence that characterize manic mourning prevents the *working through* of mourning. (See "Mourning and Its Relation to Manic-Depressive States," in *Contributions to Psychoanalysis 1921–1945* [London: Hogarth Press, 1950]. See particularly pp. 322 and 336.

35.   Foster, "Signs," p. 83.

36.   Ross Bleckner, *Philip Taaffe* (New York: Pat Hearn Gallery, 1986), p. 7.

37.   Hal Foster, "Signs," p. 91. Peter Halley is perfectly aware of this, as is shown by most of his texts and particularly by his brilliant article entitled "The Crisis in Geometry," *Arts*, Summer 1984. But he believes that this state of affairs can be represented, and through representation, criticized. Both of these claims are dubious (and contradictory with his Baudrillardian theory).

38.   Roland Barthes, "Réquichot et son corps," in *L'Obvie et l'obtus, Essais Critiques* III (Paris: Seuil, 1982), p. 211.

39.   Robert Musil, "Considérations Désobligeantes," *Oeuvres préposthumes* (1936), French tr. Philippe Jaccottet (Paris: Seuil, 1965), p. 87.

Painting as Model

This essay reviews *Fenêtre jaune cadmium, ou les dessous de la peinture,* by Hubert Damisch (Paris: Editions du Seuil, 1984).

1.   Jacques Lacan's text on Rouan, illustrated with some seventeen figures of knots, began as follows: "François Rouan paints on bands. If I dared, I would advise him to change this and paint on braid." This text, originally published in the catalogue of the Rouan exhibition at the Musée Cantini (Marseilles, 1978), was reprinted in the catalogue of the Rouan exhibition at the Centre Georges Pompidou (Paris, 1983), a catalogue for which Damisch wrote the preface, reprinted in *Fenêtre jaune cadmium*. Damisch's answer is simply that the braids were there all along in Rouan's painting for those who were able to see them.

2.   "What is real, as one should never tire of stating, are the results of the brushstrokes, the layer of paint on the canvas, its texture, the varnish that is applied over the colors. But all of this is precisely what does not become the object of aesthetic appreciation" (Jean-Paul Sartre, *L'Imaginaire* [Paris: Gallimard, 1940], p. 240).

3.   On the notion of *optics* and the "relative indifference to the material process of elaboration" of the work, typical of Clement Greenberg and Michael Fried, see Jean Clay, "La Peinture en charpie," in "Dossier Ryman," *Macula*, no. 3–4 (1978), pp. 171–172.

4.   See especially Jean Clay, "Pollock, Mondrian, Seurat: La profondeur plate," in Hans Namuth, *L'Atelier de Jackson Pollock* (Paris: Macula, 1982).

5.   I refer to the excellent collection *Autour du "Chef d'oeuvre inconnu" de Balzac*, ed. Thierry Chabanne (Paris: Ecole Nationale Supérieure des Arts Décoratifs, 1985) (cf. particularly Jean-Claude Lebensztejn, "Cinq lignes de points," pp. 149–171). For a still different approach, see Georges Didi-Huberman, *La Peinture incarnée* (Paris: Minuit, 1984).

6.   Cf. Hubert Damisch, *Théorie du nuage* (Paris: Seuil, 1972), pp. 214–248.

7.   Leo Steinberg, "Other Criteria" (1972), reprinted in the collection of the same name (New York: Oxford University Press, 1972), pp. 55–91. For a reading of Giacometti's "surrealist" oeuvre, based on the *informe* of Bataille and analyzing in it the vertical/horizontal reversal under discussion here, see Rosalind Krauss, "No More Play," in *The Originality of the Avant-Garde and Other Modernist Myths* (Cambridge: MIT Press, 1985), pp. 43–85.

8.　　My essay on Mondrian's *New York City* (reprinted in this volume) owes much, entirely unconsciously, to Damisch's text on the Dutch painter, as to a good number of texts reprinted in *Fenêtre jaune cadmium*.

9.　　"It would be misleading to imagine, therefore, as so many ethnologists and art historians still do today, that a mask and, more generally, a sculpture or a painting may be interpreted each for itself, according to what it represents or to the aesthetic or ritual use for which it is destined. We have seen that, on the contrary, a mask does not exist in isolation; it supposes other real or potential masks always by its side, masks that might have been chosen in its stead and substituted for it. In discussing a particular problem, I hope to have shown that a mask is not primarily what it represents but what it transforms, that is to say, what it chooses *not* to represent. Like a myth, a mask denies as much as it affirms. It is not made solely of what it says or thinks it is saying, but what it excludes" (Claude Lévi-Strauss, *The Way of Masks*, tr. Sylvia Modelski [Seattle: University of Washington Press, 1982], p. 144).

10.　　"Hence the fiction—basically ideological—according to which art, or whatever goes under that name, would today have reached its end, a fiction whose only meaning is to confuse the end of this or that match (or series of matches) with the end of the game itself (as if a game could have an end): the rule requiring henceforth that all matches (or series of matches) have an end, even in the highly symptomatic manner of the *impasse*, while the moves follow each other at an ever increasing pace" (p. 171).

"Resisting Blackmail" was written in English for this collection of essays.

"Matisse and Arche-drawing," previously unpublished, was translated into English by Greg Sims. This essay benefited from conversations with Angelica Rudenstine, to whom it would be dedicated if the book as a whole had not already been dedicated to others.

"Kahnweiler's Lesson" first appeared in English in *Representations,* no. 18, Spring 1987 (translated by Katharine Streip and edited by Barrett Watten). A slightly longer version, on which the one published here is based, appeared in French in *Cahiers du Musée National d'Art Moderne,* no. 23, Spring 1988. The essay was written in memory of Jean Laude.

"The De Stijl Idea" was written for the *Encyclopaedia Universalis* in 1982, but did not appear there until 1984 (new edition, vol. 17). My English translation was checked by Maria Gough. Fragments of an earlier version of this essay were interspersed in a review bearing the same title which I wrote for *Art in America* (November 1982), and which was translated by Craig Owens.

"Strzemiński and Kobro: In Search of Motivation" appeared in French in *Critique,* no. 440–441 (January–February 1984). Fragments of an earlier version of this essay were interspersed in a review translated into English by Craig Owens and published later in *Art in America* under the editor's title "Polarization" (April 1984). My translation of the present text was checked by Mary-Alice Lee.

"Piet Mondrian, *New York City*" first appeared in French in *Cahiers du Musée National d'Art Moderne,* no. 15, 1985. Slightly augmented, it was published in English in *Critical Inquiry,* vol. 14, no. 2 (Winter 1988). The translation of this later version, published here, was done by Amy Reiter-McIntosh and edited by James W. Williams with the help of Michael Fried.

"Perceiving Newman," written in English and edited by Michael Fried, was published as the preface for the catalogue of the Barnett Newman exhibition organized by the Pace Gallery, New York, Spring 1988. It was dedicated to Annalee Newman. It is reproduced here with the permission of the Pace Gallery.

"Ryman's Tact" was written as a preface for the catalogue of the Robert Ryman exhibition at the Centre Georges Pompidou, Fall 1981. It was published in English in *October,* no. 19 (translated by Thomas Repensek).

"Painting: The Task of Mourning," written in English and edited by David Joselit, first appeared in the catalogue of the exhibition *Endgame—Reference and Simulation in Recent Painting and Sculpture,* at the Boston Institute of Contemporary Art, Fall 1986.

"Painting as Model" first appeared in English in *October,* no. 37, Summer 1986 (translated by John Shepley).

Index

Page numbers in **boldface** indicate illustrations.